THE ADMINISTRATIVE FOUNDATIONS OF THE CHINESE FISCAL STATE

On subjects ranging from trade to democratization, there has lately been a wave of laments about China's development belying Western expectations. Yet these disappointments often come with misunderstandings of the very institutions that China was expected to adopt. Chinese taxation offers a sharp illustration. When China introduced a tax system suited for the market economy, it fully intended tax collection to rely on self-assessment, audits, and the rule of law. But this Western approach was quickly jettisoned in favour of one that emphasized the monitoring of taxpayers and ex ante interventions, at the expense of deterrence and truthful reporting norms. The Chinese approach surprisingly matches recommendations made by recent economic scholarship on tax compliance and state capacity. China's massive but little-known explorations in taxation highlight the distinct types of modern state capacity, and raise challenging questions about the future of taxation and the superiority of institutions based on rule of law.

WEI CUI is Professor at Peter A. Allard School of Law, University of British Columbia, Vancouver. He has authored over 100 academic and professional articles on tax law and policy and Chinese law and is a co-author of *Value Added Tax: A Comparative Approach* (2015). He practiced tax law at elite firms in New York and Beijing, and served as a consultant to China's National People's Congress, Ministry of Finance and State Administration of Taxation.

Cambridge Tax Law

Tax law is a growing area of interest. It is included as a subdivision in many areas of study and is a key consideration in business needs throughout the world. Books in this series expose the theoretical underpinning behind the law to shed light on taxation systems, so that the questions to be asked when addressing an issue become clear. These academic books, written by leading scholars, are a central port of call for information on tax law, with content illustrated by case law and legislation. The books will be of interest to those studying law, business, economics, accounting and finance courses.

Series Editor

Professor Peter Harris, Law Faculty, University of Cambridge, Director of the Centre for Tax Law

Professor Harris brings a wealth of experience to the series. He has taught and presented tax courses at more than a dozen different universities in as many countries and has acted as an external tax consultant for the International Monetary Fund for over twenty years.

THE ADMINISTRATIVE FOUNDATIONS OF THE CHINESE FISCAL STATE

WEI CUI

University of British Columbia

CAMBRIDGE
UNIVERSITY PRESS

CAMBRIDGE
UNIVERSITY PRESS

University Printing House, Cambridge CB2 8BS, United Kingdom

One Liberty Plaza, 20th Floor, New York, NY 10006, USA

477 Williamstown Road, Port Melbourne, VIC 3207, Australia

314–321, 3rd Floor, Plot 3, Splendor Forum, Jasola District Centre, New Delhi – 110025, India

103 Penang Road, #05–06/07, Visioncrest Commercial, Singapore 238467

Cambridge University Press is part of the University of Cambridge.

It furthers the University's mission by disseminating knowledge in the pursuit of education, learning, and research at the highest international levels of excellence.

www.cambridge.org
Information on this title: www.cambridge.org/9781108491426
DOI: 10.1017/9781108868648

First published 2022

A catalogue record for this publication is available from the British Library.

Library of Congress Cataloging-in-Publication Data
Names: Cui, Wei, 1970– author.
Title: The administrative foundations of the Chinese fiscal state / Wei Cui, University of British Columbia, Vancouver.
Description: Cambridge, United Kingdom ; New York, NY : Cambridge University Press, 2022. | Series: Cambridge tax law | Includes index.
Identifiers: LCCN 2021042342 (print) | LCCN 2021042343 (ebook) | ISBN 9781108491426 (hardback) | ISBN 9781108812153 (paperback) | ISBN 9781108868648 (ebook)
Subjects: LCSH: Tax administration and procedure – China.
Classification: LCC KNQ3558 .C85 2022 (print) | LCC KNQ3558 (ebook) | DDC 343.5104–dc23/eng/20211105
LC record available at https://lccn.loc.gov/2021042342
LC ebook record available at https://lccn.loc.gov/2021042343

ISBN 978-1-108-49142-6 Hardback

To
Simone & Adele

CONTENTS

FIGURES

TABLES

ACKNOWLEDGMENTS

The idea of this book came to me in 2016, when I discovered that Chinese tax agencies in several provinces were designing tax administration reforms to promote practices of taxpayer self-assessment and greater tax administrator specialization. I had published an article in the *University of Toronto Law Journal* in 2015 that used the lack of self-assessment and specialization in tax administration to synthesize many observations I had accumulated of the Chinese tax system. It was thrilling to discover that these ideas were not merely the musings of an academic, but were being independently articulated by many tax administrators across China and driving new undertakings. Although I had been fortunate to have worked on many national tax policy projects in China when teaching and practicing tax in Beijing during 2006–2013, it dawned on me in 2016 that I needed to revise my understanding of Chinese taxation from a less Beijing-centric perspective.

The highlight of this process of re-learning was definitely the many interviews and conversations I had with Chinese tax administrators in provincial, city, and district-level bureaus. I am grateful to them all, although the world they live in may seem very remote to many readers of this book, and it would not make sense to list all of their names. I would like to specifically thank Mr. Wei Guoqing, however, for introducing me to a world rich with opportunities for social scientific investigation and moral and political reflection.

Many academic colleagues and mentors also helped me in thinking through the subjects of this book, as did participants in several academic seminars and conferences where I presented the book's materials. Again, it may be better to thank most of them elsewhere, for example, when I develop my arguments further in specialized journal articles. Here, I want to thank Jeff Hicks, Camden Hutchison, Jiwei Qian, and George Yin for comments on various chapters of the book, and Jinyan Li for overall comments.

Sadly, one reader of the entire book, Professor Richard Bird, died after I submitted the manuscript to the publisher. Richard was a founder of and a giant in the field of tax and development; few in the world matched his knowledge of and passion for the subject. It was difficult to accept that my correspondence with him in the spring of 2021 would be my last opportunity to benefit from his unique mind. Despite this loss, I know that Richard's prodigious scholarship will inform and inspire scholars and students around the world for many years to come.

The research presented in this book was supported by an Insight Grant from the Social Sciences and Humanities Research Council of Canada. I am grateful for the help of many capable research assistants in the last few years, especially Xin Mu, Tina Qian, Desmond Wang, Xuerui Wang, German Vega Acuña, Joanne Xu, and Yi Zhao. Audrey Chen edited and prepared the book manuscript, saving me from many grammatical embarrassments.

This book was written mostly after the outbreak of the COVID-19 pandemic in Canada. As billions of people around the world discovered during 2020 and 2021, working during the pandemic is possible only with the extraordinary support of their families. I could not have enjoyed better support than the understanding and affection I received from my wife Jie Cheng, my daughters Simone and Adele, and (remotely) my parents George and Sharon Cui. To commemorate the experience of researching for and writing this book, I dedicate the book to Simone and Adele, who have made life in these last few years truly lovely.

ABBREVIATIONS

BT	Business Tax (*yingyeshui*)
B2B	business-to-business
CCP	Chinese Communist Party
CIT	corporate income tax
CNY	Chinese yuan/renminbi
COE	collectively owned enterprise
COVID-19	coronavirus disease
DS	Local Tax Bureau (*difang shuiwuju*)
EIT	Enterprise Income Tax
EITL	Enterprise Income Tax Law
GDP	gross domestic product
GS	State Tax Bureau (*guojia shuiwuju*)
GTP	Golden Tax Project
IMF	International Monetary Fund
IRS	Internal Revenue Service
IT	information technology
LTU	large taxpayer units
MOF	Ministry of Finance (China)
NPC	National People's Congress
OECD	Organisation for Economic Co-operation and Development
PIT	personal income tax
PITL	Personal Income Tax Law
RCT	randomized controlled trial
SAT	State Administration of Taxation
SI	social insurance
SMPE	small and micro-profit enterprise
SOE	state-owned enterprise
TPIR	third-party information reporting
UNDP	United National Development Program
VAT	value-added tax
WTO	World Trade Organization

Introduction

China's staggering economic growth in the past forty years is one of the most fascinating and important stories of social change in recent world history. Social scientists from around the globe have produced vast literatures to explore the story's countless dimensions. Invariably, the government's actions lie at the center of the narratives that emerge. The Chinese state nurtured the early growth of private entrepreneurship in township and village enterprises. It made dazzling investments in infrastructure projects and is responsible for a model of investment-led economic growth that dominates to the present day. It has tried, although with various degrees of success, to either build or revamp gigantic systems of public education and public health, of old age, medical, and unemployment insurance, and of poverty assistance. China has, of course, also expanded its military power and foreign operations. To do all these and many other things, the Chinese government has had to accumulate and deploy vast amounts of social resources. Certainly, it has done so partly by exercising control over the nation's banking sector, manipulating its capital markets, and owning large quantities of productive assets through state-owned enterprises. Yet these forms of state ownership and state control are dwarfed by the government's most important access to social resources: the power of taxation.

Taxation is not only an integral part of the story of China's breathtaking economic rise. It is also, in many ways, an astonishing story in itself. During the 1990s and early 2000s, China's ratio of tax revenue to gross domestic product (GDP) – which public finance specialists call the "gross tax ratio" – recovered from a low of 10 percent to over 20 percent (Figure 0.1). In terms of this ratio, China now easily surpasses many other countries (such as Taiwan, Malaysia, and Mexico) that have been classified as middle income for longer periods. Indeed, China's capacity for taxation is comparable to that of numerous high-income countries such as Chile and Ireland, and not far behind that of the United States. For all but a couple of years since 1997, tax revenue grew at annual rates even higher than the country's already-high

Figure 0.1 Evolution of tax-to-GDP ratio in China, 1985–2019

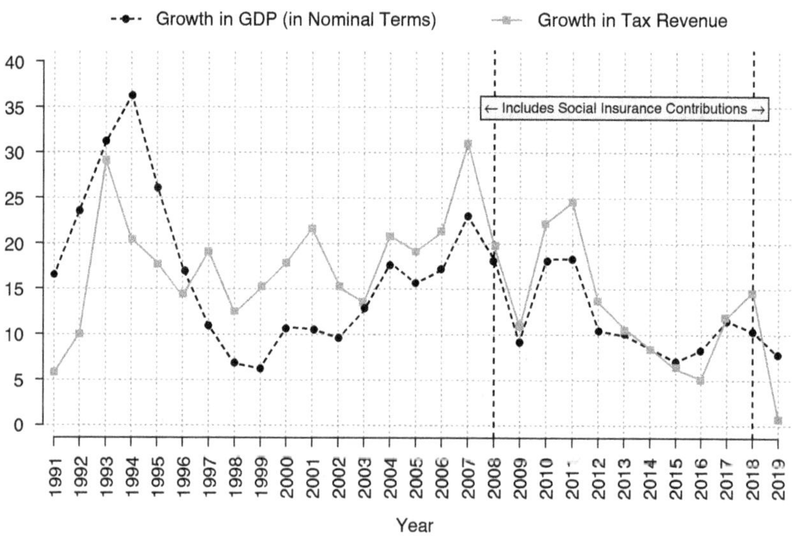

Figure 0.2 Growth of GDP and tax revenue in China, 1991–2019

rates of GDP growth (Figure 0.2). In recent years, this has allowed the Chinese government to adopt many tax cuts – even though prior to these cuts, China had neither adopted higher tax rates, nor imposed them on larger tax bases, nor used a larger variety of taxes, than is normal from a comparative perspective. If strong tax collection has not dampened China's spectacular economic progress in the past, the power of cutting taxes to stimulate future growth in China appears formidable.

Despite the unquestionable centrality of taxation to the modern Chinese state, and notwithstanding many of the unusual features and outcomes of China's tax institutions that deserve careful study, Chinese taxation has received very limited social scientific attention. The number of scholarly books and articles on Chinese taxation, even cumulated over thirty years, is small. Topics like China's state-owned enterprises, banking sector, and capital markets have received more extensive coverage in the social scientific literature. Notably, the lack of knowledge about Chinese taxation is not confined to the general public, news media, and public commentaries, but also characterizes the economics profession (in and outside of China), legal scholarship, and other social scientific disciplines.[1]

This book offers an account of certain foundational aspects of China's contemporary tax system. The book has two basic aims. The first is to answer the question: What aspects of Chinese taxation might be of general interest to policy makers and social scientists in other countries? In particular, I will explain what policy makers, administrators, and international organizations helping poor countries build their tax systems might learn from the Chinese experience. There are many lessons to be drawn, although they are quite different from what social scientists or international organizations providing technical assistance have previously emphasized. The book also seeks to provide new ideas to social scientists who do not study China in particular, but who are interested in identifying the determinants of fiscal capacity of modern states in both developing and developed countries.

[1] Indeed, an accurate and nuanced understanding of the Chinese tax system has been difficult to assemble even among tax specialists. International organizations such as the International Monetary Fund (IMF), the Organisation for Economic Cooperation and Development (OECD), the World Bank, and United National Development Program (UNDP), specialize in technical assistance in tax matters to developing countries. Their tax specialists usually have the capacity to see through countries' tax systems – often designing them themselves – and therefore characterize such systems in easily accessible terms. Yet although many of these organizations have been sending missions and training personnel to China for decades, they also offer inadequate information about China's tax system. For some such sources of information, see Lou and Wang 2008 (the most recent anthology on Chinese public finance published by the World Bank), Brys et al. 2013 (the most recent survey of Chinese tax policy by the OECD Center for Tax Policy and Administration), Brondolo and Zhang 2016 (a recent survey specifically dedicated to Chinese tax administration offered by the IMF Fiscal Affairs Department), and IMF 2018 (a report on a recent tax policy mission to China).

Second, for readers who are more interested in China for its own sake, the book sketches out a framework for understanding the policies and politics of taxation in China. The framework is new, rather than a synthesis of existing narratives. I believe that given China's economic and political power, the understanding of Chinese taxation should no longer be left to the unfortunate combination of academic neglect, desultory media coverage, and Chinese government propaganda. Indeed, the book will seek to dispel many myths about Chinese taxation and highlight the inadequacy of much conventional wisdom.

Because of these two aims – to identify what might be generalizable about the Chinese experience and to delineate a new framework for both public policy debate and further academic research about Chinese taxation – the approach I take in this book is highly selective. I will focus on arguments and explanations, rather than descriptions of the endless facets of Chinese taxation. While I do lay out substantial and previously unknown details about the Chinese tax system, I will also omit many others.

In fact, it is critical to state, at the outset, a single choice that I made in writing this book that fundamentally shapes the scope of its discussion. I anchor my study of Chinese taxation in analyses of an often-neglected set of institutions: those that organize grassroots tax administration. I argue that ground-level tax administration is the key to understanding the entire edifice of China's tax system. Therefore, more than half of the book is about tax administration, while the remainder explores what light tax administration sheds on China's tax policymaking process, recent tax policy choices and debates, and the politics of taxation.

To describe any country's tax system from the perspective of its tax administration is unusual. Consider the United States' Internal Revenue Service (IRS). For most Americans, and indeed for many people around the world, the IRS symbolizes the governmental power to tax. Yet I suspect that very few scholars would be inclined to present an overview of the US federal tax system by putting the IRS at the center. For one, the enactment of tax laws by the Presidents and Congresses of the United States seems far more important. Both the politics and the substance of these enactments occupy most of the attention of businesses, policy analysts, lawyers, economists, and political scientists. Further, understanding the economic and social consequences of US tax policies requires careful research. These seem intellectually far more significant than how the IRS administers tax policies on a routine basis and how taxpayers file returns and send checks to the IRS. What, then, can one expect from a book that describes Chinese taxation chiefly from the perspective of tax administration?

In the rest of this Introduction, I lay out the main arguments of the book by answering this last question.

China as an Alternative Paradigm in Revenue Mobilization

From a social scientific perspective, initially the most significant aspect of China's tax system is its success in raising revenue. In the past two decades, social scientists have offered extensive and compelling evidence that a government's capacity to provide law and order as well as other public goods – financed by taxation – is vital for economic development. Tax collection has come to be seen as a most fundamental aspect of modern "state capacity."[2] China's success at "revenue mobilization" reflects a strong and fundamental form of state capacity. For developing countries seeking to replicate China's economic success, it is necessary to understand how China built this capacity, as well as the potential costs and negative consequences of China's approach in building state capacity.

Specialists writing about taxation in developing countries have long emphasized the first-order importance of tax administration.[3] In poor countries, tax policy design plays second fiddle to tax administration: a strong tax administration can make any number of policy instruments roughly effective, while a weak tax administration severely limits the effectiveness of most policy instruments. More recently, political and developmental economists have tried to go beyond this pragmatic wisdom, rigorously analyzing the factors that determine the success of tax administration. As a result of this research agenda, economic research on tax administration has mushroomed into a thriving field. However, my own efforts at understanding Chinese tax administration have taught me that, collectively, we still have few useful hypotheses about tax administration in developing countries. Because of this, the claim that tax administration lies at the core of state capacity can appear, to a skeptic, either a vaguely defined truism or simply an article of faith among some researchers.

A few limitations in existing economic research on tax administration are especially relevant for this book.[4] Most notably, researchers have poured considerable analytical resources into a very small set of conjectures. For

[2] Burgess and Stern 1993; Besley and Persson 2013; Keen 2013; Bardhan 2016.

[3] Slemrod 1990; Gordon and Li 2009; Gordon 2010; Bird and Martinez-Vazquez 2014.

[4] I further elaborate on the following arguments in Chapter 8, where I discuss the general implications of the book's findings for developing countries.

instance, one prominent idea in the literature surmises that because third-party information reporting will curtail tax evasion, developing countries should more widely adopt and strengthen such reporting mechanisms.[5] Another theory is that tax collectors need to be effectively incentivized.[6] But while the empirical evidence generated to support these conjectures is impressive, the conjectures themselves seem inadequate. For one, do we know that developing countries are particularly bad at implementing information reporting, or at incentivizing their civil servants? Suppose they worked hard to improve their tax administration along these dimensions, will their tax systems come to resemble those of the developed countries? There is actually abundant evidence that developing countries have generally adopted information reporting and civil servant incentives just as extensively as developed countries. If they put greater emphasis on these aspects of tax administration, they may or may not collect more tax revenue, but they will certainly become *more different* from developed countries. This is because developed countries do not rely on manipulating the incentives of their tax collectors for raising revenue. They also rely on information reporting to a much lesser extent than some researchers have claimed.

It is tempting to respond to this first criticism by saying that, of course, information reporting and incentivizing tax collectors are not the only things that developing countries need to do to strengthen tax administration. They must boost taxpayer morale,[7] enhance their audit capacity and therefore the credibility of audits as a form of deterrence,[8] and pursue other improvements as well. This type of response threatens to blur the vision of empirical inquiry, sending us back to the traditional advice given by international organizations to developing countries about "best practices" in tax administration.[9] In other words, the question of how to build state capacity remains unanswered; it is simply tautological to say that if developed countries become "more like us" by adopting all of the recommended best practices in developed countries, they will acquire the state capacity that typifies developed countries. How do they get to there from where they are now?

In writing this book, I learned that because there is a paucity of useful conjectures in existing scholarship, the process of carefully describing tax

[5] See, for example, Pomeranz 2015; Kleven et al. 2016; Naritomi 2019.

[6] Khan et al. 2016, 2019; Finan et al. 2017.

[7] OECD 2013; Luttmer and Singhal 2014.

[8] Carrillo et al. 2017; Brockmeyer et al. 2019.

[9] My point is not that such advice is not valuable, but instead that they cannot substitute for social scientific understanding.

administration is not a matter of mechanically sorting through obscure facts. Instead, new concepts need to be invented; intellectual discoveries may emerge. I believe the discoveries from studying Chinese tax administration can substantially enrich the range of social scientific hypotheses that can be fruitfully tested in studying tax and development generally.

I would summarize these discoveries in terms of three related *trade-offs* faced by tax administrators in many parts of the developing world. The notion of trade-offs is critical. The compliance environment in poor and even middle-income countries like China is quite different from the compliance environment in rich countries like the United States and Canada. In the former, there are many more small or micro firms and many workers laboring in informal jobs, for whom complying with tax and other regulations is often not the best choice. In such an environment, tax administrators cannot follow the same approach to administration as their counterparts in richer countries; instead, they must make some difficult choices. The distinctiveness of Chinese tax administration can be defined in terms of choices regarding the following three trade-offs.

The first is how much government and society value the norm of truthful reporting. Because tax administration is such a multifaceted exercise, enforcing the norm of truthful reporting is not necessarily the most effective way of raising revenue in many circumstances. One can adopt other administrative tactics that advance the objective of revenue raising at least as effectively. This means that there can be a trade-off *between raising revenue and enforcing the norm of truthful reporting*. On closer scrutiny, Chinese tax collectors put much less value on truthful reporting than on ensuring taxpayer registration and tax payments. To put it bluntly, taxpayers who lie on their tax returns mostly go unpunished. However, Chinese practice also highlights the surprising sustainability of approaches that de-emphasize truthful reporting.

Describing this form of administrative practice turns out to be challenging. In the professional vocabularies of public economics, accounting, and tax law that have international currency, as well as in the policy advice routinely dispensed to developing countries by organizations, certain basic elements in the experiences of taxation in developed countries are taken for granted. The norm of truthful reporting is a central example. Not only do we value compliance with that norm, the very language we use for discussing tax administration also assumes that norm. The notion of a tax audit, for example, is widely taken to be universally applicable. That notion, however, makes sense only when describing the enforcement of the norm of truthful reporting. When applied to contexts where such norm is secondary, it quickly loses accuracy. Studying the Chinese case reveals basic assumptions in the very vocabulary we use to discuss tax administration. Once a more reflective vocabulary is developed, the contrast between tax collection practices that rely on the norm of truthful reporting and those that do not becomes very stark.

Because of the de-emphasis on norms of truthful reporting, Chinese tax administrators engage in a second trade-off. They devote much of their time to taxpayer registration. This sharply reduces what might be called "firm informality" in the Chinese economy, as most business firms now show up on the government's radar. At the same time, many practices typical of the informal economies elsewhere in the world remain: informal work arrangements, under-reporting of sales and profits, and dodging of regulatory requirements. The economist Gabriel Ulyssea calls this latter form of informality "labor informality." Chinese tax administration thus illustrates a trade-off between reducing firm and labor informality, or between enforcement along the extensive and along the intensive margins of formality. The Chinese choice is to enforce the extensive margin of formality. This choice goes a long way in explaining the character of Chinese tax collection.

Third and finally, Chinese tax administration has heavily invested in incentivizing civil servants – including grassroots tax collectors, senior managers at tax bureaus, and local politicians – in tax collection. Indeed, in tax administration and elsewhere, China offers a paradigm for providing incentives to civil servants. Interestingly, the intense incentives structures faced by Chinese tax administrators both engender and reinforce practices that de-emphasize the norm of truthful reporting. This is because compliance with the norm of truthful reporting lies largely beyond the control of tax administrators, and depends on many other social institutions that either reward or create indifference to compliance with the law. To effectively incentivize civil servants, one must forego emphasizing goals that lie beyond their control. This, I will argue, has led to a trade-off between incentivizing civil servants in tax collection and incentivizing taxpayers (especially business firms) in self-assessment.

These three trade-offs have rarely been recognized in mainstream scholarship and policy discourse on tax administration in developing countries.[10] Insofar as China's choices with respect to these trade-offs

[10] The first trade-off, between raising revenue and enforcing the norm of truthful reporting, is recognized in the analysis of auditor incentives offered by Di Porto et al. 2013. While

differ from choices familiar in developed countries, it represents an alternative archetype in revenue collection. To illustrate how these trade-offs shed light on building tax capacity in the developing world, consider a few seemingly unrelated examples, from recent economic research.

In the past few years, the economist Jonathan Weigel has run a number of elaborately designed experiments on tax collection and political participation in the Democratic Republic of the Congo.[11] Weigel describes Congo as a country with very low capacity for tax collection. In one of his experiments, a property tax collection campaign was launched across neighborhoods in the city of Kananga in 2016. Prior to the collection campaign, the level of compliance with the tax in question was essentially zero. In the experiment, some randomly selected neighborhoods received a particular "treatment": tax collectors went door-to-door collecting taxes. The remaining neighborhoods, representing the "control group," stayed in the old system where citizens pay at the bank themselves.

What was the outcome of the campaign? It raised property tax compliance from 0.1 percent (observed in the control group) to 10.3 percent (observed in the treatment group). That surely is an increase. But it also means that even when showing up at the doors of taxpayers, Congolese tax collectors came away empty handed *90 percent of the time.* Weigel reports that certain groups of people (e.g. wealthy, male, educated, and employed) were more likely to pay tax to the collectors, but such greater likelihood seemed only statistically, but not economically, significant. According to Weigel, the program did not even appear to increase bribes to tax collectors. It is hard to imagine how this could be anything but a thoroughly demoralizing experience for the tax collectors.[12]

the distinction between the extensive and intensive margins of informality is introduced by Ulyssea 2018, he does not discuss choosing among these margins for enforcement. The contrast between incentivizing civil servants and incentivizing businesses, to my knowledge, has not previously been drawn.

11 Weigel 2020. Weigel's experimental method – the randomized controlled trial or RCT – won three of its original proponents the Economics Nobel Prize in 2019.

12 This was not the focus of Weigel's study. Instead, in the second stage of his experiment, Kananga citizens were given opportunities to attend town hall meetings in which taxation and public spending were discussed, and to submit anonymous evaluations of the government. Weigel found that citizens from the treated neighborhoods – those who had tax collectors knocking on their doors – were more likely to pursue either or both types of political engagement. Interestingly, those individuals who refused to pay any tax to the tax collectors were just as likely to show up at the town hall meetings as those who actually paid. Weigel's interpretation of these results is that the tax campaign sent a signal of state capacity that raised the expected benefits of participation.

Like many other randomized control trials (RCTs) recently carried out in developing countries, Weigel's experiment has a clockwork-like quality: it has many components, each delivering precise formulations about what might have motivated real-world individuals to act. However, it is important to highlight some background features of Weigel's study that might otherwise escape notice. The first observation may seem obvious: the tax collection capacity of the world's rich countries today does not generally depend on knocking on taxpayer's doors. Business firms remit most of the tax revenue directly to the government – whether in the form of business taxes like the corporate income tax (CIT) or the value-added tax (VAT), or in the form of withholding on wage and financial payments to individuals. Because of this, we simply do not know what would happen if the IRS (or the Canadian Revenue Service) sent officers door-to-door to collect taxes from American (or Canadian) taxpayers.[13]

This shows that when researchers talk about "state capacity," they are often using a very abstract notion. In the Congo, it means door-to-door tax collection, while in developed countries, it means making sure – or doing whatever is compatible with the expectation – that most taxpayers will file tax returns and remit taxes without direct government prompting.[14]

Is there something wrong with this way of talking? Here, we can make the second observation regarding Weigel's study. State capacity can vary substantially in respect of specific mechanisms, and not just outcomes. It is possible for much stronger state capacity than is observed in the Congo to take the form of door-to-door tax collection. As we will see in this book, tax collection in China has a strong door-to-door flavor. Tax collectors routinely visit taxpayers, and tax bureau offices where payments can be made are always nearby. However, in contrast to the discouraging outcomes in the Congo, tax administrators across China have reported – for two decades now – rates of timely tax return filings of over 95 percent, and similarly high rates of timely tax payments.[15] Imagine dialing up the compliance rate in Kananga from 10 percent to

[13] Or actually, we could know, but only by learning about a thoroughly different and unfamiliar world of tax collection in nineteenth century America. See Hickman and Kerska 2017.

[14] Perhaps by "state capacity," scholars are merely talking about outcomes (i.e. how much tax is collected), not mechanisms (i.e. how tax is collected). But this would render the question, "How do we build state capacity to achieve the goal of raising more revenue?" tautological.

[15] These facts are detailed in Chapters 3 and 5.

95 percent! Such a result would seem to amount to a vast enhancement of state capacity. If door-to-door tax collection is the kind of state capacity countries like the Congo want to invest in, China should be their model.

Similar observations apply to other prominent recent studies of strengthening tax capacity in poor countries. For example, Adnan Khan, Asim Khwaja, and Benjamin Olken carried out several well-designed RCTs among Pakistani property tax collectors.[16] They show that both performance pay and bureaucratic rotations can generate significant incentives for tax collection, and they present these policy interventions as ways of improving state capacity in developing countries. Again, we can note two things. First, while the world's rich developed economies collect a large percentage of their GDP in taxes, very little of this has to do with property taxation. Hendrik Kleven, Claus Kreiner, and Emanual Saez have presented evidence that what distinguishes the modern tax systems in rich countries is a switch from property taxes and tariffs, which are directly collected by tax collectors, to taxes remitted by business firms.[17] They showed that the tax capacities of rich and poor countries today – in terms of the ratio of property tax collection to GDP – do not significantly differ from one another's. It is in the collection of the personal income tax (PIT), payroll taxes on wages, VAT, and the CIT – which the authors call the "modern taxes" – that poor countries fall far short of rich countries.[18]

This raises the awkward question: If developing countries like Pakistan are already as good as developed countries in raising property tax revenue, should they use this as their primary means to improve state capacity? One plausible answer is that Pakistan will not attain the taxing capacity of rich countries simply by improving property tax collection. Moreover, the organizational techniques that enhance government capacity in property tax collection may not be useful when collecting business or individual income taxes. Whether or not one agrees with this assessment is irrelevant; the point is that the question itself would go unrecognized if we talked about "state capacity" in taxation merely in the abstract, without looking at the mechanisms underlying such capacity.

A second observation regarding the Pakistani property tax collection studies, analogous to the earlier comment on the Congo study, is that civil servants face powerful incentive structures within Chinese tax

16 Khan et al. 2016, 2019.

17 Kleven et al. 2016.

18 Similarly, looking back into the history of rich countries, it was not until the countries started collecting the modern taxes that their tax-to-GDP share went up. Property tax and tariff collection contributed little to the growth of modern tax states.

administration. In this book, we consider many examples of the ways in which these incentives are manipulated: performance pay and promotions through rotation are just two of the many techniques that have been employed over the years. And although no rigorous study of the effectiveness of these incentives has been carried out in China, the reality is that they will continue to be used, until the government figures out better ways of raising revenue (by trial and error, if not by RCTs). If strengthening civil servant incentives is key to building state capacity, China again should be a leading example.

I refer to these recent studies of tax administration in developing countries not because the behaviors and institutions that they examine have counterparts in China. Instead, I want to make a conceptual point that is central to this book. Tax administration is multifaceted and rests on a variety of institutions and practices. Because of their vastly different compliance environments, developed and developing countries also tend to rely on rather different tax policy instruments. This creates a dilemma for developing countries seeking to build strong state capacity. Is the goal to build tax systems like those in OECD countries, where large businesses remit the bulk of taxes, or is it to make tax inspectors more successful in cajoling taxpayers into paying something during in-person visits? In the existing academic literature as well as much policy discourse, it is invariably assumed that no choice needs to be made between these two goals. But what if it does? What if countries like Congo face a choice between two diverging strategies in growing their state capacities: Increasing the compliance rate for door-to-door visits, or rendering door-to-door visits unnecessary? Too often, we have simply hoped that the latter would happen. But as I will argue, the Chinese example shows that Congo can do quite well, in the short or even medium term, by increasing the door-to-door collection rate. However, this path may lead the Congo further away from, rather than closer to, the tax systems in traditional developed countries. This would have enormous implications for our understanding of tax and development.

In summary, Chinese tax administration is interesting because it has succeeded in raising revenue, but has done so in a manner that substantially deviates from rich countries' approaches to tax administration. Moreover, China's approach is far from obvious: it escapes from view by virtue of the very vocabulary with which we are used to describing the goals and structure of tax administration. This book develops a new set of concepts to highlight the uniqueness of Chinese practice and for understanding such practice as a positive matter. These concepts will also help identify the practice's advantages and disadvantages, allowing one to evaluate, as a normative matter, which aspects of it are worthy of emulation.

Next, I want to explain how the focus on Chinese tax administration is also crucial for developing a framework for understanding China's fiscal politics.

A Perspective on China's Fiscal Politics

China's economy is already the world's second largest and is expected to surpass even the United States soon. Consequently, research published in English on Chinese taxation will likely grow in both volume and prominence in the next decade. Because China offers fertile grounds for empirical research – thanks to the possibility of large amounts of data becoming available, the rich internal variations within the country, and frequent tax policy changes fueling such research – economic research on Chinese taxation is already rapidly growing. However, how can such research contribute to our understanding of China's internal policy debates, or the nation's circumstances in general? Unfortunately, there are widely divergent scholarly approaches to the topic of Chinese taxation. Wider still are the gaps between scholarly research and public policy discourse on the subject. Frameworks that bridge some of these gaps and diverging approaches are sorely needed.

To give an example, in early 2006, after several years working as a US tax lawyer for big law firms in New York City, I moved to Beijing to take up an academic position at a university. At that time, China had just abolished its agricultural tax.[19] Over drinks at one of the social events during my first days in Beijing, a journalist asked me what I thought about this development. I told him that the agricultural tax had generated only a tiny portion – just slightly over 1 percent – of China's overall tax revenue. Its abolition did not seem earth shattering to me.

In speaking these words, I expressed a form of reasoning typical for tax specialists, which also virtually guarantees our irrelevance to popular discourses about tax policy. The Chinese government gave great publicity to the agricultural tax's abolition. Moreover, in 2006, the main scholarly book in English about contemporary Chinese taxation was about the

[19] For a masterful account of the politics of the agricultural tax reform, see Göbel 2010. See also Alm and Liu 2013 for an empirical assessment of the policy impact of the agricultural tax reform, and Chen 2017 for its impact on the enforcement of other taxes.

agricultural tax, depicting taxation as generating tremendous social conflict in rural China.[20] Journalists and most commentators following China generally thought then that the agricultural tax reform *was* a big deal, notwithstanding a tax lawyer's indifference to it.

Just a few months later, China's National People's Congress announced a plan for new legislation to fundamentally reform China's CIT (also referred to as the Enterprise Income Tax [EIT]). The new EIT Law, passed by the national legislature in March 2007, substantially reduced the tax rate for domestic firms but raised the rate for foreign-invested firms and ushered in other extensive changes. From a tax policy angle, it was indisputably important. The EIT Law, of course, also had a resounding impact on the Chinese tax professions' businesses and human capital: I myself devoted the next few years to writing about the EIT. However, although a small body of empirical research has analyzed isolated features of the Chinese CIT, academic interest remains very limited. The frequency with which the EIT was covered by media stories (even in business media) is also negligible. Neither social scientists nor policy commentators have offered views about how important the EIT may be for understanding China's economy or politics.

Most of the rest of China's recent tax reforms have met with the same public and social scientific indifference. China made a major step in reforming its VAT in response to the Global Financial Crisis in 2009. One subsequent study of the impact of the 2009 reform, jointly authored by American and Chinese scholars, assessed it as delivering one of the largest investment incentives in recent world history.[21] China then went on, between 2012 and 2016, to carry out a complete overhaul of its indirect tax systems, merging what was called the Business Tax (*yingye shui*) into the VAT. This, by many measures, was the largest VAT reform in the world during this period. These changes amounted to very substantial bodies of new economic policies, which preoccupied Chinese businesses, tax administrators and tax professionals, and local governments year after year. Yet it is difficult to identify how public opinions have formed around these policies, or what the press has

[20] Bernstein and Lü 2003.

[21] Chen et al. 2019. The 2009 VAT reform (transforming China's VAT from the "production type" to the "consumption type") implements across China a type of policy that was first adopted on a regional pilot basis in 2004, roughly around the same time as the agricultural tax abolition. However, while official press covered the pilot reforms in 2005, the VAT reform was generally ignored by both Chinese and foreign news media and commentary on contemporary China.

conveyed about policy analyses and debates. Meanwhile, for economists, these recent reforms have generated at most a series of "natural experiments" for testing some specialized hypotheses in public economics. Do these policy changes really have no greater social scientific relevance?

In this book, I argue that tax administration offers a new perspective on Chinese fiscal politics that helps identify what is of broader interest about the past two decades of tax policy making in China, and sheds light on some of the key institutions that public economic scholars may need to consider for their work to become more informative about China. I make three specific claims to show how the mundane material of tax administration speaks to the grand subject of politics.

First, tax administration highlights our incomplete understanding of the operation of political incentives in the Chinese state. Existing research by political scientists has supplied various evidence that Chinese subnational political leaders are promoted on the basis of political loyalty and performance, the latter being measured by certain crude and all-encompassing metrics such as GDP growth.[22] Securing tax revenue is understood to be one of the "key performance indicators" that political leaders are evaluated upon. However, these thoughtful accounts tell an incomplete story. Provincial or city political leaders need to mobilize lower-level politicians to generate career-advancing outcomes for themselves. Moreover, while economic growth is all-encompassing, many policy outcomes, such as raising tax revenue, fall in the purview of specialized bureaucracies. Yet relatively few scholars have examined how political incentives work within bureaucratic agencies, especially at the lowest administrative levels. A county tax bureau chief in China may supervise tax collection from hundreds of thousands of taxpayers, but, within the steep bureaucratic hierarchy, he/she is one of the pettiest officials. His/her subordinates are, even more undoubtedly, political nobodies. What motivates these civil servants to deliver the results asked of them by their bosses? After all, it is they who collect tax revenue, not the city mayors or provincial governors who are promoted (in part) based on revenue collection.

In fact, the following dilemma faces the study of the personnel politics of the Chinese state. Suppose, on the one hand, that the incentives of political leaders at different subnational levels differ substantially

[22] See, for example, Li and Zhou 2005; Jia et al. 2015; Yao and Zhang 2015; Ang 2016; Landry et al. 2018.

(vertical heterogeneity). Suppose incentives also significantly differ between political leaders and bureaucrats (horizontal heterogeneity). In that case, subnational politicians should not be treated as a homogenous "local" class. Justification should be offered for focusing on one group (e.g. provincial leaders) as opposed to others (e.g. county leaders). Moreover, to use personnel politics to explain outcomes in particular policy areas (be it environmental protection, workplace safety, or taxation), one must understand the personnel politics of specialized agencies, not just of government leaders. Suppose, on the other hand, that the incentives of political leaders at different subnational levels are similar (so that one group's behavior is representative of others), and the differences between political leaders and bureaucrats do not matter. If that is the case, then insofar as policy outcomes are secured at the grassroots level, one must study the personnel politics at this level as well, to draw any causal connection between politics and policy outcomes.

Tax administration represents more than 10 percent of China's civil service and is one of the largest arms of the state in terms of personnel, likely coming behind only the police and other security forces. It thus offers an excellent case for examining incentives within the Chinese state at the grassroots level.

Second, fiscal politics have led to substantial changes in China's tax structure in the past two decades but remain largely invisible to public consciousness and scholarly inquiry. I argue that this is in part due to the impact fiscal politics have had on tax administration. For instance, China's urban affluent class has been stunningly successful in forcing the central government to dismantle the PIT in the past fifteen years. This has severely undercut incentives for local tax agencies to invest in PIT administration, which in turn makes it impossible to gather information about individual taxpayers. In turn, such lack of information at once makes it harder to grasp the growth of income and wealth inequality in China, and easier for media outlets catering to the country's white-collar class to propagate falsehoods about income inequality and the PIT. Similar stories can be told about other vital components of China's tax system, such as urban employer-based social insurance (SI) schemes.

More generally, fiscal politics shapes the type of state capacity that China has built around taxation, in which severe information bottlenecks for policy makers arise. Most importantly, the way in which the tasks of tax administration – like many other aspects of Chinese governance – are so relentlessly pushed down to the bottom of the state apparatus implies that little information about taxpayers and about the economic consequences of policies is transmitted to national decision-makers. This severely restricts the extent to which national policies are based on expertise. The central government deploys crude policy instruments, which introduce existential instabilities to the fiscal system. Uncovering the often-invisible information constraint on national policy making can radically alter our understanding of policy making and policy implementation in China.

Third and finally, law features prominently in political discourse. In tax administration, the Chinese state has, to its own detriment, been unable to rely on legal norms and institutions. However, appeals to law are a dominant tool of bureaucratic control. Moreover, the rich and powerful also appeal to law to protect their wealth from taxation, while giving little support to the rule of law when that is not in their interest. Thus, the common observation that an authoritarian state often tramples upon the rule of law does not come close to capturing the law's *political* nature and significance. It is likely that, increasingly, political rivalries among the powerful groups in China will be carried out in the rhetoric of law. An important objective of this book is thus to deconstruct this discourse in terms of the realities of the Chinese fiscal state, and put future studies of Chinese fiscal politics on a sound footing.

State-Sponsored Social Order without Law

My pursuit of the twin aims of the book – explaining what lessons the Chinese experience holds for building tax capacity in developing countries and setting out a framework for understanding Chinese fiscal politics – is informed by a new, critical perspective about law. I depict contemporary Chinese tax administration as sustaining a special type of social order: it is secured by a state apparatus and allows very large-scale social coordination; however, to a substantial extent, this type of social order dispenses with the benefits of law. It illustrates, at a grand scale, a basic distinction between the coercive power of the state and law-based social ordering.

The relation between the state's coercive power and the law is one of the most enduring subjects in legal theory. Whether private subjects abide by the law because disobedience will be observed and punished by the sovereign, or whether they do so because they have internalized the norm of law following, was central to the debate between legal philosophers like John Austin and H. L. A. Hart.[23] In the past three decades,

[23] See Austin 1832; Hart 1961. In Chapter 3, I characterize China's state-sponsored social order without law, in the sphere of taxation, by the concept of "atomistic coercion." The

many scholars, especially those pursuing law and economics analysis, have identified both the conceptual possibility and concrete empirical manifestations of "law without the state."[24] The idea is that a social order can be simultaneously characterized by distinctively legal norms and sustained without the state apparatus. This idea is of clear social scientific importance. But it can be further grasped if we can also better understand "state without law." My study of Chinese tax administration illustrates what is distinctive about law as a form of social order, by presenting a type of large-scale social coordination from which law is absent.

It is tempting to imagine a lawless state as arbitrary, violent, and plundering. Especially for Western readers, to say that a state operates without the law inevitably sounds damning. But this is mistaken. I will show that a state that is organized, peaceful, and in many ways compatible with modern market economies may nevertheless largely dispense with legal norms. Specifically, while my depiction of Chinese tax administration as coercive and based on substitutes for law will almost certainly sound critical, I would remind readers that the Chinese tax system has been successful in many respects. It has raised substantial revenue without violent opposition and has allowed the Chinese government to promote economic growth and even redistribution in many ways. It is not even in any obvious way more unjust than tax systems in some developed countries, or other countries enjoying greater rule of law. Therefore, writing as a legal scholar, I think it is not implausible to claim that the violation of the rule of law in Chinese tax administration shows merely that law may be an inessential instrument for governance, and that the rule of law is not the only social value that matters. Not coincidentally, a state that dispenses with law is unlikely to be compatible with the protection of individual rights and democratic rule. But more interestingly, its grip on society is at the same time ever present and tenuous.

State-sponsored social orders that dispense with the law pose deep intellectual challenges apart from their conflict with our moral sensibilities. There is a widespread perception across the social sciences that law is simply what legislatures announce and what courts adjudicate; it may not reflect what people *actually do*. This nearly universal discrepancy between what is "on the books" and what happens in practice may lead social scientists to suppose that they can afford to ignore the law: if law

conceptual and the real-world contrasts between such coercion and rule-based governance largely track these philosophical distinctions.

24 For a recent synthesis and accessible account, see Hadfield 2016.

exists merely in fiction, it is unimportant for the positive enterprises of social science. Moreover, if the rule of law is only one of the many values we hold – as it undoubtedly is – and especially if its significance issues only from its indirect contribution to social welfare, considerations of law become secondary.

I believe this unreflective view about law is wrong and harmful for the social scientific enterprise for two reasons. First, law is not just what is written "on paper." Law is a distinctive form of social practice; social cooperation structured by legal norms has a fundamentally different character from such cooperation organized without legal norms. Law is thus an essential way of *describing* what people do. This fundamental notion has pointed illustrations in taxation. The filing of tax returns, and the reporting of one's tax attributes and computation of tax liabilities on such returns, are quintessential *rule-following* behavior. They would not exist – they could not be described as return filing, and so forth – if there was no expectation of conformity to some norm of truthful reporting. The same is true for the concept of an audit. Thus, even the basic set up in economic models of tax compliance follows a way of describing the world that assumes the relevance of legal norms. If the concepts of return filing and audits are applied in contexts where following the law is largely irrelevant, then we immediately misdescribe social reality. Because much of the vocabulary for describing modern taxation incorporates assumptions about law, to describe a world without law requires a different vocabulary, one that this book attempts to piece together for readers.

Second, without recognizing the deep significance of legal norms for modern taxation, economists risk offering policy recommendations without understanding their implications. For example, much recent economic literature takes it as self-evident that governments must obtain information about taxpayers' activities to collect tax. But if the government possessed perfect information about taxpayers, self-assessment would become unnecessary. In this sense, economists are more interested in substitutes for law-abiding behavior than in such behavior itself. In this book, I depict Chinese tax administration as tasking hundreds of thousands of grassroots tax collectors to gather as much information as they can about taxpayers. Most Chinese tax administrators' efforts can be seen as devoted to discovering substitutes for law. Many readers may find the Chinese practice as I describe alien, even dystopian. But having studied closely both economic theories of tax compliance and Chinese practice, my conclusion is that the match between the two is greater than the match between such theories and taxpayer experience in developed countries.

The arguments I advance in this book also have many implications for the large and growing body of scholarship on Chinese law, although I will be able to discuss them only briefly in Chapter 9. Much of this scholarship concerns what I would call the superstructure of law: legislatures, courts, legal principles, and doctrines that scholars would like to persuade legislatures and courts to adopt. While I participate in such discourse as a legal scholar, I believe it is fundamentally blind to much of Chinese social reality. While it is a mistake to assume that *law* is irrelevant to describing social reality, the claim of irrelevance is more apt when applied to the superstructures of law. This is because, in China, state-sponsored social ordering often marginalizes such superstructures. For example, Chinese administrative law scholars have written for decades about fair procedures in the government imposition of penalties. The reality of Chinese tax administration, however, is that tax collectors rarely bother to impose penalties – and this is highly likely to be true in other fields of Chinese governance. Similarly, scholars studying the judiciary to assess the advance of the rule of law in China ignore the vast state apparatus that makes private parties unlikely to litigate in the first place. For these reasons, even scholars who are critical of China's legal system may overestimate the significance of law in the country, and unwittingly subscribe to a discourse (sponsored by the Chinese government) that pretends law matters. To avoid this error, it is vital to identify the systematic alternatives to law that actually support daily governance.

Outline of Chapters

Chapter 1 tells the story of a forgotten reform – a tax administration reform in 1997 – that is also one of the most momentous in the recent history of Chinese taxation. The Chinese government began to build a tax administration workforce in the 1980s. During this time, the taxpayer population comprised mainly state-owned enterprises (SOEs) and collectively owned enterprises (COEs), and tax collectors handled most taxpayers' compliance tasks. A major tax reform in 1994 introduced fundamentally new taxes that were expected to require the wide adoption of taxpayer self-assessment. Reforming tax administration therefore was essential. This reform, begun in earnest in 1997, remarkably was abandoned in just a few years. By 2005, an approach largely modeled on pre-1994 practice, called the "revenue management" system, was instituted, which gave priority to tax administrator initiatives over taxpayers' in compliance. I suggest it is precisely this unexpected survival of the pre-1994 tax administration approach – the retention of a native paradigm to implement policies borrowed from advanced economies – that defines the uniqueness of China's modern fiscal state. Chapter 1 also considers two other institutions often taken as central to Chinese taxation: (1) the separation of tax administration into two branches (one nationally controlled and the other provincially controlled) and (2) the investment in information technology. I highlight differences between the *guoshui* versus *dishui* branches of tax agencies, arguing that they are more complex than researchers previously recognized and afford no general predictions. Likewise, the contributions of technological investments are unclear. Instead, I present a third feature of China's tax administration – a high degree of decentralization – as a crucial background.

Chapter 2 offers the first full illustration of the trade-off between raising revenue and enforcing the norm of truth reporting. I begin by examining a branch of Chinese tax administration that ought to be the most comparable to other countries. In traditional theories of tax compliance, audits are the primary tool of enforcement. It has been assumed that audits in China are carried out by tax inspection (*jicha*) bureaus. However, drawing on archival material and a novel dataset, I show that the practice of mandatory taxpayer "self-inspections" prevails in the *jicha* system. Self-inspections allow tax collectors to raise revenue by foregoing penalties on noncompliant taxpayers, but erode the government's deterrence power. By making self-inspections a permanent practice, Chinese tax inspectors largely abdicate from enforcing the norm of truthful reporting and the goal of deterrence. Chapter 2 then pivots to the much larger segment of Chinese tax administration called "revenue management." Revenue managers routinely process tax returns, but they are even less likely than tax inspectors to enforce truthful reporting norms, because of the competition with tax inspection to meet revenue targets and because of a lack of specialization. Therefore, what one might have thought was an immutable component of tax administration – audits – is largely absent from Chinese practice.

Chapter 3 first explains how the revenue management system engenders non-rule-based tax collection: revenue is raised not according to the letters of the law but by informal agreements between tax administrators and taxpayers. Such practices are prevalent in many developing countries, but I argue that the strongest concern they raise is not the opportunities for corruption. Instead, it is their capacity to convert what would have been highly compliant taxpayers (e.g. large and medium firms) into "quasi-compliant" ones, that is, compliant with the dictates of low-level government employees rather than the requirements of tax law.

I then lay out a conceptual framework for analyzing the revenue management system, captured by the idea of "atomistic coercion." By "atomism," I mean that (1) instead of a government organization, the authority that taxpayers obey is better described as atomistic individuals; (2) individual tax collectors acquire information about taxpayers that they (the tax collectors) need not share with the state apparatus. "Coercion," meanwhile, conveys the idea that taxpayers perform specific compliance activities only because they are monitored by specific authorities to do so, and not because of some social norm of complying with the law. Coercion secures compliance through government *observation* and *intervention*. Intervention can secure compliance along behavioral margins that are accurately observed. But because the state's powers of observation and intervention are bounded, compliance can prove very low along the vast portions of taxpayer behavior not observed by the state or where the state's capacity for intervention is necessarily constrained. One striking example is where taxpayers file tax returns but their information is obviously inaccurate. Another phenomenon involves taxpayers formally registering with tax authorities and paying some tax, while dodging most specific compliance obligations. The trade-offs among the extensive and intensive margins of informality thus offer stark examples of both the powers and the limits of coercion.

Chapter 4 argues that atomistic coercion generates a behavioral "equilibrium": it would not make sense for any individual actor to change their behavior unless all actors change their behaviors at the same time. I analyze an important attempt to reform tax administration in one province between 2012 and 2016. Echoing the 1997 national tax administration reform agenda (which national policy makers had abandoned), reformers in Jiangsu advocated for "returning responsibilities to taxpayers," that is, enforcing truthful reporting norms. But they faced a predicament. In the pre-reform environment, information on tax returns was very inaccurate, making it difficult to improve audits. The government's overall capacity for observing taxpayers could not hope, at least in the short term, to surpass that of revenue managers. But as direct personal monitoring of taxpayers declined as a result of reform, the government risked lowering compliance. Because securing tax revenue was politically paramount, tax administrators faced pressure to continue relying on traditional means of coercion. This undermined the government's ability to threaten punishment for noncompliance beyond the traditional, minimal set of requirements. Consequently, the objective of holding taxpayers accountable for truthful reporting remained elusive. Chapter 4 illustrates this dynamic through a novel dataset on the outcomes of a new type of audit function that Jiangsu reformers instituted. Moreover, I argue that just as truthful reporting norms have no place in the low-information equilibrium of atomistic coercion, attempts to reform tax administration also struggle against crucial, background political institutions.

Chapter 5 turns to these background institutions and offers an original examination of the complex system of performance incentives within China's tax bureaucracy. What emerges is a picture of substantial heterogeneity as one moves down the bureaucratic hierarchy. When the national State Administration of Taxation evaluates provincial tax bureaus' performance, the metrics deployed are few and tend to equalize outcomes. By contrast, provincial performance evaluations of city-level tax bureaus are comprehensive and extremely detailed. Intriguingly, meeting revenue targets receives relatively little weight. The lowest tiers of management in tax agencies, and the "foot soldiers" in revenue management and tax inspection units in particular, face yet another set of incentives. While promotion opportunities are scarce, they can extract pecuniary rewards from the lowest-ranked leaders in the political branch of the state. Meanwhile, they are subject to performance targets in respect of other measurable outcomes. While scoring high on these outcomes may not be the most efficient way to raise revenue, the metrics facilitate top-down management, and are consistent with keeping enforcement discretion at the grassroots. Overall, it is the political organization of the state that ultimately determines the character of tax administration, not the instrumental relationship that the latter bears to policy implementation.

Chapter 6 elaborates the implications of the previous chapters' study of tax administration for Chinese tax policy. A main argument is that the relationship between tax administration and tax policy is highly endogenous: policy decisions can directly affect tax administration, which in turn constrain subsequent policy options. For example, political decisions to cut the PIT for the rich in China directly undermined PIT administration, which in turn made it seemingly infeasible to expand the PIT. I also offer a novel explanation for low compliance with urban employment-based SI schemes: I argue that conflicting incentives among the central and provincial government lie at the root of perennially lackluster enforcement, whereas enforcement capacity is a secondary factor. In both cases (PIT and SI), the policymaking process suffers from severe information bottlenecks, but these bottlenecks are endogenous products of what one might call information-destroying politics.

But the subtlest, yet most pervasive, causes of information constraints in Chinese tax policy are the structures of relentless delegation and governance through atomistic coercion discussed in earlier chapters. In the largest sphere of Chinese taxation – business taxation through the VAT, turnover taxes, and the CIT – information bottlenecks imply that considerations of economic efficiency are rarely applied. Instead, modifying the overall level of taxes is the chief policy lever. This introduces tremendous fiscal instability: while the government's recent resolve to lower taxes could increase efficiency in the economy, it also threatens to throw government budgets into crisis.

Chapter 7 deconstructs the discourse on the rule of law in Chinese taxation. The significance of such discourse lies in its importance to China's political actors, but the political use of the rhetoric of law implies that a more reflective account of law than is customary must be given. Legal theory suggests that every legal system must have basic *rules of recognition*: commonly known criteria for determining which social norms are legal norms. I show that such a set of rules of recognition exists in China, but the government mostly bypasses the use of legal instruments. This *disuse* of law fundamentally marginalizes the roles of China's legislative bodies and courts, without the need for the government (or Chinese Communist Party) to directly intervene or subvert their operations. Along with the marginalization of law comes selective, political invocations of law: I offer dramatic examples of this in recent PIT, CIT and property tax policy changes. Finally, I show that the political rhetoric of law stands in contrast to the government's invocations of law during the 1980s, when the concept of law in taxation supported the notions of consistency, the legitimate use of the state's coercive power, and social norms of compliance. After tax administration practices evolved to substitute for law, however, the latter became relegated largely to political discourse, particularly for maintaining political control within the state machinery.

Chapter 8 explores the implications of the previous chapters' findings for the study of taxation in developing countries. The most distinctive feature of Chinese tax system is the adoption of taxes that are designed to be administered through self-assessment, while minimizing reliance on self-assessment. This fundamental modification of the modern taxation paradigm has deep implications. First, it suggests substantial revisions to economic theories of tax compliance: to articulate the difference between China's approach to tax administration and those prevalent in developed economies, one must recognize the deep connections between modern taxation and legal systems. Second, the evolution of Chinese tax administration provides a rare case study for exploring the conjecture that, to properly analyze tax and development, one must consider not only state capacity in tax collection, but also view such state capacity as endogenous with politics. I show that my account of Chinese taxation partially affirms, as well as enriches, this conjecture. Finally, technological developments could strengthen the tendency of China's tax system to continue on its recent path. Indeed, instead of the Chinese tax system converging to more familiar paradigms of modern taxation, tax administrative practices around the world may show convergence towards the Chinese paradigm.

In Chapter 9, I explain some implications of the book's investigations for legal scholarship and scholarship on Chinese politics. Many legal scholars have speculated about whether China might adopt "rule by law" without embracing "rule of law." This stylized discourse, however, assumes that the Chinese government is willing and able to implement "rule by law." However, because coercive substitutes for the law are often available and preferred, even "rule by law" is optional, and discussions of rule of law norms are on even shakier grounds than legal scholars realize. Relatedly, I explain how the Chinese bureaucracy can incorporate elements of meritocracy and even autonomy, without being "Weberian." Finally, I argue that a better understanding of China's fiscal politics is critical for predicting and imagining the nation's future.

1

The Forgotten Reform

This book is about foundations: What are the most important structural features of China's contemporary tax system, and what are its fundamental determinants? In 1994, Chinese political leaders engineered a major tax reform that continues to define the key elements of the country's public finance system. This book focuses almost entirely on taxation in China *since* 1994,[1] an approach that invites some questions. The 1994 tax reform may itself be an important part of the explanation of China's success in collecting revenue in the past quarter century. If so, would an account of Chinese taxation not need to situate the post-1994 tax system within a longer time horizon? In other words, what are the key decisions of the 1994 tax reform, and how do they correspond to the structural features of the system that emerged?

Past commentators have habitually given extensive attention to the 1994 tax reform. In fact, among educated people – who are not tax specialists – whom I have talked to in China, the single institutional feature of Chinese taxation that they are most likely to identify is the revenue-sharing system (*fenshuizhi*) established in 1994. Under this system, the national (central) government agreed with provincial governments on sharing ratios for revenues from different types of taxes; these ratios varied across taxes but were uniform across provinces. Provincial governments then proceeded to agree with their own sub-provincial units on ways of sharing revenue not claimed by the central

[1] There are at least two reasons to believe that it is China's post-1994 tax system that matters to readers interested in tax and development generally. First, the 1994 tax reform roughly coincided with – in fact, it was motivated by – China's decision to embrace the market economy for its urban sector. Moreover, the role of taxation within a market economy is of much greater general significance than tax systems, such as China's before 1994, that are part of a planned economy. Second, it is under the post-1994 tax system that the country's tax collection succeeded, as measured by a rising tax-to-GDP ratio during decades of unprecedented economic growth. It is this stellar performance that policy makers and scholars may want most to understand.

government. The sharing percentages for different taxes have changed over time.

One problem with privileging this aspect of the 1994 tax reform, however, is that revenue-sharing arrangements are quite common around the world, especially among federalist countries (such as Canada, Australia, and Germany). While intergovernmental revenue transfers are important to the politics of taxation in many countries, there is no reason to believe that they are *more* important in determining China's tax system than they are in defining other tax systems. Moreover, while there are long-standing bodies of scholarship that study intergovernmental transfers, subnational tax competition, and other related topics, they are relatively specialized subjects that assume a background of state capacity for revenue extraction. If revenue sharing were the most remarkable feature of the Chinese tax system, the system itself would not be that remarkable.

There is also the problem, of course, that revenue must be raised before it can be shared. One aspect of the 1994 tax reform that obviously requires comment before we turn to revenue sharing is the taxes China decided to impose. Given that China had only just decided to abandon its planned economy in the early 1990s, one might expect that the taxes it introduced in 1994 were new. This was indeed the case. The 1994 tax reform launched many taxes, all of which were relatively unfamiliar to the country. These included, among others, a unified corporate income tax (CIT) that would apply to all domestically owned firms (a parallel CIT regime for foreign-owned firms was retained); a personal income tax (PIT) that would theoretically apply to the entire populace; a value-added tax (VAT) applicable to the production and sale of goods; and a broad-based turnover tax applicable to all services (Business Tax, or *yingyeshui*).[2] Specialists refer to this portfolio of tax policy instruments and their relative importance as the "tax structure" of a country; China's current tax structure is a product of this 1994 tax reform.

However, tax structure is a topic that tends to be relegated to specialists. Few people outside public economics or the tax and business professions seem to think that the relative importance among a country's PIT, payroll taxes, CIT, or VAT is of fundamental *institutional* significance. Also, what a specialist *can* say is that China's chosen tax structure is, at least on its surface, somewhat conventional from a comparative perspective. Most importantly, the PIT plays a relatively small role in raising

[2] China's social insurance (SI) regime, which imposed substantial payroll taxes that have gained prominence in the past two decades, was introduced later. See Chapter 6 for an extended discussion of the SI regime.

revenue, while the CIT, VAT, and Business Tax lift most of the weight in filling the government coffer. There are generally accepted explanations for the prevalence of similar tax structures among developing countries, to which we will turn in Chapter 6. But because of such similarities, it follows that describing this tax structure when explaining the 1994 tax reform would still not identify what is unique about Chinese taxation.

Finally, the 1994 tax reform set up two separate branches of tax administration: the State Tax Bureau (*guojia shuiwuju*, which I abbreviate as *guoshui* or GS) and Local Tax Bureau (*difang shuiwuju*, *dishui*, or DS) systems.[3] The former collected several taxes that had a greater or entire share of their revenue claimed by the central government (most importantly, the VAT), while the latter collected other taxes, including especially the PIT, Business Tax, and, in some provinces, social insurance (SI) contributions.[4] This bifurcation of tax administration, creating what has been known as the *guoshui* versus *dishui* dichotomy, was for fourteen years a key feature of Chinese tax administration. However, the bifurcation was abolished in 2018, and its legacy is unclear. While the *guoshui* versus *dishui* tax administration split has fewer counterparts in other countries, we will see that it too yields few general implications.

This chapter aims to answer the following question: Is there some aspect of the 1994 tax reform that helps define what is relatively unique about the Chinese fiscal state? I offer an affirmative answer, but the answer's details have to do with a core vision of the reform that unraveled, was gradually abandoned by the early 2000s, and became virtually unspoken of. In other words, the most distinctive part of the reform is a part that failed, and consequently, was forgotten.

An Earlier Foundation

While the politics of the 1994 tax reform was extraordinarily complex,[5] consider one basic question that Chinese national policy makers – from Premier Zhu Rongji to his advisors in the Ministry of Finance (MOF) – must have faced. How should China go about, practically, collecting the

3 It is a pervasive feature of contemporary Chinese discourse that two meanings of "state" are conflated in the term *guojia*: the first connotes public authority and governmental power, while the second connotes country/nation. In the term "state tax bureau," "state" connotes national. Correspondingly, in the term "local tax bureau," "local" means subnational, including government entities at the provincial and sub-provincial levels.

4 Responsibility for collecting the CIT is split between the GS and DS systems.

5 See Liu and Jia 2009.

multitude of new taxes? There are two equally stylized and contrasting answers. The first is that *one needs bodies*. That is, the government needed to ensure that there were tax collectors around the country ready to enforce the new taxes. This answer, focusing on personnel capacity, seems intuitive and compelling. Many scholars and commentators have followed this idea to explain subsequent developments in Chinese tax collection. For example, they have examined the *guoshui* and *dishui* tax bureaus – with some scholars positing differences in incentives between tax collectors in the two administrative branches – and used such differences to explain tax administration outcomes.

While I will consider these arguments later, it is important to note that before 1994, the "bodies" were already largely there. Figure 1.1 plots the long-term evolution of the size of the Chinese tax administration workforce, based on the *China Taxation Yearbook* (for years after 1993) and information gathered from various archival sources (for earlier years). What we see is a striking and steady rise in tax collection personnel beginning from 1979, the start of China's economic reform. This workforce was not bifurcated into two systems before 1994, and in Figure 1.1 it is represented by the black line until 1993. By 1988, the overall personnel size of Chinese tax administration had already risen to around 463,000 individuals, a 160 percent increase from the 1979 level. By 1993, formal employment in the tax

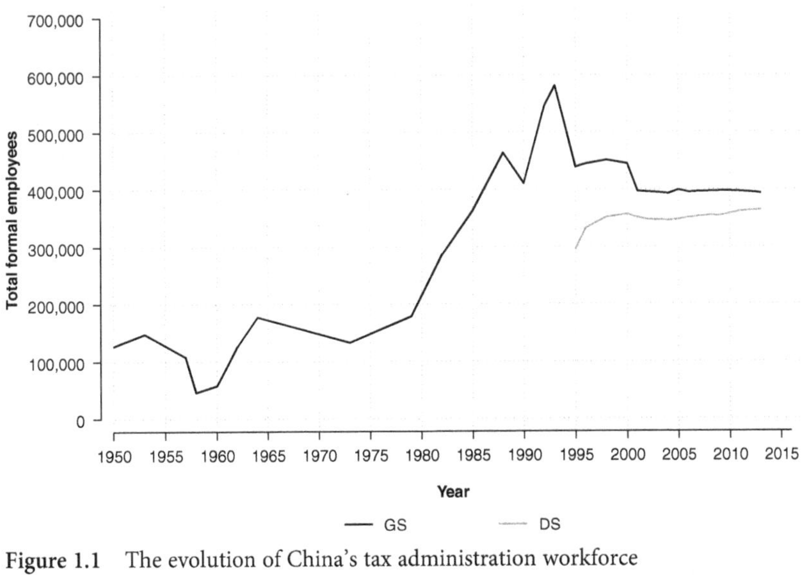

Figure 1.1 The evolution of China's tax administration workforce

administration apparatus reached 581,000, or 325 percent of the 1979 level. In 1994, this workforce was split into the GS and DS branches, with the GS system keeping most existing personnel. The DS system, taking over a smaller portion of the preexisting army of tax administrators, began to hire more staff. The GS system experienced a significant personnel reduction in 2001, but the size of Chinese tax administration remained steady in the following years.[6] In 2013, the total number of tax administrators in China was 756,592, only 30 percent higher than what the country had in 1993. The basic message of Figure 1.1 is that whatever the Chinese government did to organize personnel for enforcing a new tax system, it did so upon a foundation laid down before 1993. The primary challenge facing policy makers in 1993 was not the shortage of personnel. Instead, it was how to make an existing army of tax collectors collect new taxes.

What were the 581,000 Chinese tax administrators in 1993 doing, if they were not collecting the taxes later introduced in 1994? It is possible to answer this question, without going into much detail into the evolution of the Chinese tax system up until 1993,[7] in three steps.

First, between the 1970s and 1993, tax policy making in China was considerably decentralized. Although the national government enacted a series of taxes after economic reform began in 1978, the obligation to enforce these taxes fell on subnational governments and was often treated as nonbinding. This was because regardless of the specific taxes in use, most provinces were only accountable to the central government for transferring fixed amounts negotiated in advance for each year, under what was known as the "fiscal contracting" system.[8] Because provincial and sub-provincial governments carried out tax collection, and because the central government's main lever of control was negotiating targets for revenue transfers to itself, the rules by which taxes were collected were hard to dictate.

This was exacerbated by the fact that the rules requiring enforcement left much to discretion. A majority of the new taxes introduced by the central government in the 1980s were taxes on the profits of SOEs and COEs that

[6] I will return to the post-1994 personnel story later in this chapter, as it provides a useful heuristic for explaining numerous background features of Chinese tax administration.

[7] Important summaries of the history of Chinese taxation from the 1950s to 1993 can be found in World Bank 1990; Oksenberg and Tong 1991; Wong 1991; Lou and Wang 2008; Liu and Jia 2009.

[8] For details see Oksenberg and Tong 1991. The heydays of fiscal decentralization in 1980s China represented the background of an earlier social scientific literature on "market-preserving federalism." See Jin et al. 2005.

still dominated China's urban economy at the time. These profit taxes replaced the surrender of profits by state- or collectively owned firms to their government shareholders under the planned economy. Notably, firms under the planned economy had not kept much of their profits. Consequently, the taxes that initially replaced the profit distribution regimes were characterized by high rates, as well as pervasive firm-specific negotiations with the government regarding the applicable rate. Regional tax competition and grants of local tax preferences further fueled a tendency for tax liabilities to be determined on an individual firm basis. To a substantial extent, there was no set of "national laws" enforced by tax collectors around the country.[9] Instead, low-level tax offices often directly participated in negotiations between local governments and local SOEs and COEs about how much tax each had to pay. The line between tax administration and tax policy making was tenuous. This was one of the core practices that the central government tried to curtail by launching the 1994 tax reform.

Second, apart from the risk – a source of notable concern to the central government – that individual tax collection offices would decide what policies applied to, or could be waived for, particular taxpayers, the role of the Chinese tax collector in the 1980s generally involved intensive contact with taxpayers. Large taxpayers (many of which were SOEs and COEs) were often each assigned a dedicated tax administrator (*shuishou zhuanguan yuan*), an agent who determined what and how much taxes a firm needed to pay, and literally saw through payments from the firm to the government. Very early on, Chinese tax administrators recognized a stark contrast between this emerging mode of tax collection and the style of tax administration that foreign experts were beginning to describe in relation to developed countries: it was often observed that in China, there was no separation between "administration," "inspection," and "collection" in taxation. In the 1980s, this all-in-one role of the tax administrator had come to be known among Chinese tax officials as "nanny-style" (*baomushi*) tax administration: taxpayers were like children, with their tax compliance taken care of by tax administrators.[10]

[9] China gradually centralized tax policy-making power in the 1980s; see Cui 2012a.

[10] Some Chinese tax officials describe "nanny-style" tax administration as the prevailing tax-collection style imposed under China's planned economy from the mid-1950s to the late 1970s. It bears emphasis that this was not just a matter of tax collectors going to market fairs or street vendors to collect payment that would not otherwise be made. The practice applied to the largest taxpayers in each tax office's jurisdiction as well.

Chapters 3 and 4 explore how a more technologically advanced Chinese tax administration still struggles to exorcise the spirit of "nanny-style" administration. "Returning responsibility to taxpayers," for example, has been the core principle and ringing slogan in tax administration reforms pursued by some provinces in the past decade. However, in 1980s China, "nanny-style" tax administration was a very practical arrangement. For SOEs and COEs in particular, paying tax was just a continuation of the prior practice of transferring profits to economic planners. Both tax and accounting rules were still underdeveloped, so the intervention of government agents was often necessary for determining tax liability. Budgetary units within the government were also decentralized, fragmented, and continuously changing. Having tax collectors help each business navigate such a system and shepherd tax payments through may have seemed a natural additional task.

Third, as the Chinese urban economy began to liberalize in the late 1980s, many SOEs and COEs began to fail: tax revenue from such firms plummeted.[11] Increasingly, the government needed to raise revenue from a growing population of private firms that were much more resistant to the demands of tax administrator "nannies." Moreover, the sheer number of new firms implied that tax administrators could not remain "dedicated" to a single or a small number of taxpayers. It did not take long for the government to figure out that the "dedicated tax administrator" system could not continue. Consequently, discussions about reforming tax administration emerged just a few years after such administration was implemented. In the early 1990s, before the 1994 tax reform, two practical ideas were widely discussed.[12] One was that tax administrators should not handle payments; taxpayers should remit taxes directly at banks to government accounts. The other was that tax administrators should increasingly focus on "examining" businesses' tax affairs. The underlying assumption was that, by then, one could speak of *correct* ways of determining tax liability, which taxpayers could follow themselves. Tax administrators would simply verify and monitor taxpayers' self-assessment.

[11] Wong 1991.

[12] The State Administration of Taxation (SAT) is reported to have issued certain "Opinions on Reforming Tax Administration throughout the Country" in December 1989, after running reform pilots in 1988 in three provinces. The text of the 1989 tax administration reform plan, however, cannot be located. It appears to be an earlier example of a reform designed within one government agency and overtaken by larger political events (in this case, the 1994 tax reform). Analogies thus can be drawn with the abandonment of the 1997 tax administration reform.

In summary, China already employed close to 600,000 tax administrators in 1993. Most of these individuals were hired in the 1980s; they enforced a transitory set of taxes that would soon become obsolete and dealt with a tax base (i.e. the profit and turnovers of SOEs and COEs) that was rapidly shrinking. While the 1994 tax reform would soon centralize both tax policy making and government budgetary affairs on the political front, there is an entirely separate question that needed to be answered: How would the work of frontline tax administrators change? This leads us back to the question, described earlier, that likely confronted Chinese tax policy makers in 1993: How should China go about collecting so many taxes that it had not collected before?

There is a second stylized answer to this question, which does not hinge on the existence of tax administrators (they were already there), and not even, at least not primarily, on tax administrators doing things in particular ways. In fact, this second answer ought to be easy to grasp, but it has eluded many commentators on modern tax administration.

Specifically, among the variety of taxes that China considered adopting in the early 1990s – which were also taxes widely observed in other countries in the late twentieth and early twenty-first centuries – some depended on the actions of tax administrators more than others. Taxes on real property and custom duties on imports, for example, required tax administrators' intervention in the completion of compliance obligations: a tax assessor often needs to assess property value before a property owner's tax liability can be determined and paid; the confirmation of duties paid is needed for customs to be cleared. Other taxes, however, are *self-assessed*: tax administrators intervene only in some cases, such as to audit a taxpayer, to correct mistakes, or to provide a refund. Generally, the taxpayers themselves determine the amount owed, make payments, and complete compliance tasks without interaction with tax administrators. The CIT, VAT, Business Tax, and the withholding of PIT and payroll taxes by employers – examples of major sources of tax revenue in post-1994 China and most developed countries – are characterized by this reliance on self-assessment.

To make this system work, then, a radical shift needed to happen: taxpayers had to start filing tax returns and follow the law themselves.

Reforming Administration to Enforce New Taxes

To see how vital taxpayer compliance was to the way Chinese political leaders envisioned the 1994 tax reform, one only has to read one of the two key official documents that laid out the reform's agenda: the notice issued by the State Council on December 25, 1993, to all Chinese provincial governments and all central government ministries regarding "the Approval and Transmission of the Implementation Plan for the Reform of Industrial and Commercial Taxation Proposed by the State Administration of Taxation."[13] About two-thirds of the document was devoted to the various taxes that the reform would introduce. The next lengthiest portion of the document, however, proposed the principles for a *tax administration reform.*

Practical, but New, Principles

The State Council's careful formulation of these principles in 1993 is worth quoting at length:

> 1. *Widely establish a tax declaration system.* Making tax declarations is the first key step for taxpayers in fulfilling their tax obligations. Establishing a tax declaration system would facilitate the formation of a self-restraining mechanism among taxpayers and enhance the tax-paying awareness among citizens. It is a foundational project that enables tax authorities to implement effective tax collection and management. After the establishment of the tax declaration system, any delays or false declarations shall be regarded as tax evasion and strictly punished according to the law.
> 2. *Actively promote a tax agent/representative system.* In accordance with internationally accepted practices, a tax agent system shall be implemented, where accounting and law firms and other private intermediaries represent taxpayers in handling tax affairs. These agents will gradually become an indispensable link within the tax collection and management system.
> 3. *Accelerate the process of computerizing tax collection and management.* International experience has proven that the use of computers and other advanced technologies in tax collection is the only way to establish a rigorous and effective tax monitoring network, while also reducing the cost of tax collection. As the country has a large number of scattered taxpayers and a weak foundation in computerized management, the computerization process may begin in cities and in the collection and management of key tax types. A nationwide comprehensive computer network for tax collection and management would be gradually established.

[13] *Guofa* [1993] 90. A parallel document, the State Council Decision to Implement the Revenue Sharing System of Public Finance Management (*Guofa* [1993] 85), was issued ten days earlier. That document described the tax reform in a more abbreviated fashion, focusing on revenue sharing and especially on reforms to the budgeting and transfer payment systems.

4. *Institute a strict tax inspection system.* Following the wide establishment of a tax declaration system and a tax agent system, the main focus of the tax authorities would shift to carrying out routine as well as key inspections. Tax collection would be founded on the three-part configuration of declaration, assistance by tax agents, and inspection. These approaches shall be supplemented by heavy penalties for tax evasion.
5. Separate central and local tax agencies will be established to meet the needs of the revenue sharing system.
6. *Establish the basic tax norms that suit the needs of the socialist market economy.* At this stage, it is particularly necessary to emphasize the following. Taxpayers must pay tax in accordance with the law. Tax authorities must collect taxes in accordance with the law. Taxes must be calculated based on the rates set out in the tax law. No one shall apply a "tax farming" (*baoshui*) approach or arbitrarily adjust the tax rates. All *ad valorem* taxes must be calculated based on actual price, the practice in some industries of not changing tax after price increases must be eliminated. Except for tax reduction and exemption prescribed by the tax law, governments at all levels and various departments shall not approve additional tax reduction or exemption.
7. Lawmaking power for both central taxes and local taxes that are to be implemented nationwide will be exclusively held by the central government.
8. Strengthen the rule of law in tax collection, expedite the legislation process for tax laws and regulations; gradually establish a tax system where legislation, judicial review, and law enforcement are mutually independent and mutually constraining.

   "*With the implementation of the above measures, the country's tax administration will transform into a new configuration which puts equal emphasis on legal rules, collection, inspection, and appeals and litigation, with the four aspects coordinated with and binding each other.*" (Emphasis added)

Three comments must be made about these striking pronouncements. First, they describe a style of tax administration characterized by several interlinked elements, all of which were missing from the Chinese tax system when the pronouncements were made. That is, on the eve of the reform, most Chinese taxpayers did not declare their liabilities on tax returns filed with tax authorities; tax professions did not exist to assist taxpayers in such tasks; tax authorities rarely engaged in audits (since there were no declarations or returns to audit); the norm of complying with the law was not established among either tax administrators or taxpayers; and there existed only rudimentary tax rules and regulations. Additionally, while the Chinese legal system allowed citizens to file lawsuits against the government starting in the late 1980s, judicial involvement in tax collection had mainly been in the criminal procedure sphere. In short, these proposed mechanisms of tax administration were as new to China as the taxes introduced by the 1994 tax reform.

Second, as revealed by the references to international experience in the second and third principles, the State Council's and SAT's vision of tax administration reform borrowed from foreign practice.[14] The Chinese government received substantial technical assistance from the World Bank, International Monetary Fund, and other international organizations and foreign governments in designing the 1994 tax reform. Such foreign advice appeared to have convinced the Chinese government of the necessity of implementing a rather alien vision,[15] within which tax administration was, non-trivially, about promoting norms associated with legal systems. Specifically, it was not just that how tax liabilities were determined needed to be written into the law: it needed to be written into the law because that was how taxpayers would know what rules to follow, which in turn was important because taxpayers taking their own initiative to apply the law was how the new taxes would be collected. The tax professions were necessary to help taxpayers apply the law. Similarly, the role of tax administrators was reconceptualized: tax administrators must follow the law instead of exercising discretion, and their primary task now was to check whether taxpayers correctly applied the law to themselves, rather than applying the law *for* taxpayers.

This novel language of law may nevertheless have sounded practical to Chinese government officials. Compare the reference to law with the idea of computerization: China was still a poor country in 1993; the widespread use of computers could only be described in aspirational terms. Law, by contrast, was not some expensive technology, but a social practice that a government might adopt should it fit its country's needs. Although the State Council did allude to what one might call the superstructure of law (i.e. legislatures and courts), its focus was on such grassroots appliers of law as tax administrators and taxpayers. Moreover, since the 1980s, the Chinese government had already increasingly emphasized rule-based tax collection, and had especially wanted to use law to limit local government

14 Contrast this with the very brief mentions of the creation of a bipartite (i.e. GS vs. DS) tax administration, or of the exclusive claim to policy-making power by the central government. Neither arrangement was based on foreign experience.

15 The fact that the State Council, near the top of the administrative reform agenda, prescribed a flourishing tax profession seems positively quaint.

discretion. Consequently, policy makers already possessed some familiarity with the invocations of law.[16]

Third, and most importantly, the State Council's 1993 pronouncements conveyed a vision that has *not* been realized: China currently does not have the system of tax administration contemplated in 1993; it has instead taken a different route, one that will preoccupy us for much of this book. Readers previously exposed to discussions about the 1994 tax reform will likely be surprised to learn that tax administration was a core of the reform agenda,[17] or that the implementation of legal norms was considered central to the transformation of tax administration. The fact that the administrative reform described in 1993 did not fundamentally transform China's tax collection and compliance explains why. This history in itself should also puncture any presumption that the principles the State Council endorsed in 1993 are anodyne recitations of what would more or less happen automatically. Instead, the principles articulate choices about fundamental institutions. The abandonment of these choices, as the rest of this book will show, has had radical consequences.

Of course, the State Council's policy pronouncements are sometimes mere rhetoric, echoed by subordinate government units for some time, but not necessarily pursued in practice.[18] However, the State Council's 1993 pronouncement about reforming the nation's tax administration was no empty talk. If its fundamental logic has not been reflected in China's current tax administration practice, it was not because no action was taken. In January 1997, the Office of the State Council released a plan for reforming tax administration proposed by the SAT.[19] The 1997 plan

[16] See Cui 2012a. In Chapter 7, I discuss how the practical invocations of law in the early 1990s were gradually replaced by politically motivated rhetoric of law.

[17] The portion of the reform agenda devoted to tax administration reform was approximately the same length as the prescription for revenue sharing in Guofa [1993] 85.

[18] Legal scholars are especially familiar with this type of rhetoric, as the State Council has exhorted government agencies to follow the rule of law for decades, which has in many senses gone ignored.

[19] Notice of the State Council Forwarding the SAT's Agenda for Deepening the Reform of Tax Administration (*Guobanfa* [1997]). The delay of implementing tax administration reform was no doubt because of the overwhelming personnel task of creating the separate GS and DS branches of tax administration during 1994–1996. Information on this task can be gleaned from State Commission Office for Public Sector Reform, Ministry of Personnel and SAT, Notice regarding Personnel Plan in the Guoshui System and Dishui Tax Offices and Related Issues (*Zhongbianbanfa* [1996]10, August 1, 1996). In addition, other aspects of the 1994 reform, especially the budgetary transition to the revenue sharing regime for government units across the country, preoccupied Chinese political leaders.

called for "deepening tax administration reform." Reform would be gradually rolled out in the country, first in urban centers and then in rural areas. The goal was to "strive to largely complete" the plan by 2010. This formulation and the fourteen-year time horizon indicate that what the SAT had in mind was ambitious. It could not be quickly executed, as it was a matter of fundamental institution building.

Building a System of Self-Declarations

The SAT summarized its administration reform program succinctly, in what some Chinese tax administrators came to call the "thirty-character strategy." This new approach would have "as its foundation taxpayer declarations" (i.e. self-assessment) and "enhanced taxpayer service"; it would "rely on a computer network"; "tax collection would be centralized" (i.e. taken away from individual tax collectors); and the emphasis in tax administration would "shift to audits." The SAT then outlined the concrete measures for implementing each element of this strategy. For instance, it set five targets for urban tax administrators for 1997. First, all firms and sole proprietors were to begin filing tax returns that year. Second, tax agencies needed to open public-facing offices that would allow taxpayers to submit returns, make payments, and handle other tax matters, instead of relying on tax administrators to perform these tasks for them. Third, based on the transition to self-assessment and more centralized payments and services, grassroots tax administrators would begin to specialize. In particular, at least 40 percent of tax administration personnel should be assigned to audit tasks. Fourth, new internal divisions would be created in tax bureaus to replace existing ones. Fifth, and finally, while no particular target for computerization was stipulated for 1997, tax bureaus were responsible for setting up files or accounts for each taxpayer, so that the compliance activities of each could be recorded and monitored.

Both in the State Council–approved version of the 1997 SAT reform program, and in subsequent directives for implementing the program, the SAT provided further instructions about return filing, taxpayer services, and centralized collection.[20] I will turn to the implementation of these instructions shortly. It is useful to note, however, that in comparison to these aspects of tax administration, the SAT's instructions for computerization

[20] An important further omnibus directive was the SAT Notice regarding Implementing the Plan for Deepening Reform of Tax Administration Forwarded by the State Council (*Guoshuifa* [1997] 27, February 21, 1997).

and audits were vague. With respect to computerization, the SAT expected that technological upgrades would be gradual as well as decentralized. Specifically, there was no concrete plan for information systems to be developed at the provincial, let alone national, level.[21] Indeed, the primary role for computerization delineated in 1997 was one of assisting the new daily functions of Chinese tax administration: maintaining taxpayer accounts, handling tax returns, and tracking payments as well as other interactions between taxpayers and tax bureaus. Insofar as these administrative tasks would remain decentralized, it only made sense for the cost-saving, efficiency-enhancing use of computers to be decentralized as well. While the decentralized building of information systems would forego the benefits of the economy of scale, it allowed flexibility and avoided waste in a fast-evolving administrative environment. A nationwide information system that would allow data sharing across regions was not part of the plan.

With respect to building audit capacity, the SAT's 1997 reform program offered several general guiding principles. First, like computer networks, audit units would be established in urban areas at the district and city levels. The lower audit units would regularly examine taxpayer affairs, while the city units would deal with important cases as well as process whistleblower claims. Second, tax authorities would begin to conduct routine audits (potentially of any taxpayer), special issue audits (where select issues would be examined in connection with a group of taxpayers), and special case audits (focusing on important cases of noncompliance detected through the two previous types of audits). Third, only one measurable outcome of audit capacity-building was prescribed: at least 40 percent of all tax administration personnel should be assigned to audit units.

The actual implementation of the 1997 tax administration reform involved the mobilization of extensive public and private resources. A tangible example is the construction and opening of taxpayer service halls (*nashui fuwu ting*) across the country. By the mid-2000s, these government premises had become ubiquitous features of China's urban landscape, often housed in impressive buildings occupied by tax bureaus. While the advent of online filing and e-government in the past decade means that taxpayer service halls are no longer the bustling places they used to be, they were the high-speed railways of yesteryear in Chinese taxation: they allowed a massive population of Chinese taxpayers to perform compliance

[21] The SAT called for an infrastructure, by the early twenty-first century, comprising two-tiered computer networks in urban areas. The first tier would be at the district/county level, the second at the level of prefectural cities.

obligations in an unprecedented fashion. Not only could taxpayer registration, return filing, payments, tax invoices, and applications for tax preferences all be handled at these centers, but taxpayers would also often obtain information about tax law and policy. Indeed, they arguably made taxpayer service one of the strongest components of Chinese tax administration.[22]

Less visible than the hardware of tax service centers, but no less important, is the system of processing taxpayer information. Tax returns, along with their respective instructions, were designed and published according to the 1997 reform plan. Often, the next step required proactive problem-solving on the part of local tax bureaus. Consider the story of one lowly tax bureau in the district of Huanggu, one of the ten districts in Shenyang, the capital city of Liaoning Province in northeast China. In 1995, the Huanggu GS branch bureau had jurisdiction over a taxpayer population that included close to 8,000 private firms. The branch bureau boasted of a 200-square-meter taxpayer service hall, but even this could not accommodate the crowd when all taxpayers came to file tax returns in person. Even with twenty staff members and ten desktop computers, handling in-person filing required the service center to open "without lunch break and late into the evening." Long queues lined up.

To solve this problem, the Huanggu branch bureau entered into an agreement with the district's postal bureau so that taxpayers could submit tax returns by mail. Special arrangements had to be made for this to work. For one, if taxpayers had to weigh their heavy envelopes stuffed with tax returns at post offices, the latter would themselves be clogged! In response, the Huanggu postal bureau agreed to offer a special, single rate for all mail sent to the local tax office regardless of weight. Indeed, the tax and postal bureaus found it worthwhile to print a new kind of envelope for mailing tax returns within the district. Special daily delivery services between taxpayers and the tax bureau were also launched. With these arrangements, the Huanggu branch bureau was able to invest in automatic envelope openers and scanners to process tax returns, in lieu of building a larger taxpayer service hall. This purportedly increased the speed of return processing by twenty times, helping to reduce the service center personnel from twenty to five.[23]

This special arrangement with the postal service was adopted in the entire province of Liaoning by 1997. The SAT included a report of the

[22] As we will see, the physical accessibility of Chinese tax offices is comparable to that of post offices.

[23] One benefit from this arrangement apparently was that the personnel staffing the taxpayer service halls could now be assigned to audit tasks instead.

practice in a national circular, promoting tax and postal bureau cooperation across China in the processing of tax returns.[24] Likewise, the coordination of grassroots tax bureaus and bank branches (in setting up taxpayer accounts that allowed direct bank transfers to government accounts) formed another theme of local experimentation.[25] Many similar stories can be told. The general point is that establishing a taxpayer self-declaration system was itself no simple feat. It required not only the undertakings of multiple government agencies but also massive mobilization among taxpayers. At least in the late 1990s, tax administration reform was not just talk. It was a radical transformation.

There is strong evidence from official statistics that the late 1990s saw several highly unusual years in Chinese tax administration. The government reported some of the highest numbers of taxpayer inspections in the country's history, as if tax collectors around the country answered the call to increase audit activity.[26] Tax auditors also appeared to have had ample material to work with: in 1998, an aggregate of 220,519 whistleblower reports about tax evasion were filed across 5,879 whistleblower centers in the nation.[27] Even the State Council's reference to tax dispute resolution as one of the four equal pillars of tax administration resonated in practice: close to 6,000 first-instance lawsuits were filed by taxpayers against tax agencies between 1998 and 2000.[28] This may not seem much in a country with over a billion people. But for comparison, the annual average quantity of tax cases in China for the 2006–2013 period was fewer than 400. The late 1990s, with an annual average of 2,000 cases, was practically the golden age of tax litigation in China.[29]

There is a rich story to be told here. The activities of processing tax returns, providing services to taxpayers, and facilitating tax payments may seem quotidian, but they are foundational to modern tax systems.

24 SAT and National Postal Bureau, Measures for the Postal Handling of Tax Returns (*Guoshuifa* [1997]14, September 26, 1997).

25 See SAT, People's Bank of China and the Ministry of Finance, Notice Regarding Strengthening Work in Return Filing and Payments (*Guoshuifa* [1997] 100, August 7, 1997). While the 1997 SAT reform program contemplated replacing taxpayers' cash payments with the use of checks and credit cards (another idea from foreign experts), such payment methods would largely not materialize.

26 The subsequent decline of audit coverage is discussed in the next chapter.

27 This and the subsequent decline in tax whistleblowing are documented in Cui and Wang 2019.

28 Cui 2017a.

29 Cui 2017a. Even in 2016, the total number of lawsuits in China against tax agencies was only 653. Cui et al. 2019.

The institutionalization of such practices in China in the late 1990s is critical for understanding the system's ensuing success. Or, at least, they are of equal significance as other features of Chinese tax administrations that have received more attention (e.g. the division between GS and DS bureaus). I have dwelled on the 1997 tax administration reform, however, not because of its richness and significance. Instead, I have done so because, despite its role in implementing practices that form the bedrock of China's taxation system, very few people in China talk about the reform in the years that followed, and most scholars do not even acknowledge that it happened.

Reform Abandoned

There exists little to no scholarship, from Chinese or non-Chinese writers, on China's 1997 tax administration reform. By contrast, less sweeping tax administration changes have attracted more commentary. For example, in 2002, the central government adjusted its revenue-sharing agreement with provinces to allocate a greater share of CIT revenue to itself. In connection with this change, for the period between 2002 and 2008, all new firms registered in China were required to remit the CIT to GS bureaus instead of DS bureaus. This change in CIT administration is examined in several scholarly studies, even though it is more piecemeal relative to the 1997 reform.[30] Similarly, several recent studies have probed the impact of the Golden Tax Project between 2000 and 2002 on firms' VAT compliance.[31] Generally, Chinese scholars postulate that tax enforcement has steadily improved after 1994, and most attribute this improvement to the changing jurisdictional scope between DS and GS bureaus, the Golden Tax Project, or simply various government units' "tax effort."[32] The onset of the self-declaration system in 1997 is rarely mentioned.

[30] Tian and Fan 2016 hypothesize that the lowered revenue share for subnational governments after 2002 reduced the incentives of DS bureaus to collect CIT, but not that of GS bureaus. They provide evidence that they interpret as showing that firms subject to DS jurisdiction came to engage in greater tax evasion. Cai et al. 2018, by contrast, show that firms established immediately after the 2002 policy change (thereby coming under GS jurisdiction) displayed substantially lower effective tax rates compared to firms established just before the policy change. They interpret this as firms being subject to more lax enforcement under GS.

[31] Fan et al. 2018. The Golden Tax Project is briefly discussed at the end of this chapter.

[32] Lü and Guo 2012; Fang and Zhang 2013; Xie and Fan 2015. As I will discuss in Chapter 2, scholars have also examined the tax inspection system, partly due to the ready availability of data.

I believe the Chinese government's abandonment of key objectives in the 1997 tax administration reform may be a principal reason for the reform's academic oversight. In China, the national media is dominated by the voice of the government. If the national government wants to elevate some reform to public prominence, such as the 2002 modification of CIT revenue sharing or the Golden Tax Project, the successes and societal impact of such reforms naturally occupy scholarly attention. By contrast, if the national government decides to relegate a policy that has fallen from favor to obscurity, scholars are unlikely to take notice.

There are various ways of tracing the gradual abandonment of the 1997 reform. For instance, in 1999, the Chinese government decided to embark on an overall reduction in government personnel across agencies. This exogenous shock certainly impacted tax administration: the GS system's staff size shrank by over 48,000 in 2000. When the SAT set out the organizational and personnel plan for the GS system in 1997, implementing the tax administration reform was a central objective.[33] Yet the SAT's next organizational plan, issued in 2000, made no mention of the reform (which was supposed to be ongoing until 2010), and focused instead on the new objective of reducing personnel and handing mass government layoffs.[34] From this point on, the goal of dedicating at least 40 percent of total staff to audit tasks ceased to receive mention in SAT documents.

But a more important development, referred to only obliquely in official documents, was the emergence of a critique of the 1997 reform agenda. According to this critique, the 1997 reform vision led to "the neglect of management, and the weakening of accountability" (*shuyu guanli, danhua zeren*). This critique never received an official exegesis. Commentaries circulated within Chinese tax administration suggest that it had two components. First, the "neglect of management" referred to a problem that arose from the separation of tax collection, audit, and the supervision or "management" of taxpayer affairs. This practice, as we saw earlier, had been advocated since the 1980s. The critique argued that while the 1997 reform entrenched the roles of tax collection and audits, tax administrators were becoming too removed from taxpayers: they simply waited for taxpayers to

[33] SAT Opinions Regarding Modifying the Allocation of Functions, Internal Departments and Personnel Quota of Provincial Guoshui Bureaus (*Guoshuifa* [1997]144, September 3, 1997).

[34] SAT Rules on the Allocation of Functions, Internal Departments and Personnel Quota of Provincial Guoshui Bureaus, Implementation Measures for Fixing Quotas and Positions, and Implementation Measures for Arranging Personnel Streams (*Guoshuifa* [2000]162, September 25, 2000).

file returns and remit taxes, but no longer had the capacity to routinely control the level of taxpayer compliance. In essence, although audits were being conducted, they came only after infringements of tax laws had already occurred. Taxpayer compliance needed to be monitored more "dynamically," according to the critics, and tax administrators needed to do more than completing audits (or providing taxpayer services) to ensure that taxpayers complied. But because of the "regrettable" emphasis on allocating personnel to audits and taxpayer services, taxpayer "management" had become thinly staffed.

Second, "the weakening of accountability" referred to the dearth of incentives within tax administration. Critics observed that when collection, audit, and taxpayer supervision were separated, it became harder to motivate tax administrators themselves. Administration outcomes now depended on multiple functions and agency units, making it harder to pin down the under-performance of individual persons and units. Additionally, performance metrics were harder to design. This problem of internal management was apparently aggravated by demographic factors. Many employees in the tax collection workforce had been hired in the 1980s. They had unsurprisingly low levels of education – the country's education system was suspended during the Cultural Revolution – and were getting older. Career incentives were thus weak for a sizeable portion of the staff. Moreover, the general personnel reform being pushed across the government was affecting employee morale.

These arguments are puzzling. The "weakening of accountability" amounted to a management or human resource problem and did not seem to impugn the basic design of the new tax system. The accusation of the "neglect of management" appears even stranger. Chinese tax revenue grew at an average annual rate of 16 percent between 1997 and 2001, despite the Asian financial crisis in 1998 (see Figure 0.2). This rate of revenue growth was sustained during a period when an unfamiliar set of taxes and system of self-declarations were freshly introduced. Certainly, revenue could have grown even faster if Chinese taxpayers had been more compliant, but the reformers in 1997 had anticipated a fourteen-year timeline for building a modernized tax administration. Compliance was not supposed to improve overnight. Finally, in both the 1993 and 1997 reform statements, audits and penalties were envisioned as the main way (aside from taxpayer services) for ensuring taxpayers' compliance, presumably through the power of deterrence. The suggestion that this was an inadequate form of taxpayer monitoring thus seems surprising.

Despite these possible replies, the charge that tax administration at the end of the 1990s was "neglecting management and weakening accountability" became influential. It was explicitly acknowledged in a SAT proposal issued in 2001 "to experiment with using information technology (IT) to promote tax administration reform."[35] According to this proposal, tax administration across China should begin to adopt more uniform software, standardize administrative protocols through computerization, and move toward a more integrated information system. And along with developing this information system, clearer specialization among administrative roles would be delineated. The payoff of investing in IT was framed mostly in terms of improving internal management, seemingly responding to the complaint about "the weakening of accountability." Its intended impact on taxpayers was not clear. Other SAT documents between 2000 and 2003 also indicate that tax administration reform entered an inward-looking phase, emphasizing the enhancement of IT, reorganization and centralization of administrative functions, and improvement of specialization and internal accountability.[36] The outlines of the four fundamental pillars of tax administration described by the State Council in 1993 (i.e. legislation, collection, audit, and dispute resolution) became obscured. Likewise, the emphasis on taxpayer self-declarations, service, centralized collection, audits (and IT to serve these tasks) faded.

However, none of these developments definitively signaled the reversal of the 1997 reform. After all, setting up a self-declaration system, along with the taxpayer services and audit capacity that complemented it, involved both large upfront investments and subsequent ongoing improvements. The phase of physical construction and taxpayer mobilization in the late 1990s represented the upfront investment. As these are naturally more dramatic than subsequent improvements, a quieter ensuing phase is just what one would expect.

The main reason to believe that the 1997 tax reform met its demise was that, beginning in 2003, the SAT came to advocate administrative changes that decidedly deemphasized taxpayer services and audits, while elevating taxpayer "management" to the highest prominence. According to this new

[35] *Guoshuifa* [2001]137, December 3, 2001.

[36] Several important SAT documents regarding tax administration improvements can be described this way. See SAT Notice on Pilot Regions Making Reports on Plans for Accelerating the Use of Information Technology in Tax Administration to Advance Tax Administration Reform (*Guoshuifa* [2002]100, August 9, 2002); SAT Notice Regarding a Strategic Plan Outline for the Management of Chinese Tax Administration 2002–2006 (*Guoshuihan* [2003]267, March 10, 2003).

position, there existed certain tasks in tax administration that were "more foundational" than taxpayer services and audits.[37] As a result, SAT officially augmented its thirty-character reform agenda from 1997: tax administration must now also "strengthen management" (*qianghua guanli*). The decision to switch from practices that "neglected management" to ones that prioritized management was associated with the arrival of a new Commissioner of the SAT, Xie Xuren, in 2004. Xie was perceived to be a critic of the initial results of the 1997 reform,[38] and he championed efforts to institute a "revenue manager" system throughout China.[39] The effort culminated in the adoption of two sets of "trial measures" by the SAT in 2005: the "System of Revenue Managers" and the "System of Taxpayer Evaluation."[40]

In subsequent chapters, we examine the 2005 institutions in some detail, studying both the letters of the 2005 SAT directives and how they worked in real practice. At this point, what is important to grasp is the systems' general significance. The SAT's 2005 announcement of the revenue management and taxpayer evaluation systems represented a clear abandonment of the 1997 reform, because the revenue manager system largely revived the "nanny-style" tax administration of the 1980s.[41] Tax administrators returned to overseeing particular taxpayers as opposed to performing specialized tasks. Their performance also came to be evaluated based on the compliance activities of these taxpayers. The main differences between the "dedicated taxpayer managers" of the 1980s and the "revenue managers" promoted in 2005 were that the latter did not physically collect tax returns or payments, and did not enjoy discretion in determining what policies applied to taxpayers. Moreover, revenue managers worked in parallel to a separate

37 SAT Opinions of the concerning Some Issues on Further Strengthening the Foundational Work of Tax Administration (*Guoshuifa* [2003]124, October 22, 2003).

38 Leadership change can of course matter a great deal to the fate of reforms. Xie's predecessor, Jin Renqing, had assumed the post of SAT Commissioner in April 1998 after serving as a deputy mayor of Beijing (and earlier as a deputy governor of the Province of Yunan). Jin went on to become the country's Minister of Finance from 2004 to 2008. A powerful politician, it is not clear how invested Jin was in the tax administration reform. Xie was a deputy Minister of Finance until 1998 and headed the China Agricultural Development Bank and the China Economics and Trade Commission before his leadership at the SAT.

39 An initial manifesto can be found in the SAT's "Certain Opinions Regarding Further Strengthening the Work of Tax Administration" (*Guoshuifa* [2004]108, August 24, 2004).

40 SAT, The Tax Revenue Manager System (for Trial Implementation) (*Guoshuifa* [2005]40, March 17, 2005); SAT, Measures for the Management and Evaluation of Tax Payments (for Trial Implementation) (*Guoshuifa* [2005]43, March 11, 2005).

41 The SAT 1997 reform program thus fell into oblivion by 2005, even though it was formally pronounced as obsolete only in 2016.

"tax inspection" system that specialized in formal audits and were supposed to use penalties more frequently. In other words, revenue managers were to ensure that taxpayers carried out their compliance activities, generally without using formal audits and imposing penalties. And, of course, revenue managers no longer supervised mainly SOEs and COEs. Instead, they were to "manage" large populations of private firms.

I want to stress the novelty of the story I have related so far. It is unclear whether most of China's younger generation of tax policy makers and administrators today know about the 1997 tax administration reform. The reform's astounding obscurity, despite its dramatic immediate impact, is what prompted me to use it as a centerpiece for discussing the administrative foundations of the Chinese fiscal state. What is equally surprising is the obscurity of the revenue management system. If one examines Chinese government directives about tax administration after 2005, it would be impossible to avoid reading at length about the bureaucratic details of revenue management. These details are further elaborated on and debated among the 800,000 tax administrators across China. Yet the system receives little acknowledgement in commentaries on Chinese taxation and is ignored in social scientific and legal scholarship. I believe this is because scholars have lacked the conceptual apparatus for understanding this quintessential aspect of Chinese taxation – and of the Chinese state. This book will gradually develop such an apparatus to bring out the practice's social scientific significance.

The foregoing story raises the following key questions: What is the revenue management system, and why is it felt in China to be superior to a system that relies on voluntary taxpayer compliance and audits? The 1997 national tax administration reform and its subsequent demise illustrate the competition between these two paradigms of tax administration. The revenue management paradigm, having its roots in the 1980s (when China was still substantially closed to the world), may be considered native to China. The self-declaration-plus-audit paradigm, in contrast, may plausibly be viewed as imported: it is a style of tax administration that came with the new taxes that China decided to introduce in the early 1990s. The imported paradigm is easier to talk about, even in China – and most certainly for the readers of this book – because it is more internationally prominent. Yet it is the native paradigm that has the most tenacious hold in real-world practice in China. Indeed, the fate of the 1997 national reform is not the only example illustrating the triumph of the native paradigm. In Chapter 4, we will see that the competition between the two paradigms was staged again during 2012–2015, in a self-initiated tax administration reform in Jiangsu province. The native paradigm again turned out to be the winner in that competition.

Before diving into these topics, however, the remainder of this chapter comments on three features of Chinese tax administration that may be somewhat more familiar to readers because of existing scholarship and policy discourse: (1) the GS versus DS distinction, (2) bureaucratic decentralization, and (3) the use of IT. These are important features of the Chinese fiscal state, and I will have much to say about them in the rest of the book. But it is important to put them in place and define their relationship to the dominance of the revenue management system.

Bifurcated Administration, Decentralization, and Technology Use

Guoshui *versus* Dishui

The bifurcation of Chinese tax administration into the state tax bureau (GS) and local tax bureau (DS) systems lasted between 1994 and 2018. Both systems implemented tax law and policies set by the national government (as elaborated by the MOF and SAT). The best-known distinction between the two systems is political. The central government determined the budget, personnel, and leadership appointments of GS units in the country, whereas provincial governments controlled these matters for DS units within their respective provinces. In Chinese terminology, the GS system was subject to "vertical control" by the national government, while the units in the DS system were "vertically controlled" by provincial governments. There is no *a priori* answer to the question of how the national (as opposed to the provincial) determination of agency budgets might have affected administrative capacity. However, it is reasonable to postulate that appointments matter. Leaders of DS units were ultimately answerable to political bosses in their respective provinces. Leaders of GS units, by contrast, participated in a nationwide bureaucratic hierarchy with the SAT at its head. Senior bureaucrats in the GS system thus enjoyed career opportunities (e.g. taking up positions in different provinces or at the SAT) not available to their DS counterparts.

Does this political distinction between GS and DS bureaus carry significant implications? Many Chinese scholars have viewed "vertical control" by the national government as a solution to problems arising from excessive decentralization in many policy areas. In viewing the GS versus DS distinction through this lens, they suggest that the GS system exemplifies a superior form of organization.[42] But this is based on misunderstanding. These same scholars usually contrast "vertical control" by the central government with "tiered control," where a government agency at a low (e.g. county) tier of government is accountable – for example, because of appointments – primarily to the political bosses at the same low tier. But the DS system does not present an instance of "tiered control": DS units at all tiers in a province are accountable to the provincial leadership, which is at best a slightly lower level of leadership than the SAT. The better view is that the differences in incentives for lower-tier bureaucrats in the DS and GS are multidimensional, and not dominated by whether the SAT wields the power of appointment.

There are, in fact, many significant but lesser-known institutional differences between the GS and DS systems. Figure 1.1 showed that overall the GS system is larger in terms of staff size. The discrepancy is even larger in terms of revenue collected. The upper-left panel in Figure 1.2 shows that from 1997 to 2009, the GS system consistently raised about two times the revenue as the DS system. Furthermore, although the budgets of the DS and GS systems are not easily located, the GS system appears to command better resources in many ways. The upper-right panel shows that more of GS personnel is concentrated in tax bureaus at the county level and above, and the lower-left panel shows that, at these levels, GS bureaus are allowed to host more internal divisions. Both facts suggest higher levels of specialization for GS employees in these bureaus and potentially better career opportunities. The GS system also enjoys a far greater number of information centers (lower-right panel), as well as employees working in nonadministrative units that provide training and logistical support.

The DS system, however, has some of its own advantages. Figure 1.1 showed that the DS system experienced a much smaller personnel reduction than the GS system during the government reorganization in 2000. Because the DS system was built starting from 1994, it also benefitted from a workforce that is somewhat younger and better educated, as shown in Figure 1.3.[43] Moreover, since budgets are controlled by provinces in the DS

[42] For an influential account, see Zhou 2008.

[43] It can be seen from Figure 1.3 that Chinese tax administration overall is highly educated: employees receiving degrees beyond high school represent close to 90 percent of both the GS and DS workforce.

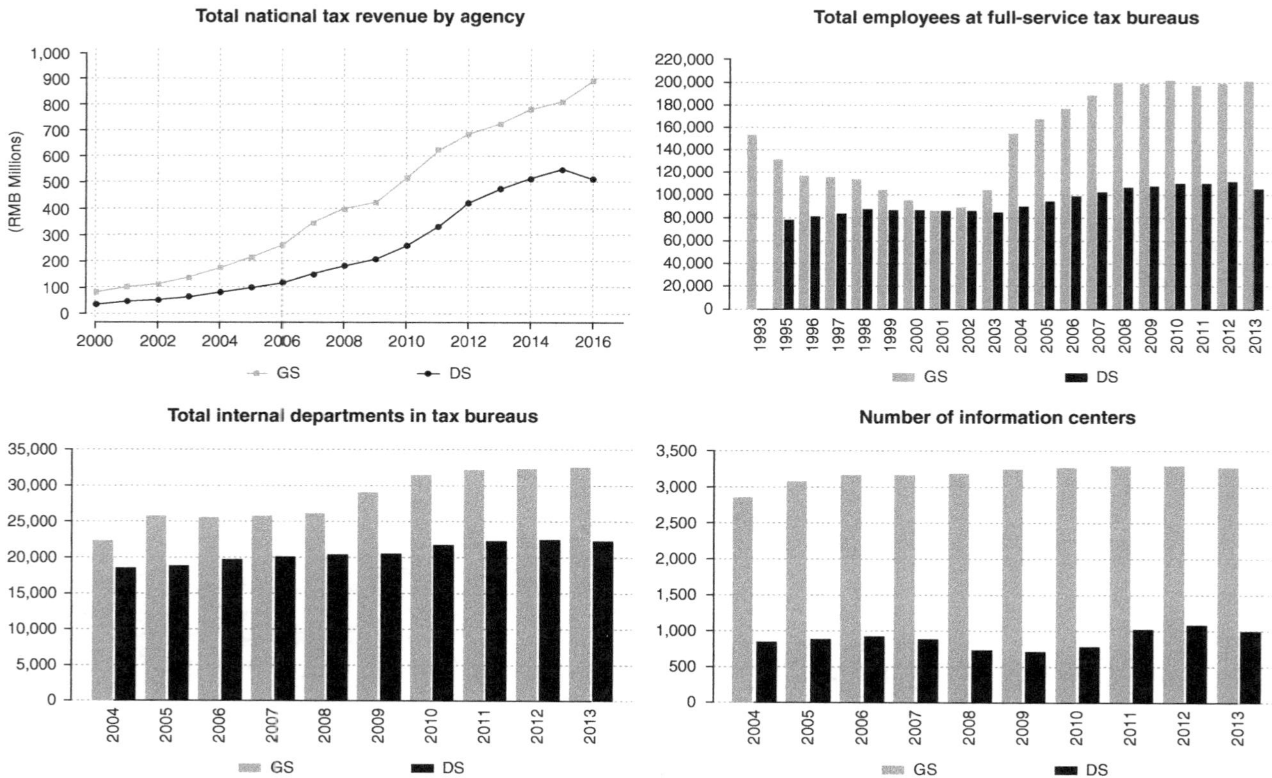

Figure 1.2 Comparisons between GS' and DS' resources

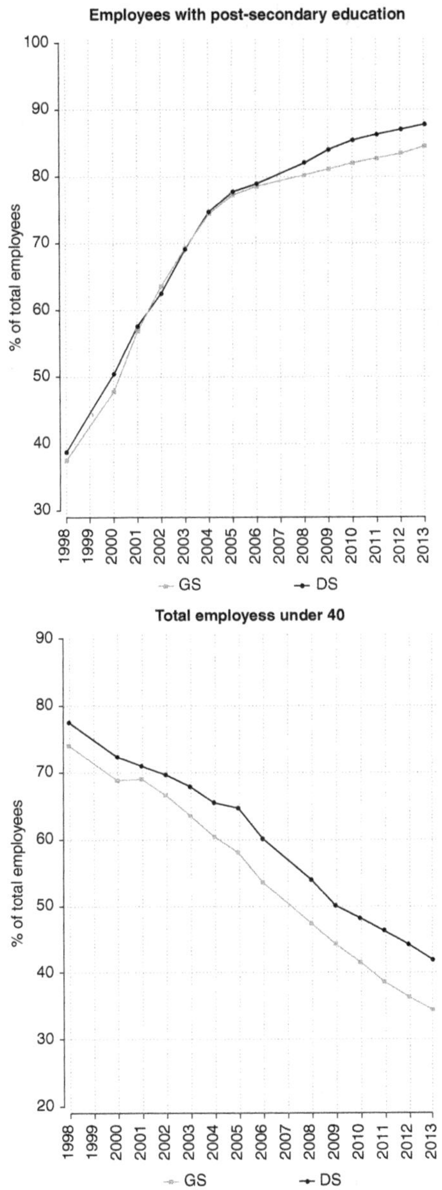

Figure 1.3 Education and age composition in GS versus DS bureaus

system, there is likely to be greater variation in pay across provinces. This means that incentive pay for tax administrators can be arranged in ways that would not be feasible in the GS system.

Historically, the DS system was substantially more decentralized: it had more branch bureaus and outposts than GS bureaus and assigned more of its staff to these grassroots units. This is significant, especially when it interacts with the operation of the revenue management system. For these and other additional reasons,[44] without careful research design, it would be hard to attribute any observed differences in administrative outcomes between GS and DS bureaus to a single institutional factor (such as the fact that DS bureaus are more accountable to local political leaders). The most one can say about Chinese tax administration's bifurcation into the GS and DS branches before 2018 is that it is always one of the factors to consider while analyzing Chinese tax administration; however, its predictive value is sensitive to context. And, most importantly, the competition between the native and imported styles of tax administration discussed earlier applies to both the GS and DS systems. Understanding either system requires a better grasp of these basic approaches to tax administration.

Administrative Decentralization

The decentralization of tax administration is one of the most striking features of Chinese taxation. Unfortunately, this feature has long been obscured by the way scholars (both in China and elsewhere) use the term "local" (*difang*) to describe Chinese governance. This term is often used to draw a line between national and subnational governments. When used so broadly, "local" may denote the provincial, prefectural/city, or district/county levels of government, which are the next three tiers of government (in descending order) in China.[45] Or it could denote governance activities at even lower levels, such as neighborhoods/townships. Failing to distinguish between these

[44] Further challenges arise from variations across provinces as well as over time – the GS system, for instance, has undergone substantial organizational changes before 2008.

[45] In the basic classification used to describe the hierarchy of administrative units in China, four cities (Beijing, Shanghai, Tianjin, Chongqing) occupy the first rank below the national government, along with twenty-seven provinces and autonomous regions. In the next tier, most prefectural jurisdictions are categorized as "cities." Districts in urban areas and counties in more rural areas occupy the third rank below the national level (some counties are confusingly also called "cities"). The fourth tier below the national level, comprised of urban neighborhoods (*jiedao*) and rural townships, is typically the lowest tier with government units and civil servants.

four tiers of subnational governance, however, omits essential facts about China's administrative decentralization.

The GS and DS systems (before they merged in 2018) each established tax bureaus at the provincial, prefectural/city, and district/county levels. This implied totals of about sixty provincial bureaus in the thirty-one provinces, close to 700 city bureaus in the more than 300 prefectures across the country, and close to 6,000 district/county bureaus. But this count of bureaucratic units only includes full-service bureaus (*quanneng ju*) or bureaus that manage subordinate units (*ju jiguan*). Such bureaucratic entities supervise a much larger number of specialized or subordinate units: specialized units include inspection bureaus (discussed in Chapter 2), and subordinate units include branch bureaus and tax offices assigned to finer geographical jurisdictions within districts and counties. The number of subordinate outpost units is staggering. The left panel in Figure 1.4 shows that in 2013, the GS system had 10,128 below-county units and the DS system had 16,791. In 1995, these numbers were 26,715 and 32,723, respectively.

Virtually each of these below-county units is a physical premise at which taxpayers interact with tax administrators to fulfill compliance obligations. What this means is that in 1995, there were close to 60,000 grassroots tax offices (i.e. not counting the full-service or management-oriented higher-level bureaus) that Chinese taxpayers could visit. This was comparable to the total number of post offices (61,898) China had that year! Although the number of tax outposts declined significantly over time (while the number of post offices grew), in 2012, Chinese taxpayers still enjoyed one tax office open for every three post offices. And China's postal network is denser than many other countries. The US Postal Service, for example, had 30,825 post offices and locations in 2017, close to the total number of tax bureaus and offices in China. This staggering comparison with post offices is what one needs to understand the sweeping meaning of "local" tax administration in China.

This extraordinarily dense network of grassroots tax offices has enormous implications for both government personnel arrangements and taxpayer experience. China's workforce of tax administrators comprised approximately 757,000 civil servants in the last fifteen years. Although

An even lower, fifth tier comprises urban resident committees (*jumin weiyuan hui*) and rural villages, at which government-controlled civil organizations operate.

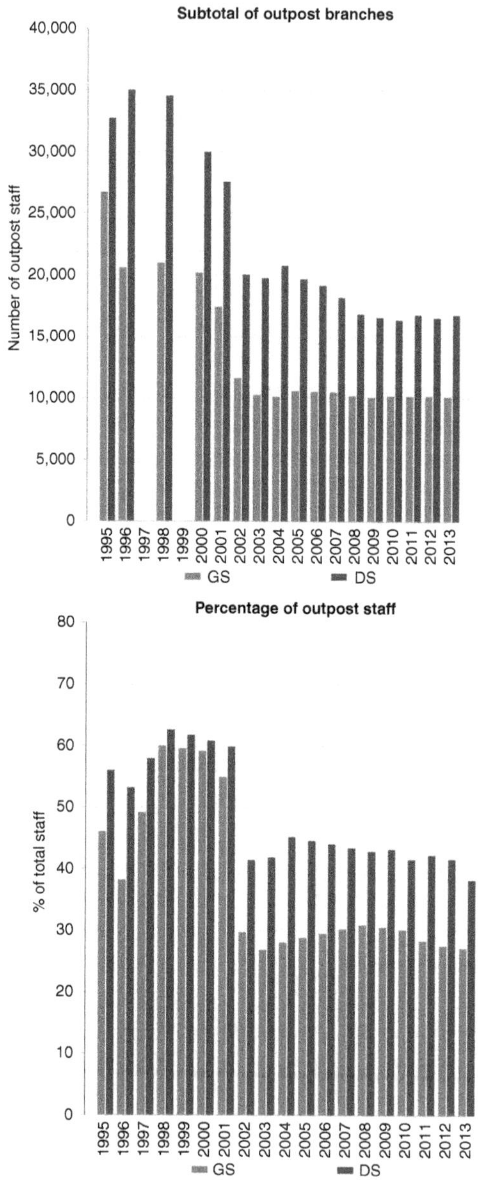

Figure 1.4 Decentralization in GS versus DS bureaus

this is certainly the largest tax bureaucracy in the world by absolute size, it is not so in per capita terms: the number of tax administrators relative to the size of the country's general workforce is much lower than the OECD average.[46] However, by being organizationally bottom heavy, China's tax administration permits most taxpayers to easily contact tax collectors.

Consider the following: at the national level, the SAT hosts just over 800 staff members – a mere 0.1 percent of the army of tax administrators. By contrast, in 2013 the US IRS National Office in Washington D.C. employed close to 5 percent of total IRS staff.[47] At the provincial level, China's tax bureaucracy has 11,000 employees. Thus, even when the national and provincial offices are combined, employees at these levels represent only 1.56 percent of the tax administration.[48] Data compiled by the SAT shows that in 2003, 16 percent of subnational tax administrators were posted at prefectural tax bureaus, with the remaining 80 percent working at the county level or below. The right panel in Figure 1.4 graphs two longer time series capturing the proportion of the administrative workforce staffed at below-county units. Although this proportion declined generally over time – it was around 60 percent for both the GS and DS systems in the late 1990s – it was still well over a quarter in the GS system, and 40 percent in the DS system, by 2013.

Imagine what the US IRS would be like if it were structured like China's tax bureaucracy. Most notably, the Washington D.C. National Office would essentially be empty. There would also be no counterparts to the seven IRS regional offices, each of which oversees matters across several states. Instead, the current 139 IRS district offices,[49] which are field offices that deal directly with taxpayers, would become high-level offices giving commands to three additional layers of subordinate offices, where most personnel would be located. Instead of having twenty Taxpayer Assistance Centers in the entire state of New York (or twenty-eight in California),[50] there would be twenty such centers just for upper Manhattan. Rather than having two or three hundred field offices in the entire country, the IRS would possess this same number of offices in just one metropolitan area. Instead of mailing their

[46] See Robinson and Slemrod (2012), where analysis of OECD data shows that developed countries tend to have a much higher number of tax administrators relative to population than developing countries.

[47] OECD (2015), at 83 (Table 2.4).

[48] Among the thirty-five OECD countries and seventeen non-OECD countries/regions surveyed in OECD (2015), China has by far the smallest percentage of tax staff working either at headquarters (i.e. national offices), or at national and regional offices combined.

[49] Id. (Table 2.4). The IRS has 139 "regional offices" and 119 "local/branch offices."

[50] IRS, Contact Your Local IRS Office (www.irs.gov/help/contact-your-local-irs-office).

returns and writing checks to distant "return processing centers," US taxpayers would be able to dial-up local IRS service hotlines where someone always answers the phone. If they wished, taxpayers could also simply handle their basic tax compliance and obtain taxpayer services in their neighborhoods.

The coming chapters examine what exactly happens at these extremely "local" sites of interaction. For now, we can label this type of state organizational structure as "administrative decentralization," defined by the following two features. First, there is a single bureaucratic hierarchy, and government functions viz-a-viz citizens are performed at the lowest levels of this hierarchy. By contrast, higher levels of the bureaucracy do not exercise government power directly over citizens but instead issue commands to bureaucratic subordinates. Second, the lower the bureaucratic rank, the smaller the geographical reach of units in the rank. Decentralization thus implies that the jurisdiction of a citizen-facing government unit is geographically quite limited. What is unusual about China is first, how deep (i.e. multilayered) the bureaucratic hierarchy is, and second, how resolutely the tasks of government administration are placed at the bottom ranks of the hierarchy.

The Golden Tax Project

Like many other organizations, tax administration can benefit from a well-educated workforce and use of advanced IT. Chinese tax administrators are generally highly educated (Figure 1.3). China's tax authorities have also invested heavily in IT since the late 1990s. The reason to discuss IT use here, however, is that a particular form of technology has gained special attention in recent social scientific research.

Specifically, the Golden Tax Project (*jinshui gongcheng*) is a nationwide IT project launched in the late 1990s that is far more ambitious than the computer networks contemplated by the SAT 1997 tax administration reform. It had a short unsuccessful pilot phase in 1994–1995 called Phase I. GTP Phase III, which attempts to integrate tax authorities' IT systems across the country – allowing, among other things, automatic taxpayer data transmission to the SAT and across regions within the entire tax administration – did not become operational until 2017. It is GTP Phase II, which began implementation in 2000 and became fully operational across the country in 2003, that has attracted scholarly attention. GTP Phase II is a VAT anti-fraud system that requires large VAT-remitting firms to use special encrypted VAT invoices, deploy an extensive network of physical devices for the regular de-encryption and authentication of these invoices, and, to a more limited extent, perform cross-matching of invoices between business sellers and buyers.[51] The implementation of GTP Phase II helped the Chinese government staunch an alarming rise in VAT fraud in the 1990s and played a significant role in shaping China's VAT policy.[52]

But scholarly attention to GTP Phase II has arisen for a very different reason – and possibly on the basis of a misunderstanding. Researchers in developmental economics have in recent years portrayed the cross-matching of invoices as a key feature of the VAT, one that is particularly relevant to developing countries because of their low levels of tax compliance.[53] Since Chinese policy makers invested billions of yuan in GTP Phase II and believe that they have improved VAT compliance as a result, China's practical experience seems to resonate with this new scholarly understanding. The problem is that Chinese policy makers are aware – contrary to the belief of scholars advocating extensive VAT invoice cross-matching – that invoice cross-matching is not part of the VAT's traditional design. The vast majority of developed countries that initially adopted the VAT (including countries in Europe, Canada, Australia, and Singapore) do not have an invoice cross-matching system under their VATs. And it was based on the successful experience of VAT implementation (*without* cross-matching) in these rich countries that the VAT was promoted to many developing countries.[54] When China considered adopting a VAT anti-fraud system, there was little international experience to borrow from.[55] GTP Phase II, therefore, was very much an indigenous creation.

The launch of GTP Phase II was backed by Chinese Premier Zhu Rongji. It was probably the single most expensive IT project that the SAT invested in. Not surprisingly, national political leaders and the SAT gave it heavy promotion and much press coverage. An objective evaluation of the actual

[51] Detailed discussions of China's VAT anti-fraud system (GTP Phase II) can be found in Winn and Zhang 2013 and Chapter 14 of Schenk et al. 2015.

[52] See Schenk et al. 2015, Chapter 14.

[53] See, for example, Pomeranz 2015; Naritomi 2019.

[54] That invoice cross-matching is not intended to be an essential feature of the VAT is especially clear from the writings of tax specialists at the IMF, the international organization most responsible for the propagation of VAT across developing countries. See Ebrill et al. 2001; Harrison and Krelove 2005; Keen and Smith 2006; Schenk et al. 2015.

[55] Two developed economies in Asia – South Korea and Taiwan – had experimented with VAT invoice cross-matching earlier but had abandoned the experiments by the 1990s.

impact of the VAT anti-fraud system, however, still awaits thorough investigation.[56] In fact, assessment of the system by Chinese taxpayers and tax administrators is quite mixed.[57] For taxpayers, the VAT anti-fraud system created high compliance costs, even for many firms that would have been compliant already. For tax administrators, it created a technological arms race between the government and criminals that the former is never assured of winning. None of this, though, is unique to China. The VAT's vulnerability to criminal fraud, including in developed countries, is well documented, and tax administrators in many countries must weigh the benefit of anti-fraud measures against their compliance costs. What I want to note here is that while China practices the use of IT in VAT invoice cross-matching, it is controversial domestically. The merit of VAT invoice cross-matching is also highly controversial internationally, despite its recent popularity among developmental economists.

The role of information in tax administration is a central topic for this book. In the following chapters, we will systematically investigate the institutions and practices that generate information. For example, if tax administrators enforce the norm of truthful reporting, the information transmitted from taxpayers to the government's database is more likely to be reliable. The non-enforcement of truthful reporting, on the other hand, may render much of the government's data useless, whatever advanced IT is used. It turns out that the revenue management system has a major impact on how information is gathered by Chinese tax agencies and the type of information gathered. To use a favorable term of economists, information is *endogenous*. Different approaches to tax administration will generate different types of information.

[56] Fan et al. 2018 provide important evidence that GTP Phase II increased VAT remittance in the short term, partly by reducing input claims. The long-term impact was less clear. The authors also interpret the short-term impact as falling on tax evasion by regular firms, and do not consider the possibility that GTP Phase II exerted its impact mainly through curbing forms of criminal VAT fraud prevalent in China in the early 2000s.

[57] See Winn and Zhang 2013; Schenk et al. 2015 (Chapter 14).

2

What Is an Audit?

When scholars write about Chinese tax administration, they tend to focus on a particular arm of the tax collection apparatus: the Bureaus of Tax Inspection (*jicha ju*). Two factors explain this tendency. First, the Chinese term *jicha* (which literally means to examine, investigate, or check) connotes the idea of audits. In ordinary discourse, audits are widely taken to be one of the most important aspects of modern tax administration. The notion of audits crystalizes the view that taxation is intrinsically a coercive exercise, and that compliance with tax payment obligations needs to be secured through deterrence. Influenced by this familiar discourse, it is natural to infer that audits are the most important task conducted by Chinese tax administrators. With the further assumption that the Bureaus of Tax Inspection carry out tax audits, it seems to follow that tax inspection is the most important arm of Chinese tax administration.

Second, the Chinese government appears to emphasize the role of tax inspection bureaus in measuring tax administrator performance. While the government publishes data on tax revenue in its budget reports and through the China Taxation Yearbook, these sources of data contain relatively little information about tax administration itself. The main source of data on tax administration is found in the China Tax Inspection Yearbook, the annual volumes of which contain tables and reports describing how tax inspectors have dealt with taxpayers.[1] As this is the only official source of aggregate information on Chinese tax administration, one might infer that the information it contains must be representative.

However, these assumptions and inferences are mistaken. It is erroneous to conflate Chinese tax administration with tax inspection. It is also substantially wrong to assume that Chinese tax inspectors carry out audits

[1] The Tax Inspection Yearbook may be analogized to the *Internal Revenue Service Data Book* published annually in the United States. There is one notable difference: the IRS only has centralized operations, while Chinese tax administration is decentralized. The Tax Inspection Yearbook thus contains reports from all Chinese provinces and is consequently much more voluminous.

similar to audits in the United States or elsewhere. Notably, these mistakes and errors are in part factual and in part conceptual. Factually, it is easily shown that tax inspection bureaus represent only a small portion of Chinese tax administration. The much larger portion – in terms of both staff resources and impact on taxpayers – is the revenue management (*shuiyuan guanli*) arm of tax bureaus. This chapter offers an introduction to the revenue management system, which remains extremely obscure despite its dominance in administrative practice.[2] However, even though the institutional distinction between tax inspection and revenue management will become obvious, the conceptual distinctions between the two are less so. To properly understand either system, one needs greater conceptual clarity about the basic concept of an audit.

This chapter first examines the activities of tax inspection bureaus – despite the overall conclusion that, institutionally, they are much more marginal than is commonly assumed. I will argue that most of what Chinese tax inspectors do cannot properly be characterized as audits. That is, we must question the very assumption that Chinese tax inspectors mainly carry out audits. The reason for this surprising conclusion is that Chinese tax inspectors generally do not enforce the norm of truthful reporting. Instead, they are focused on generating revenue in the present, not on establishing deterrence that produces compliance in the future. For instance, Chinese tax inspectors infrequently examine tax returns; what taxpayers report on their tax returns is largely immaterial. Most tellingly, Chinese tax inspectors rely extensively on taxpayer "self-inspections," which, I will argue, is most appropriately analogized to tax amnesties in other countries.

The wide use of self-inspections in China critically illustrates the trade-off between raising revenue and upholding the norm of truthful reporting – one of the three key trade-offs identified in this book's Introduction as marking the unique choices made by Chinese tax administrators. Understanding this trade-off is vital. After all, governments in developing countries may for good reasons focus on, at least for the short term, collecting revenue in a peaceful fashion, and postpone the goal of nurturing particular social norms.

To my knowledge, few scholars (or policy makers for that matter) have analyzed Chinese tax administration in this way. This is remarkable in itself. The Chinese government has never tried to hide its use of taxpayer self-inspections: indeed, it is rather difficult to hide, because the effectiveness of self-inspection campaigns depends on communication with

[2] Chapter 3 offers a conceptual scheme for more thoroughly analyzing the revenue management system.

a wide swath of taxpayers. Nonetheless, taxpayer self-inspections have not been documented in previous scholarship, as though they have hidden in plain sight. I believe the reason is that the vocabulary for describing them is not readily available. The first task of this chapter is thus to engage in such documentation and build the relevant vocabulary. The chapter then argues that practices that similarly deemphasize the norm of truthful reporting are pursued, at a much larger scale, in the revenue management arm of tax administration.

The Shrinking Tax Inspection Workforce

The tax inspection (*jicha*) system can be contextualized with some simple personnel statistics. The left panel in Figure 2.1 displays, separately for the GS and DS systems, the total number of tax inspectors across China from 2000 to 2016. The right panel then plots the national trends for the proportion of tax inspectors to the total tax administration workforce from 2000 to 2013. From these graphs, it is obvious that tax inspection personnel shrank over time in both absolute and relative terms. In recent years, inspectors represented only 10–12 percent of total tax administration personnel. Even at their heights in 2003, the proportion of tax inspection staff to total tax administrators was less than 15 percent.

Figure 2.2 displays measures of the same proportion at the provincial level for the years 2003–2007. While there are differences across provinces, provinces that have greater than 20 percent of their tax administrators occupying tax inspector roles are rare outliers. Meanwhile, a significant minority of provinces have fewer than 10 percent of their tax administrators in tax inspection bureaus. What is clear is that after 2000, no province came even close to the goal declared by the SAT in 1997 to staff one-third to 40 percent of all tax administrators in tax inspection positions.

We will soon see that the decline of tax inspection in recent years can be observed in terms other than personnel: the number of taxpayers covered, as well as the proportion of tax collected through tax inspections to total tax revenue, also dwindled.[3] These trends are consistent with the narrative

[3] These declining trends occurred during a period when the total number of inspection bureaus in China held steady. Most tax bureaus that are large enough to afford some degree of specialization – referred to as "all-purpose bureaus," and essentially, tax bureaus at the county level and above – have an inspection bureau or division. In the GS system, the total number of inspection bureaus ranged between 73 percent and 81 percent of the total number of all-purpose bureaus, while for DS the range was between 74 percent and 83 percent.

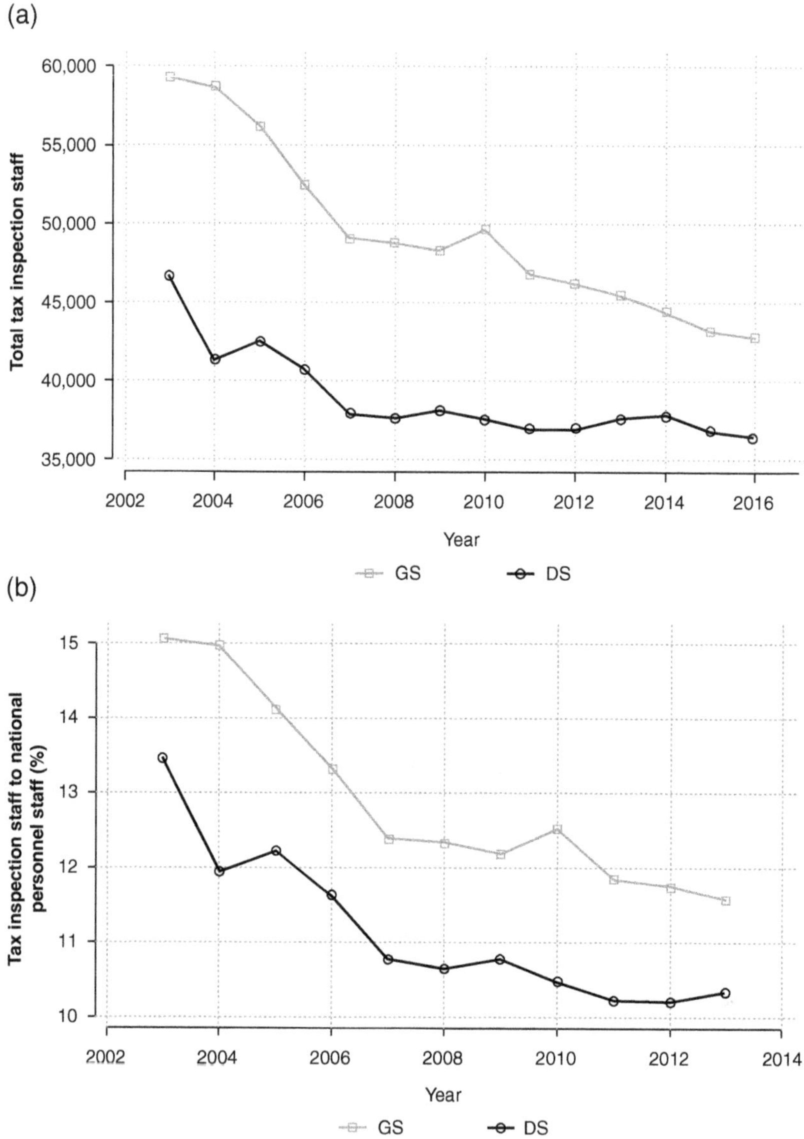

Figure 2.1 National trend in tax inspection staff, total and relative to total tax administration staff

in Chapter 1. At least in terms of the SAT's national directives, there was a shift from an over-the-top emphasis on tax inspections in the late 1990s to a solid focus on revenue management roles by 2004. Moreover, as we

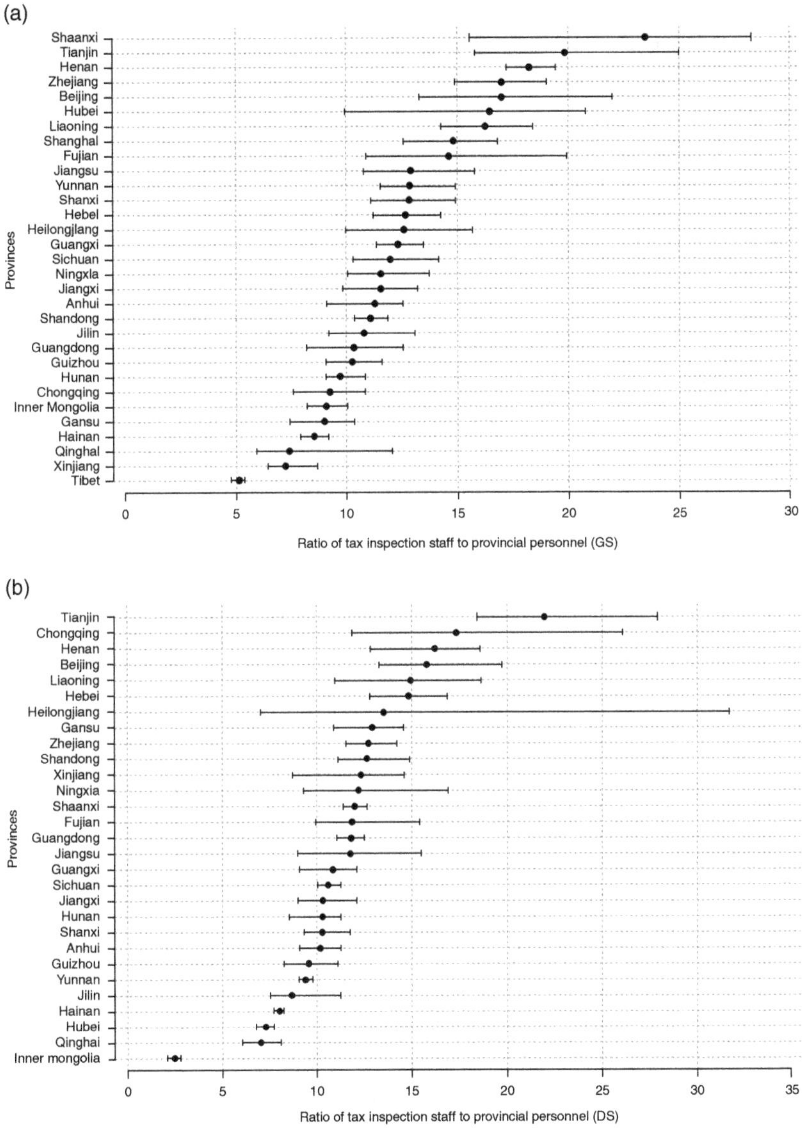

Figure 2.2 Provincial variations in ratio of tax inspectors to total tax administration staff

will discuss later, functions labeled obscurely as "tax risk management" and "taxpayer evaluation," but which can be interpreted as audit-like, began to emerge in the revenue management system and may have partially substituted for tax inspections.[4] In any case, had it been recognized that inspection forms only a marginal part of Chinese tax administration, the Tax Inspection Yearbook would probably not have been taken as the most obvious starting point for understanding Chinese tax collection.

Nonetheless, the Tax Inspection Yearbook does contain critical information, some of which has escaped scholarly attention. An important example is the phenomenon of taxpayer self-inspections. Unbeknownst to most, an extremely prevalent practice sponsored by Chinese tax inspection bureaus is mandatory self-inspections (*zicha*), a type of review carried out by taxpayers themselves about whether they have paid taxes according to official requirements. This review is entirely separate from normal return filing and compliance activities, and is carried out upon the order of local tax inspectors. Notably, self-inspections are performed under the incentive that any additional reported tax liabilities do not attract penalties. By combing through the obscure corners of the Tax Inspection Yearbook, one can assemble a picture of the practice of self-inspections that challenges our understanding of what an "audit" amounts to in China.

The Evolutions of Self-Inspections

The practice of having taxpayers carry out self-inspections in order to collect more taxes has no ground in Chinese tax law. However, the practice goes far back, and was extensively documented already in the early- to mid-1990s. A brief examination of this history will shed light on self-inspections in general, and dispel any conflation of self-inspections with administrative practices adapted to larger taxpayers alone.

Expanding Audit Coverage

In the first half of the 1990s, when China's tax system was newly established, the level of taxpayer noncompliance was very high. Consequently, tax administrators were eager to extend audit coverage, both to collect tax and to create deterrence, and find low-cost audit techniques to achieve this goal. Asking taxpayers to "self-inspect" emerged as one core technique. Because there were "not enough tax inspectors" – a common complaint found in reports from subnational tax bureaus – taxpayers were asked to inspect themselves. Self-inspections were "coupled with" government

[4] Nonetheless, as we will see later in the text, the introduction of audit functions in the revenue management divisions of tax bureaus faced serious challenges.

inspections, which were labeled "selective inspections" (*choucha*) or "intensive [or key] inspections" (*zhongdian jiancha*). The terminology implied that self-inspections were broader in coverage but came with a lighter touch. This reduced the cost of inspections so much that, in reports from this period, it was sometimes claimed that for a given sector targeted for inspection, the coverage of self-inspection had reached "100 per cent."

By the early 2000s, provinces across China began to develop and publish guidance for the practice of self-inspections. According to these reports, taxpayer self-inspections were not to be used in investigations based on whistleblowers and other referrals with specific allegations of violations. These latter investigations, however, have always represented a relatively small portion of tax inspection. Self-inspection *was* used for all inspections with broad coverage. Broad-coverage inspections included "special-issue examinations" (*zhuanxiang jiancha*), which targeted particular sectors (e.g. real estate developers, gas stations, and peddlers' markets) or particular tax issues (e.g. wage withholding, withholding tax on royalty payments to foreign licensors) for inspection.[5] They also included examinations of particular taxpayer segments (e.g. large taxpayers). Altogether, broad-coverage inspections made up greater than 80 percent of all inspections carried out by tax inspection bureaus. In these areas of activity, self-inspections thrived.

Official reports on self-inspections typically describe a pre-inspection stage during which one or more of the following things happen. First, tax inspectors would widely advertise an upcoming inspection among the targeted taxpayer population (e.g. a particular sector or taxpayer type). These publicity initiatives would stress the importance of paying tax according to law. Second, tax inspectors could arrange individual or group meetings with taxpayers (called "interviews," or *yuetan*) to outline the tax law and policies that inspectors expected to enforce. Third, in some places, taxpayers could receive a formal notice setting out procedures and taxpayer rights. Taxpayers selected for self-inspection would then have a limited period of time for carrying it out (e.g. ten days to a month), at the end of which additional tax liabilities would be declared, sometimes on a "self-inspection report."

Self-inspection campaigns are followed by government inspections of select taxpayers that potentially carry penalties; these are necessary as a threat to back up self-inspections. Consistent with this, tax bureaus often

[5] The choice of issues differs from year to year and may depend on either SAT instructions (i.e. national campaigns) or subnational bureaus' own initiatives.

specify minimum ratios of taxpayers to be subjected to government inspections after the self-inspection phase – as high as 20 percent or 30 percent. This is much higher than the coverage ratio of tax inspections in general.

How are taxpayers who have carried out self-inspections selected for subsequent government inspection? Sometimes, the selection process is explicitly said to be randomized. But it is more commonly claimed that a subset of taxpayers is selected for "intensive" government inspections "depending on the outcome of self-inspections." The criteria used for such selection, however, is rarely spelled out in government internal reports. Does it depend on the sufficiency of aggregate revenue collected from the previous round to meet revenue targets? Or does it depend on whether particular taxpayers are likely to have been truthful? How is this latter type of selection carried out?

It is unlikely that tax inspectors carry out meaningful selection based on the veracity of self-inspection reports: these often are too crude to support effective selection. Unlike regular tax returns, self-inspection reports typically list additional tax liabilities for various types of taxes and contain no information about items relevant for determining the basis of taxpayers' liability. Moreover, although government reports imply that there is a selection process between self-inspection and government inspection, such selection is described not as part of a general audit strategy/algorithm that the government has in store, but as specific to each inspection campaign (and thus *ad hoc*). Some officials have all but explicitly stated that there is little effective selection prior to or following self-selection. For example, Ma Yimin, the commissioner of the National Tax Inspection Bureau, urged in 2013 that "the inspection of key revenue-source firms should not be allowed to go their own way" (*shunqi ziliu*). "It is necessary to focus on one or two firms before or during firm self-inspections. It is only by understanding typical cases that tax authorities could foresee possible tax issues of a firm, and therefore better guide the firm's self-inspections."[6]

Indeed, Ma's exhortation points to a radical deficiency in the audit capacity of Chinese tax inspectors. While they conduct inspection campaigns every year – and while the threat of their direct inspections is what, supposedly, generates incentives for declarations in self-inspections among taxpayers – they lack familiarity with taxpayer affairs outside these campaigns. By their nature, tax inspection campaigns rarely

[6] Speech at the National Training Courses for Tax Inspection Department Directors, May 8, 2013 (2014 Tax Inspection Yearbook, p 16).

hinge on what taxpayers previously declared on their tax returns: inspection targets are generally not selected on the basis of individual tax returns, but are instead based on issues and features common to groups of taxpayers. Yet outside inspection campaigns, Chinese tax inspectors do not even routinely see tax returns, because of the division of labor with "revenue management" functions. How, then, do Chinese tax inspectors gain experience in detecting evasion on tax returns?

Self-inspections versus Collaborative Compliance

Even Chinese tax inspectors who do claim to exercise audit skills express trepidation at inspecting large taxpayers. China's tax inspection regime pivoted toward large taxpayers around 2008, for two reasons. First, during the Global Financial Crisis, the government anticipated a loss of tax revenue. This led to the SAT issuing revenue targets in 2009 specifically for its provincial tax inspection systems.[7] While tax inspection bureaus had always been driven by revenue targets – a fact discussed later in this chapter – before 2009, the targets were imposed by subnational political leaders. The year 2009 was the first time that the SAT also imposed such targets. It is likely that this led subnational tax inspectors to rely on self-inspections not just to achieve broad inspection coverage, but also to extract revenue from large taxpayers. Second, a Large Taxpayer Division was set up at the SAT in 2008,[8] and large taxpayer units (LTU) were gradually formed at provincial and city tax bureaus as well. Although LTUs were organizationally distinct from tax inspection bureaus, they, as new units, were not prepared to carry out audit functions. Collaboration likely emerged between LTUs and inspection bureaus, again leading the latter to focus on larger taxpayers.

Tax inspection's shifting focus to larger taxpayers after 2008 began to transform the rationales offered in tax agency reports for self-inspections. Many reports observed that the tax affairs of large firms were complex and too challenging for tax administrators to audit; taxpayer self-inspections might thus be more effective in generating positive adjustments. Instead of laboring to detect misreporting taxpayers, tax administrators simply needed to re-explain what rules and policies taxpayers had to comply with. Earlier, self-inspections had been justified because they broadened audit coverage (even if at the expense of low per taxpayer adjustment).

[7] See Cui 2012b.
[8] Brondolo and Zhang 2016.

Now, self-inspections are said to "deepen" audits for a narrow group of large taxpayers, allowing an increase in per taxpayer adjustments.

For many tax professionals in China – especially those at international accounting firms – the SAT's decision to intensify tax collection against large corporate groups *after* 2009 was what first exposed them to the practice of self-inspections. (Indeed, this is how I, as a tax lawyer, first learned about it.) Tax directors of multinational companies expressed discomfort at the lack of legal basis for such inspections, as well as the element of bargaining that was almost explicit in self-inspection requests. However, self-inspections long predated the focus on large taxpayers.[9] This point is important because, in the past decade, some Chinese tax administrators have tried to rationalize self-inspections by reference to a tax administration practice that is internationally referred to as "collaborative" or "enhanced relationship" compliance.[10] Under collaborative compliance, large taxpayers would (1) disclose more of their tax-relevant information to the government; (2) receive better services (including private advance rulings, unavailable to other taxpayers, that specified how the government would apply the law in particular circumstances); and (3) be exempt from most penalties. The premise underlying such practices is that since the selected taxpayers are already predisposed to compliance, the threat of penalties becomes unnecessary. Instead, enhanced service and prompt information disclosure would allow revenue to be collected with low compliance and administrative costs.

Yet three basic facts belie any purported analogy between Chinese self-inspections and collaborative compliance. First, tax inspection bureaus are the divisions within China's tax collection apparatus that are the most responsible for creating *deterrence* effects. Taxpayer education and service are tasks handled by other, much larger departments in tax bureaus. If tax inspection bureaus do not impose penalties, no opportunity is left for creating differential treatments (in terms of the likelihood of penalties) between compliant and noncompliant taxpayers. In other words, penalty-free self-inspections supervised by tax inspection bureaus undermine a basic premise of collaborative compliance. Second, it does not appear that taxpayers required to conduct self-inspections disclose any further information

[9] The format of taxpayer self-inspections to this day bears the mark of their earlier origin. For instance, self-inspection continues to be preceded by taxpayer education campaigns, which supposedly increase taxpayers' knowledge of the law. In reality, large taxpayers are likely to know tax law better than low-rank tax inspectors, and the taxpayer education campaigns are useful only for smaller firms.

[10] See De Simone et al. 2013; OECD 2013.

about themselves: their self-inspection reports contain much less information than regular tax returns. Third, self-inspections apply to both large and small taxpayers, and there is no general presumption that targets of self-inspection are more compliant than taxpayers subject to other types of inspection (or the vast majority of taxpayers who are subject to no inspections at all).

Chinese tax administrators themselves are quite candid about the primary motivation for self-inspections: in the short term, they generate revenue at a low cost. In a speech in 2012, the then-chief of the SAT Tax Inspection Bureau, Xie Xuezhi, identified as a "major issue in contemporary tax inspection" the fact that "law enforcement in tax inspection is obviously revenue-driven."[11] He offered as evidence the increase in the use of self-inspections that year:

> The ratio of government-inspected firms to self-inspected firms is reduced to 55%, from 58% in 2011. Revenue collected through self-inspections increased to 59% of the total revenue from inspections; the ratio was 51% in 2011. This means that tax inspection has focused more on organizing firm self-inspections – to secure more revenue.

Xie warned that "if left unchecked, [such practices would] inevitably hinder the fairness and justice of tax inspection." In a report the next year, Xie similarly observed that "firm self-inspections are favored, indicating that the inspections are revenue-driven and lack rigor in enforcement."[12]

The next SAT Tax Inspection Bureau Chief, Sun Ruibiao, made a similar critique of self-inspections in 2014:

> In recent years, we have established an inspection approach for large enterprises that are key revenue sources, where tax inspection is led by self-inspection and ensured by key inspection. The approach has reduced the burden on taxpayers, saved inspection costs, improved inspection efficiency, and led to positive results. At the same time, however, some local tax authorities over-rely on self-inspections. They gave too much leeway to taxpayers during self-inspections and hindered strict law enforcement, which, to a certain extent, has weakened the authority of law enforcement. Local tax authorities should attach great importance to this issue and make improvements accordingly. In carrying out inspections of key tax-source enterprises, local tax authorities need to clarify the policies and the enterprises' responsibilities during self-inspections. It is also necessary to follow up

[11] Xie Xuezhi, Speech at the 2012 Forum on Tax Inspection in Some Regions, August 22, 2012, 2013 Tax Inspection Yearbook, p 14.

[12] Xie Xuezhi, Speech during the Investigation of Tax Inspections in Northeastern and Northwest China, 22 July 2013, 2014 Tax Inspection Yearbook, p 10.

> with key inspections. Without key inspection as the backup, self-inspection will be mere formality, and the authority of tax inspection will be undermined. In the future, aside from inspections of key tax-source enterprises or industry-specific inspections, the approach of self-inspection should not be adopted.[13]

There is little evidence, however, that the practice of self-inspections subsided.

The Prevalence of Self-inspections

China's Tax Inspection Yearbooks make available, in tabulated form, data about various provincial outcomes from tax inspections in the late 1990s to 2007. Starting in 2008, such tabulated data were omitted from the Yearbook. Consequently, most Chinese scholars empirically studying tax inspection rely on pre-2008 data. However, the Tax Inspection Yearbooks published from 2009 onward contain extensive reports produced by provincial tax inspection bureaus, from which one can hand-gather data on tax inspection outcomes. Specifically, for many province years, one can locate separate information on inspection outcomes for two kinds of inspections: taxpayer self-inspections and tax inspections carried out by tax officials. By contrast, tabulated data from the Tax Inspection Yearbooks up to 2007 did not distinguish between these two inspection types.

The next few graphs illustrate the evolution of self-inspections on the basis of such hand-gathered data. Figures 2.3 to 2.5 present overall time trends for three types of inspection outcomes, separately for the GS and DS systems. In each figure, I combined the tabulated data up to 2007 and the hand-gathered data from 2008 to 2016; self-inspections and government inspections are represented in grey and black, respectively.[14] Figure 2.3 shows the evolution of the provincial average of the number of taxpayers inspected. There is a pronounced trend of decline before 2008. After 2008, the decline of total taxpayers inspected became more gradual. Notably, at least on average, the number of taxpayers inspected through "self-inspections" dominate coverage by government inspections in every year. This makes perfect sense, given the lowest cost of taxpayer self-inspections and the explicit goal of self-inspections to broaden inspection coverage.

[13] Sun Ruibiao, Address at the National Tax Inspection Conference, February 25, 2014, 2015 Tax Inspection, Yearbook, p 9.

[14] Note that the pre-2008 data are based on complete provincial panels, while the post-2008 data are based only on a subset of provinces (the composition of which also changes from year to year).

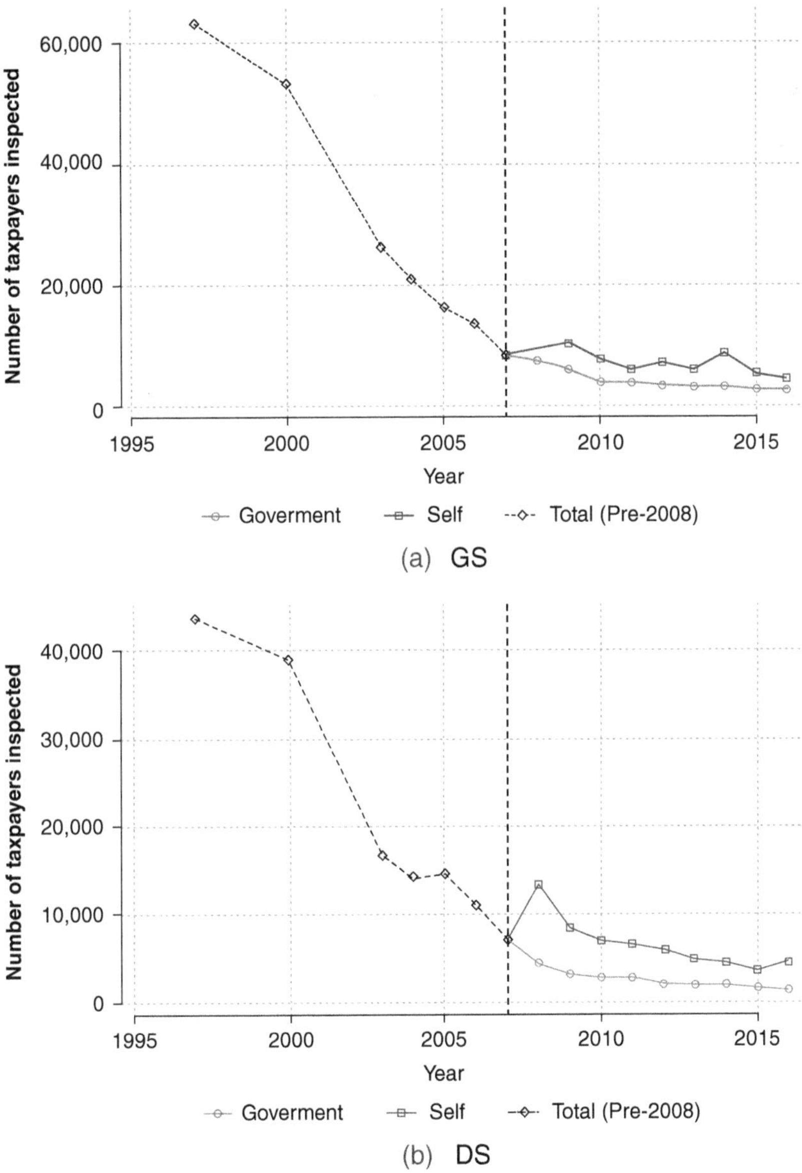

Figure 2.3 Trends in tax inspection coverage

Figure 2.4 shows similar trends for another measure of tax inspection outcomes – the contribution of revenue collected directly through inspections to overall tax revenue intake. The ratio is calculated

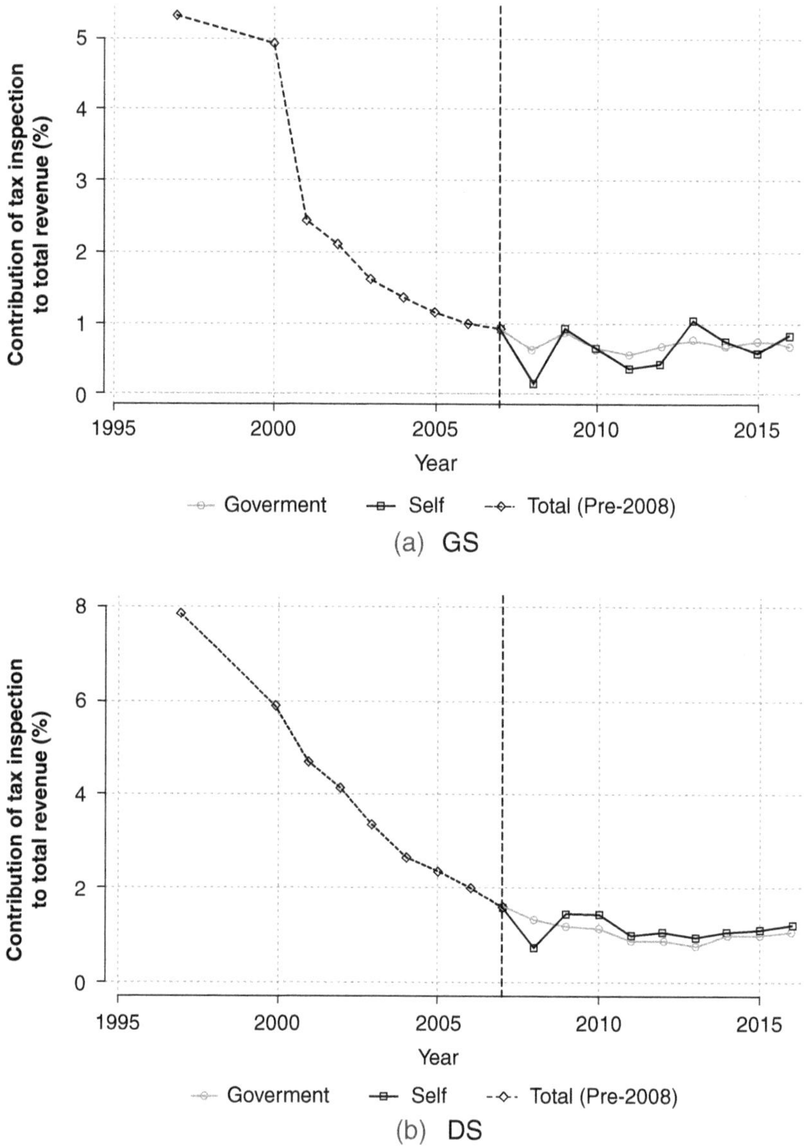

Figure 2.4 Trends in tax inspection contribution to total tax revenue

(separately for DS and GS) at the provincial level and then averaged across provinces. The average revenue contribution of tax inspections was in the 5–8 percent range in the late 1990s, but dropped to less than

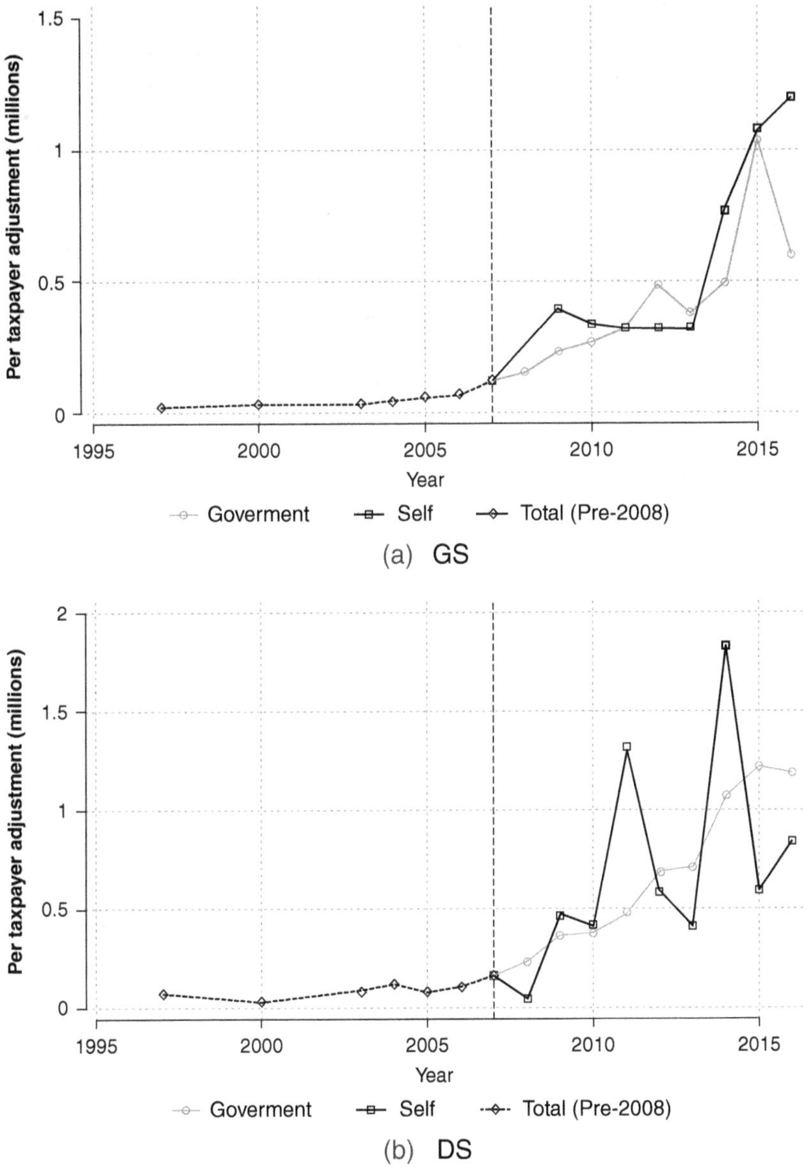

Figure 2.5 Trends in tax inspection per taxpayer adjustment

2 percent by 2007. The ratio has held steady since 2008. Significantly, the average revenue contributions of self-inspections and government inspections are similar.

Figure 2.5 depicts trends in average taxpayer adjustment per inspection (first calculated at the provincial level and then averaged across China). There has been a substantial increase in such adjustments in the past decade, which is likely driven by an increasing focus on large taxpayers. Meanwhile, while there are large fluctuations in the average adjustment from self-inspections, the overall trends and magnitudes of inspection outcomes are similar to government inspections.

To summarize, since 2008, in terms of taxpayer coverage and revenue contribution, taxpayer self-inspections have been at least as important as government inspections. Reports on pre-2008 practice indicate that self-inspections may have been even more prevalent before 2008. Overall, self-inspections have been a constant feature of the tax inspection system.

Audits, Amnesties, and Pure Bargaining for Revenue

Instead of "collaborative" or "enhanced relationship" compliance, the foreign practice that bears the closest analogy to Chinese taxpayer self-inspections is tax amnesties. These are episodes during which governments offer taxpayers a temporary opportunity to declare past unpaid taxes without being subject to penalties. Amnesty campaigns are sponsored by tax authorities with some frequency even in developed countries like the United States and Germany.[15] They are also quite common in developing countries.[16] These leniency programs tend to be temporary, and policy commentators advise against their routine use: while amnesties may appear to increase revenue in the short term, they are feared to lower compliance in the long term by detracting from the government's deterrence power.[17] At least in law, China does not have tax amnesties and voluntary disclosure programs. And to my knowledge, aside from the type of taxpayer self-inspections examined here, there are none in practice. While this fact has not been previously noted, it is also not surprising, once we recognize how often de facto tax amnesties are *already* offered through self-inspections.

[15] See Andreoni 1991, 1992; Malik and Schwab 1991; Bayer et al. 2015; Langenmayr 2017.

[16] Baer and Le Borgne (2008). In developed countries, the targets of tax amnesty programs are typically individuals (i.e. regarding their personal income tax obligations), while in developing countries, the targets tend to be businesses.

[17] One prominent practice in the sphere of international taxation – namely, voluntary disclosure programs where taxpayers are allowed to declare previously undeclared foreign asset holdings (without penalty if declaration occurs before any audit) – is a form of permanent tax amnesty.

One potential dis-analogy between Chinese self-inspections and tax amnesties elsewhere is that a taxpayer who participates in self-inspection and reports a positive additional tax liability may still face a subsequent government audit. By contrast, it is often assumed that taxpayers participating in amnesties will not be further audited for the same periods. However, this difference is arguably one of degree. On the one hand, the ability of Chinese tax administrators to make additional adjustments in the subsequent round of government inspections may be limited. On the other hand, it is unlikely that tax collectors administering amnesty programs in other countries make no judgment about whether their participants fully disclosed prior liabilities.

The more fundamental difference between Chinese self-inspections and taxpayer amnesties, I believe, is that the latter are carried out against some robust background regime of tax audits: amnesties are recognizable *deviations* from the norm of audits. Audits enforce the norm of truthful reporting and raise revenue by creating greater compliance via deterrence. Amnesties extract revenue from taxpayers but allow them to depart, without penalty, from the norm of truthful reporting. That is, taxpayers are not exempted from paying tax under amnesties; they are simply forgiven for lying in the past. Both the benefits and the costs of amnesties follow from this divergence from audits. Although amnesties potentially undermine the credibility of future audit threats, as well as leave the norm of truthful reporting vulnerable, they still assume that audits are generally carried out. What is radical about the Chinese practice is that self-inspections are carried out as an important form of *tax inspection*. That is, amnesty-like techniques erode, eclipse, and replace practices that uphold the norm of truthful reporting.

When audits no longer serve as the background practice, however, the character of amnesty-like practices also changes. It is here that we need to sharpen the conceptual vocabulary for describing tax administrative practices. Consider Table 2.1, which illustrates how tax administration techniques may differ along two important dimensions. The first is whether taxpayers are responsible for disclosing private information. The second is whether the government verifies the true liability of taxpayers. Normal tax audits belong in the upper-left cell of Table 2.1. That is, they are the product of two arrangements captured by the corresponding column and row: taxpayers are

Table 2.1 *Two dimensions of revenue-raising techniques*

	Taxpayer accountable for disclosing private information	*Taxpayer not accountable for disclosing private information*
Government verifies true liability	Normal tax audits	Assessments without audits (e.g. of property tax)
Government does not verify true liability	Tax amnesties	Pure negotiation

responsible for disclosing private information, *and* the government verifies true liability.

These two components are distinct, because not all tax collection practices that require the government to verify true liability also require taxpayers to disclose private information. In some important areas, such as property tax assessments,[18] the government can directly determine the tax base, without waiting for taxpayer reporting. This type of administrative technique is represented in the upper-right cell. Within the same scheme, tax amnesties are represented in the lower-left cell. Taxpayers are still responsible for disclosing private information, both upon the original filing of tax returns and during amnesties. The government, however, foregoes the verification of true liability in an amnesty, by not auditing anyone participating in amnesty.

If the government does not verify true tax liability, *and* if the taxpayer is not expected to disclose private information, we would no longer have an amnesty. Instead, we would be in the lower-right cell of the table. It seems that tax collection of this kind can only be interpreted as a pure form of negotiation for payment.

How should we characterize taxpayer self-inspections in China? Because self-inspections can occur in respect of all taxes, we are not looking at the special contexts of the upper-right cell. Yet at the same time, because the self-inspections are carried out as a tactic of regular inspections, it becomes unclear where we can find the background practice that enforces the norm of truthful reporting. The key question

[18] Property tax assessments are the focus of several recent randomized controlled trials carried out in developing countries. See Khan et al. 2016, 2019; Brockmeyer et al. 2020; Weigel 2020.

becomes: Do tax administrators enforce the norm of truthful reporting enough for it to be understood as a relevant background in China's tax inspection regime?

Through our examination of the revenue management system later in this chapter and in Chapters 3 and 4, we will conclude that the answer is largely "No." The practice of genuine audits – defined as the government verifying and holding taxpayers accountable for failures to disclose private information through tax returns – is very fragile. Because of this, it is hard to distinguish between self-inspections from pure negotiation for payment. It is worth stressing again that Chinese tax inspectors disregard tax returns not only in the penalty stage, but even in the inspection selection stage. Tax inspection campaigns in general, and self-inspection campaigns in particular, do not hinge on what taxpayers have previously declared on their tax returns, rendering taxpayers' prior obligations to truthfully report on their returns irrelevant.

To summarize, while there are striking analogies between taxpayer self-inspections in China and tax amnesties elsewhere, an important difference is that self-inspections in China substantially substitute for regular audits, whereas tax amnesties assume the continuance of audits. This underscores the former's more radical abdication of the responsibility to enforce truthful reporting norms.

Researchers studying tax amnesties elsewhere have found that they often occur as a result of fiscal pressures.[19] Interestingly, it has been observed in China that audits also respond to fiscal pressures. In prior research, Chinese scholars used three measures of fiscal pressure to study the impact of such pressure on tax collection by subnational governments: (1) a province's GDP growth rate, (2) a province's revenue growth rate, and (3) the difference between (2) and (1). The logic is that lower GDP growth rates threaten lower revenue growth: because tax collectors face revenue targets, both spur them to intensify collection. Moreover, lower revenue growth relative to GDP growth (i.e. a lower positive or a larger negative difference) may be especially prone to an interpretation of lackluster performance in tax collection – and therefore further incentivize collection efforts. Chinese scholars have found that these variables are correlated with tax inspection outcomes.

19 Bayer et al. 2015.

I tested such a correlation using hand-gathered data from the Tax Inspection Yearbooks for 2008–2016. Specifically, I examined two measures of inspection outcomes: the number of taxpayers inspected (normalized by provincial population), and the ratio of direct revenue contributions from inspections to total tax revenue. While prior research by Chinese scholars has analyzed pre-2008 inspection outcomes, I used post-2008 data. Moreover, I separately examined outcomes for self-inspection and government inspection.

For taxpayers inspected (Table 2.2), I found that the coefficients of correlation with the fiscal pressure variables are generally of the predicted signs: the lower the GDP growth rate, the lower the revenue growth rate, and the lower the revenue growth rate relative to the GDP growth rate, the larger the number of taxpayers inspected. Self- and government inspections are generally similar in this regard, although it appears that revenue pressure may lead GS tax inspectors to expand self-inspection coverage more. I found similar results when regressing contribution to total tax revenue on the fiscal pressure variables using 2008–2016 data on self-inspections (Table 2.3). The negative correlation with GDP growth rate is statistically significant. And GS tax inspectors generally appear to be more sensitive to revenue pressure than DS inspectors.

Such empirical evidence only confirms widespread anecdotes, as seen in remarks made in 2003 by one top SAT official about the organization of tax inspection:[20]

> Tax collection efficiency and inspection capacity are primarily determined by our basic institutions. [Under the current system], tax inspection, from the SAT down to the county levels, focuses on generating revenue. The system was designed for such a goal. Consequently, in a year when the SAT cannot meet its revenue targets, we resort to tools including inspections and special inspections. The same approach would be adopted by tax authorities of provincial, city and county levels that could not meet their revenue targets. Such inspections usually set eyes on "lucrative" industries . . . . They are not designed to prevent and curb tax violations.

[20] Liu Taiming, Director of the Tax Inspection Bureau at the SAT, Address (Speech at the National Taxation (Local Taxation) Training Courses on Tax Inspection, 9 December 2003), 2005 Tax Inspection Yearbook, p 14.

Table 2.2 *Correlation between inspection coverage and fiscal pressure*[21]
Correlation between tax inspections per capita and the listed variables. GS data, 2008–2016.

	(1)	(2)	(3)	(4)	(5)	(6)
Self × GDP growth rate (percent)	−5.346 (4.026)	−5.003 (3.908)				
GDP growth rate (percent)	3.826* (2.151)	−4.303 (3.151)				
Self × Diff. between revenue and GDP growth rates (percent)			−3.295* (1.923)	−3.676** (1.866)		
Difference between revenue and GDP growth rates (percent)			−0.104 (0.558)	−0.100 (0.543)		
Self × revenue growth rate (percent)					−2.827* (1.627)	−3.788** (1.608)
Revenue growth rate (percent)					0.143 (0.545)	−0.225 (0.539)
Year FEs		X		X		X
Observations	406	406	406	406	406	406
Adj R-squared	0.215	0.282	0.215	0.281	0.214	0.285
F-test	0.000	0.000	0.000	0.000	0.000	0.000

[21] The dependent variable is taxpayers inspected (scaled by provincial population). For each fiscal pressure variable, the table reports a baseline coefficient corresponding to government inspections, and a coefficient for the interaction between a self-inspection and the fiscal variable, representing self-inspection's difference from the baseline. The results for the GS and DS systems are separately displayed. Columns 2, 4, and 6 use year fixed effects and represent the preferred specifications. Values in parentheses are standard errors. * $p<.1$, ** $p<.05$.

Table 2.2 (*cont.*)

Correlation between tax inspections per capita and the listed variables. DS data, 2008–2016.

	(1)	(2)	(3)	(4)	(5)	(6)
Self × GDP growth rate (percent)	1.516 (2.242)	2.401 (2.220)				
GDP growth rate (percent)	1.626 (1.386)	−4.255** (2.093)				
Self × Difference between revenue and GDP growth rates (percent)			1.281 (1.329)	1.323 (1.291)		
Difference between revenue and GDP growth rates (percent)			0.531 (0.852)	−1.813 (1.164)		
Self × revenue growth rate (percent)					1.045 (1.012)	1.242 (0.987)
Revenue growth rate (percent)					0.672 (0.645)	−2.456** (1.041)
Year FEs		X		X		X
Observations	442	442	442	442	442	442
Adj R-squared	0.115	0.167	0.114	0.164	0.118	0.170
F-test	0.000	0.000	0.000	0.000	0.000	0.000

Revenue Managers as Competing Auditors?

Although tax inspection bureaus are often assumed to typify the tax collection apparatus of the Chinese state, we saw that they house only around 12 percent of the total tax administration workforce. What does the

Table 2.3 *Fiscal pressure and tax inspections' contribution to revenue*[22]

Correlation between contribution of tax inspection to total revenue and the listed variables. Self-inspections, 2008–2016.

	(1)	(2)	(3)	(4)	(5)	(6)
GS × GDP growth rate (percent)	−0.022*	−0.027**				
	(0.013)	(0.013)				
GDP growth rate (percent)	−0.010	−0.022*				
	(0.008)	(0.012)				
GS × difference between revenue and GDP growth rates (percent)			−0.001	−0.007		
			(0.006)	(0.007)		
Difference between revenue and GDP growth rates (percent)			−0.002	0.004		
			(0.005)	(0.006)		
GS × revenue growth rate (percent)					−0.001	−0.006
					(0.004)	(0.005)
Revenue growth rate (percent)					−0.003	0.002
					(0.004)	(0.005)
Year FEs		X		X		X
Observations	379	379	379	379	379	379
Adj R-squared	0.134	0.161	0.116	0.141	0.122	0.144
F-test	0.000	0.000	0.000	0.000	0.000	0.000

remaining bulk of Chinese tax administration do? How can we define the respective roles of tax inspectors and other tax administrators? Do tax administrators other than tax inspectors enforce the norm of truthful reporting?

22 DS serves as a baseline while the difference of GS from DS is reflected in the coefficients of an interactive term. Values in parentheses are standard errors. * p<.1, **p<.05.

The most central function in Chinese tax administration (*shuishou zhengguan*) is denoted in official documents as "revenue source management" (*shuiyuan guanli*, or revenue management for short). Correspondingly, the most typical role of an employee in a frontline tax agency is as a "tax revenue manager" (*shuishou guanli yuan*). Revenue managers routinely monitor taxpayer compliance and exercise coercive power to deter or prevent noncompliance, long before the tax inspection system comes into play. The basic reason why few tax inspections are initiated by examining tax returns is that tax inspection bureaus are simply not in the business of examining returns. That task falls, at least purportedly, within the "revenue management" system.

As we began to see in Chapter 1, "revenue management" is the product of a specific sequence of policy decisions made in the 1990s and 2000s. But what does it mean specifically? We can begin by referencing a paradigm used by the OECD to compile comparisons of tax administration features across more than sixty countries. Generally, one can divide the taxpayer-facing units of modern tax administration into the following functions: taxpayer services, account management, audit and investigations, collections, and other support functions (such as dispute resolution).[23] Although each of these bureaucratic functions is easy to understand – I will briefly define the function of account management below – their organization is subtle and varied. In the Chinese revenue management system, the key observation is that revenue managers have historically performed – and in most of China, continue to perform – *all* of these functions with respect to any given taxpayer. Revenue managers are *defined* by their lack of specialization.

That Chinese frontline tax administrators do not specialize contrasts with some basic assumptions about tax administration – or, for that matter, about most modern bureaucratic organization – typically used in most developed countries. We normally assume that taxpayer services, audits, and so forth are different units of government agencies: the audit division of a tax agency examines the tax returns and compliance of all taxpayers within a particular jurisdictional scope, whereas other divisions carry out taxpayer services and collection activities. Moreover, we associate these various bureaucratic functions with organizations, not with particular individuals. By contrast, the standard approach of Chinese tax bureaus is to combine and personalize these functions in one tax revenue manager (or a small group of them), for any given taxpayer.

[23] See "Allocation of staff resources by functional groupings," p. 189 of OECD 2015.

The most important reason for this personalization and lack of specialization in Chinese tax administration is the primacy of account management and collection. "Account management," as used by the OECD (and the US IRS), denotes the function of maintaining the accuracy of registration information about a taxpayer in the tax administration's data system, and keeping track of the taxpayer's compliance activities (e.g. whether returns are timely filed and whether outstanding tax liabilities are timely paid). "Collection," of course, denotes ensuring that a taxpayer that is delinquent on tax payments pays as early and/or as much as possible. As is typical for developing countries, the vast majority of Chinese taxpayers are small businesses. The Chinese government places a high priority on keeping such taxpayers registered, monitoring the timeliness of their filings and payments, and ensuring that they do not default on their tax obligations – despite the high propensity of such taxpayers to default along all these margins. It follows that account management and collection consume substantial bureaucratic resources. In many places in China, these two functions are denoted by the term "basic management" (*jichu guanli*). Traditionally, the most effective way of carrying out "basic management" is believed to be assigning individual revenue managers to individual taxpayers, a practice that explains why tax administration in China is personal as opposed to impersonal.

We will analyze the primacy of "basic management" in the next few chapters. For example, taxpayer services are relatively easy to separate from the core functions of account management and collection. In China's more affluent regions, there are now well-staffed call centers at city levels to answer taxpayer questions. In addition, easily accessible taxpayer service halls also handle payments, tax invoices and vouchers, and various approval procedures – to the extent that they have not been moved online. Thus, unless a local tax bureau cannot afford a robust taxpayer service function – in which case revenue managers assigned to specific taxpayers still deliver taxpayer services – good progress has been made in peeling off the taxpayer services role from revenue managers. Indeed, even account management tasks have been substantially simplified, with reminders for filing and payments sent increasingly by email, text messages, or notifications on phone apps. The bureaucratic resilience of the basic management function in the age of smartphones – and indeed of rapidly advancing surveillance techniques – can only be explained by certain deep organizational features of the Chinese state.

But even recognizing (without rationalizing) the basic structure of the revenue management system is already helpful for contextualizing the tax inspection system. The former is responsible for ensuring that taxpayers timely file tax returns and make tax payments. In this process, revenue managers would inevitably carry out some audit-like functions. Insofar as they do so, the corresponding "audit" coverage of revenue management could be much wider than the tax inspection system.[24]

Unfortunately, the revenue management and tax inspection systems are often uncoordinated. The former faces its own separate revenue targets, engendering a competition for revenue with the tax inspection system that bears on the understanding of the use of self-inspections in the latter system. As discussed earlier, self-inspections are often initiated with a taxpayer education campaign and are often said to have a taxpayer service component. Some readers may have found it strange that tax inspectors simultaneously deliver taxpayer education and taxpayer services. Indeed, Chinese revenue managers believe that they should supervise taxpayer self-audits (at times of their own choosing), since taxpayer education and services are a routine part of *their* work. Tax inspectors should instead solely carry out government field inspections. However, given that self-inspections broaden coverage and raise substantial revenue, inspection bureaus have understandably resisted being deprived of such a tool.

The oddity of separating revenue management and tax inspection and subjecting them to separate revenue targets goes further. Leaders of China's tax administration emphasize the aspiration of using audits to improve future compliance so that tax inspections do not play out as yearly scrambles to raise revenue from a persistently noncompliant taxpayer population. But organizationally, this means that tax inspections would discover patterns of noncompliance, which would then be dealt with during the revenue management process: an idea captured by the official phrase "using tax inspection to improve management" (*yicha cuguan*). This, of course, is in tension with the specific use of tax inspection (and the specific incentives imposed on tax inspection bureaus) to achieve annual revenue targets.

The possibility that the revenue management and tax inspection systems compete more than they coordinate is striking. Causality between this and the fact that the two systems face separate revenue targets can go in both directions. On the one hand, it may be that revenue targets are what cause tax inspectors to incorporate taxpayer services and education into their toolkit. If such administrative techniques help generate revenue, then tax

[24] As a consequence, taxpayers may also be examined separately by revenue managers and tax inspectors in the same period (and by such personnel separately from the GS and DS systems), while these different tax administrators may fail to share information among themselves.

inspectors have more incentive to use them. On the other hand, it is conceivable that tax inspectors had given up their specialized role as pure auditors, with the result that they already perform functions similar to those assigned to revenue managers. In that case, setting revenue targets could be an effective way of evaluating performance across the entire tax administration. Therefore, it is not clear that tax inspectors abdicated their auditor roles *because of* their separate revenue targets.

In any case, just as Chinese tax inspectors have tried to use the tools of taxpayer education and service, Chinese revenue managers have tried to introduce audit functions into their arsenal. Given the compromised nature of the "audits" that tax inspectors actually carry out, as well as the fact that revenue managers do have regular access to tax returns, this might appear beneficial. However, the separate existence of tax inspection bureaus has required attempts at establishing audit functions within revenue management to be disguised by opaque terminology. Two extremely elusive terms are used for quasi-audit functions within revenue management: taxpayer evaluation (*shuishou pinggu*) and risk management (*fengxian guanli*).[25]

Taxpayer evaluation is meant to assess whether taxpayers have reported truthfully on their tax returns, and whether there are risks of noncompliance beyond routine filing and payment. It is a task to be completed by tax revenue managers in addition to their taxpayer service, account management, and collections operations. In recent years, the SAT has urged tax revenue managers to shift their focus to, and engage more in, taxpayer evaluation. We can infer the meaning of "taxpayer evaluation" by reference to the OECD functional division set out earlier: Which of the tasks might taxpayer evaluation correspond to? The answer is, clearly, audit and investigation, that is, a type of interaction with taxpayers that is conditional on an assessment of the taxpayers' degree of compliance. And by urging more emphasis on taxpayer evaluation, the SAT acknowledges that audits can often hold low priority for revenue managers.

The term "risk management" is even more elusive, bearing multiple meanings in an organizational context.[26] Internationally, "risk management"

[25] The terms are so elusive that there is a tremendous amount of confusion even within Chinese tax administration on their meaning. For example, various proposed revisions of the Law on Tax Collection and Administration that have been debated since 2011 have referred to "taxpayer evaluation," but many debates have quickly bogged down because participants do not share an understanding of the term.

[26] A substantial amount of discussion among Chinese tax administrators over the past decade has been about managing the risk of *official* malfeasance, for example, corruption

in tax administration has in recent years been associated with the idea of sorting among different types of taxpayers. Because the nature of the risks arising from high-compliance taxpayer populations differs from the risks arising from low-compliance populations, such populations should be treated differently in many phases of tax administration. For example, taxpayer services and penalty regimes should all vary between high-compliance and low-compliance populations, an idea that encompasses the "collaborative compliance" targeted at large taxpayers discussed earlier in this chapter. Like many other bureaucratic organizations, the SAT likes to brandish new management practices and echo international trends. But what the SAT means by "risk management" is in truth much more staid. For the most part, "risk management" in China does not mean differentiating among types of taxpayers, but creating greater specialization and differentiation among administrative functions. Most importantly, the emphasis is on differentiating audit and investigations from "basic management" tasks.

Take, for example, a tax administration reform proposal that the SAT issued in October 2010.[27] In a set of "Guiding Opinions," the SAT announced a number of pilot initiatives across the country for "specialized revenue management" (*shuiyuan guanli zhuanyehua*). The SAT explained that the direction of the proposed reform was to "enhance risk management" in tax administration. Moreover, the reform would make greater use of information in tax collection, adopt taxpayer segmentation and the vertical division of labor (among different tiers of tax bureaus), and, tellingly, give greater emphasis to improving "the truthfulness of tax returns."[28] However, the SAT offered few practical methods for implementing these ideas. For example, tax collectors were merely urged to "better establish the goals of revenue management" and make better use of "taxpayer evaluation" to ensure truthful reporting. For improving risk management, the SAT simply instructed subnational bureaus to set up (according to their own design) protocols for risk management, as well as develop new institutions that largely did not exist within the revenue management system. These included risk identification strategies, models for evaluating taxpayer behavior, and guidance for audits.

or failures to enforce the law. In other words, the "risk management" discourse fails to focus even on risks arising from taxpayers.

27 SAT Guiding Opinions on Launching Pilot Experiments on Specialized Revenue Management (*Guoshuifa* [2010] 101, October 18, 2010).

28 In addition, administrative protocols would be clarified and standardized, and professionalism among tax administrators nurtured. Both points speak directly to the issue of lack of specialization.

The SAT's announcement also repeated numerous objectives for specialization in tax administration that it had advocated more than a decade earlier, thus implicitly acknowledging that the objectives had not been achieved.[29] Relative to previous efforts to reform tax administration, the SAT 2010 Guiding Opinions did promote additional ideas. One was to make taxpayer segmentation an important component of administration strategy: tax administration resources should focus largely on "risky" taxpayers, including specific sectors and large taxpayers. However, it was unclear how specialization with respect to different types of taxpayers would work out, prior to the specialization of tasks. Would revenue managers assigned to large taxpayers again carry out the whole range of administrative tasks?

Talks of "risk management" in recent years, therefore, are largely new bottles into which the old wine of enhancing specialization is poured. Regarding the introduction of greater audit capacity into the revenue management system, this new label serves two purposes. First, it obscures the competition between revenue management and tax inspection: revenue managers do not conduct tax inspections; they simply do more "risk management." Second, it puts a new spin on an old, stagnant effort – audits and investigations continue to be the weakest aspect of the revenue management system.

What ultimately is of greater importance, however, is not the competition between the two parts of the tax administration, but the challenge of establishing more robust audit functions *anywhere in the system*. Note that insofar as revenue managers mainly register taxpayers and pursue non-filers and delinquents, they also do not hold taxpayers accountable for the accuracy of their returns. For both revenue managers and tax inspectors, audits are a distant aspiration, forever postponed by current exigencies. This leads inevitably to the critical question: If Chinese tax

[29] Compare the following excerpt from the 2010 proposal, for example, with the 1997 tax administration reform proposal discussed in Chapter 1: "Tax bureaus should standardize the basic procedures of tax administration and collection in various steps, including tax return reception, taxpayer evaluation, tax inspection, and legal remedy. Upon receiving tax return filings, tax agencies should utilize both computers and manual power to conduct initial review of the tax returns based on filed tax information, risk indicators, and evaluation models, and make the appropriate dispositions. For those potentially non-compliant taxpayers after the initial review, revenue managers could further inspection by mail, appointment, or on-site visit, and make dispositions accordingly. If revenue managers discover instances of tax evasion, tax avoidance, or tax fraud, they should refer the cases to the tax inspection department, which shall, upon opening the case, investigate the claims thoroughly and fully realize its functions."

administrators do not secure compliance through threatening and conducting audits, then *how do they do it*?

The short answer to this question is that audits are far from being the only or even the most powerful means of coercion at tax administrators' disposals. While audits enforce the norm of truthful reporting, they only indirectly help generate tax revenue. Chinese tax administrators have opted out of such indirect means for extracting revenue. As we will see in the next chapter, they apply, tirelessly and incessantly, other tools of coercion.

3

Atomistic Coercion

The organization of grassroots tax administration is crucial for understanding the functioning of the Chinese fiscal state. But the topic is an unfortunate combination of the esoteric and the mundane, which has invariably misled scholars – including those in China – to describe it as commonplace. The reality is almost the opposite. The structure of frontline tax administration in China is quite unusual when compared to tax administration in advanced economies. At the same time, Chinese tax authorities adopt a particularly opaque terminology in describing this structure – such as "revenue management," "taxpayer evaluation," and "risk management" – that connotes very different things to different people. When an opaque terminology hides subtle but important features, in a sphere of social organization that strikes most scholars as banal, we have a perfect recipe for misunderstanding.

This chapter takes a close look at how Chinese tax administrators and taxpayers conduct themselves within the revenue management system. I start with features of the system that have provoked the most discussion among tax administrators: the lack of specialization; an impossible demand on the span of control of frontline officers; and opportunities for corruption and malfeasance. I then zero in on a more fundamental consequence of the system, the practice of non-rule-based tax collection, and analyze the practice in terms of a novel concept, atomistic coercion.

Specialization and Span of Control

A 2005 SAT circular, "The Tax Revenue Manager System (for Trial Implementation),"[1] laid out the revenue management system's intended mode of operation. The document is informative, but not because it accurately presents how things have subsequently worked in practice. For one, the circular was neither legally nor bureaucratically binding. It did not dictate any particular reorganizations at grassroots tax bureaus or personnel

[1] *Guoshuifa* [2005] 40, March 17, 2005.

reallocations; it did not even specify metrics for evaluating the extent of implementation, in the way the 1997 tax administration reform came with timelines and measurable outcomes. Moreover, even the text of the circular has a surreal quality, it takes a considerable suspension of disbelief to accept that it describes something that *could* be implemented in practice.

The circular begins concretely enough and explicitly defines a "grassroots tax agency" (*jiceng shuiwu jiguan*) as one that has direct contact with taxpayers and is responsible for tax collection and administration. A grassroots tax agency may have a "revenue management department," which can include a branch bureau, an outpost office, or teams within these low-tier offices.[2] A revenue manager, in turn, is defined as an employee in such a department who is assigned to supervise particular taxpayers on the basis of geographical allocation or taxpayer type. The circular then goes on to delineate the (purported) responsibilities of this type of frontline tax administrator.[3] The job description includes comprehensive responsibilities in five areas and seventeen major tasks:

> • Giving publicity to and implementing tax laws, regulations and policies; providing taxpayer services; offering taxpayers consultation services relating to tax law and instructions on the handling of tax affairs; prompting taxpayers to file tax returns and remit tax payment in a timely fashion and accurately, to establish sound accounting policies and procedures, and to enhance the management of the accounting books and supporting vouchers in accordance with the relevant regulations;
> • Investigating and verifying the validity of assigned taxpayers' tax registration information; acquiring information on taxpayers' amalgamation, division or bankruptcy; acquiring information on taxpayers' changing circumstances such as operation of business in other jurisdictions, the dissolution or suspension of business, etc.; acquiring information on changes in taxpayers' household registration; investigating and verifying taxpayer's tax returns (including applications for tax reduction, exemption, deferral or refund) as well as verifying and determining the authenticity of other items relevant in the determination of tax liability; and acquiring basic information on taxpayers' production, business operation and financial accounting;

2 Figure 1.4 showed that in 2005, there were around 20,000 such offices in the DS system and 10,000 in the GS system. These numbers represent a decline from 35,000 for DS and 20,000 for GS in the mid-1990s. Thus, after much effort had been expended to centralize tax administration by reducing the number of outpost offices, the 2005 SAT circular envisioned a central role for employees at such offices. It should not be surprising, then, that both the number of outpost offices and their staffing level have remained steady since then.

3 I deliberately chose "revenue manager" as an awkward, non-colloquial translation of the term "*shuishou guanli yuan*," in the hope that it would remind the reader of its very specific connotations, in a way that the more bland translation, "tax administrator," may not.

- "Prompting assigned taxpayers to file overdue tax returns and remit unpaid taxes; acquiring information on tax debts owed by taxpayers and their disposition of assets while tax debt is outstanding; performing routine management and inspection of taxpayer's use of invoices and conducting on-site audit and inspection of unusual invoices; prompting taxpayers to install and utilize tax control systems in accordance with the requirements of tax agencies;
- "Conducting evaluations for assigned taxpayers, identifying irregularities through general utilization of relevant information as well as assessment criteria and red flags, and screening for key targets for assessment and analysis; conducting preliminary determination of the validity and accuracy of tax returns; based on issues identified through such evaluation, conducting individual interviews with taxpayer and on-site investigations; providing recommendations for dispositions in cases of violations of tax legislation and regulations; and
- "Maintaining and updating files for assigned taxpayers in the tax agency's internal system, which files would contain timely collected taxpayer information such as production, business operation and financial accounting, and which would be regularly organized, updated and stored in order to facilitate information-sharing."

One tax administrator in charge of designing computerized protocols in his province to implement this list told me that it includes sixty-eight subtasks. For good measure, the SAT adds a residual, catchall category, "the completion of other tasks assigned by superiors" – which, according to the same tax administrator, forms "a major part of the job for frontline officers!"[4] The only tasks revenue managers are exempted from are "direct participation in handling tax remittances, tax inspections, the approval of tax reductions, exemptions, deferrals, credits against tax liabilities, and refunds, and the imposition of penalties for violations."

Given how the 2005 SAT circular spelled out revenue managers' roles, it seems fair to say that there was no expectation for revenue managers to specialize. Within Chinese tax administration, the debate about specialization has long been carried out in terms of whether tax administrators should be assigned to taxpayers (*guanhu*) – thus handling all tax matters rising from the assigned taxpayers – or assigned to specific types of tasks in connection with unspecified taxpayers (*guanshi*). The 2005 SAT circular heavily favored taxpayer assignment, and paid only lip service to task assignment (and specialization). Insofar as the 2005 SAT circular is implemented, any further discussion of specialization among frontline

[4] In Chapter 5, I discuss the importance of such "other tasks" for the evaluation of bureaucratic performance.

tax administrators is arguably empty talk.[5] The circular offered a recognizable example of the fluffy language common to such empty talk, by declaring that under the revenue manager system, taxpayer- and task-base assignments would be "integrated."

In truth, even if the SAT (under Commissioner Xie Xuren) did not so heavily promote the revenue manager system, specialization within Chinese tax administration would have been difficult to realize, for two structural reasons. First, the decentralized network of branch bureaus and outpost offices that directly engage with taxpayers – discussed in Chapter 1, and explicitly recognized in the 2005 SAT circular as "grassroots tax agencies" – implies that each of these low-tier government entities is precluded from the economy of scale that often is necessary for specialization. While the team of revenue managers in each branch bureau or outpost office struggle to keep up with thousands of taxpayers, thousands of taxpayers is often too small a population for fine divisions of labor. Consider examples from tax law: many detailed tax rules apply to relatively small portions of taxpayer populations. The smaller the taxpayer population within a jurisdiction, the less frequently are these rules applicable. Consequently, it may not make sense for a team of twenty or thirty tax collectors in a branch bureau to designate a corporate tax or VAT specialist, or for a county- or even a city-level bureau to house specialists in international taxation, corporate reorganizations, and financial institutions. Very often, it is already too much to expect these frontline tax administrators to be fluent in the nuances of tax returns. To ask them to engage directly with the interpretation of tax law, when these interpretation issues arise rarely, would be unreasonable.

I came to appreciate this fact through a personal experience. In 2006, the SAT invited me to teach a one-day course on tax treaties at its training center in the city of Yangzhou. I prepared a day's worth of introductory material that I hoped would hold the interest of experienced tax administrators. When I entered the classroom at the Yangzhou training center, I learned that my audience was about 100 tax administrators from Qingdao, a large, prosperous coastal city in Shandong Province. At some point during our morning discussion, I asked my students how often they had to work with tax treaty issues. I expected the answer to be "a lot," as Qingdao was a major location for foreign direct investments in China. But my question was met with a moment of silence. Some members of the

[5] This critique of official rhetoric about specialization applies to the 2010 SAT Guiding Opinions on Launching Pilot Experiments on Specialized Revenue Management (*Guoshuifa* [2010] 101), discussed in Chapter 2.

audience began shaking their heads. One of them eventually spoke up and answered that treaty law issues came up only very occasionally. I blurted out in response, "So why do you have to learn this esoteric stuff?!" It seemed to me that it would have been much more efficient for the training course to be offered to treaty specialists from different cities, with perhaps one or two from each city.

This was not an incident of misallocation of training resources that just happened to a junior academic. The day after my course, the director of the SAT's treaty division gave a one-day course to the same group on the same subject. I sat in on it. The lecturer was the same SAT official who then led a team of six staff members to negotiate and manage China's network of tax treaties with close to ninety countries.[6] I asked her why, given her presumably very busy schedule, she would spend a day teaching frontline tax officials basic treaty law. Her answer was as surprising – and illuminating – as the answer I got the previous day from the Qingdao officials. She said that she found such teaching stints quite useful, as her team at the SAT did not regularly get to find out what issues arose "on the ground" in the application of tax treaties.

Episodes like this helped me understand the transmission of legal information within China's tax bureaucracy. The officers who directly deal with taxpayers may not have enough reason to learn about the law's specialized details. But the specialists who know more about law, in the upper tiers of administration, may not know how law is actually applied, as they do not directly deal with taxpayers. The problem was not how training sessions were organized. Even if the SAT specialist trained specialists in provinces and cities, these provincial and city specialists would still have to train the lower-tier agencies' revenue managers, as long as the latter are in charge.

During the same teaching stint, I was exposed to the second structural difficulty for cultivating specialization among revenue managers. After our one-day course (and a delicious dinner), some of the Qingdao tax officials invited me out for a group foot massage, a service that Yangzhou was famous for. As we hung out together that evening, I ended up talking to the leader of the Qingdao delegation, Mr. Zhang, a nice man in his late forties or early fifties. His colleagues referred to him deferentially as "Zhang *Kezhang*." I subsequently learned that *kezhang* is a typical rank for the leader of an internal division of a city-level tax bureau. It has an

6 Recall from Chapter 1 that the SAT has fewer than 800 staff members. The SAT's International Department has less than forty staff members, and the Treaty Division (a subunit of the International Department), in having six members, is typical of other SAT divisions.

equivalent rank to a county-level tax bureau chief. But it is also between three and five ranks below the rank of the SAT treaty division chief who lectured the next day. In the regular promotion system for Chinese civil servants, it could easily take up to ten years for even well-performing civil servants to rise through this many ranks. Moreover, Mr. Zhang was at least seven or eight years older than the SAT treaty specialist.

In other words, even though Mr. Zhang was well respected by his peers, he was fifteen to twenty years behind in career progress relative to the SAT official. Most of this had to do with where Mr. Zhang started, that is, as a revenue manager in a grassroots tax agency. This meant that absent exceptional performance and truly good luck, he would never rise to the rank of the average employee in the SAT in their early forties. The other members of his delegation, whether older or younger, similarly belonged to the very bottom ranks of China's bureaucratic hierarchy. What reasons do they have for investing efforts in the nuances of law, given these career prospects?

These considerations indicate that the decentralized structure of Chinese tax administration creates serious barriers to specialization. Because decentralization in tax collection follows to a large extent the general structure of the Chinese state, one might think that it is something that China's tax bureaucrats could not do much about – and therefore constitutes an exogenous factor that explains the lack of specialization.[7] But as we saw earlier, the 2005 SAT circular also suggests that China's policy makers may not really want revenue managers to specialize, even if that were possible. This points to the possibility that bureaucratic decentralization is not a fact arbitrarily given, but serves some underlying purpose.

To elaborate on this claim, consider the other obvious challenge the revenue management system presents, namely, the ever-expanding span of control it requires. As we saw in Chapter 1, the number of Chinese tax administrators has been stable since the early 2000s. But the number of firms has grown dramatically: in one province I studied, the taxpayer population nearly doubled between 2010 and 2016.[8] Tax administrators' workload has also grown explosively. One tax administrator explained the implication for the revenue manager system in one city in 2016:

> In the urban parts of City Y, the Local Tax Bureau oversees 51,848 registered taxpayers (28,474 normal business entities and 16,487 sole proprietors) and

[7] Cui 2015 advanced this hypothesis. These barriers to specialization exist in the GS system as well as the DS system: the former generally adopts the same revenue management system as the latter.

[8] Cui et al. 2021.

> 15,472 businesses registered as employers liable for social insurance (SI) payments. Revenue managers responsible for account management tasks are predominately located in the Third and Fourth Tax Branch Bureaus. Not counting bureau executives and support staff, there are a total of 56 revenue managers, each of whom is responsible for, on average, 979 taxpayers (including 508 business entities) and 276 SI registrants.
>
> Let's forget the fact that among the revenue managers, 43% are over the age of 45 and 21% are ex-military cadres. Let's also not consider the geographical spread of taxpayers, the time devoted to dealing with 'abnormal' taxpayers,[9] or even SI premium collection. If a revenue manager devotes efforts to acquire the information [listed in the 2005 SAT circular] at the rate of one taxpayer per day, there is not enough time in a year to cover the taxpayers assigned to him. Simply relying on unspecialized management . . . even the basic duty of acquiring taxpayer information is already quite burdensome, [let alone] the other duties and responsibilities listed by the SAT.

In other words, revenue managers are expected to juggle an impossible number of tasks with respect to each of hundreds of taxpayers. This objection to the SAT's delineation of the revenue manager's role could easily have been raised in 2005: even in the 1990s, many tax bureaus already faced taxpayer-to-tax-administrator ratios in the hundreds. To be clear, I have not omitted mentioning any mechanism – for example, computer technology that renders the seemingly complex task descriptions easily implementable in reality – that would explain the sense of impossibility away. What, then, is the point of this impossible job description?

The best way to read the 2005 SAT circular, I believe, is not as a document that describes pragmatic steps in tax administration, but as one that announces a certain logic or vision. As a first component in this vision, there is a long list of requirements imposed upon taxpayers, compliance with each of which is observable by the government. The message of the 2005 SAT circular is that the government must always stand ready to secure such compliance. For example, even though the law requires taxpayers to file tax returns and pay taxes on time, it is also the job of tax administrators to make sure that such compliance actually happens. It is not enough, for instance, to penalize taxpayers for failures to comply. The government must preempt noncompliance as much as possible. Similarly, even though maintaining sound accounting records and installing tax control hardware and software are primarily taxpayers' responsibilities, tax administrators should also attempt to get taxpayers to the compliant state. Nor is the accuracy of

9 Abnormal taxpayers are those who are nominally registered with the tax authorities but who cannot be contacted and who are persistently delinquent (even if only for small amounts).

taxpayer registration information some by-product of taxpayer compliance. Instead, government agents must diligently check such accuracy in each individual case. Even if the government does not intend to provide nanny-style hand-holding to taxpayers, it establishes at least a nagging adult presence.

The second component of the SAT's logic is that revenue managers in direct personal contact with taxpayers may be best positioned to establish such adult presence. Suppose, for example, that email – or, nowadays, smartphone – reminders are sent to taxpayers who are at risk of failing, or who have already failed, to submit tax returns on time. That may be a good substitute for in-person reminders. But if taxpayers fail to respond to the electronic reminders, an official could step in and cause corrections to be made.

There is also a large list of compliance obligations the fulfillment of which is not easily observed, such as whether information that determines tax liabilities is accurately disclosed. Because of this, the government should acquire maximal information about taxpayers. Here again, the SAT's logic is that agents in personal contact with taxpayers may be able to acquire information that other agents (e.g. tax inspectors) could not. Therefore, personal contact has the advantage both of carrying greater persuasive authority (where needed) in securing compliance and of an expanded range of observation.

The point of the SAT circular was to state this vision. As long as the vision is accepted, how it is to be actualized is a matter of ongoing trial and error. Technology could make a difference: for example, if electronic reminders are sufficient for most returns to be filed and taxes to be paid, government agents would have lesser need to be in personal contact, reducing the revenue manager's required span of control. But Chinese tax administrators have also long thought about other methods of maximizing the actualized span of control. One is to better train revenue managers for their comprehensive portfolios. This is why the comments quoted earlier sound resigned about City Y's revenue managers being too old and insufficiently educated: the implication is that they are not that trainable.[10]

Although one can criticize the SAT's delineation of the revenue manager's role as unrealistic, such criticism would not necessarily challenge the goals spelled out in the vision. Are the goals themselves unobjectionable, or

[10] Of course, such notes of resignation are ironic: China's tax administration workforce is likely one of the best educated in the world (see Figure 1.3), and, comparatively, most trainable.

are they misguided? This is the critical question. Lest readers think that the SAT's goals are platitudinous, it is worth noting that they deviate from tax administration protocols in many other countries. The Internal Revenue Manual used by the IRS in the United States, for example, explicitly instructs IRS account managers *not* to take calls from taxpayers except during the three and a half months of the annual return-filling season. It further instructs most IRS employees *not* to answer taxpayer questions about law, or give directions to taxpayers about how to complete tax returns. IRS employee must direct taxpayers to self-help resources instead. Personal contact with taxpayers (even by phone) is explicitly discouraged, as well as most types of direct assistance with taxpayer compliance.[11] These IRM instructions are based on the premise that certain taxpayer responsibilities – learning the law, seeking advice from specialists, and so forth – *are not* tax administrator responsibilities, and that taxpayers' attention should be called to the existence of these boundaries. In the performance of taxpayer responsibilities, taxpayers, not tax administrators, are in control. It is this distinction that the revenue manager system declines to maintain.

Corruption, Familiarity, and Quasi-Compliance

We now know that Chinese revenue managers are frequently in contact with local taxpayers by design. The risks of bribery and other illegal behavior seem to be high. However, the designers of the revenue management system are aware of such risks. The SAT dictates that taxpayer assignments among revenue managers must rotate at least every two years, and further requires at least two government agents to attend many types of revenue manager visits to taxpayer premises. There are also extensive documentation requirements for such visits, aiming to capture most incidents of interactions with taxpayers in the government's computer systems. Further, when lip service is paid to specialization within revenue management, a key benefit emphasized is that by allowing the tax affairs of a single taxpayer to be handled by different specialized agents, different agents can also monitor one another.

The effectiveness of these official measures in curbing corruption is unknown. But there are in any case other reasons not to posit corruption

[11] See Internal Revenue Manual, Part 21 Customer Account Services; Chapter 1. Accounts Management and Compliance Services Operations; Section 1. Accounts Management and Compliance Services Overview (last revised September 11, 2019): www.irs.gov/irm/part21/irm_21-001-001.html. See in particular the lengthy Exhibit 21.1.1-1, Out-of-Scope Topics and Forms.

as the most important outcome of personal contact. Social scientists often portray a high level of – and a high tolerance for – corruption in the developing world. But, without making little of the problem of corruption, I would argue that there is also a tendency for scholars in developed countries to overcompensate for their own irregular exposure to corruption, by being too willing to accept that corrupt motives characterize government officials in poor countries. They seem to believe that a studied cynicism provides heuristics to understanding otherwise unfamiliar social practices. But it is important to reflect on two facts before adopting such cynicism.

First, a prerequisite for much corrupt behavior (e.g. petty bribery) is in-person contact. It is difficult to bribe anonymous officials whom you never meet. The shortage of tax revenue in poor countries, however, often implies that the size of their civil services is too small. This should make it harder for citizens in these countries to contact – or bribe – government officials than in developed countries. Second, whether government employees are personally reachable by citizens is often a matter of institutional design, and not a choice that petty government officials themselves get to make. In the Chinese system, for instance, revenue managers do not choose themselves to be close to taxpayers; instead their *bosses* (all the way up to the SAT) decide that they need to be so situated. The accessibility of government employees – especially when the size of the civil services is relatively small – likely serves some governmental purposes, with corruption only being a side effect. Such official purposes – like the ones pronounced in the 2005 SAT circular – may be legitimate but unfamiliar to those in developed countries. Without trying to understand such purposes, it would be wrong to posit that corruption opportunities are the *reasons why* personally reachable government officials are put in charge in the first place.[12]

It is also worth noting that the application of the term "corruption" in particular contexts is subjective. One experienced Chinese tax administrator explained the material incentives of some revenue managers to me in terms of the following calculation. Suppose that in the portfolio of a revenue manager in charge of 500 to 1,000 taxpayers, 100 are businesses whom the manager regularly interacts with – think of these as small or medium firms that, in their compliance activities, benefit from the taxpayer

[12] A standard portrayal of corruption in developing countries is that rent-seeking officials adopt institutional design specifically to allow them to extort businesses and citizens, with such institutional design serving no other compelling purpose. This, for instance, is the view of "red tape" presented in Rose-Ackerman 1999.

services that the revenue manager is responsible for providing. Suppose that among these 100 taxpayers, 70 percent choose to communicate their goodwill toward the revenue manager during major holidays like the Chinese New Year. Suppose further that, on average, each taxpayer offers gifts of no more than CNY 500 (or about eighty US dollars) per year. In prosperous places in China, gifts in such amounts would be quite modest compared to what family members, colleagues, and neighbors routinely exchange with one another. Even if brought to the attention of an anti-corruption official in the Chinese Communist Party's disciplinary apparatus, such ordinary gifts would not trigger scrutiny. But such gestures of goodwill would allow the hypothetical revenue manager to reap an annual total of CNY 35,000 in material benefits from the taxpayers he supervises – a substantial income supplement! Such a system cannot be viewed as the cleanest government, but to call it corrupt, and to describe the revenue manager as engaging in illegitimate quid pro quo (let alone extortionate conduct), seems more captious than insightful.

This last example also suggests a first-order effect of personal contact is that it may generate a social environment characterized by familiarity between the regulator and regulated. There are many ways in which such familiarity can be undesirable beyond corruption. The phenomenon of "capture" – where a regulator gives more weight to the preferences of the subjects he regulates than the general preferences of the public – is observed in modern governments worldwide. In addition, government officials might fail to enforce the law against subjects with which they are on friendly terms. Indeed, among Chinese tax administrators, the risk of official "nonfeasance" or "dereliction of duty" (*duzhi*) is discussed more often than the problem of corruption as an evil of the revenue management system. Dereliction on the part of a revenue manager brings private benefits to him even without bribery: he could simply spare much personal effort.

Further, the personal contact and familiarity between Chinese revenue managers and taxpayers arguably result in systematic deviations from written rules and norms for a reason that is related to petty corruption, capture, and the dereliction of duty, but distinct from all three. What emerges is the practice of non-rule-based tax collection, or, as I would put it, taxpayer behavior characterized by "quasi-compliance."[13]

The idea of quasi-compliance can be explained by the opposite effects that revenue managers can have on two types of taxpayers. On the one hand, for

[13] I offer a detailed discussion of taxpayer incentives underlying the phenomenon of quasi-compliance in Cui 2015.

taxpayers that have low capacity and willingness to comply with the law – such as micro-firms and individual proprietors – revenue managers may help raise their compliance levels by putting a floor in compliance: fewer taxpayers can get away with complying with no official requirements, when revenue managers are frequently chasing after them. This is easy to understand. On the other hand, and more subtly, for taxpayers who have high capacities for compliance – for example, large firms that can afford, among other compliance costs, to hire accounting and legal professionals to determine the legal rules applicable to them – revenue managers may *lower* their level of compliance. This is because while such taxpayers are capable of complying with all or most of the requirements of law, they may conclude that they need not do so. All they have to do instead is to comply with the requirements expressed by the revenue managers. After all, it is the revenue managers who have the greatest responsibility in the government apparatus for ensuring compliance, and who have the most extensive observations of taxpayer activities. Good enough for the revenue manager is good enough for the system.

I directly witnessed many instances of such "quasi-compliant" behavior by large institutional taxpayers when teaching and practicing law in China. A couple of stories suffice as illustrations. In 2010, I learned that all the research grants my university colleagues and I received from the government, which were processed by our academic employers, would begin to be subject to a 5 percent Business Tax (BT). BT (which I will discuss more in Chapter 6) was a turnover tax that substituted for the VAT in the taxation of services. It would begin to be replaced in China by the VAT in 2012 and was entirely eliminated by 2016. Through my policy work, I had already heard in 2010 that BT would soon become obsolete. So I was surprised to hear that it was suddenly being collected on more transactions.

When I looked into the rules, however, I quickly realized that nothing whatsoever had ever exempted our grants – a major source of cash flow for universities – from BT. So why had my university, a state-owned institution, not been remitting this tax? All I could gather from my university's accounting department was that the Local Tax Bureau in Haidian – the university district in Beijing where our employer was located – never asked for the tax to be remitted. I obtained similar responses after making inquiries at some of China's top universities. No one appeared to have previously thought about whether the tax had been due. Though some faculty members grumbled, all of the universities of course proceeded to remit the tax. But neither did anyone worry about the consequences – penalties and late payment interests – of not having previously remitted a legally required tax. Only compliance with the requirements of the Haidian bureau mattered.

In 2010, I also worked part time as an in-house tax lawyer at a large Chinese state-owned enterprise, which frequently entered into complex cross-border financial transactions. The Chinese tax law governing such transactions was either extremely vague or simply nonexistent. In such situations, large financial institutions like the one I represented would often engage with administrators and policy makers in the SAT to discuss the range of rules that could potentially apply. Taxpayers and tax advisors also communicated among themselves about what range of practices might be commercially acceptable. But one day, a big accounting firm shared a memo about some transaction for which there was no clear rule. Instead of analyzing how specific tax treatments would be consistent or inconsistent with existing rules and market practices, the memo described a conversation that the accounting firm's professionals had with an anonymous tax official in a branch office of the Xicheng District Local Tax Bureau. Xicheng is where Beijing's equivalent of Wall Street is located, and the particular branch office of the tax bureau in question was the "revenue management department" for many of China's largest financial institutions. It was conceivable that an employee in such a tax bureau might be more familiar with complex financial transactions than frontline tax administrators elsewhere in China. But the memo offered no reason why the view of the particular official was credible – there was nothing informative about the official's view quoted. Instead, the premise of the memo was that because the official's branch bureau was in charge of the taxpayers for whom the memo was written, the official's view should be considered.

While lawyers may object to this approach to determining what rules to follow, savvy business people quickly adapt. In China, there is a good amount of market demand for access to local tax officials. This is because very often, by virtue of low-level officials' ignorance or lack of responsibility for the general implications of their positions, the discretion of such officials may be more taxpayer favorable relative to the rules written on paper (or what can be inferred from the latter). It is a bonus to taxpayers to have the choice to comply with either the requirements of law or the requirements of low-level officers – whichever is more advantageous. Although lawyers often invoke the specter of abuse when they see government discretion outside the bounds of law, businesses – that is, taxpayers – may more often see opportunities for gain through strategic action.

The foregoing anecdotes are of course incapable of proving any general claim about how China's large taxpayers behave: the prevalence of quasi-compliance, whether in the form of my former university employer's blissful indifference to what the law required, or in the form of large businesses' strategic choice between following the law or official discretion, is not easy to establish empirically.[14] Even harder to evaluate is any claim about whether quasi-compliance results in overall revenue losses to the government. However, while it would be intellectually satisfying to provide quantitative evidence of this phenomenon – and the related but distinct phenomena of petty corruption, capture, or dereliction of duty – all these phenomena are results of a behavioral ecosystem that has more fundamental consequences for the government's capacity to tax. I would describe the logic of this ecosystem as the logic of *atomistic coercion*.

Atomism

A basic feature of the revenue management is its atomism. By this I mean, first, that the individual tax collector assumes a paramount significance in exercising the authority of the state. In attempting to comply with the requirements of the state, many Chinese taxpayers need to heed only the demands of a single tax official assigned to them, or at most a handful of officials stationed at a local tax office. What tax legislation is adopted by the national parliament, what tax regulations and administrative guidance are issued by national ministries, and even what information provincial and sub-provincial tax agencies generally provide regarding tax law and policy, are of secondary importance, compared to the views of the tax collectors whom taxpayers directly deal with. Conversely, from the state's perspective, the government apparatus reaches each individual taxpayer, for the most part, through an assigned revenue manager. Most importantly, the revenue manager is the main or even the sole arbiter of whether the taxpayer is in compliance.

The revenue manager is thus a decisive link between the taxpayer and the state. But while this link is sustained through physical proximity and personal contact, it is also highly fragile. This lies behind the second meaning of atomism. Revenue managers receive many instructions from their superiors, but, as we will see in Chapter 5, they are effectively

[14] In Cui 2015, I argue that the observed low level of tax litigation in China and languishing tax professions can be seen as evidence for – because they follow logically from – the idea that most Chinese taxpayers choose to pay more attention to revenue managers' views than what the law says. One does not go to court when one rarely considers the content of law, and professional knowledge can only have law as its subject – not what each of hundreds of thousands of tax officers thinks.

measured only by a few key performance metrics, such as meeting revenue targets. It is especially hard to set performance targets for the transmission of taxpayer information. Each revenue manager can perhaps be motivated to monitor his or her assigned taxpayers closely. But by the same token, other tax administrators not assigned to the same taxpayers would not be motivated to monitor them. When a revenue manager records information about a taxpayer in the tax bureau's computer system, he or she knows that it is unlikely that anyone else will read this information. Any effort to transmit knowledge gleaned from his or her direct observations of taxpayers to the government's database would be for transmission's own sake, and, therefore, pointless. Consequently, not only do the individual tax collector's observations about a taxpayer often represent the whole extent of the state's knowledge about the latter, but that knowledge may also reside only in the individual tax collector's own mind. Whatever he knows about the taxpayer may stop with him.

Our earlier anecdotes about quasi-compliance illustrate the first aspect of atomism – how state authority may be degraded to individual authority. The second aspect, the degradation of the state's information gathering capacity, has a striking illustration in a perennial internal management issue that China's tax agencies struggle with. In endless internal documents, "reform proposals," and official speeches, bureaucratic leaders speak of the need to enhance agency "management of taxpayer records" (*dang'an guanli*). That is, the tax collection apparatus should have a single record for all the information that has been gathered regarding a particular taxpayer. It is easy to see how this is essential to managing large populations of taxpayers: before the wide adoption of electronic return filing, handling, scanning, or otherwise inputting information from paper tax returns represented a large chunk of menial tasks for tax administrations around the world. It is partly why account management exists as a distinct function in tax collection. And even after electronic filing, organizing taxpayer information so that it is easily accessible for tax administrators is a basic goal for tax administrations' IT systems. What is critical to grasp is that even in the past decade, Chinese tax agencies have mostly operated without such a system.

In 2013, for example, the provincial tax bureau of Jiangsu province – a province held in high regard by tax administrators from elsewhere in China for its competent tax administration – urged "greatly strengthening taxpayer records management." Provincial instructions to subordinate agencies in this regard contained the following to-do items: (1) each city or county bureau should have either an internal division in charge of "records management" or dedicated personnel to implement records management; (2) such division or dedicated personnel should store and scan all paper records that are needed for revenue management and tax inspection; and (3) taxpayer service divisions should scan and electronically store paper records and reduce usage of paper records in taxpayer management. In connection with these requirements, a provincial bureau leader remarked in an internal speech:

> For many years we have ignored taxpayer record management. Such records are now scattered and chaotically distributed; some records are impossible to locate. This is because we didn't need taxpayer records, we made no or only rare use of them. This is also why our taxpayer service divisions cannot achieve the objective of not asking taxpayers repeatedly for the same documents . . .. We are so handicapped . . . it is as though we do not know how to use computers . . . [Inadequate record management] also makes it impossible to reduce the burden on taxpayers [to submit information to tax bureaus].[15]

How is it possible, in an age when Alibaba, Tencent and other digital platforms in China have converted much of the Chinese economy into a world of cashless transactions, and when Chinese businesses and citizens increasingly manage customers, investments, and savings through smartphones, that heavily computerized tax bureaus across China still struggle with maintaining taxpayer accounts and locating taxpayer records? The explanation clearly lies not with technological capacity. The key is that there have been few occasions for different actors in the tax administration to make use of the same taxpayer records: revenue managers gathering information about taxpayers are, for the most part, the only ones using such information.

Atomism in tax administration can also be found outside China. What historians refer to as "tax farming" – mostly studied in connection with tax collection in Europe before the eighteenth century, although economists have come to see analogous techniques in developing countries today – is a form of atomistic tax collection.[16] The analysis of revenue management I have given so far shows that the logic of tax farming, that is, atomism, is confined neither to history nor to

[15] A national directive issued by the SAT in 2014 echoed the theme of enhancing record keeping so as to reduce taxpayer burden in submitting information. See Notice Regarding Further Standardizing the Management of Tax Documents and Returns (*Shuizongfa* [2014] 50).

[16] The title of Khan et al. 2016, "Tax Farming Redux," which studies twenty-first century property tax collection in Pakistan, invokes such a historical analogy.

corners of the developing world where governments are desperately trying to raise revenue. More importantly, it highlights a consequence of atomism that scholars studying tax farming have not previously identified, but which has unrivaled relevance in the twenty-first century: atomism may severely constrain a government's capacity to gather information.

Figure 3.1 illustrates the atomism of the revenue management system graphically. The following are key features in the diagram that I have already elaborated upon:

- Tax inspection operates as a separate system from revenue management, does not select audit targets based on tax returns, and widely adopts self-inspection;
- Revenue managers are assigned to specific taxpayers instead of being differentiated in terms of the tasks they perform;
- The taxpayer service function has gradually been removed from the workload of revenue managers;
- Revenue managers focus on taxpayer registration, account management, and collections; their undifferentiated role prevents the introduction of significant audit responsibilities.[17]

In Figure 3.1, the taxpayer database is depicted as "dormant." This captures two facts that we have discussed so far: (1) tax inspectors do not examine tax returns, and generally do not select inspection targets based on information taxpayers provide to the tax authorities; (2) the information collected by revenue managers often lays idle – no one else makes use of such information. But there is a further and crucial reason why the government's information system about taxpayers lays idle. This has to do with the coercive aspect of revenue management.

Coercion

By saying that tax collection in China is coercive, I do not mean that taxpayers are routinely intimidated or threatened with violence, or that they are forced to do what they are not required by law to do. That surely happens with greater frequency in China than in some other countries. But I use the term "coercion" to convey two ideas that are more fundamental. First, the requirements of the "law," or at least of general rules

[17] I return to the issue of local politicians' monitoring of revenue targets in the operation of the traditional revenue management system in Chapter 5.

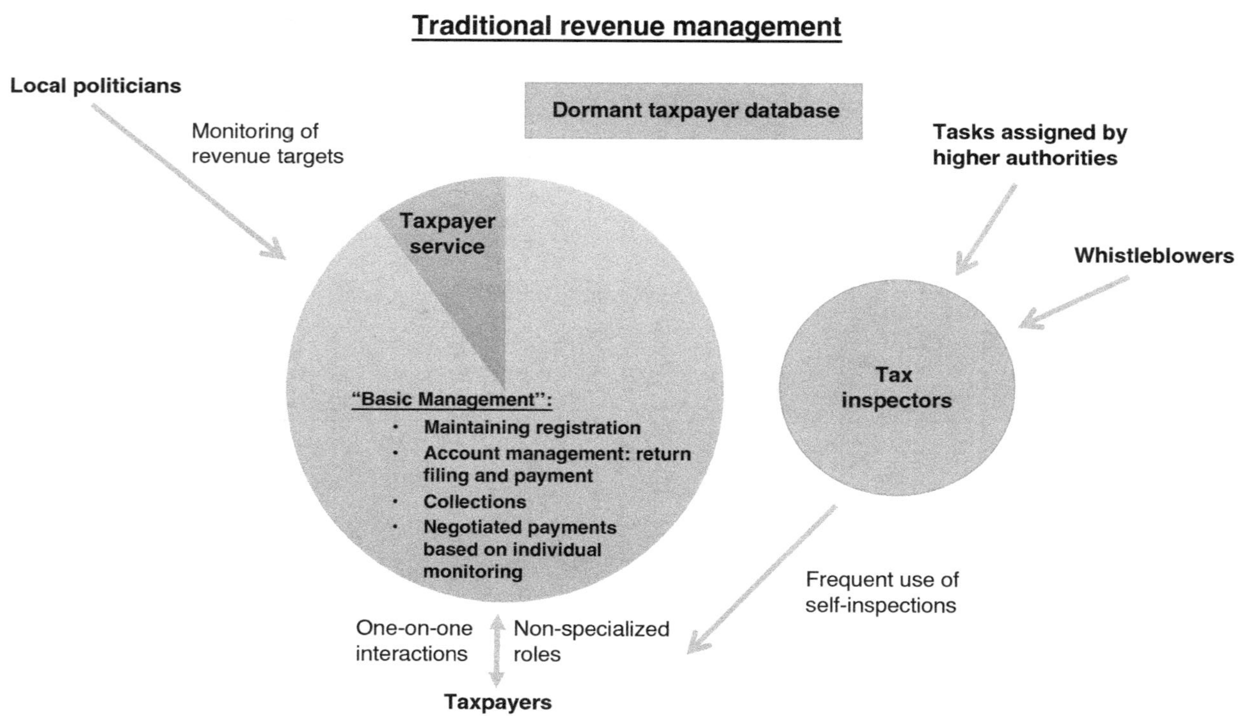

Figure 3.1 The basic structure of China's grassroots tax administration

promulgated by the government, are enforced primarily by government agents. Such enforcement can take the form of *ex post* sanctions, such as penalties, but it more often takes the form of *ex ante* interventions, which prevent taxpayers from failing to comply in the first place. Second, there is a general social expectation for the government to intervene in regular compliance requirements, such that one can say, for large populations of taxpayers, that a main reason why they file tax returns and make tax payments is that the tax collectors assigned to supervise them monitor and cajole them to do so. As a consequence, compliance depends on government intervention. This dependence characterizes the psychological motivation of taxpayers; it also fits the empirically observable patterns of compliance.

To elaborate on the notion of coercion, consider first the distinction between *ex post* and *ex ante* government interventions. Penalties are *ex post* interventions: taxpayers act first, and the government then detects infringements of the law and penalizes the infringers. Penalties shape taxpayer behavior through *deterrence*: some taxpayers may choose to follow the law only because the expected losses from penalties are greater than the expected benefits of cheating. For the deterrence effect to take hold, the combination of the perceived probability of being detected for cheating and the perceived magnitude of penalties must be sufficiently great. This is how economists have generally thought about the way government intervention may produce tax compliance.[18] But *ex post* sanctions is not the only tool at the government's disposal: the government can also intervene before taxpayers act. For example, if the government has access to taxpayers' bank accounts and periodically withdraws amounts that correspond to the appropriate tax liabilities, no *ex post* sanction is needed:[19] taxpayer noncompliance need not be deterred, as it can simply be disabled.

Notwithstanding differences between these two forms of government intervention, both must satisfy two conditions to be effective: the government must be able to detect whether the private subject (e.g. taxpayer) has complied, and it must have the resources or willingness to impose a cost on non-compliers through penalties or disable noncompliance. When either of these two conditions fails to be satisfied, government

[18] As discussed in Chapter 2, an additional assumption is also in play but often goes unrecognized: it is not only the timely payment of tax but also the norm of truthful reporting that is enforced.

[19] The distinction between *ex ante* and *ex post* government interventions features in the expositions that law and economics scholars give to the dichotomy between "property rules" and "liability rules." See Shavell 2004, chapter 25, for a concise general discussion.

intervention alone cannot secure compliance. These two conditions represent the limits of the power of government intervention.

How do Chinese tax administrators choose between these two modes of intervention, and where are they most likely to apply their limited resources? Table 3.1, which is condensed from a lengthier set of tables in the 2002 Tax Inspection Yearbook, helps to answer these questions. It summarizes a 2000 SAT evaluation of the quality of tax administration across China's thirty-one provincial-level jurisdictions and five important cities with a "quasi-provincial" status. For reasons of space I present only some of the performance outcomes that these regional tax administrations were evaluated upon, and I omit the explicit scores that provinces received for reporting these outcomes – the topic of performance evaluations will be discussed in Chapter 5 instead. I also present only the outcomes in the GS system – tables for the DS system would have supported similar conclusions.

In the first three pairs of columns, the values reported are the percentages of taxpayers, within each of the two categories of business entities and individual proprietors in business, that (1) properly registered with the tax authorities; (2) filed tax returns on time; and (3) made timely payments of declared taxes. The denominators for the computation of values in the first pair of columns are the numbers of firms or individuals that began operation in 2000 and therefore were required to register for tax purposes. Not shown in Table 3.1, but displayed in the original Tax Inspection Yearbook tables, are the national totals of new firms and of individuals in 2000: 2,317,760 and 6,078,170, respectively. Of these 8.4 million new businesses in China, the reported national average rate of prompt registration was 98.5 percent for firms and 96.4 percent for individuals. Inner Mongolia reported the lowest rate of timely registration for both firms (91.7 percent) and individuals (83.5 percent).

For readers who even briefly consider these numbers, the most likely response is amazement, if not sheer disbelief. How could any country, with a 2000 GDP per capita of less than 1,000 US dollars, register almost 100 percent of its 8.4 million new businesses in a year? This astonishing statistic is consistent with what one sees in the next two pairs of columns. The denominators for the next pair are the total numbers of firms and individuals required to file tax returns in China. Again not shown in Table 3.1 but locatable in the original official tables are the national numbers of firms and individuals: 14,810,106 and 33,309,573, respectively. For this giant population, the reported national average timely filing rate was 96.6 percent for firms and 95.4 percent for individual proprietors. Again, the reported level of compliance was uniformly high

Table 3.1 *Regional tax administration outcomes, state tax bureau (GS) system, 2000*

Region	Percent of tax payers registered		Percent of tax payers filed returns		Percent of timely payment		Late payment interest imposed where applicable		Penalty imposed where applicable	
	Firms	Individuals	Firms	Individuals	Firms	Individuals	Percent of tax payers	Percent of amount	Percent of tax payers	Percent of amount
Beijing	99.90	99.70	96.00	93.70	96.29	98.44	99.79	99.42	27.43	13.84
Tianjin	99.20	96.50	95.70	92.30	96.42	99.42	88.99	24.22	66.75	16.61
Hebei	99.70	97.70	98.90	95.80	97.31	98.19	86.46	58.22	56.75	15.69
Shanxi	99.60	99.70	96.60	95.70	92.15	97.67	99.45	89.65	80.67	27.85
Inner Mongolia	91.70	83.50	97.40	96.50	96.76	99.93	98.58	94.38	90.40	19.07
Shanghai	97.80	92.30	97.20	96.40	98.43	97.82	84.05	40.47	30.22	6.33
Jiangsu	98.20	95.20	97.10	95.60	94.60	98.96	86.47	82.67	87.05	56.02
Shandong	99.00	92.00	97.00	95.00	95.00	99.88	93.00	94.00	86.44	17.81
Zhejiang	96.60	94.39	97.80	97.30	96.34	98.04	94.81	96.81	96.12	23.72
Fujian	99.30	95.60	93.00	90.50	95.08	95.57	89.87	72.34	73.01	10.81
Anhui	100.00	98.50	98.30	93.10	94.23	98.01	90.18	87.71	69.78	13.26
Jiangxi	100.00	99.00	97.90	95.10	97.51	98.93	87.74	93.35	38.44	19.93
Ningbo	97.40	94.20	96.50	94.80	96.40	97.61	96.77	67.68	89.86	27.85
Qingdao	100.00	95.20	98.00	95.00	104.02	100.00	85.92	87.50	99.21	27.24
Xiamen	97.66	94.20	94.00	82.40	94.76	98.43	92.94	88.17	73.01	9.10
Guangdong	97.90	95.00	90.50	92.80	91.97	96.63	42.23	3.83	55.55	19.75
Guangxi	97.50	96.90	91.80	92.90	80.13	99.47	82.97	56.26	65.92	11.16
Hunan	99.90	97.40	97.30	94.00	96.20	97.73	92.00	82.17	69.02	12.83
Hubei	99.80	98.00	96.00	98.00	88.00	99.00	91.00	65.04	65.73	14.89

Table 3.1 *(cont.)*

Region	Percent of tax payers registered		Percent of tax payers filed returns		Percent of timely payment		Late payment interest imposed where applicable		Penalty imposed where applicable	
	Firms	Individuals	Firms	Individuals	Firms	Individuals	Percent of tax payers	Percent of amount	Percent of tax payers	Percent of amount
Henan	99.10	98.80	88.30	86.10	98.13	99.90	99.13	84.87	86.39	22.78
Hainan	99.90	99.50	90.40	95.20	93.53	98.42	97.93	87.60	64.85	15.54
Shenzhen	97.70	91.30	96.70	91.20	99.40	100.00	100.00	98.73	100.00	20.50
Chongqing	95.70	95.40	96.00	91.80	92.99	96.33	88.29	0.21	90.89	10.19
Sichuan	99.40	97.50	95.40	93.20	96.32	98.92	89.19	88.79	42.12	8.97
Yunnan	100.00	98.60	98.00	97.00	99.24	99.64	91.87	95.98	52.13	14.30
Guizhou	95.30	94.90	94.90	93.70	95.01	98.32	57.55	1.25	83.09	16.90
Tibet	98.50	97.80	95.30	93.10	98.56	84.99	96.42	98.55	67.30	16.63
Liaoning	100.00	99.50	98.30	99.10	97.32	99.75	87.49	17.62	52.70	8.86
Jilin	99.60	97.00	97.70	99.10	96.09	99.48	93.29	84.06	47.24	11.58
Heilongjiang	99.60	99.30	98.00	96.10	96.22	99.60	97.96	83.19	70.41	6.77
Dalian	98.30	99.60	97.90	99.70	96.90	99.99	98.46	93.91	20.17	14.57
Shaanxi	99.70	97.80	97.80	96.10	98.76	99.73	95.79	97.26	77.43	16.13
Gansu	99.10	94.80	96.30	92.20	90.45	97.17	0.00	0.00	63.66	10.15
Qinghai	100.00	98.70	97.90	97.80	90.62	99.87	97.94	86.41	47.68	11.19
Xinjiang	98.10	98.50	95.60	91.80	95.64	99.68	65.39	94.75	92.23	17.80
Ningxia	97.70	96.80	98.50	97.30	93.63	98.62	98.50	100.00	62.02	21.08
Total	98.50	96.40	96.60	95.40	95.65	98.48	80.28	66.88	66.74	17.07

across China: the lowest rate of timely filing for firms was 90.5 percent (reported in Guangdong Province), and for business proprietors, 82.4 percent (reported for the city of Xiamen). For Xiamen, this meant that 133,472 out of 162,010 of its individual proprietors in 2000 – most of whom were likely to be street vendors and small shop owners – made timely filings of tax returns. With respect to the timely payment of tax liabilities, no count of taxpayers was provided in official statistics, but the third pair of columns show percentages in terms of the amounts of tax liabilities. The national averages of promptly paid funds were 95.65 percent and 98.48 percent for firms and individuals, respectively.

Only a few seasoned tax administrators will have comparative figures for other countries at their fingertips, so it is useful to quote some information from an OECD report published in 2008 (OECD 2008). According to that report, the Canadian Revenue Agency set a target of 90 percent for rates of timely filing of corporate income tax returns among Canadian taxpayers, but only achieved a rate of 86–87 percent during 2002–2007. The French tax authorities secured timely filing of VAT returns from only 84.2 percent to 90.7 percent of taxpayers during the same period. In the United Kingdom, even by one year after the due dates of company tax returns, a total of less than 88 percent of firms would complete their return filing obligations. Only the Dutch authorities achieved a similar rate of timely filing as China did in 2000 (around 97 percent).

It may be tempting to dismiss outright the Chinese reports of the incredibly high levels of compliance in 2000: either the reporting provinces and cities are lying, I expect some readers to say, or the labels they use do not mean what we think they mean. Note, however, that the reports of these 2000 tax administration outcomes are published as parts of official statistics. Although statistics on these particular administrative outcomes were never published again in subsequent volumes of the Tax Inspection Yearbook, I have seen similar tables in many internal reports filed by provinces with the SAT, by cities with their respective provinces, and by tax bureaus and branch bureaus with their respective cities. I was struck by the consistency of such reports, over many years and across many regions. Moreover, to my knowledge, the Chinese government has not touted these numbers to demonstrate Chinese taxpayers' law-abiding tendencies. Indeed, Chinese tax administrators themselves may see some absurdity in these numbers, for they constantly complain about a highly noncompliant taxpayer population. Yet it does not follow that the numbers are made up.

I would argue that it is possible to interpret these stunning numbers at face value, and they in fact demonstrate certain extraordinary achievements. First, it is surely relevant that timely registration, timely filing of tax returns, and timely payment of declared tax liabilities are outcomes that subordinate tax agencies are evaluated upon by their superiors. Achieving a high rate in any of these dimensions could potentially be rewarded – though it does not mean that Chinese tax administrators across the country would lie their way to the reward. Instead, a second step to the interpretation is to accept that grassroots tax agencies in China may indeed be extraordinarily successful at registering businesses. They work very hard at it, after all, and keeping businesses registered for tax purposes is one of the central missions of the revenue management system, with its heavy investment in account management. Third, once businesses are properly registered, what remains is ensuring that they file and pay the liabilities on tax returns. As Chapter 2 had suggested, Chinese tax administrators may be quite lax in enforcing the norm of truthful reporting and may largely dispense with what are regarded as normal audit techniques. If the truthfulness of tax returns is not the object, then timely filing and timely payment of whatever is declared on the tax returns may still require strenuous efforts, but could be within revenue managers' reach.

Before I offer evidence for the foregoing interpretation, consider the last two pairs of columns in Table 3.1. These contain measures of two types of *ex post* government interventions: the impositions of late payment interests and penalties. Significantly, the zeal with which these two types of actions are taken varies more widely across the country. Nationally, only 80 percent of taxpayers who were liable for late payment interests were actually charged such interest, and only 67 percent of the amount of such interest was actually collected. Guangdong Province collected late interest from around 40 percent of taxpayers owing such interest, and four provinces collected less than 10 percent of the interest that was legally due. The variance in the collection of penalties is even greater. Nationally, an average of 66.74 percent of taxpayers that should have received penalties actually did, and only 17.07 percent of penalties due were actually collected. Beijing is an example of a region that made starkly different choices among the different mechanisms of intervention: it scored very high on all three *ex ante* measures and even on the collection of late payment interests, but penalized only 27.43 percent of taxpayers who deserved penalties, and collected less than 14 percent of penalties that were due, more than 3 percentage points below the national average.

However one wants to interpret the incentives of misreporting within the government (and in published statistics), what seems to emerge from Table 3.1 is that Chinese tax administrators prefer the use of *ex ante* modes of intervention to *ex post* ones. In Chapter 4, we further interrogate explanations for this preference.

The Extensive versus Intensive Margins of Compliance

If the rates at which Chinese business taxpayers meet their return filing deadlines far exceed our expectations, what do we expect concerning the accuracy of the returns filed? Working with tax authorities from one large Chinese province, I examined the confidential corporate tax returns (with taxpayer identities removed) for the period 2010–2016. Among the many tax returns and documents that provincial businesses filed with local tax authorities, we observed annual balance sheets, income statements, and parts of the corporate income tax return that comprised of a main return and several schedules. We found that among the over-one-million firms that filed their balance sheets, close to 20 percent of firms entered zero on or left blank *all entries* on the form. Only until recently, Chinese companies were subject to registered capital requirement that mandated shareholder contributions of a minimum of equity capital at the time of registration;[20] as a result, it is highly unlikely that so many firms had exactly zero assets or liabilities. This means hundreds of thousands of balance sheets were filed that were blatantly inaccurate – they contained no information whatsoever about the filers.

Using the term "zero-reporting" to denote the behavior of a firm where it enters zero on or leaves blank all entries of a form filed with tax authorities, we found that almost 25 percent of firms zero-reported on their income statements. That is, these firms reported not only zero revenue, but exactly zero expenses of whatever kind. And of the firms that filed corporate income tax returns, nearly 30 percent zero-reported on the main income tax return, and even higher proportions zero-reported on the other schedules. Of course, firms that do not zero-report may still provide inaccurate information on their tax returns, but zero-reporting seems to be a strong indicator of inaccuracy.

In our analysis we also identified several intuitive determinants of zero-reporting. Newly registered firms were more likely to zero-report: compared to the first year of its formation, a firm in its fifth year of operation was 23.3 percent less likely to zero-report on any of its main filings with tax agencies and 34.4 percent less likely to zero-report on all such filings. "Dying" firms were also likely to zero-report: compared to

[20] Cui and Wei 2021.

firms that were in their final year before dropping out of the database (i.e. filing no forms at all), a firm that was two years before dropping out were 9.6 percent less likely to zero-report on any of the tax filings. The lowering of entry barriers also elevated the level of zero-reporting. China eased its business registration requirements in 2014 by amending its Company Law and simplifying registration procedures. As a result, new firms formed in 2016 were 50 percent more likely to zero-report on all forms than new firms formed in 2012. Nonetheless, these factors do not explain all instances of zero-reporting: some firms persist in zero-reporting, and some of them are even rather large.[21]

These findings support three claims I advanced earlier. First, Chinese tax administrators have a very high tolerance for inaccurate tax returns, and Chinese taxpayers have a very high willingness to file such returns. The extent of zero-reporting we observed in actual tax returns vindicates the account given in Chapter 2 about how Chinese tax inspectors and revenue managers pay little attention to the tax returns' accuracy. For zero-reporting to be so rampant, persistent, and even growing in recent years, the norm of truthful reporting needs to be very weak.[22]

Second, there are likely to be trade-offs between zero-reporting and actions taken by tax administrators to register businesses as soon as possible and for as long as possible. If newly formed firms were allowed to register just a year or two later, or not to file tax returns from the get-go, the zero-reporting percentage would certainly go down. Similarly, if dying firms were allowed to de-register and stop filing tax returns earlier, the proportion of zero-reporters would also drop. Zero-reporting is thus in part the cost of registering businesses and prompting them to file tax returns early on and persistently. Therefore, the extent of zero-reporting makes Table 3.1's numbers on other administrative outcomes – the high levels of registration, timely filing and timely payment – more credible.

Third, although we identified some determinants of zero-reporting behavior, we have trouble discerning the exact nature of zero-reporting behavior from the tax returns. Young firms or firms that are about to go under are likely to have no positive income tax liabilities, but what exactly leads them to think that, in such circumstances, it is acceptable to file obviously false returns? Alternatively, more than one of the Chinese tax administrators I have talked to claim that revenue managers often filed

21 Cui and Hicks 2021 further investigate determinants of zero-reporting, including the geographical and sectoral distribution of zero-reporting and other firm characteristics.

22 Persistent zero-reporting is also consistent with the absence of deterrence effects due to the disuse of penalties and other sanctions.

the tax returns *for* the taxpayers they were assigned to in order to meet performance targets regarding timely filing. But how often does this occur, and what is the revenue manager's calculus in submitting obviously inaccurate tax returns on behalf of "his" or "her" taxpayers? Moreover, aside from young and dying firms, many firms zero-report on a persistent basis. If they are tax evaders, would they not worry that their non-compliant behavior is easily identifiable? Or do they actually take comfort in the fact that so many other firms also zero-report, for very disparate reasons?

The prevalence of zero-reporting confirms the thrust of the concept of "quasi-compliance" I introduced earlier. The revenue management system produces a convergence among taxpayers who otherwise have very different capacities for compliance. Firms that have very low capacities for compliance are forced or helped to comply with at least a few official requirements (e.g. timely filing). Firms with high capacities for compliance, on the other hand, get away with (and indeed may be expected to get away with) complying with far fewer requirements than they are able to manage.

Zero-reporting also gives a hint of why, as suggested in Figure 3.1, the government's taxpayer database might stay dormant. Both zero-reporting itself, and the ways it shows a general indifference to truthful reporting among Chinese taxpayers and tax administrators, do not bode well for the reliability of the taxpayer data system. We return to this topic in Chapter 4. But to conclude this chapter, I want to emphasize the most important conceptual point that zero-reporting illustrates: the limitation of government intervention as a means of securing compliance.

As stated earlier, two conditions underlie such a limitation: the government's power of observation and its ability to impose costs on or preclude noncompliance. Filing a tax return before a given date is a discrete behavioral dimension of the taxpayer observable by the government. The government can monitor taxpayer actions along this dimension even before the filing deadline, and intervene *ex ante* if necessary to preclude a taxpayer from failing to take the right action. It seems that the high rates of timely filing among Chinese taxpayers combined with the relatively low frequency of penalties (both presented in Table 3.1) can be explained and accepted at face value only if the government intervenes *ex ante* with some frequency. At the extreme, at least as anecdotes among Chinese tax administrators have it, some revenue managers submit returns on taxpayers' behalf. As outlandish as this seems, it is clearly physically feasible.

Contrast the act of submitting a return with the act of entering accurate information on the tax return. Like business income tax returns in many other countries, China's corporate income tax return contains tens of lines on the main return and hundreds of lines in supplementary schedules. On each line, taxpayers need to provide accurate information in a legally prescribed manner. Completing each line accurately is thus an act of compliance. By the same token, each line is also a margin of noncompliance. What would it mean for the government to monitor and intervene on each and every one of these margins? In countries with longer experience of modern taxation like the United States, the most comprehensive monitoring of compliance on tax returns would be a "line-by-line" audit. But such audits have never been applied to more than a tiny portion of all taxpayers. They are also *ex post* interventions, and would convert into compliance only through the deterrence effect of penalties. Moreover, effective audits of tax returns themselves require extensive information: they are usually based on auditors' experience in examining returns and in algorithms developed from taxpayer data. But we do not know of cases where such experience and algorithms are developed without a lot of filed tax returns that already provide accurate information.

In short, the government can both observe and intervene in the requirement of filing a return, but it can do neither in securing accurate information on tax returns. If, in addition, taxpayers comply only if they are effectively monitored by the government (and precluded from noncompliance if necessary), then we would have an explanation of the stark difference in the compliance outcomes among Chinese taxpayers along the filing and accuracy dimensions.

The *timely filing* versus *accuracy* dichotomy is one of many illustrations of the dichotomy of two types of behavioral margins – dimensions along which compliance can be secured purely through government interventions, and those along which it cannot. For instance, this dichotomy can be used to interpret an important distinction recently drawn by developmental economists between two basic forms of informal economic activity. On the one hand, *firms* may be formal or informal, depending on whether they register with government authorities and subject themselves to the latter's scrutiny in terms of compliance with tax and regulatory requirements. On the other hand, *transactions* may also be formal or informal, in that firms can comply or not comply with tax and other legal requirements in entering into them. While the transactions that informal firms enter into are likely to all be informal, formal firms have more room to vary the extent of formality in their transactions. Because of this, firm formality can be thought of as the "extensive margin" of formality – firms can be located either above or below a minimum threshold of transactional formality.

Above this threshold, variations in the degree of transactional formality are variations in the "intensive margin." For example, how many workers a formal firm hires in compliance with labor regulations, how many of these labor relationships meet minimum wage requirements, and how much the firm pays social security contributions for their workers – the degree of "labor formality" in the firm's operations – may vary greatly.[23]

These distinctions do not just provide plausible descriptions of the varieties of informality; they correspond to different types of government interventions to address informality that, according to a model by the economist Gabriel Ulyssea, can have significantly different macroeconomic consequences. For example, firm informality can be reduced either by cutting business registration costs or by having government officials stringently enforce against non-registrants and drive them out of business. Labor (or other transactional) informality can be reduced if the government either reduces the tax and regulatory burdens on paper or if it ramps up enforcement of existing requirements. Ulyssea derives different combinations of changes in wages, firm productivity, economic output, and social welfare corresponding to the adoption of each of these interventions. These consequences become even more interesting when we realize that the different types of intervention Ulyssea considers also have different probabilities of securing compliance. For example, the first two columns on business registration in Table 3.1 suggest that the revenue management system dramatically reduces firm informality. But the same system may well fail to reduce labor informality – or other types of transactional informality, such as the amount of sales not reported to tax authorities.

The combination of high firm formality and high labor (and other transactional) informality is in fact a key feature of the Chinese economy. For example, the Chinese government estimates that less than 70 percent of its urban workforce is covered by employment-based SI – an estimate confirmed by independent scholarly studies. This is because many firms that have registered for tax purposes and paid some of their taxes do not participate in SI for the benefit of their employees. Working with the confidential taxpayer dataset mentioned earlier, my colleagues and I found that even among firms that did not zero-report on their financial statements and income tax returns, a high percentage did not contribute to SI and therefore were highly informal in their employment arrangements.[24] A plausible explanation is that because the SI contribution burden is

[23] See Ulyssea 2018.
[24] Cui, Hicks and Norton 2020b.

especially high in China, firms are especially resistant to it, making revenue managers' interventions ineffective.[25]

Indeed, the SI example shows that talks of the *extensive* versus *intensive* margins of compliance are somewhat arbitrary. When there are so many different dimensions of compliance (as on each line of the hundreds of lines in an income tax return), pointing to any one dimension as "the" threshold may be hard to justify. Which dimensions form "the" extensive margin may merely depend on the actions that the government can take to enforce legal requirements along various dimensions.

This chapter has suggested that the revenue management system – at the costs of sacrificing specialization among tax administrators and norms of truthful reporting among taxpayers, and at the risk of elevated corruption and malfeasance – has achieved extensive taxpayer registration and a form of quasi-compliance among a very large population of taxpayers. Many readers may wonder how this immense trade-off can be justified – surely we have left out some important benefits and costs? Is the revenue management system worth it in terms of the state capacity to extract revenue and information from its people? The next chapter begins to tackle this difficult question.

[25] Chapter 6 considers this and other explanations.

4

Returning Responsibilities to Taxpayers

Tax administrators from all over the world seem always to want more information about taxpayers. With more information, they can better exercise their coercive power to detect actual or potential noncompliance, and to deter or preempt such noncompliance. But the discussion of China's revenue management system in Chapter 3 points to a phenomenon that we might call the "paradox of taxpayer information": When good-quality information is most needed to secure compliance, it is most likely to be unavailable; when good-quality information is available, it is less needed.

This paradox arises whenever good-quality information is a product of taxpayer compliance. When taxpayers adhere to the norm of truthful reporting, the information on tax returns is reliable and yields high-quality data. By contrast, if taxpayers do not adhere to the norm of truthful reporting, tax return information may be forged, misleading, or, as we saw in the phenomenon of zero-reporting, blatantly missing. Assuming that one can make better inferences with good-quality data than with poor-quality data, tax administrators facing a noncompliant population are less able to observe the world through taxpayer-provided data. Tax administrators facing a compliant population have better observations, but they also have less need for intervention to secure compliance.

If effective government intervention to reduce noncompliance depends on the power of observation – this, I argued in Chapter 3, is the logic of coercion – then the government's power of observation cannot presume compliance. But a government that can gather information when *no one* willingly provides such information is a radical conception. Unless we persuade ourselves of the plausibility of such a conception, we must attribute the revenue-raising capacity of governments in developed countries to something other than government coercion.[1] Tax administrators

[1] In Chapter 8, I discuss this radical conception in connection with claims recently made by economists that there can be no taxation without information, and explain why this view must be rejected.

in developing countries often express envy about what they perceive as high rates of compliance in developed countries, and, just as frequently, conjecture that such compliance is explained by rich countries' access to extensive taxpayer information. But the causality may actually run the other way: developed countries have good information about taxpayers only because they are already mostly compliant.

In this chapter, we examine how this conundrum of information has both tempted Chinese tax administrators to break away from the mode of atomistic coercion and dealt them setbacks in such attempts. The picture that emerges is that atomistic coercion constitutes a behavioral equilibrium, a pattern of interactions that no one has incentives to deviate from in the absence of radical change.

A Reformer's Journey

In Chapter 1, I described a series of positions adopted by China's top tax administrators in the SAT: A fundamental reform of tax administration was launched in 1997, encountered resistance and internal critique in the early 2000s, and was ultimately abandoned by 2004. Since then, the SAT has promoted the revenue management system while preaching incompatible goals like specialization. Chapter 1 also emphasized, however, that Chinese tax administration is highly decentralized. This means that on virtually all fronts of policy implementation – including the organization of tax administration – there may be a divergence between the requirements announced by policy makers in Beijing and grassroots government operations. Considering this point, how faithfully has the revenue management system been implemented?

In 2004, around the time the SAT began advocating for "strengthening the foundational work of tax administration" through the revenue manager system, the Local Tax Bureau in the prefectural city of Huai'an, Jiangsu Province, began its own tax administration "reform." This local effort is documented in a book by Mr. Chen Jianpu, the Commissioner of Huai'an's DS Bureau from 2001 to the mid-2010s. Chen's manuscript, *On a Journey: Explorations and Reflections on Innovations in Tax Administration*, was published in 2011 and proselytizes his attempt to bring changes to Huai'an's tax administration. While the author's claim about the reform's success requires verification, the book is notable for two things. First, the author engages in extensive polemics against the failings of China's tax bureaucracy and singles out the SAT's promotion of the revenue manager system for criticism. Second, one-third of the book reprints internal directives associated with actual reform measures Chen directed. This choice was ostensibly made to enable other local tax administrations to emulate Huai'an's reform. But it also provides both an official chronology and the details of Huai'an's reform that can be read and interpreted independently of Chen's account of his own accomplishments.

Chen's book bluntly casts the revenue manager system as a step backward in the development of Chinese tax administration. He argues that like dedicated tax managers in the 1980s, revenue managers implement "nanny-style" tax administration: they "exercise the rights and carry out the obligations of taxpayers on behalf of the latter." They embody a "double encroachment," acting *ultra vires* in spheres that should have been reserved for two sets of other actors. First, revenue managers take responsibility away from taxpayers. According to Chen, the idea that revenue managers, in addition to tax inspectors, should verify the truthfulness of tax returns submitted – but make corrections without imposing penalties – implies that taxpayers are not responsible for the veracity of their returns. Second, revenue managers encroach upon the sphere of tax inspectors. Although underreporting tax liabilities on tax returns is treated as tax evasion (*toushui*) under Chinese law,[2] Chen claims that few revenue managers think of themselves as wielding the power of sanctions, given the revenue management system's emphasis on taxpayer services. From Chen's perspective, the role of revenue managers amounts to a negation of the SAT's decision in the early 1990s to separate collection, administration, and inspection.[3]

Chen believes that the future of tax administration lies with a paradigm centered on self-assessment and effective tax audits – he thus echoes the calls of the SAT's 1997 tax administration reform agenda. But according to Chen, China is not yet ready to adopt this paradigm, because the country lacks some critical institutions that he believes advanced economies enjoy: a high degree of rule of law, rigorous monitoring of taxpayer financial information, and extensive information sharing about taxpayers among government authorities. Nonetheless, Chen believes China can move toward the "audit-based" paradigm by first going through an intermediate stage based on taxpayer "alerts." That is, while taxpayers will eventually fulfill their own

[2] Chen refers to Articles 63 and 64 of the Law on the Administration of Tax Collection (*Shuishou zhengshou guanli fa*, or LATC), but the LATC is arguably ambiguous about what type of misreporting on tax returns is sanctionable – in particular, about whether the intent to misreport needs to be present.

[3] Chen 2011 at 5–9.

compliance obligations, they can initially be helped by receiving government-issued alerts about their mistakes. Tax administrators would then gradually withdraw from intervening in the process of compliance and move toward *ex post* interventions.

As the commissioner of the Huai'an DS bureau, Chen had the power to direct substantial reorganization among his subordinates (which numbered over a thousand). To implement his vision, he claims to have abolished the revenue manager system, by which he seems to mean two groups of specific measures. First, he centralized taxpayer services. Before 2004, the Huai'an city tax bureau had five branch bureaus, each of which hosted a taxpayer service center. In 2004, Chen allocated taxpayer services to a single branch bureau, thus removing the function from the other units. Chen was particularly proud of this step, because it reduced revenue managers' contact with taxpayers and therefore opportunities for corruption.[4] As he also appeared to be successful in promoting other steps to simplify compliance, he coined a slogan for Huai'an's reform and had it carved into a giant ornamental rock in front of the city bureau: "Offer convenience to taxpayers to the maximal extent; eliminate opportunities for tax administrators to make mistakes."

Second, in 2007, Chen created a new branch bureau that specialized in assembling and analyzing taxpayer information. "Taxpayer evaluation" would no longer fall within the portfolio of individual tax administrators but was institutionalized in the new unit, which began to issue alerts about potential noncompliance in 2008.[5] To strengthen this unit, Chen pushed for more information-sharing between his DS units and Huai'an's State Tax Bureau (GS) system. Even more impressively, he persuaded the Huai'an city government to bring twenty-five local government agencies together to reach an interagency taxpayer information-sharing agreement. Agencies would send close to seventy types of taxpayer information to the taxpayer analysis unit in the city DS bureau.[6] Chen claims that the city government imposed a hard performance standard on the other agencies' participation in the agreements: inadequate participation in a given year

4 According to Chen, because the new service bureau handled most taxpayer registration, it precluded the other units from competing for new taxpayers (i.e. new revenue sources).

5 Chen 2011 at 11–13 and Appendix 2.

6 Chen's narrative seems to imply that the GS bureau in Huai'an did not house a similar taxpayer analysis unit. If this was indeed the case, it would be a striking example of DS administrators using their ties to local governments to improve tax administration, and would also illustrate the need for caution, highlighted in Chapter 1, in drawing any systematic conclusions about the relative incentives and strengths of the *DS* versus *GS* systems.

would result in that agency's elimination from the annual performance tournament in which city government units regularly take part (and which affect agency leaders' chances of promotion).

Some of these actions to create and strengthen a separate taxpayer data analysis unit were laid out in a 2007 internal directive ironically titled "Notice Regarding Further Strengthening of the Foundational Work of Tax Administration"– a title that is identical to the title of a 2003 SAT circular that harbingered the SAT's turn in *favor* of the revenue management approach.[7] Using the same opaque bureaucratic language, Chen stood the revenue management approach on its head. According to Chen, revenue managers that were now relieved from taxpayer registration and evaluation tasks were expected to perform two remaining types of tasks: One was "basic management" (*jichu guanli*), which involved information acquisition and collection with respect to delinquent taxpayers; the other was "risk response" (*fengxian yingdui*), which comprised the government follow-ups on the new taxpayer analyses.

Chen provides relatively few details about the new "risk response" function in Huai'an, except that it was differentiated according to three categories of risk: low, intermediate, and high. "High-risk response" was to be carried out by Huai'an's tax inspection bureaus. In contrast to traditional tax inspection, Huai'an's "high-risk response" units would select inspection targets on the basis of feeds from the new taxpayer data analysis unit, rather than running broad campaigns by sector.[8] "Low-risk" and "intermediate-risk" responses would be carried out in the units traditionally implementing revenue management. Chen has the least to say about the difference between these two types of tasks. He mainly suggested that "low-risk" items, once identified by the taxpayer analysis unit, could be incorporated in alerts to taxpayers for self-correction. "Intermediate-risk" response, by contrast, would carry a greater flavor of *ex post* sanctions, and require tax administrators in traditional revenue management units to enforce the law in parallel to tax inspectors.[9]

Regarding these last measures, it is hard to distinguish between Chen's statements of aspiration and statements of accomplishment: Some of the measures were implemented in 2011, not long before his book was published, and one cannot determine their success or failure from the book

[7] Id, Appendix 3.

[8] Id, Appendix 8. Chen even instituted a process to have local tax professionals recommend strategies for tax inspections, fearing that tax inspectors lacked expertise about complex taxpayer affairs. Id, at 49–50.

[9] Id, at 27–33.

alone.[10] In any case, Chen's reputation as a successful reformer seems to have stayed largely local, and his book may have already fallen into oblivion. In the Afterword to the book, Chen remarked that the road of innovation is never ending, and his reform was only a small step to satisfying taxpayer needs and in the transformation of government operations. He also alluded to setbacks and controversies that confronted his reform advocacy, which seemed to have inspired the book's title, *On a Journey*.

Whatever incidents led to these remarks, Chen's book did attract one important endorser. The then-commissioner of the Jiangsu Provincial Local Tax Bureau, Li Xiaoping, wrote the Foreword for the book, and praised Chen's ideas for improving tax administration and his spirit of innovation. In 2012, Li, along with a small team of fellow provincial leaders, began to implement a province-wide tax administration reform that strongly resembled what Chen described for Huai'an. Figure 4.1 captures the critical common aspects between the Huai'an reform and the province-wide reform, depicting a reorganized structure of tax administration that starkly contrasts with the atomistic arrangement depicted in Figure 3.1.

In this reorganized structure:

- Taxpayers are no longer assigned individual revenue managers but obtain taxpayer services from institutionalized functions in local tax bureaus.
- The taxpayer database is activated, incorporating tax return data and augmented by taxpayer information from third-party sources. It is actively analyzed by a team dedicated to "risk identification" (*fengxian shibie*).
- Tax inspection units are relabeled "high-risk response" units, increasingly use results from taxpayer data analysis, and thus finally benefit from tax return data.
- A new type of unit – "intermediate-risk response" – is created. Tax administrators in such units will not contact taxpayers unless they have received information from a taxpayer analysis unit about risks associated with specific taxpayers (or, occasionally, from the residual "basic management" function). Although tax inspection ("high-risk response") and "intermediate-risk response" remain separate, the latter now also enforces the law and uses penalties: its goal is to hold taxpayers accountable for the truthfulness of self-assessments. Indeed,

[10] Abolishing the revenue manager system was only one of several reforms that Chen carried out during his time in office. His book also discusses personnel reform, some relevant aspects of which we will return to in Chapter 5.

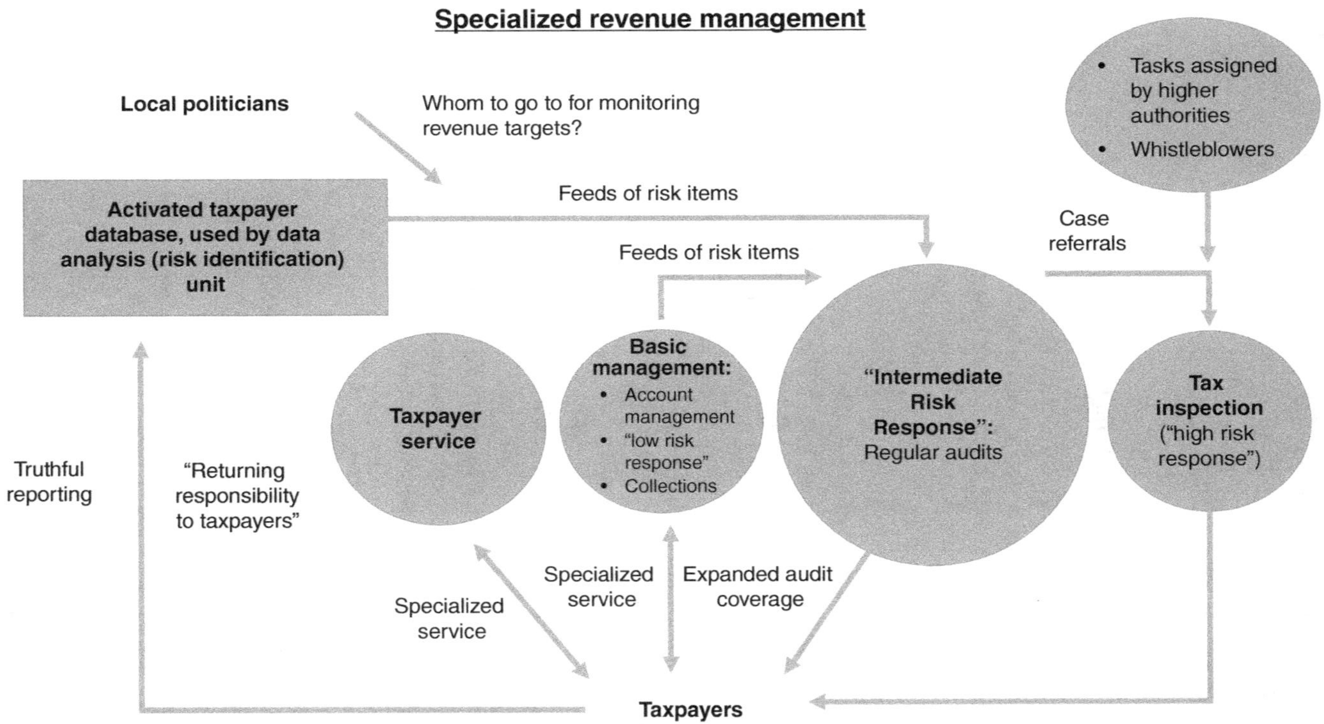

Figure 4.1 Structure of reorganized tax administration: reforms strategies in Huai'an (2007–2011) and Jiangsu (2012–present)

the most important slogan of Jiangsu's provincial-wide reform would be "returning responsibilities to taxpayers."

- A "basic management" arm of revenue management remains, but its scope of tasks is increasingly limited (possibly only to delinquent taxpayers).[11]

Building Audit Functions from Scratch

The impetus for Jiangsu's reform came from the SAT's 2010 Guiding Opinions on Launching Pilot Experiments on Specialized Revenue Management (discussed in Chapter 2). Although the SAT chose only a handful of provincial tax authorities as reform "pilots" in 2010,[12] it encouraged non-pilot agencies to engage in "spontaneous experimentation" in accordance with the Guiding Opinions' spirit. The SAT never published an account of how subnational agencies implemented these "experiments," with or without a SAT mandate. Without specific investigation, one could not know what happened in each jurisdiction. For example, the Jiangsu GS system did not undertake substantial reform before 2013, despite being chosen as a pilot agency in 2010. By contrast, although the DS system in Jiangsu was not among the SAT-designated pilot agencies, leaders in that system (including Commissioner Li Xiaoping and Deputy Commissioner Ni Hongri) took up the call for spontaneous experimentation with their own reform plans. In 2011, DS bureaus in five prefectural cities launched reform pilots for the province, but other Jiangsu cities also began their own versions of reform.

The outcome of top-down reform efforts in Chinese tax administration – like top-down reforms in other policy areas and arms of the state bureaucracy – is generally hard to predict for several reasons. First and foremost, the instructions for reform tend to be vague, provide little concrete guidance, and frequently set out mutually irreconcilable objectives. As I argued in Chapter 3, the revenue manager system discourages and disables specialization in frontline tax agencies. It also produces behavioral convergence among the different segments of the taxpayer population to a common state of quasi-compliance, making it hard to differentiate between more and less compliant taxpayers. The key themes in the 2010

[11] I return to the issue of how local politicians could monitor revenue targets in the reorganized tax administration in Chapter 5.

[12] The pilots chosen were the GS systems in Shanghai, Jiangsu, Anhui, Henan, Guangdong, and the city of Qingdao, as well as the DS systems in Guangdong and Shandong.

SAT Guiding Opinions, however, were the promotion of specialization and differentiated risk management. How could these objectives be advanced without abandoning the revenue management system? Bureaucratic subordinates were left to their own devices to figure this out.

For instance, the Jiangsu Provincial Local Tax Bureau, in announcing its 2011 reform pilots, merely proclaimed that revenue managers should cease to rely on atomistic one-to-one contact with taxpayers and begin to adopt an "assembly line" model where each tax administrator performs specialized tasks.[13] Instead of specifying such an assembly line, it left city-level bureaus to fill in the blanks. Such vagueness implies that the actual reform outcomes must be separately verified. At the extreme, there may even be actions contrary to the declarations of higher-tier policy makers. Just as Commissioner Chen Jianpu in Huai'an turned a SAT slogan for entrenching the revenue management system into one for its demolition, it is possible for city-level bureaus to subvert provincial instructions, and sometimes even for units within a city to subvert city-level instructions.

Civil servants in the system have, after all, widely diverging preferences about reform. "Reform-oriented" officials claim that many grassroots tax administrators are too comfortable with the revenue management system, either because they reap material rewards through the gifts permissible in strongly personalized relationships with taxpayers or because they have already figured out how to meet the system's requirements and are uninterested in trying anything new. Perhaps unsurprisingly, "reformers" see resistance from "vested interests" everywhere. But such accusations can be countered. The vagueness of instructions from high-level "reformers" elicits well-justified cynicism. The instructions for reform often neglect making changes to internal performance evaluations, casting doubt on the seriousness of reform proposals. In 2011, one Jiangsu tax administrator remarked in an internal discussion that "most believe that specialization is a temporary phenomenon and will blow past like a gust of wind."

In the end, however, the tax agencies in Jiangsu – in both the GS and DS branches – did push through concrete measures that made a difference to the experience of rank-and-file employees.[14] These measures fell into

[13] Jiangsu Provincial Local Tax Bureau, Guiding Opinions regarding the Launching of Pilots in Specialized Revenue Management, January 4, 2011.

[14] In the Jiangsu DS system, these organizational steps were laid out in the Opinions on Several Problems in Further Deepening the Reform of Tax Collection and Administration, promulgated by Jiangsu Local Taxation Bureau [2013] No. 1, March 19, 2013 (the "2013 Reform Recommendations") and the Notice by Jiangsu Local Taxation Bureau regarding Relevant Problems in Improving and Deepening

two groups. The first involves actions to implement the aim of "returning responsibilities to taxpayers": tax administrators would minimize contacts with taxpayers to reduce the scope of their *ex ante* interventions in compliance. These measures led to widespread disgruntlement among government employees – which offered evidence that something new was being tried. The second encompasses measures to build new audit functions premised on informative taxpayer data analysis. Like the system for "risk response" that Chen Jianpu had envisioned for Huai'an, Jiangsu tax administrators would center their work on "feeds" regarding taxpayer risks (coming out of units analyzing taxpayer information). These two groups of measures would reinforce each other, as captured by the phrase, "no risk, no taxpayer contact" (*wufengxian, buxiahu*).

Consider how Jiangsu's reform reduced tax administrators' personal interactions with taxpayers. One strategy, echoing Chen Jianpu's ideas in Huai'an, was to allocate many functions traditionally associated with revenue managers to a centralized taxpayer service unit.[15] Such allocation meant that any interaction would be initiated by the taxpayer seeking services: no revenue manager would proactively reach out to the taxpayer first to provide such services (it was hoped that this would enhance compliance). But the province-wide reform went further. In 2013, the provincial bureau moved the periodic reviews of the appropriate levels of presumptive taxation for small taxpayers away from traditional units to the new division that managed taxpayer data.[16] In addition, it eliminated the routine verification of taxpayer registration information through field visits, another time-consuming task for traditional revenue managers.[17] Consequently, although "basic management" units were retained, they became responsible only for handling de-registration and tax-related approval procedures,

Collection and Administration Reform, Jiangsu Local Taxation Bureau [2014] No.1, June 24, 2014 (the "2014 Reform Notice").

15 In the "2013 Reform Recommendations," these included the verification of taxpayers' registration information upon initial registration and subsequent modification; affirmation of categories of taxes (and fees) that a taxpayer is liable for; and decisions (affirmation, claims for, cancelling, and voiding) regarding qualifications for possession of invoices.

16 Moreover, the separate collection of two small taxes – the deed tax and the arable land use tax – which in some places had been handled by revenue management units, merged with other types of tax collection. These two types of taxes did not require the filing of tax returns and had lent themselves to one-on-one exaction.

17 The provincial deputy commissioner Ni Hongri suggested that "[eliminating] the function of verifying taxpayer registration information through field visits significantly alters the long-held approach to tax administration; we have redefined the account management functions of frontline taxation bureaus."

contacting delinquent filers and payers, providing immediate responses to reports of fraudulent invoices, delivering penalties for "ordinary" violations and infractions, and performing other "special investigative tasks."[18]

Within frontline tax offices, this resulted in substantial personnel reshuffling throughout Jiangsu. Provincial DS Deputy Commissioner Ni Hongri described the outcome as follows:

> Since the workload for basic management functions has been massively reduced, can we peel away these functions from each local bureau and create a special unit for them? We conducted an experiment in one county, and found that one separate unit could comfortably handle all basic management matters in that county. So we made the following proposal ... : combine all related basic management functions; isolate risk management functions; and set up special branch bureaus for each of these two types of functions. For instance, if there are five branch bureaus in a county, one of them would handle all basic management, while the other four would specialize in responding to risks. This implements the basic framework determined in the early stages of reform, namely, to devote 10 to 20 percent of material and human resources to basic management while freeing up the rest to engage primarily in risk response.

This reshuffling of personnel echoes a strategy promoted in the SAT's 1997 Tax administration reform, namely, to allocate a substantial amount of human resources to audit functions ("risk response" in the new terminology). In 1997, the SAT urged local tax bureaus to devote at least 40 percent of staff to tax inspection. By 2013, the staff count in newly created "risk response units" in the Jiangsu DS system stood at 137 percent of the staff count in the remaining "basic management" units.

However, as we saw in Chapters 1 and 2 in connection with tax inspection, staffing personnel in bureaucratic units that have little to do is unsustainable. For the "risk responders" to be productive, the "risk feeds" they receive must be meaningful. Here, tax administrators across Jiangsu quickly identified something that Chen Jianpu did not acknowledge in his book: their taxpayer databases were no good. When tax administrators forego direct personal observations of taxpayers and choose to be guided completely by data analysis, they are taking a large leap of faith. Unfortunately, they immediately realized that the blind was leading the blind. One tax administrator put things this way in 2011:

18 Moreover, all these remaining tasks must satisfy an additional condition to fall under the scope of basic management: they must not involve any audit aspect and therefore cannot be included under the "risk management" system.

> Data quality has generally been poor due to insufficient support by information technology. This prevents us from meaningfully building risk models and analyzing the data, and consequently prevents us from realizing the true potential of taxpayer evaluation. [The risk identification unit] often conflates poor-quality data with that of real risk of revenue loss, and referred many files on for further actions even when those files do not warrant risk management responses.

Information, in other words, turned out to be the hardest constraint on the tax authorities' push toward building new audit functions. Reformers had no choice but to accept that the new approach could not quickly succeed: it would take time to improve both the scope and accuracy of the taxpayer database. Only a better database would support the new functions of risk analysis and response.

Practically, Jiangsu's tax administrators took a number of steps to improve the gathering and analysis of taxpayer data. First, they built a province-wide taxpayer database for the first time. Second, they centralized taxpayer data analysis to the city and provincial levels, so as to improve data quality and the accuracy of risk identification. Third, they cut off other ways for tax administrators to gather and store information, so as to force frontline tax administrators to use the taxpayer database and feed more input into it. For instance, the 2013 Reform Recommendations reiterated the principle that local bureaus must not require taxpayers to submit information already contained in the provincial information system (the "Grand Unified System," *dajizhong xitong*, or GUS). Only the provincial bureau had the authority to expand the scope of information collection. Moreover, the provincial bureau required most administrative tasks, including those involving contacts with taxpayers, to be inputted in the IT system developed by the provincial bureau. Because the provincial computerized protocol reflected the reformers' scheme of new tax administration, each frontline unit would increasingly converge, through technology, to newly designed procedures.

Finally, as a concrete measure to promote self-assessment, the new system would offer taxpayers annual opportunities to verify their own tax account information. This would operate through a system of "soliciting confirmation" [*tuisong queren zhi*]. Tax bureaus would send taxpayers their basic information as stored in the GUS and solicit confirmation by signature or corporate seal at the beginning of each year.[19] Taxpayers

[19] The Reform Recommendations proposed to add an "Important Notice" section in all information collection forms to alert taxpayers of their obligations and duties to provide true and accurate tax-related information.

would be held responsible for any inaccurate information.[20] While audit or inspection units would verify such basic information during any audit procedures, there would be no separate routine verification. Commissioner Ni explained the significance of these measures as follows:

> Taxpayers should be held responsible for their own tax-related filing, because taxpayers, not tax officials or tax authorities, should be held responsible for their tax-related conduct in general . . . We should not obscure or diminish taxpayers' responsibilities for the accuracy and legality of their filed information by investigation and verification through field visits. It must be made clear that each taxpayer is responsible for his or her own doing. If we engage in such investigation and verification, then it would not be merely for verifying some information but for imposing legal sanctions on any discovered inaccurate filing as part of inspection functions.

Outcomes of the New Audit System

The organizational achievements of Jiangsu's tax administration reform during 2012–2015 were considerable. I could cite many more official speeches, extensive internal bureaucratic directives, and ample anecdotes collected through interviews to illustrate Jiangsu's remarkable performance. However, one feature of the reform requires a more systematic empirical account: Jiangsu's new *audit system*. New units across the province – called "intermediate-risk response" departments – would engage with taxpayers identified as potentially guilty of misreporting or underpayment, and aim to verify and correct, *ex post*, such misreporting or underpayment. Because analyses of tax returns were the basis of "risk identification," and because "risk response" was clearly separated from other functions (such as taxpayer service, account management, and collections), it seems appropriate to use "audit" to refer to the operation of these new units. I will adopt this label in distinction from traditional tax inspection[21] and from "low-risk response," a range of tasks handled by tax administrators performing traditional, "basic management" functions. City tax bureaus across

[20] Ni argued, "This could improve our data management functions, since the need for information correction is drastically reduced. For small sole-proprietorships or taxpayers hardly operating with a profit, we also do not need to devote much human and material resources to verifying their information and can opt for some simple and efficacious alternative."

[21] Note, though, that during Jiangsu's reform, even tax inspection bureaus (in the new functional role of "high-risk response") supposedly benefitted from the new analyses of tax returns.

Jiangsu produced quarterly and sometimes monthly internal reports about the outcomes of these new "audit" functions. I use statistics extracted from these reports – covering thirteen cities and about ten quarterly periods from 2013 to 2016 – to describe the outcomes of the new audit system. The statistics provide a detailed, ground-up view of what the reform did and did not achieve. The picture that emerges is complex and, in many ways, unexpected.

A first set of facts to consider concerns the new system's overall audit coverage and contribution to revenue. The new system resulted in audits of around eighty-seven to eighty-nine thousand business taxpayers a year in 2013, 2014, and 2015, equivalent to over 5 percent of the province's business taxpayer population. For "key taxpayers" that represent large sources of revenue, this audit rate was on average 39 percent. From an international and comparative perspective, these are high and respectable rates of audit coverage. And relative to the coverage of traditional tax inspection, the new regime expanded the coverage of audit-related government interventions by six to ten times. Moreover, the new audit function directly resulted in revenue collection amounting, on average, to about 4 percent of total tax revenue; this compares favorably with the 1 percent average contribution to total tax revenue made by the tax inspection system in recent years (see Figure 2.4).

But a second set of facts reveal more unusual patterns. In international terminology, additional tax liabilities detected through audits are called "adjustments" – as in, adjustments to the amounts declared on tax returns. Figures 4.2(a) and 4.2(b) show, respectively, the proportion of all Jiangsu audits that resulted in adjustments – sometimes called the "target rate" – and the portion of adjustments of various sizes. It is understandable why, from the perspective of the auditor, coming away from an audit emptyhanded may feel unsatisfying. Both these metrics thus seem to measure the effectiveness of audits.[22]

Astonishingly, Figure 4.2(a) shows that the mean target rates in Jiangsu's audits exceed 95 percent. In terms of amounts, Figure 4.2(b) indicates that the most frequent group – on average, almost 45 percent – of audits resulted in adjustments of between CNY 100 and 10,000. Adjustments for over CNY 10,000 are the next largest group (more than 30 percent of all audits). But adjustments for less than CNY 100

[22] They only *seem* this way, because in theory the point of audits is not to catch and punish wrongdoing, but to deter wrongdoing by implementing a promise to catch and punish it. Thus, it is possible that the more successful deterrence is, the more likely that auditors will come away empty handed.

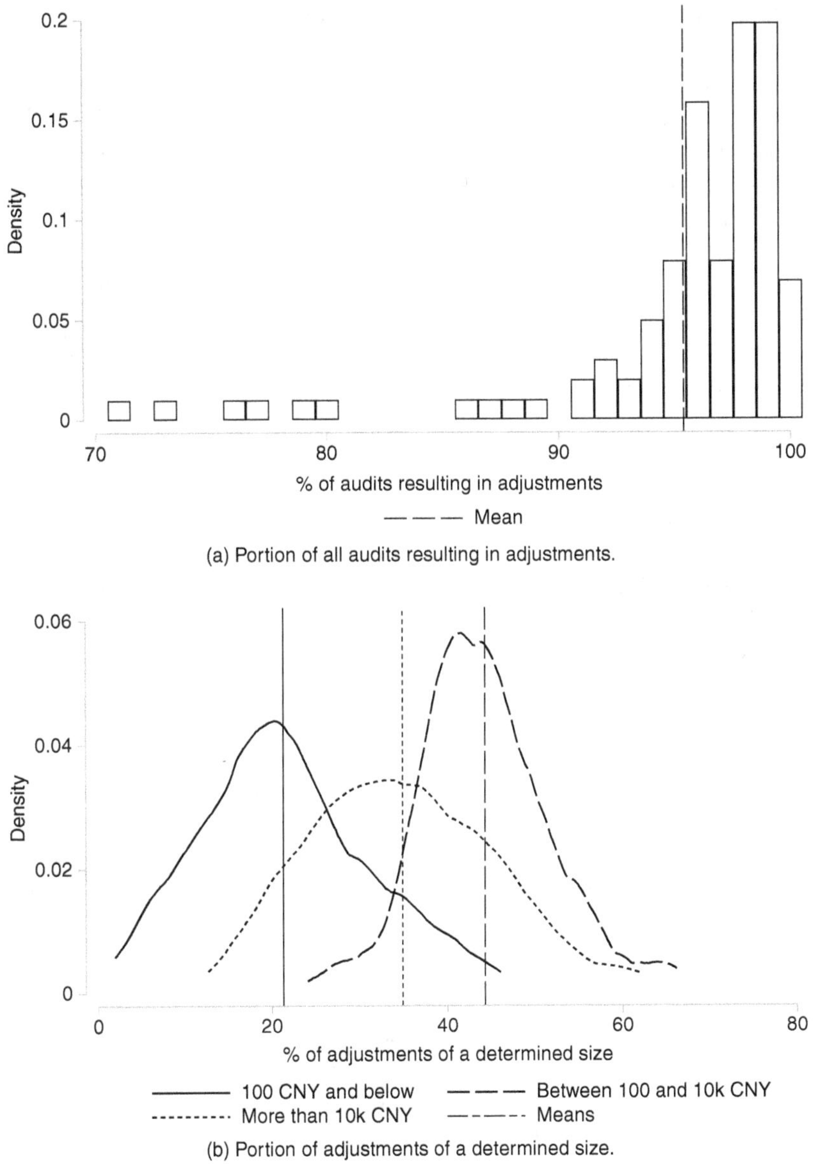

Figure 4.2 Target rates and distribution of audits by adjustment size[23]

[23] In both panels, the distributions report observations of fourteen jurisdictions in Jiangsu over nine quarters in 2014–2016.

still represent a significant portion of audit outcomes – on average, over 20 percent of all audits.

How should one interpret these facts? Consider first the target rate. Conceptually, a high target rate could arise for two reasons. Either the selection of audit targets is very accurate (so that taxpayers selected for audits are precisely those likely to have underpaid tax), or most taxpayers underpay tax (so that *anyone* being audited is likely to show unpaid tax liabilities). One reason to think that the latter factor – widespread noncompliance – is more relevant to outcomes in Jiangsu is the following: if we compare Jiangsu's new audit regime with the tax inspection regime, the latter ought to be more selective. This is reflected in the fact that a tax inspector handles on average only two cases a year, whereas a tax auditor in Jiangsu handles on average fifteen audits in just half a year.

Moreover, Figure 4.3(a) shows the portions of tax inspections that resulted in adjustments of different sizes. Comparing Figure 4.3(a) with Figure 4.3(b), it is clear that tax inspections tend to generate higher adjustments: on average, only 4 percent of tax inspections result in adjustments of less than CNY 100, and only 20 percent result in adjustments of between CNY 100 and 10,000. The remaining 75 percent of tax inspections result in higher adjustments. Figure 4.3(b) shows that the distribution of average adjustments per investigation for tax inspections lies far to the right from that for regular audits: the mean is CNY 1.7 million for the former, compared to CNY 220,000 for the latter. This is all consistent with the idea that tax inspection targets are carefully chosen for more dedicated examination, in the expectation of greater revenue recovery. However, even though tax inspection is evidently more selective in its targets, its target rate is not higher than the target rate of audits – and can hardly be higher, given the level of the latter. Thus, the high target rate of audits cannot be explained primarily by effective target selection.

A third set of facts brings us closer to how Jiangsu's new audit system actually operated. In other countries, taxpayers may be familiar with the experience of receiving letters from tax authorities requesting further information to substantiate reporting on tax returns. Such letters are part of what are often referred to as "correspondence audits." In China, although email and smartphone alerts were recently adopted to notify taxpayers of potential underpayment of tax, there has not been a tradition of "correspondence audits." The tax agencies are generally located so close to taxpayers – much like post offices – that a more natural means of communication is to require taxpayers to show up for meetings at the local tax bureau's office. Most audits thus start with such a meeting or interview (*yuetan*).

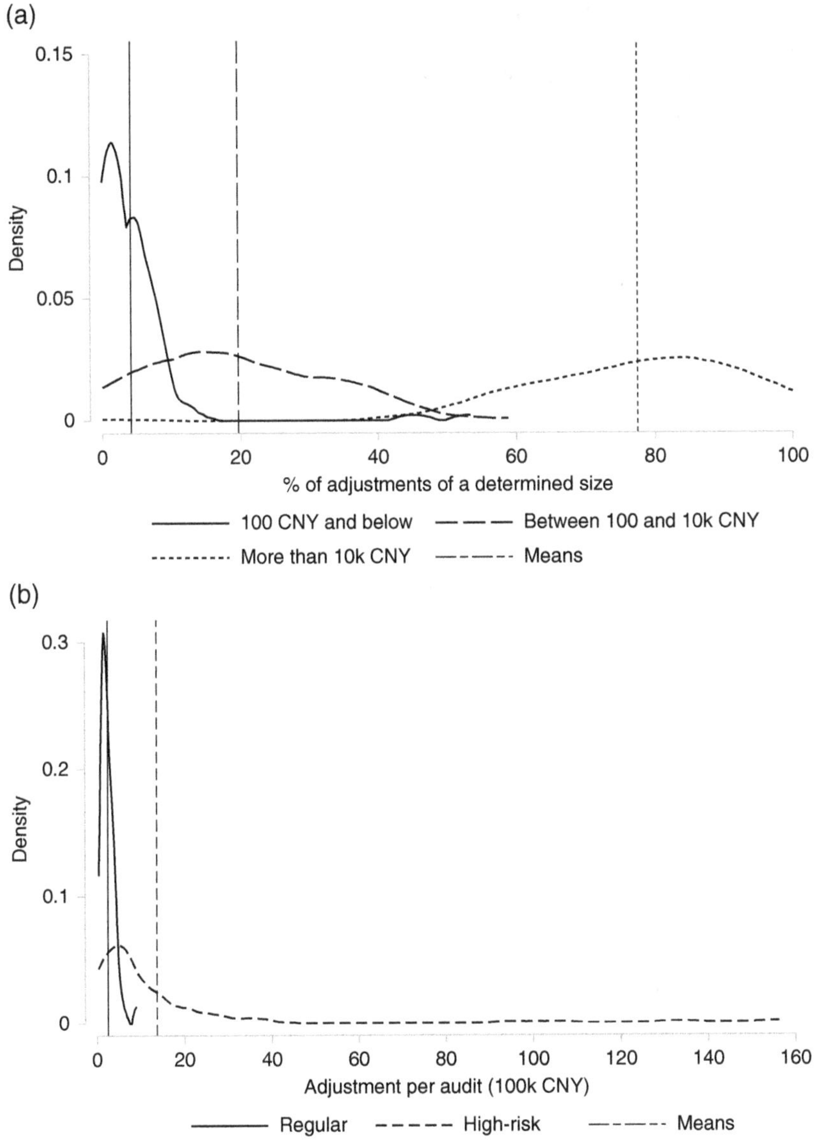

Figure 4.3 Adjustment size: tax inspections versus audits[24]

[24] Panel (a) reports the distribution of tax inspection outcomes by adjustment size. Panel (b) compares the distribution of adjustment size between tax inspection and audits. As in Figure 4.2, both panels report observations of fourteen jurisdictions in Jiangsu over nine quarters in 2014–2016.

In countries like the United States, an in-person interview with the tax authorities for audit purposes is often referred to as an "office audit" or "desk audit." If taxpayers adequately answer questions during such an audit, or if the reason for underpayment is successfully identified and agreed upon, an audit could end right away. In Jiangsu, however, only a tiny portion (less than 2 percent) of cases concludes after such an interview.[25] Figure 4.4(a) shows that instead, most audits (around 80 percent) are completed during a phase called "self-audit" or "*zicha*," a term also used for self-inspections supervised by tax inspectors. That is, the taxpayers report additional amounts of tax payable *after* a meeting at the tax office, as a result of further "self-examination." Field audits (*shidi hecha*) – where auditors visit the physical premises of taxpayers – represent the third way in which an audit can be completed. However, only 5 percent of all audits proceed directly to the field audit phase after the office interview; most field audits are initiated only after a self-audit phase (Figure 4.4(b)).

In other words, the new audit regime in Jiangsu remarkably replicates some of the core features of China's tax inspection system discussed in Chapter 2. Legally, self-audits and field audits under the audit regime are distinct in the same way as self-inspections and government inspections are distinct: additional tax liabilities reported through self-audits do not attract penalties but only late payment interests. Recall that tax inspection bureaus usually stipulate a minimum ratio – typically 20 percent or more – of government inspections to self-inspections, in order to incentivize taxpayers under inspection to report previously unreported tax liabilities. The ratio of field audits following self-audits seems to correspond to this minimum ratio.

All this is surprising for several reasons. First, unlike the use of self-inspections by tax inspection bureaus, there was no explicit instruction in the Jiangsu reform directives for the use of self-audits in the new audit system. Instead, as the quote of Commissioner Ni Hongri earlier suggests, reformers contemplated taxpayer "self-correction" mainly for "low-risk response" issues, whereas "intermediate-risk response" would enforce the law and generate deterrence. This suggests that the wide adoption of self-audits emerged contrary to the reformers' intent. Second, the purpose of the new audit system was not to (directly) generate additional revenue; it was instead to enforce the norm of truthful reporting and "return responsibilities to taxpayers." Chapter 2 showed that self-inspections

[25] Although no separate statistics are available, my discussion with Jiangsu tax officials indicates that those cases concluding with an office interview usually result in no adjustments.

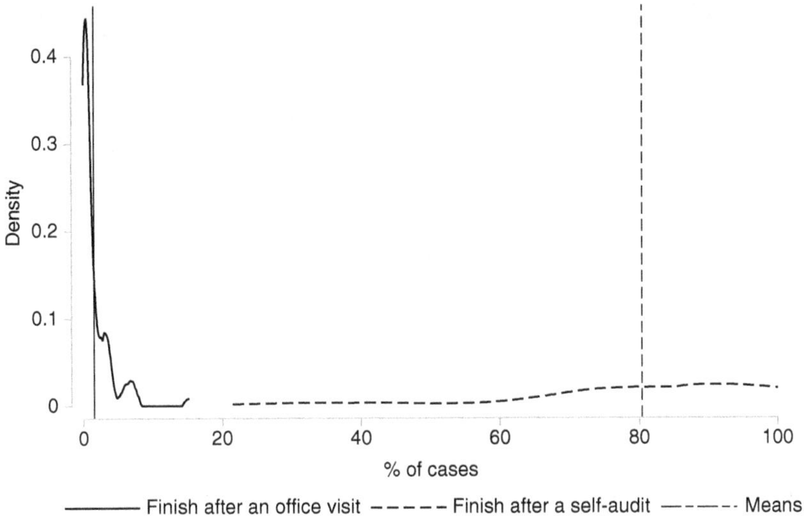

(a) Portion of audits finished after office visits and self-audits.

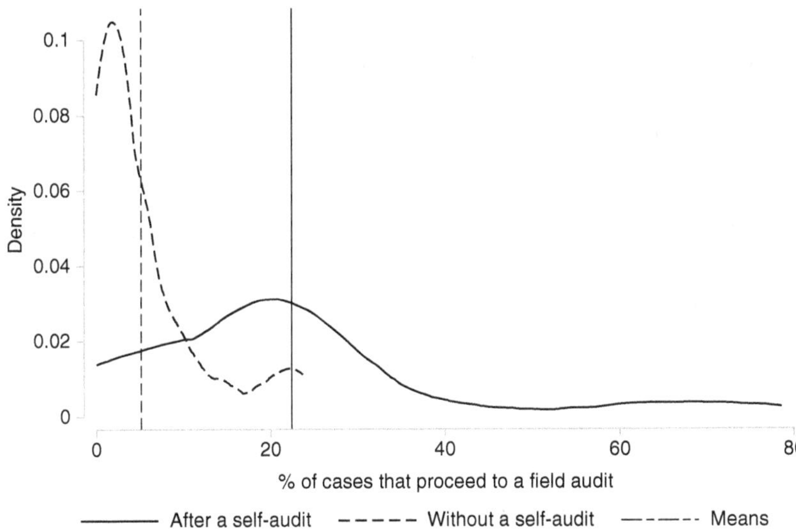

(b) Portion of cases that proceed to a field audit after a self-audit or without a self-audit.

Figure 4.4 Relative frequency of office audits, self-audits, and field audits

across China were adopted to raise revenue during revenue-raising campaigns at low cost to tax administrators. In Jiangsu's reform, however, though reformers had hoped that increased compliance would lead to greater revenue, meeting revenue targets was not the reform's rationale.

A fourth and final set of facts is relevant for assessing why self-audits became the preferred way in Jiangsu to conclude "intermediate-risk responses." It turns out that across cities and periods, aggregate adjustments from self-audits represented on average around 95 percent of all adjustments from Jiangsu's new audit regime. Moreover, although I have data only for one year (2014) in this regard, that year saw a significantly higher proportion (on average > 95 percent) of self-audits ending with adjustments than the proportion of field audits ending with adjustments (on average < 75 percent). The effectiveness of self-audits versus field audits can also be compared in terms of the magnitudes of adjustments resulting for those audits that did come with adjustments. On average, 40 percent of field audits end with trivial amounts of adjustments (< CNY 100), whereas only 20 percent of self-audits end up with such amounts (Figure 4.5(a)); 10 percent of self-audits generate large adjustments (> CNY 100,000), whereas only 5 percent of field audits do so (Figure 4.5(b)). Moreover, as Figure 4.5 shows, the outcomes of self-audits are also more consistent in these regards, whereas the outcomes of field audits are much more dispersed.

Interestingly, for one quarter in 2014, Jiangsu's cities reported on outcomes of audits that contained two phases: self-audits (phase 1) and field audits (phase 2). In these cases, adjustments in phase 1 averaged a higher proportion of larger adjustments (> CNY 10,000), while adjustments in phase 2 averaged a higher proportion of trivial adjustments (< CNY 100). That is, even when auditors are dissatisfied with a self-audit, they end up issuing adjustments in the field audit phase that are far smaller than what the taxpayers concede in the self-audit phase. Similarly, in audits that involve both phases, phase 1 more frequently delivered large adjustments than audits that proceeded directly to field audits.

It is difficult to avoid the conclusion that under Jiangsu's new audit regime, penalty-free self-audits lifted most of the weight. The explanations for these outcomes that I have heard from Jiangsu tax administrators are not fully satisfying. I will come to some of them in this chapter, but first, I want to analyze two questions related to aggregate revenue. First, did Jiangsu, after launching its tax administration reform, raise more tax revenue overall than it would have raised without such reform? Second, did the establishment of the new audit system affect the revenue raising capacity of the preexisting tax inspection system? The answers to these two questions would permit the following inference. If Jiangsu *did*

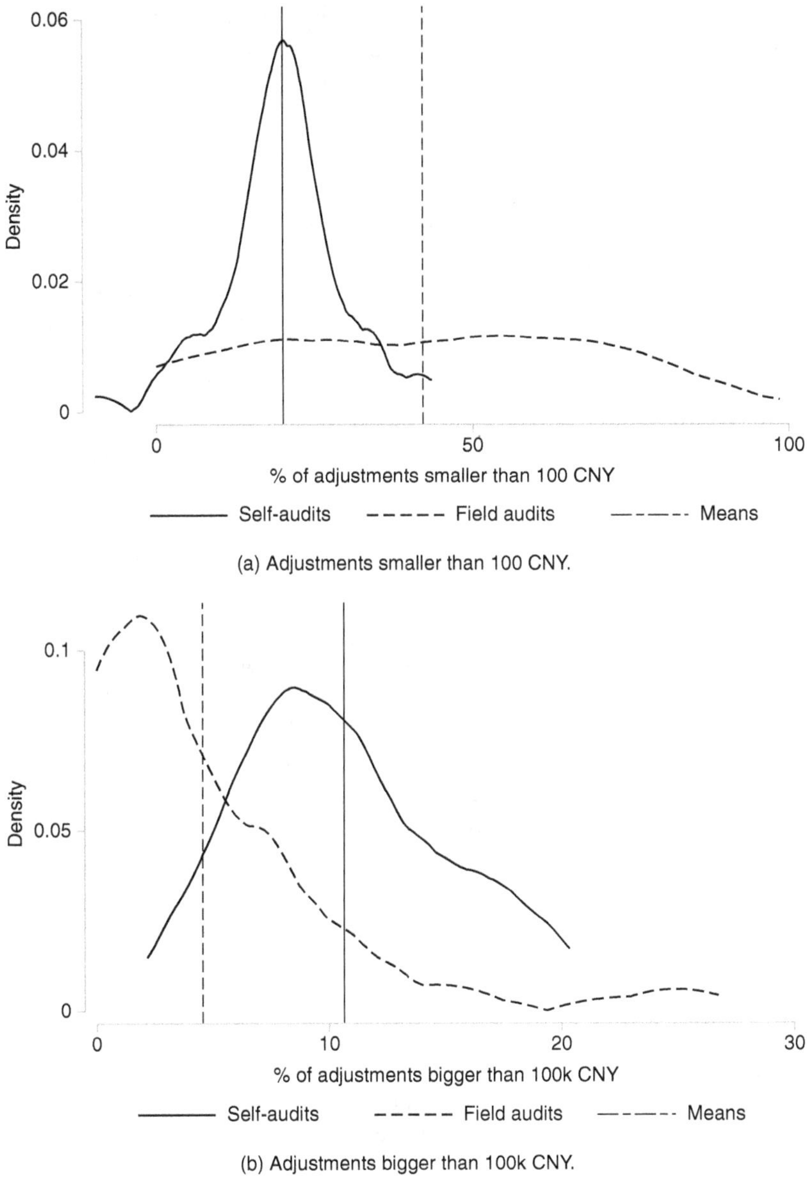

Figure 4.5 Size of adjustments: self-audits versus field audits

not raise additional tax revenue overall compared to what it would have raised without reform, then the revenue reportedly raised through audits (about 4 percent of total revenue) must come from either or both of two sources. First, it may represent revenue that would have been raised through the tax inspection system. Second, it may represent revenue that would have been raised through the traditional revenue management system.[26]

Figure 4.6(a) compares the trend of year-on-year revenue growth in Jiangsu during 2008–2018 with the trend of revenue growth in China as a whole. This comparison is informative because, notwithstanding the 2010 SAT Guiding Opinions on promoting "specialized revenue management," most Chinese provinces did not go through tax administration reform during the 2012–2016 period. Therefore, Jiangsu's reform can be thought of as a "natural experiment," in which Jiangsu was "treated" by a new approach to tax administration, while other provinces represent the "control group" that did not receive such treatment. Any effect on revenue of the reform, therefore, may be detectable by comparing the treated and control groups. Figure 4.6(a) shows, however, that changes in revenue growth in Jiangsu largely track changes in national revenue growth during this entire period. There was no visible revenue "bump" in any of the years after 2012 relative to the rest of the country.

Figure 4.6(b) again compares national and Jiangsu trends in respect to one measure: the percentage contribution to total revenue made by tax collected during tax inspections.[27] Jiangsu's trend largely tracked the national trend from 2005 to 2012, but the province's revenue contribution ratio of tax inspection dropped in 2013, and the gap with the national ratio persisted afterward. This suggests that Jiangsu's tax inspection system may well have been affected by the new audit system: the expansion of the latter partly eroded the ability of the former to raise revenue. However, because the tax inspection system generally contributes not much more than 1 percent of total revenue, the 4 percent revenue contribution of the new audit system cannot be entirely attributed to the substitution of new audits for traditional tax inspections. Since we know that the new audit system was intended as a substitute for traditional revenue management, it is plausible to conclude that the revenue raised by the new system would have been wrangled from taxpayers, through atomistic coercion, under revenue management.

[26] In other words, if the new audit system did not negatively affect revenue intake through the preexisting tax inspection system, then we can regard the revenue raised by new audits as coming from the revenue management system that the new audit system replaced.

[27] In Chapter 2, I used this measure as one indicator of the importance of tax inspections. As there, the data for Figure 4.6(b) comes from the Tax Inspection Yearbook.

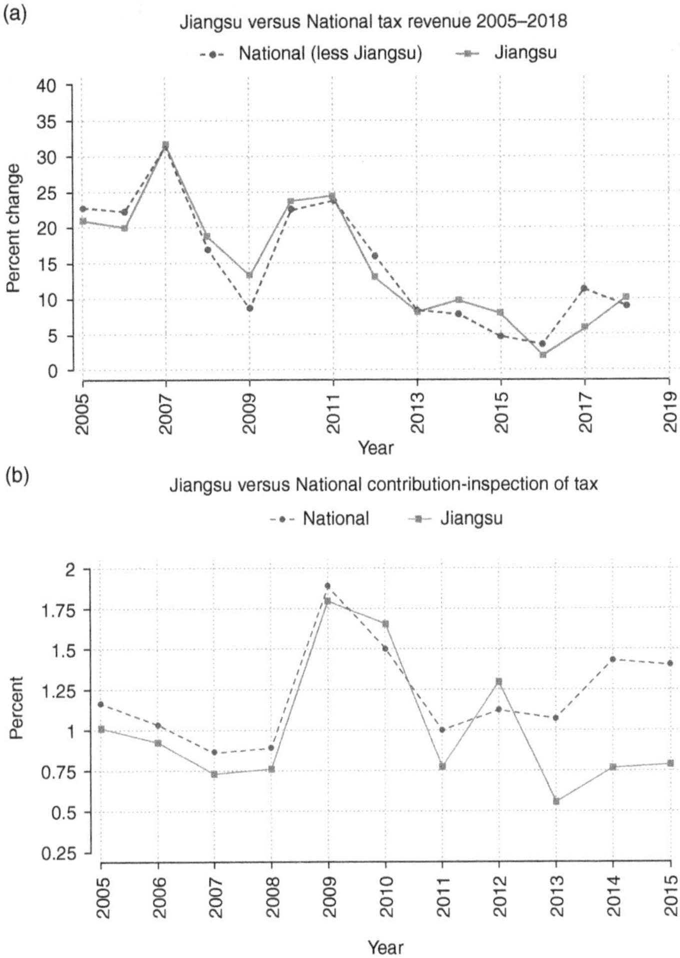

Figure 4.6 Impact of tax administration reform on overall revenue and on tax inspections

This suggests an interpretation of the predominance of self-audits in Jiangsu's "intermediate-risk response" operation: Tax administrators simply continued to do what they did well – namely, cajoling taxpayers into paying more tax, while imposing penalties very sparingly. Despite continuing this prior practice – albeit under a new system of "risk response" – frontline tax collectors may have experienced several differences. On the one hand, they could tell taxpayers selected for "risk response" that the government's data system had identified them as "risky," implying that tax agencies now possessed superior information about taxpayers. This may enhance their capacity to extract concessions from taxpayers. On the other hand, because of the abolition of the revenue management system, the new audit personnel would not have been assigned to the audited taxpayers on a regular basis. They would thus not have enjoyed the benefit of persistent monitoring.

The potential advantage of superior information about the taxpayers was probably weak, perhaps even in appearance only. It seems that such information did not allow tax administrators to make either frequent or substantial adjustments during field audits. Nor did it embolden them to use penalties more often. Indeed, it is likely that the new auditors, or "risk responders," had to exercise substantial judgments on their own about what the "risk-identification feeds" they received actually meant – and even, in conducting examinations, to substitute their own judgments for the supposed clues that the system identified. Indeed, if risk identification was highly unreliable, auditors were likely better off asking taxpayers to self-audit rather than pursuing field audits.

In short, Jiangsu tax auditors' strong preference for self-audits over field audits, as well as the evident superiority of self-audits in catalyzing more frequent and larger adjustments, are both consistent with the low quality of taxpayer information that was being used for the province's data analysis. And in the absence of reliable information, tax auditors substantially perpetuated preexisting practices, though within new organizational structures.

The Information-Compliance Dilemma

Is there anything inevitable about the reform outcomes described in the last section? The evidence available for answering this question is inconclusive. This is because while Jiangsu's reform strategies had become clearer and more entrenched in 2014, the reform also began to lose political momentum, for two reasons. First and perhaps most importantly, the national anti-corruption campaign pushed by the Chinese Communist Party (CCP) leader Xi Jingping had rapidly ramped up by 2014, generating deep political tensions throughout the Chinese bureaucracy. Instead of routine policy goals, institutional innovation, and professionalism, the anti-corruption campaign emphasized political purity and loyalty. It also promised to severely reduce material rewards to civil servants. This was widely reported to have reduced morale among Chinese bureaucrats. Second, Jiangsu's reform did not immediately raise additional revenue, which had been presented as one of the potential benefits of reform. Thus, although reform measures announced in 2013 and 2014 stayed in place for the next few years and were never reversed, they became more vulnerable to pushback by opponents. By 2016, Jiangsu's tax administration reform was largely suspended, if not undone.

The patterns in Jiangsu's new audit system shown earlier can be interpreted in two opposite ways, but insofar Jiangsu's reform was suspended for reasons unrelated to the nature of the reform itself, one simply cannot tell which is correct. On the first interpretation, these patterns reflect just what one might expect in the early stages of a reform. Recall that Mr. Chen Jianpu from Huai'an argued that for China to adopt an approach to tax administration that relies on taxpayer self-assessment backed up by audits, there needs to be a transition stage, where taxpayers are alerted to their wrongdoings without penalty. Perhaps the dominance of taxpayer self-audits in Jiangsu's "intermediate-risk response" regime reflected this transition stage: neither taxpayers nor tax administrators were ready for the large-scale imposition of penalties, especially given the very extensive noncompliance uncovered by audits. Nonetheless, this view would hold, neither the increased use of penalties nor improved analysis of taxpayer data is infeasible, if the reform is continued. On the second interpretation, by contrast, the early results simply provided evidence for the unavoidable: Jiangsu's reform was doomed to failure. It is clear why reformers would prefer the first interpretation, while opponents of the reform would embrace the latter.

I will start by elaborating on the first interpretation. When I asked reformers in Jiangsu why self-audits became so prevalent, one answer I got was that many reported self-audits were in reality field audits. It was just that many auditors chose to report them as taxpayer self-audits instead. The reasons for this choice were not only that the imposition of penalties would provoke antagonism with taxpayers, but also that the procedures for imposing penalties were cumbersome. Chinese law provides that taxpayers have the right to appeal any penalties either within the executive branch or to courts. Litigation would clearly take up resources. Appeals within the executive branch, on the other hand, would initially be handled by an internal division within the county- or district-level tax bureaus – low-level bureaucratic units that essentially operate side-by-side with the auditors. For readers who are legally-minded, this might suggest that taxpayers are unlikely to get a neutral and fair hearing when appealing proposed penalties. But from the front-line tax administrators' perspective, this arrangement produces the opposite effect: they would prefer not to impose penalties in the first place, as that would merely produce additional and time-consuming work for their colleagues that may not yield much revenue. That is, with a decentralized appeals system, it is as if individual metermen need to simultaneously run an appeals operation after issuing parking tickets. It is obvious how this might lead to more sparing punishments of parking infractions.

If this was the problem, then the fix would be obvious: one could centralize the appeal of administrative penalties, possibly to the city level, so that county- or district-level bureaus can focus on auditing and detecting noncompliance, without fear of being bogged down by disputes. Some reformers in Jiangsu believed that this was the necessary next step in reform. If the main reason for the rarity of field audits was that bureaucratic protocols required the imposition of penalties in such audits, but auditors were averse to imposing penalties too often, then the prevalence of self-audits would be less troubling. It would not necessarily imply that auditors were ineffective in identifying noncompliance. And if auditors were effective in such identification, then the threat of audits itself, even if accompanied only by low or rare penalties, may be enough to produce deterrence.

The aversion to the use of penalties could have other explanations, too. To begin, it is hard to impose harsh penalties when widespread noncompliance is common knowledge. Moreover, at least under the revenue management system, tax administrators and taxpayers have frequent contact, and this sense of personal familiarity may embolden many taxpayers to try – directly by themselves or through their social networks – to persuade tax administrators to drop penalties. Even during Jiangsu's reform, which limited direct contact between tax administrators and taxpayers, the local social networks that embedded such relationships persisted. I was told by tax administrators that taxpayers were willing to leverage all kinds of personal connections to prevent the enforcement of law against them.

Also requiring consideration is the fact that tax administrators may have wanted to reserve penalties for those violations that they cared most about. That is, tax administrators may feel that the quantum of penalties they can hand out to each individual taxpayer is limited. As mentioned earlier, many of the preexisting performance metrics used within the Jiangsu tax bureaucracy were retained during the reform years, notwithstanding the fact that tax administrators had begun to pursue a new style of administration. Taxpayer registration, timely filing, timely payment, and many other compliance targets remained important for internal evaluations. Tax administrators therefore may have wanted to reserve the use of penalties to secure outcomes under these other metrics.

But these last considerations also lend support to the opposite interpretation: namely, Jiangsu's reform was doomed to failure. When I talked to sceptics about Jiangsu's reform, they relished the enumeration of purportedly necessary preconditions of success that the reform lacked. According to them, the reformers wanted to implement "risk response," but the government lacked data on who was considered "risky." The reformers aimed to "return responsibilities to taxpayers," but Chinese taxpayers neither cared about nor understood the rule of law. The reformers proposed to implement specialization in tax administration, but the details of how to specialize were not forthcoming. It was wholly mysterious, they suggested, how voluntary compliance, reliable taxpayer information, and detailed rules guiding social behavior could be conjured out of nowhere.

These arguments were rather compelling, in light of Chapter 3's analysis of revenue management as embodying the approach of atomistic coercion. Most taxpayers neither paid attention to legal rules nor complied with the rules out of a sense of obligation. Following the judgment of individual tax collectors substituted for acquiring knowledge about the law. Revenue managers were expected to lend a hand when taxpayers failed to fulfill their own responsibilities. To collect revenue, revenue managers directly monitored and coerced taxpayers into following a minimum set of requirements (such as business registration) and making negotiated tax payments. The effectiveness of direct coercion, however, is by necessity narrow in scope, and dramatically diminishes when compliance is multi-dimensional. Consequently, deterrence for noncompliance with most provisions of tax law is low. Many taxpayers either cheat or do not commit resources to compliance, and the government neither possesses nor makes use of systematic taxpayer information. Finally, when neither taxpayers nor the government rely on rule-following – when the "demand" for rules is eroded – it is not surprising that few rules tend to be available for guidance.

To transition from such a regime to self-assessment is obviously challenging. The promotion of the latter can take two forms: limiting the use of coercive techniques that represent a "drag" on the move to self-assessment, or producing incentives for self-assessment or "accelerants" for the transition. The problem is that such accelerants are hard to come by. Not only does the dearth of reliable taxpayer information stand in the way of effective audit selection, and not only is the imposition of penalties a practice that can be adopted only gradually, but it is also unclear whether these tools at tax administrators' disposal alone are close to being sufficient to institute social norms of following the rules of law. It seems only commonsense that when there is a deficit of the rule of law in governance and social life, it is difficult to instill the rule of law just in the sphere of taxation. But if tax agencies alone cannot create enough incentives for law-abiding behavior, then abandoning other methods of government intervention to minimize the "drag" on the transition to self-assessment seems highly risky.

Skepticism about the visions of Jiangsu reformers thus seems coherent and not just fueled by vested interests. The practice of self-assessment may represent a social equilibrium: the existence of rules, the sufficiency of private parties' incentives to follow the rules, and the capacity of government agents to monitor and enforce compliance with the rules, must all hang together. Conversely, the regime of atomistic coercion may also represent a social equilibrium – a system of interconnected incentives and behaviors that makes it difficult for individual rational actors to deviate from its characteristic choices. In that case, what Jiangsu's reformers proposed is not a matter of modifying an existing practice, but one of moving from one deep social equilibrium to another.

What about the inefficiencies of the revenue management system? Do the opponents of Jiangsu's reform not recognize them, and are they completely unmoved by the polemics that reformers throw against the system? Interestingly, the focus of contention between reform advocates and opponents is the relative prominence between "basic management" and "risk response." Reformers believe that basic management – the routine verifications of taxpayer accounts to ensure accuracy, the collection of small amounts of taxes against persistently delinquent taxpayers, and so on – is a fruitless operation. The taxpayers that are unable to provide accurate basic information to tax authorities or to make timely payments tend to be fragile businesses and therefore unreliable sources of revenue in any case. The function of "basic management" should be shrunk, and both tax authority and taxpayer resources should focus on complying with and enforcing the norms of truthful reporting. Yet the opponents of reform insist that the function of "basic management" is indispensable, arguing that it is a wild dream to hope that the norms of truthful reporting would take hold. In what sense, though, is "basic management" an indispensable function for raising revenue?

The next chapter offers an answer to this question: the "basic management" function – and the system of atomistic coercion in general – may not be the most efficient approach to tax collection, but it fits into and helps sustain a political system within the state apparatus. That is, what holds the equilibrium of atomistic coercion together is the system of political incentives within the Chinese state bureaucracy. The rationality of the revenue management system cannot be judged with a view to tax compliance and revenue extraction alone. The coherence of the reformers' vision must also be reassessed in this light.

5

Organizing Revenue

Many scholars believe that China's subnational political leaders are strongly incentivized to raise tax revenue. This belief reflects not just an assumption that Chinese politicians, like politicians elsewhere, inherently aim to maximize government budgets (and thereby their power), but a more specific conjecture that China's provincial, prefectural, and county political leaders face competitions for promotion in which raising revenue, like economic growth, serves as a key metric. Since the national leaders of the CCP give great weight to raising revenue and incorporate this objective in the evaluation of provincial leaders, provincial leaders will respond, either by somehow enabling tax collection directly or by adopting similar incentives to spur their subordinates. City-level leaders are presumed to do the same with their own subordinates, and so on.

This conjecture – that raising tax revenue is a central criterion by which subnational politicians are evaluated and promoted – is consistent with much anecdotal evidence.[1] But if it is true, it is important to ask what follows. For example, is this incentive system critical in explaining the high revenue growth that China has experienced for twenty-five years – is the system of political incentives a significant *cause* of China's success in revenue collection?[2] This is a difficult empirical question: if all Chinese subnational politicians face such incentives, it would be difficult to say what *would* have happened if such incentives were removed. A different question is how the political incentives translate

[1] Systematic empirical evidence on this hypothesis is scanter. The most interesting study is Lü and Landry 2014, which finds an inverted-U-shaped correlation between per capita tax revenue collected in a prefecture and the degree of political competition in that prefecture (as proxied by the prefecture's number of counties and districts.) Lü and Landry 2014 cite prior studies that largely rely on anecdotal evidence. Many of these studies also focus on rural tax collection, which is *not* the main source of revenue growth in China. Even Lü and Landry 2014's evidence is not causally identified. Nor has it yet been corroborated by more recent empirical studies.

[2] See Figure 0.1.

into effective action: clearly, one's desire to raise revenue does not mean that one can do it. This question seems more tractable, but it has, surprisingly, not been studied in prior literature.

To identify the mechanisms linking political incentives to revenue generation, one has to bridge at least two institutional gaps. The first lies in the distinction between the state's political offices and the bureaucracy. If taxes are mainly collected by tax agencies, what levers do provincial Party Secretaries, or city mayors, or county chiefs, hold over tax administrators to meet revenue objectives? This question is important because, as I will explain in Chapter 7, subnational governments in China generally cannot design their own tax policies, and therefore cannot increase tax revenue simply by raising legal tax rates. Control over the intensity of enforcement is thus crucial. The second gap lies in the Chinese state's hierarchical structure. As we have seen, most tax administration personnel are stationed at the county level and below. How do the commands of provincial or even city political leaders manage to penetrate these bureaucratic layers, all the way down to where tax enforcement is actually carried out?

This chapter explains how political incentives for raising revenue are transmitted across the two institutional gaps just identified, and make the bureaucratic wheels turn at the lowest levels of tax administration. Unlike much existing literature, I take a perspective from *within* the bureaucracy and examine incentives at the lowest rungs of the bureaucratic hierarchy. This chapter does not speak to the question of whether strong political incentives for raising revenue caused China's success in revenue collection – such a claim would be beset by both methodological and substantive difficulties. Rather, I am interested in two other consequences of these political incentives and the bureaucratic schemes used to implement them. First, I argue that the Chinese tax administration's focus on *ex ante* interventions – especially ensuring taxpayer registration, timely return filing, and the timely payment of taxes – reflects the fact that they are types of observable outcomes that are easy to incorporate into performance metrics. That is, these interventions receive emphasis not because their execution is the most efficient way to raise revenue, but, rather, because there is an independent need within China's political system to keep the tax bureaucracy adequately managed. Second, I argue that the model of atomistic coercion in Chinese tax administration may be more consistent with the structure of political incentives than any approach that enforces the norms of truthful reporting.

National Performance Metrics

China's MOF, on behalf of the State Council and the Prime Minister, prepares budgets each year for submission to the National People's Congress for approval. Most sources of major tax revenue are reflected in the General Budget,[3] and in producing it, the MOF consults with both provinces – whose own budgets are incorporated in the national budget – and the SAT in Beijing. Both the MOF and (especially) the SAT view the collection of projected budget revenue as among their paramount objectives. They closely monitor the progress – or setback – in provincial tax collection each month.

Before going into their details, it is worth pausing for a moment to consider what revenue-related performance metrics within tax agencies implies for political actors outside the tax bureaucracy. Local politicians, to achieve their own revenue objectives, presumably need to incentivize tax agencies for tax collection. However, the vast majority of bureaucratic leaders in China's tax agencies spend their entire careers within these institutions. Their career opportunities critically depend on favorable views by tax agency superiors.[4] If tax agencies are already a part of an incentives system designed by the SAT, one can ask: Which set of incentives – those coming from local politicians or those coming from superior tax agencies (and the SAT) – matter more for tax collection? If promotion incentives are critical, then the standards set by bureaucratic superiors, not local political leaders, ought to be the most immediately relevant. It helps that local politicians do not face strong incentives *against* raising revenue, but it is far from clear that strong revenue incentives for them are necessary for tax administrators to be similarly incentivized. Incentives implemented through bureaucratic management may suffice.

If we compare the relative strengths of internal-bureaucratic and external-political preferences for maximizing revenue, a priori, it is not clear which is stronger. On the one hand, as will be seen below, the SAT

[3] As of 2020, income and expenditures from state-owned assets, as well as the nation's social insurance (SI) system, still form separate budgets from the General Budget. SI contributions by employers and employees, therefore, are not reflected on the general budget, even though they are often collected by tax agencies. In the past, many forms of government fees and charges, especially proceeds from land sales, were also excluded from the general budget. Since 2014, these items have been incorporated into the General Budget.

[4] This is especially true in the State Tax Bureau (GS) system, where the SAT directly controls personnel and appointment at provincial bureaus (which in turn controls personnel and appointment at prefecture/city bureaus). But even in the Local Tax Bureau (DS) system, satisfactory performance by the standards of SAT metrics is also likely a necessary condition for promotion.

may impose performance metrics other than meeting revenue targets, whereas local politicians may look to tax agencies mainly for revenue collection. So perhaps local politicians' single-minded focus on revenue could come across as a stronger preference. On the other hand, the opposite can also be true: many local politicians may prefer maximizing GDP growth over tax revenue. In contrast, the SAT and other bureaucratic superiors in tax administration may be indifferent to local economic growth and the welfare of local businesses, and in that sense are more focused on revenue. When the relative strengths of *bureaucratic* versus *political* preferences for particular policy outcomes are thus indeterminate, any account of policy outcomes solely by reference to politicians' incentives may be partial, even redundant. This, as mentioned in the Introduction to this book, is a major flaw with many popular social scientific stories that link promotion tournaments among Chinese subnational political leaders to specific policy outcomes. It offers a strong reason to look closely at the functioning of incentives within such specialized bureaucracies as tax administration.

By the SAT's own accounts, prior to 2000, the primary performance measure for subnational tax agencies was meeting revenue targets. In a phrase the richness of which I will later unpack, the SAT has historically described – and does so even to this day – the task of tax collection as the "organization of revenue" (*zuzhi shouru*). The SAT announced a set of performance metrics on the "organization of revenue" in 2000 that, for the first time, went beyond revenue targets.[5] In this system, the SAT would evaluate provincial tax bureaus, which would in turn evaluate their subordinate bureaus. The scheme comprised three parts: reaching annual and quarterly revenue targets; achieving a desired relationship between tax revenue and economic growth; and maintaining the quality of tax administration.

Out of 100 points, 60 pertained to the first part of absolute revenue targets. Of these 60 points, 50 were given to whether the annual revenue target was met. Any 1 percent revenue collected beyond the target would earn 2 bonus points, while each 1 percent shortfall would result in 2 points deducted. Meeting or exceeding targets every quarter would generate an additional 8 points. Failing to meet the target in any quarter would result in 0 (out of 2) points for that quarter. Finally, an absolute increase in revenue relative to the prior year would net 2 points.

[5] SAT, Trial Measures for Performance Evaluations in the Work of Organizing Revenue among State Tax Bureaus (*Guoshuifa* [2000] 39, February 28, 2020).

The annual revenue target for each province was determined by the SAT. "Significant factors" that could unexpectedly increase or decrease revenue would be considered and potentially lead to an adjustment of the target. Aside from this vaguely phrased exception, however, the revenue metrics were plain and simple. And judging from the history of their implementation, the SAT enforced the targets rigorously. For instance, in May 2003, shortly after the Chinese government brought the SARS (severe acute respiratory syndrome) outbreak under control, the SAT issued a lengthy directive urging tax agencies across the country to meet revenue targets for the year.[6] Although such work was supposed to be premised on ensuring economic recovery, no particular concession on revenue was made. A similar directive was issued in October 2008, after the onset of Global Financial Crisis: agencies across China were urged to meet revenue targets for the year despite the economic slowdown.[7]

The second part of the SAT's 2000 evaluation scheme – the relationship between revenue and the economy – accounted for a total of 10 out of 100 points. It involved two crude metrics: the ratio of revenue to GDP, and the "elasticity of tax revenue" – the ratio of revenue growth to GDP growth. For each ratio, if a jurisdiction kept it at the same level as the previous year, 5 points were earned; an increase (decrease) in the ratio of 0.1 percent would net 0.5 bonus points (deductions). Clearly, these measures also rewarded increases in tax collection.

To appreciate the strength of the SAT's revenue imperative, it is useful to consider, finally, the nonrevenue metrics introduced in 2000, which formed the third and last part of the national evaluation scheme. These related to the quality of tax administration, and accounted for 30 out of 100 points. The SAT initially introduced evaluations for the quality of tax administration (*zhengguan zhiliang kaohe*) in April 1999, two years into the tax administration reform launched in 1997.[8] Ten initial metrics were initially adopted. They are displayed in Table 5.1, along with initial targets.

The SAT acknowledged that while the majority of these metrics reflected tax administrator efforts, several (e.g. items 2, 3, and 6) measured taxpayer compliance. Although the latter were useful for understanding

[6] SAT, Notice regarding Further Strengthening Tax Administration and Succeeding in the Work of Organizing Revenue (*Guoshuifa* [2003] 55, May 15, 2003).

[7] SAT, Notice regarding Practically Strengthening Tax Administration and Succeeding in the Work of Organizing Revenue in the Fourth Quarter (*Guoshuifa* [2008] 97, October 22, 2008).

[8] SAT, Notice regarding Initiating the Evaluation of Tax Administration Quality (*Guoshuifa* [1999] 52, April 2, 1999).

Table 5.1 *Ten components of the 1999 quality-of-tax-administration index*

Nature of metric	Initial performance targets
1. Tax registration rate (i.e. out of all persons that newly obtained business licenses or otherwise ought to register, how many actually registered for tax purposes).	Firms and branches, >95 percent; sole proprietors with fixed premises, > 90 percent; others: >85 percent
2. The rate of timely return filing.	Firms and branches, >95 percent; sole proprietors with fixed premises, > 90 percent; others, >90 percent.
3. The rate of timely payment of declared tax liabilities.	Firms and branches, >95 percent; major taxpayers, >90percent; sole proprietors with fixed premises, > 98 percent; others, >95 percent; additional liabilities of inspected taxpayers: >85 percent
4. The rate at which late payment interests are collected (in terms of the number of taxpayers on whom such interests were imposed and the number of days for which such interests were tolled).	By taxpayer, 95 percent; by day: 90 percent
5. Changes in outstanding delinquencies.	at least 20 percent reduction of preexisting stock; no new delinquencies
6. Accuracy of taxpayer declarations (=ratio of declared tax liabilities to total tax ultimately determined).	70–75 percent
7. Rate at which investigations are opened into suspected noncompliance (out of all cases selected by agency databases, whistleblower reports, and referrals from other tax agencies).	85–90 percent
8. The rate at which opened cases are concluded.	>85 percent
9. The average penalty rate (= the ratio of penalties imposed to the additional tax liabilities uncovered).	>10 percent
10. The portion of decisions reversed on administrative appeal.	<30 percent

variations in compliance environments, their role in a performance evaluation system was dubious. This was only one – and likely not the most important – of the reasons why the system's implementation immediately encountered resistance. As the targets were imposed uniformly across the country, administrators from poor provinces probably resented competition with richer provinces. In just a few months, an SAT follow-up notice urged tax administrators to recognize the value of the new system, to "overcome their fears," and to refrain from "fabricating outcomes."[9] To facilitate such adaption, the SAT arranged a system of peer review, as opposed to top-down evaluation, in 1999. The standards of evaluation were also made "flexible at the beginning" – provinces were simply rated on whether they performed "satisfactorily" on each measure. Moreover, for 1999, only the first three metrics – the rates of registration, timely filing, and timely payment – would be applied.

In 2000, as it was incorporated into the overall evaluation of revenue organization, the quality-of-tax-administration index saw substantial revision.[10] Three metrics (items 7, 8, and 10) were dropped. The definitions of some remaining measures changed. And the index was converted to a score of 100 points: the rates of registration, timely filing, and timely payment each received 20 points, whereas the remaining metrics received 10 points each. Notably, the metrics determined to be the easiest to implement in 1999 also received the greatest weights. The evaluation results for provinces in 2000 were published as tables in the Tax Inspection Yearbook 2002.[11] Table 5.2 displays the points received by provincial (and select city) GS bureaus. It is telling that for the first three metrics that received 20 points each, there was less variation (as measured by the coefficient of variation) across jurisdictions than for the metrics that received only 10 points each. It shows that performance metrics can be designed to equalize, rather than to highlight differences. Gansu, one of China's poorest provinces, received the lowest overall point – 76 – but this may have sufficed as a passing grade.[12]

In 2002, the SAT stated that it would continue to publish the quality-of-tax-administration index but would no longer apply any ranking or

[9] SAT, Notice regarding Issues in the Evaluation of Tax Administration Quality and Peer Review in 1999 (*Guoshuihan* [1999] 577, August 20, 1999).

[10] SAT, Notice regarding the Issuance of "Provisional Measures on the Evaluation of Tax Administration Quality" (*Guoshuifa* [2000] 151, August 21, 2000).

[11] These include the tables used in Chapter 3 on China's registration, timely filing, and timely payment rates.

[12] The final score was divided into four ranges: excellent, good, fair, and poor.

Table 5.2 *Provincial performance outcomes on the quality-of-tax-administration, 2000*

	GS system							
Region	Total score	Registration	Filing	Payment	Accuracy	Delinquency	Interest collected	Penalties imposed
Beijing	98.36	20.00	19.00	19.40	10.00	10.00	9.95	10.00
Tianjin	83.30	19.60	18.90	19.50	9.08	0.00	6.31	10.00
Hebei	81.35	19.70	19.50	19.50	9.75	2.00	7.52	3.70
Shanxi	93.10	19.90	19.20	18.90	9.81	5.69	9.55	10.00
Inner Mongolia	95.62	17.50	19.40	19.60	9.70	10.00	9.69	9.70
Shanghai	88.78	19.00	19.40	19.60	9.65	7.50	6.66	7.00
Jiangsu	86.05	19.30	19.30	19.30	9.68	0.00	8.50	10.00
Shandong	96.80	19.10	19.20	19.40	9.81	10.00	9.34	10.00
Zhejiang	90.46	19.10	19.50	19.40	9.66	3.14	9.56	10.00
Fujian	90.72	19.50	18.40	19.10	8.76	6.75	8.29	10.00
Anhui	96.90	19.80	19.20	19.10	9.81	10.00	8.92	10.00
Jiangxi	96.41	19.90	19.30	19.60	9.81	8.74	9.00	10.00
Ningbo	90.00	19.20	19.20	19.40	9.58	4.60	8.51	10.00
Qingdao	97.50	19.50	19.40	20.00	9.86	10.00	8.66	10.00
Xiamen	92.96	19.20	17.90	19.20	9.42	10.00	9.10	9.10
Guangdong	80.37	19.30	18.30	18.80	9.84	1.97	2.69	10.00
Guangxi	82.13	19.40	18.40	17.60	9.42	0.00	7.23	10.00
Hunan	91.59	19.70	19.20	19.40	9.75	4.75	8.81	10.00
Hubei	85.92	19.80	19.40	18.50	9.30	1.00	8.06	10.00

Table 5.2 (*cont.*)

	GS system							
Region	Total score	Registration	Filing	Payment	Accuracy	Delinquency	Interest collected	Penalties imposed
Henan	95.82	19.80	17.50	19.80	9.48	10.00	9.34	10.00
Hainan	86.82	19.90	18.50	19.10	9.94	0.00	9.38	10.00
Shenzhen	92.70	18.90	18.90	19.90	9.89	5.22	9.95	10.00
Chongqing	81.82	19.10	18.90	18.90	9.68	0.00	5.31	10.00
Sichuan	83.70	19.70	18.90	19.50	9.76	5.10	8.90	1.89
Yunnan	95.09	19.90	19.50	19.90	9.49	7.33	9.35	10.00
Guizhou	89.79	19.00	18.90	19.30	9.11	10.00	3.50	10.00
Tibet	86.15	19.60	18.90	18.60	9.32	0.00	9.73	10.00
Liaoning	93.02	20.00	19.70	19.70	9.23	9.49	5.95	9.00
Jilin	87.20	19.70	19.70	19.50	9.66	0.00	8.96	10.00
Heilongjiang	94.41	19.90	19.50	19.50	9.84	10.00	9.21	6.50
Dalian	91.02	19.80	19.70	19.60	9.90	2.32	9.66	10.00
Shaanxi	95.18	19.70	19.40	19.80	9.63	6.91	9.64	10.00
Gansu	76.91	19.40	18.90	18.60	0.00	10.00	0.00	10.00
Qinghai	97.32	19.90	19.60	18.90	9.68	10.00	9.33	10.00
Xinjiang	95.11	19.70	18.80	19.50	9.85	10.00	7.74	10.00
Ningxia	87.74	19.40	19.60	19.10	9.67	0.00	9.91	10.00
Coefficient of variation	0.06	0.02	0.03	0.02	0.17	0.73	0.27	0.19

Source: China Tax Inspection Yearbook 2002

rating.[13] However, it urged provincial tax agencies to continue monitoring these metrics and attach specific incentives to outcomes.[14] In reality, because of improvements in data systems at all levels, provincial tax bureaus in recent years submit more extensive tax administration information to the SAT than they did in 2003. But in terms of explicit performance indicators that are regularly applied, most nonrevenue measures have receded in importance.

As we will see shortly, provincial tax bureaus in China design and implement much more elaborate performance evaluation schemes. The fact that the SAT itself had not sponsored extensive performance evaluations (at least not until recently[15]) can be understood in several ways. First, the reality is the SAT delegates almost all management tasks (besides promotion and overall budget and staff size) to provincial tax bureaus, even in the GS system.[16] That is, the SAT issues commands to all tax agencies in the country but is uninvolved in the implementation of any of these commands. Because it does not take responsibility for most policy outcomes, it is unsurprising that the SAT would not invest too much in performance evaluation as a management tool. Second, the SAT itself has a tiny staff of less than 800 individuals. There are very few promotional opportunities for provincial-level bureaucratic leaders to rise to national office. Thus, any SAT-designed performance evaluation scheme would not be backed up by strong promotional incentives for provincial bureaucrats.

Finally, even if the SAT cannot offer strong promotional incentives and lacks the ability to engage in extensive performance evaluations, it wields a unique political instrument: it announces many policies in the

[13] The suspension of rating was expected to reduce the incidents of falsification. The SAT also called on higher-level (i.e. provincial and city) agencies to examine the accuracy of reports from subordinate bureaus.

[14] The SAT continued to tinker with the quality-of-tax-administration index, issuing a further revised set of instructions in 2003. In this last publicized scheme, the metric of taxpayer declaration accuracy was dropped, thus reducing the index of 10 ratios to one of 6 ratios. See SAT, Notice regarding the Issuance of the Revised Measures on the Evaluation of Tax Administration Quality (*Guoshuifa* [2003] 50, August 20, 1999).

[15] In 2014, the SAT initiated a three-year, nationwide "management through performance evaluation" (*jixiao guanli*) campaign in response to a call by the Chinese Communist Party for more performance evaluation in the government bureaucracy in general. See SAT, Opinions regarding Implementing Management through Performance Evaluation (*Shuizongfa* [2013] 130, December 10, 2013). However, for many provinces, this campaign added little of substance to existing provincial performance evaluation schemes.

[16] In the DS system, appointment, budget and personnel size are determined primarily by provincial governments.

name of "law." If there is a strong law-abiding norm within the state bureaucracy, and if the SAT succeeds in reserving tax policymaking power – the power to announce general rules or "the law" – mostly to itself, then it may be able to dictate policy outcomes without performance evaluation or promotional incentives. In reality, as we have seen in Chapters 3 and 4, non-rule-based tax collection is a dominant practice in China. And, as Chapter 7 will discuss, the SAT (and the Chinese central government in general) shows little adherence to rule of law norms. However, there are endless invocations of "taxation according to law" in bureaucratic directives. Such invocations essentially serve one purpose: they express the wish on the part of the SAT – the national agency that is completely detached from actual policy implementation – to be obeyed by subordinate agencies.

Comprehensive Department Evaluations at Provincial and City Levels

Many provincial tax administrations in China engage in extensive performance evaluations (*jixiao kaoping*). Such evaluations significantly shape agency operations, and, not infrequently, even spill over into the private lives of civil servants. In the summer of 2016, I paid a one-day visit to a district tax bureau in one large Chinese city to conduct interviews. I arrived early in the morning at the bureau's office building, where my host had arranged breakfasts for me and a fellow visitor in the bureau's canteen. As we finished breakfast, we saw our host walking across the street toward the building entrance. We went up to greet her, and my fellow visitor – who had known our host for many years – complimented her for walking to work instead of driving. Our host replied: "Well, our bureau is participating in a 'healthy life' competition sponsored by the city bureau now. All of us are recording the steps we walk each day on our cellphones. This may help us with our performance rankings!"

This is just one example of the seemingly endless ways in which Chinese government agencies employ performance metrics. Thanks to government transparency efforts and the Internet, glimpses of the metrics used within many types of government agencies are available to anyone who searches online for such material. One can observe substantial variations in the evaluation schemes adopted by tax agencies, especially over time, as well as at different levels of the bureaucratic hierarchy and across regions. The challenge is to come up with a description that conveys important and generalizable patterns. To facilitate such a description, it is useful to make two distinctions at the outset.

First, both bureaucratic units and individuals can be subject to performance evaluations. Evaluations of the former type – which I refer to as "departmental evaluations" (corresponding to the Chinese term *bumen kaohe* or *zuzhi kaoping*) – measure collective outcomes, and can apply to the entire tax administration system in a prefectural city or a county, or to internal divisions of prefectural or county bureaus. Individual evaluations (*geren kaohe*), by contrast, apply to individual civil servants and normally adopt different standards according to an employee's position and rank. The two types of evaluations interact with each other: Individual evaluations of bureaucratic leaders may refer to department evaluations of the units they are in charge of; individual evaluations of rank-and-file employees, conversely, may be used by bureaucratic leaders to implement the management goals communicated through department evaluation schemes announced by higher-ups.

The second distinction is conceptual. One can think of the design of performance evaluations as communicating management priorities, and the outcomes of such evaluations as describing the degree to which management goals are achieved. Alternatively, one can view evaluation schemes as incentive devices. Thus, in addition to knowing what the evaluation criteria are, and how well bureaucratic units or individuals perform, it is important to know how the outcomes of performance evaluations matter to different actors. What is at stake in the scores or rankings they receive? To answer this latter question, one must also determine how the department and individual evaluation schemes fit into the promotion and compensation systems at tax agencies, whether for bureaucratic leaders or lower-level employees.

In practice, nearly all aspects of agency operations may be subject to performance evaluations in Chinese tax bureaus. Schemes may be adopted with respect to particular areas. For example, in 1998, the Shandong Provincial Local Tax Bureau adopted "target management" (*mubiao guanli*) separately covering internal information management, public relations, "rule of law," computerization, and other bureaucratic agendas.[17] Alternatively, different management areas may be brought

[17] Shandong Provincial Local Tax Bureau, Measures for Target Management in Information Work (*Ludishuiban* [1998] 9, March 15, 1998); Measures for Target Management in Legal Work (*Ludishuiban* [1998] 11, March15, 1998); Measures for Target Management in Computerized Taxation (*Ludishuiban* [1998] 14, March 30, 1998); and Measures for

under a comprehensive scheme. As performance evaluations became an entrenched management tool in Chinese tax agencies, the tendency has been to adopt comprehensive evaluation schemes.[18] Comprehensive evaluations across all divisions facilitate better coordination and mobilization of resources in implementing evaluations. They also allow the performance of agency leaders to be compared across management areas. Moreover, they potentially convey policy priorities through the relative weights assigned to different performance targets.

However, a notable fact about comprehensive evaluation schemes adopted by provinces and cities is that, unlike the 2000 SAT evaluation system for provincial tax bureaus, meeting revenue targets is no longer a prominent feature. For example, the evaluation scheme in Jiangsu's DS system in 2012 for assessing the performance of city-level tax bureaus involved a 1,000-point scale. The achievement of a city's revenue target earned it, remarkably, only 6 points. Even summing all metrics related to revenue targets would yield only a total of 22 points (including up to 8 that could be deducted upon any finding of revenue fabrications). The greatest weight assigned to meeting revenue targets in the Jiangsu DS system during 2012–2017 was in 2016, which only amounted to 3.5 - percent.[19] Jiangsu is by no means unique in this regard.[20] Thus, even if meeting revenue targets is a core (and unchanging) objective in Chinese tax agencies, its implementation does not seem to rely on the incentives provided by the provincial or city performance evaluation system.

Target Management in Publicity Work (dated January 1, 2000). For another example of an early use of performance evaluation within provincial tax administration, see Sichuan Provincial Local Tax Bureau, Measures for Target Evaluations in Tax Inspections (*Chuandishuihan* [1999] 335, October 10, 1999).

18 This approach has been reinforced since 2014 by the SAT's effort to promote performance evaluations. See SAT, Opinions regarding Implementing Management through Performance Evaluations (*Shuizongfa* [2013] 130, December 10, 2013).

19 As Chapter 6 discusses, this was the year in which the reform to replace the Business Tax with the VAT in China was completed. DS bureaus across the country were worried about achieving their revenue goals, given that the Business Tax was often their largest source of revenue. This may explain why the weight assigned to meeting revenue targets was higher than other years.

20 In 2007, the Hangzhou City State Tax Bureau (in Zhejiang Province) faced an evaluation scheme where meeting revenue targets was assigned 16 out of 100 points. See Notice on Allocating Responsibilities for Work Targets among Internal Divisions (*Hangguoshuiban* [2007] 392, July 19, 2007). In 2010, the Zhuhai City Local Tax Bureau (in Guangdong) assigned achieving revenue targets only 20 out of 200 points in its evaluation of its subordinate bureaus' handling of SI contribution collection. See Notice regarding the 2010 Target Evaluation Scheme for User Fee Divisions (*Zhudishuifa* [2010] 176, September 19, 2010).

Instead, performance evaluations seem to be used to convey other policy priorities. The second notable feature of Chinese tax agencies' performance evaluation schemes is that they are extensively tinkered with each year: agencies almost always face new metrics each year. The most obvious reason for this is changing management priorities announced by either the SAT or provincial bureau leaders. For example, to champion its administrative reform of "returning responsibility to taxpayers" (discussed in Chapter 4), Jiangsu's provincial bureau assigned 100 out of 600 points in its 2013 evaluation of city bureaus – by far the largest item in that year's scheme. This item disappeared by 2015. Likewise, tasks in building a new taxpayer data system received an aggregate weight of greater than 10 percent in 2013, which far exceeded what such tasks received in prior or subsequent years. New national policies are typically incorporated in subnational evaluation schemes shortly after they are announced: examples include lowering the burden of business registration and delivering tax reductions to small firms (2015), strengthening coordination between DS and GS bureaus and launching Phase III of the Gold Tax (2016), or completing VAT reform (2017).

In fact, even for the many areas of agency operations where there is no new national policy or provincial initiative, and which may receive small weights – in Jiangsu's elaborate performance evaluation system, each measured outcome could receive as little as 0.4 points out of 1,000 – new formulations for metrics may be adopted. This fact by itself suggests that the metrics have some incentive effect: otherwise, why bother changing them every year?

Comprehensive performance evaluations in Jiangsu's tax administration display several further structural features that likely characterize similar schemes in other provinces. The largest bulk of performance metrics – representing 40–55 percent of total scores – directly relate to taxpayers. They pertain to taxpayer services, processing and analyzing taxpayer data, audit-like tasks, public relations, revenue analyses, collections, and implementing specific policies such as granting tax preferences. Internal management items – representing between 20 percent and 30 percent of overall scores – usually make up the second largest group of metrics. Topics range from training and managing non-leadership staff, improving IT systems, maintaining proper accounting, promoting the rule of law, to internal supervision and monitoring – including, notably, conducting performance evaluations. A third and highly important group – aggregating to between 11 percent and 18 percent of total scores – is metrics that are political in nature or relate to the operations of the CCP within tax agencies: these include implementing anti-corruption initiatives, ideological study, training, and ideologically oriented evaluations of leaders. Finally, there is a residual category of metrics, generally changing every year, that involve implementing commands from superiors that do not fit into the first three general groups.[21]

The use of comprehensive performance evaluation in China's tax bureaucracy contrasts sharply with a portrayal, common in western social scientific scholarship on China, of how performance targets are assigned to Chinese subnational politicians by their superiors. In this common depiction, politicians and their superiors enter into individual performance contracts, which specify the key outcomes to be achieved, such as reducing pollution, preventing mining accidents, or generating a certain quantity of fixed asset investments. The politicians then proceed to secure these outcomes through all means at their disposal. The notion of private performance contracts implies a relatively small range of performance indicators, with the result that new policy priorities would immediately create incentive effects given the ease to assign them significant weight. By contrast, the vast scope of department performance evaluation schemes is impossible to duplicate in private contracts tailored for individuals. The measurements and evaluations they prescribe also must be implemented collectively, and sometimes only publicly. This is not to deny that leaders of Chinese tax agencies may also enter into private performance contracts, perhaps in parallel with collective performance evaluations. But if collective performance evaluations also matter to the individual evaluations of bureaucratic leaders, one should be cautious about the explanatory power of private performance contracts for policy outcomes.

For now, it suffices to note that departmental evaluations affect bureaucratic leaders' individual evaluations. Elements of departmental evaluations are typically carried out throughout the year, but the most important evaluation, from an incentive (as opposed to management) perspective, is made annually. An annual evaluation would typically result in a ranking of the units – for example, all city tax bureaus in a provincial evaluation, all district and county bureaus in an evaluation within a city, or all internal divisions for an evaluation carried out within a tax bureau – in terms of overall scores. It is common for departmental evaluations to

[21] Some of these superior directives have a heavy ideological tone, so metrics regarding their implementation may be regarded as political in nature as well.

choose some highest-ranked units for awards of certificates of excellence. The leaders of such winning units may also receive a monetary reward. But in the senior ranks, the amount of such reward is likely to be small relative to compensations that already come with the office. Instead, bureaucratic leaders are often themselves ranked (wholly or in significant part) on the basis of the collective performance of their units: the highest-ranked units produce the highest-ranked leaders. Such high individual rankings may bring additional monetary rewards, but, again, the one-time payments may not be large. Instead, it is the public mark of outstanding performance, which can directly enhance the leaders' promotion opportunities, that likely has the greatest value. Promotion itself would bring all types of pecuniary and nonpecuniary rewards.

This logic renders comprehensive performance evaluations in Chinese tax agencies similar to quantitative evaluations of government performance in other countries, such as the Comprehensive Performance Assessment system adopted in England for local governments.[22] The incentive effect on bureaucratic leaders is largely nonpecuniary. However, the extensive measurements of agency performance that are published – albeit internally, within a relatively large bureaucracy – do potentially provide information about leadership abilities. Such information is likely to be used in promotion decisions, and can, at least in theory, improve agency efficiency.[23]

How, then, can we reconcile the relatively light weight given to revenue targets in comprehensive performance evaluations, on the one hand, with the evidence of strong motivations to generate revenue discussed in Chapters 2–4, on the other? Two considerations are relevant. First, even when revenue targets are not prominent in performance evaluations – nor, for that matter, is any other single outcome in most comprehensive evaluations that I have examined – it does not follow that tax bureau leaders do not take such targets seriously. Rather, it is possible that meeting revenue targets is an unchanging, and therefore unspoken, priority. As long as no other management goal seriously threatens meeting revenue targets, the pursuit of such latter targets can proceed without the reinforcement of incentives provided by performance metrics applicable to upper-tier tax bureaus.

22 See Lockwood and Porcelli 2013.

23 Lockwood and Porcelli 2013 offer evidence that the English CPA system was particularly useful in generating positive outcomes in local districts characterized by weak electoral competition.

Second and more importantly, a wide range of the performance metrics adopted by provinces and cities apply to tax bureau units that do not directly engage with taxpayers. That is, they are not metrics faced by the revenue management divisions described in Chapters 3 and 4, but instead are mainly implemented by other internal divisions of "all-purpose" bureaus. This is clearly true of the categories of internal management metrics and ideologically oriented political metrics. Even for the metrics directly related to taxpayers (representing perhaps 40–55 percent of total scores), some are directly applicable only to management offices (*jiguan*). The measurable outcomes of such offices often take the form of reports providing information to superiors: a peculiar feature of many tax agency metrics is that they measure whether particular types of information are generated, at the required frequency, for review by upper management. In other cases (e.g. international taxation), the evaluation may simply be based on qualitative, and likely subjective, criteria.

A consequence of this is that the aggregate weight associated with metrics that applies to revenue management functions, and especially to functions other than taxpayer services – for example, account management, audits and examinations, and collections, which I referred to in Chapters 3 and 4 as the tasks of "basic management" – is disproportionately low relative to the personnel allocation to such functions. If, say, at least 50 percent of tax bureau employees in a city work in revenue management and tax inspection functions, the metrics corresponding to their work could be as low as 20 percent of total scores in the city's comprehensive performance evaluation. This suggests that the comprehensive department evaluations increasingly adopted in the past two decades are focused primarily on management, especially upper management, divisions. They are important only for the career opportunities for higher-ranked bureaucrats. By contrast, for the largest portion of frontline, bottom-rank tax officials, a different set of incentives dominates. In this grassroots sphere, both the observable outcomes of *ex ante* interventions discussed in Chapter 3 (e.g. taxpayer registration, timely filing, and payment) and the imperatives of raising revenue reappear as determinative goals.

Incentivizing Grassroots Tax Collectors

At the lowest ranks of the Chinese tax bureaucracy, and especially in the taxpayer-facing units in revenue management and tax inspections, monetary rewards can provide a significant incentive. The reason is that promotion is generally quite slow for employees in these units; both the pecuniary and nonpecuniary rewards of promotion materialize only infrequently. As base compensation is generally tied to rank, salaries also increase slowly. Therefore, the ability of lower-level bureaucratic leaders to arrange some forms of performance pay becomes critical.

The slowness of civil servant promotions in Chinese tax agencies is perhaps not too different from state bureaucracies elsewhere. Promotions typically are based on age, seniority, and education.[24] Each promotion also typically requires satisfactory or even outstanding performance at a given rank for three years or more. Two institutional features are slightly more distinctive of Chinese bureaucracies. First, the hierarchy is very steep. As explained in Chapter 3, it is rare for revenue managers in frontline offices – even ones with excellent performance – to rise to the position of a division chief (*kezhang*) in a city bureau, whereas such probability is significantly higher for an employee lucky enough to start in a management, as opposed to frontline, division. Second, most higher civil service ranks are associated with "leadership positions," and employees do not rotate through these positions. In the CCP political apparatus, individuals in leadership positions tend to leave only when they are promoted to a higher position, rotate to an equivalent position, or retire. Thus, promotional opportunities in the management ranks heavily depend on scarce openings in leadership positions.[25]

This is not to say that local tax agency leaders may not sometimes succeed in implementing more flexible personnel arrangements and generate greater incentives through promotion opportunities. Mr. Chen Jianpu, the DS Bureau Commissioner of Huai'an City whose book, *On a Journey*, I discussed in Chapter 4, was able to introduce an impressive scheme in his agency during the 2000s that rewarded outstanding performance with promotion. This scheme applied to all positions in the Huai'an DS system that were not subject to top-down appointments by higher-level bureaus (roughly, positions below the *kezhang* level).[26] Chen opened these positions up to competition, and designed an interesting competition system that comprised two stages. In the first, low-level employees competed for *candidacy for promotion.* To succeed in such competition, one needed to

[24] Those who have higher levels of education when entering the civil service start at higher ranks. Education or professional attainments during employment (such as becoming a Certified Public Accountant) also contribute to advancement.

[25] When raises in lower ranks are infrequent and higher-ranked positions are scarce, the use of bribery to obtain office also becomes common, not to mention cronyism.

[26] The positions of division chiefs in prefectural bureaus and (the next-rank-down) divisions in county bureaus are generally selected on a political basis by the CCP organizational apparatus. The overall quota of leadership positions is also determined by the CCP.

win votes from peers, pass oral and written tests, and face evaluations by superiors.[27] Success in this first round of competition only provided promotion eligibility for three years. To be actually promoted, an individual also had to be chosen by a bureaucratic leader at the next higher rank to form a management team. The idea was that higher-ranked leaders had incentives to make offers to capable candidates, because that would likely lead to superior team performance, which would impact the leaders' own performance evaluations. The candidates for promotion had the option to accept or decline such offers: if a leader was so unpopular that no candidate accepted his or her offer, his or her leadership position could be in jeopardy.

This system partially replaced an age- and seniority-based promotion scheme and allowed some employees in Huai'an's DS bureaus to leap through the ranks. Chen reported that upon the regime's first introduction in 2003, the average age of employees newly promoted to the *fuke* level (one rank lower than *kezhang*) was 10.5 years lower than those occupying such rank before. Between 2004 and 2011, Chen's system ensured that 92 percent of the individuals newly appointed to *fuke* positions had gone through the open competition process.[28] Further, beyond opening up promotion opportunities for the lowest ranking employees, Chen introduced some competition for mid-level management positions. Importantly, he appeared to have succeeded in introducing limited-duration contracts for such positions, with outstanding performance required for renewal.

According to Chen, the challenges of introducing promotional incentives in Chinese tax agencies are different for lower-level staff than for management personnel.[29] For frontline staff, Chen claims that administration outcomes are usually measurable, but the standard promotion system provides little upward mobility. Positive career incentives are lacking. For management personnel, by contrast, the chances of promotion are greater, but outcomes are harder to measure. Notably, negative incentives are lacking: non-performing employees will most likely keep their ranks. Thus, even if management personnel are required to enter into individual performance contracts, the effectiveness of such contracts will often depend on the availability of carrots for good performance, but not sticks for bad performance. By introducing a robust scheme for low-level staff to compete

[27] Notably, the oral and written tests were organized institutionally without personal interference from superiors or other employees, and therefore injected an objective element into the process.

[28] A similar 93 percent of the individuals newly appointed to the lower, *fugu* positions went through the competitive process. See Chen 2011 at 85.

[29] Id, at 87, 101.

for promotion, he provided significantly more positive incentives for that group, while creating, indirectly, some negative incentives for management personnel (e.g. the embarrassment of not being able to form a management team).

However, most local tax agency leaders in China are unlikely to have the political clout that Chen wielded to implement such extensive personnel reforms.[30] This means that most tax bureau leaders at the city and county levels in China face the nonoptimal personnel scheme that Chen criticizes, but lack the power to do anything about it. In such a situation, incentive schemes may be dysfunctional. A common manifestation of this dysfunction is the creation of strong negative incentives for employees at the bottom ranks – the so-called management by pressure (*yalixing tizhi*). City bureaus would issue performance targets to county/district bureaus; upper management may even insist on drafting performance contracts with lower management, claiming that the latter will be held accountable for failing to deliver. Yet the fulfillment of such contracts by lower management often relies on nothing more than transmitting the downward pressure to even lower-level units and employees. It is as though all levels of management try collectively to make the lives of their lowest subordinates truly miserable.

While such dysfunctional regimes can be found in many Chinese government agencies, there is one saving grace for frontline employees in tax agencies. Securing tax revenue is important for many low-level political leaders – especially heads of county-level governments. Such politicians are willing to provide monetary rewards to tax collectors, often even in institutionalized fashions. Consider the example of one arrangement found in a notice issued in December 2010 by the government of the Longsheng Autonomous County, in Guangxi Province. The notice was issued to the county's GS and DS bureaus, as well as its Finance Department (in charge of collecting various user fees).[31] The county government specified the respective revenue targets for the three agencies (CNY 135 million, 104.47 million, and 27.33 million, respectively) for 2010. It then provided that if the targets were met, each agency would receive "monetary rewards and fees for tax collection" of CNY 2.1 million. An additional bonus of CNY 10,000 would be paid for each additional

30 Even in Huai'an, the GS system probably enjoys less personnel flexibility than the DS system, given that personnel in the GS system is subject to approval by the SAT.

31 The People's Government of Longsheng Autonomous County of Various Ethnicities, Notice on the Rewards Used in Target Evaluations for Tax and Finance Agencies (*Longzhengfa* [2010] 34, December 3, 2010).

1 percent of the targeted amount, while a deduction of CNY 20,000 would apply for each 1 percent of revenue shortfall. This reward scheme effectively guaranteed that the collection agencies would pocket a minimum percentage (between 1.6 percent and 7.7 percent) of any revenue raised. The notice further specified that "the use of the monetary rewards and fees for tax collection" would be according to the "responsibility contract" that the agencies signed with the county government at the beginning of the year.

In cases like this, the local government pays a "fee" to county-level tax bureaus to cover "costs" in revenue collection, as a discretionary budgetary allocation. The recipient agencies would then find ways to distribute the fees (and rewards) to employees. The amount at stake can be substantial. The methods of distribution are manifold: they can take the form of office-paid vacations, banquets, and other in-kind benefits. Cash compensation can also be arranged. When I interviewed frontline tax officials in China in 2016, many expressed concerns that the anticorruption campaigns Xi Jinping started in 2014 would bring a permanent reduction to the material rewards for civil servants, precisely by shutting down most such channels of "workplace benefits." Correspondingly, the ways in which positive incentives are provided to low-rank employees also could become sharply curtailed: tax agencies would not be able to spend the bonus budget allocations offered by local governments.

There is evidence that the financial arrangements documented in the Longsheng County notice are also common elsewhere in China, even though they are generally set out in private contracts rather than published.[32] They help explain why revenue targets do not feature

[32] For some additional published examples, see Xinyang City (Henan Province) People's Government, "Decision regarding Rewards for Leading Units in Completing 2005 Revenue Targets" (*Xinzheng* [2006] 17, March 1, 2006) (announcing twenty-three monetary rewards for different tax agency units for meeting various collection targets); Fuzhou City (Fujian Province) Local Tax Bureau, Notice Regarding Key Points in 2009 Local Tax Operations (*Rongdishuifa* [2009] 2, March 11, 2009) (urging tying individual rewards and budgetary allocations to achieving revenue targets); Bengbu City (Anhui Province) People's Government, "Notice Regarding Trial Measures for Evaluating the Implementation of Comprehensive Provincial Targets for Urban Basic Pension Insurance" (*Bengzhengban* [2011] 40, June 13, 2011) (2.1 percent bonus budget allocation from city and county budgets to collection agencies for exceeding SI fee collection targets); Hebi City (Henan Province) People's Government, "Implementation Opinions regarding Strengthening Construction of Fiscal Resources and Advancing High Quality Economic Development" (*Hezheng* [2018] 19, August 14, 2018) (CNY 1 million to city tax bureau for achieving basic revenue target and up to CNY 0.5 million for exceeding target).

more prominently in top-down performance evaluations within tax agencies. Such top-down evaluations serve comprehensive management functions, and lever the promotional incentives of management personnel in tax agencies. But they may be quite ineffective in delivering incentives to grassroots employees. At the same time, tax agencies themselves may have neither the budgetary resources nor discretion in awarding compensation to such employees based on revenue. This means that, generally, top-down mechanisms within the tax bureaucracy may have limited effectiveness in incentivizing efforts at tax collection.

However, within the political branch of government, promotional incentives do trickle from the provincial level, through the prefecture and city level, and down to the county or district level. Political actors at the county level could provide horizontal, financial, and not promotion-oriented incentives to grassroots tax agencies via discretionary budgetary allocations. This explains how the following three facts can be simultaneously true:

(1) Tax agency leaders are driven primarily by promotion incentives and career opportunities within the tax bureaucracy, yet meeting revenue targets is a relatively small part of their incentives scheme;
(2) Local political leaders are driven by promotion incentives within the political branch of the state, and maintaining tax revenue growth is an important performance metric,[33] but they do not control promotions within the tax bureaucracy;
(3) Raising tax revenue, as an overriding objective for the political branch, can translate into incentives at the bottom rank of tax agencies.

This explanation is illustrated in Figure 5.1 and implies that, on average, local political leaders care more about meeting revenue targets than provincial or city-level tax agency leaders. There is much evidence consistent with this implication. A striking example is an unusual discourse within Chinese tax agencies about guarding the "quality of revenue" (*shouru zhiliang*). The quality of tax revenue is degraded when local governments fabricate tax revenue. Techniques of such fabrication include using government funds to make tax payments on behalf of existing taxpayers (*dianjiao shuikuan*), forming fake business entities (or relying on nonbusiness entities that

[33] It is likely that in the political branch, as within the tax bureaucracy, revenue generation is given greater weight in the performance evaluation of actors at the lower end of the hierarchy, whereas higher level leaders are evaluated on a comprehensive set of targets.

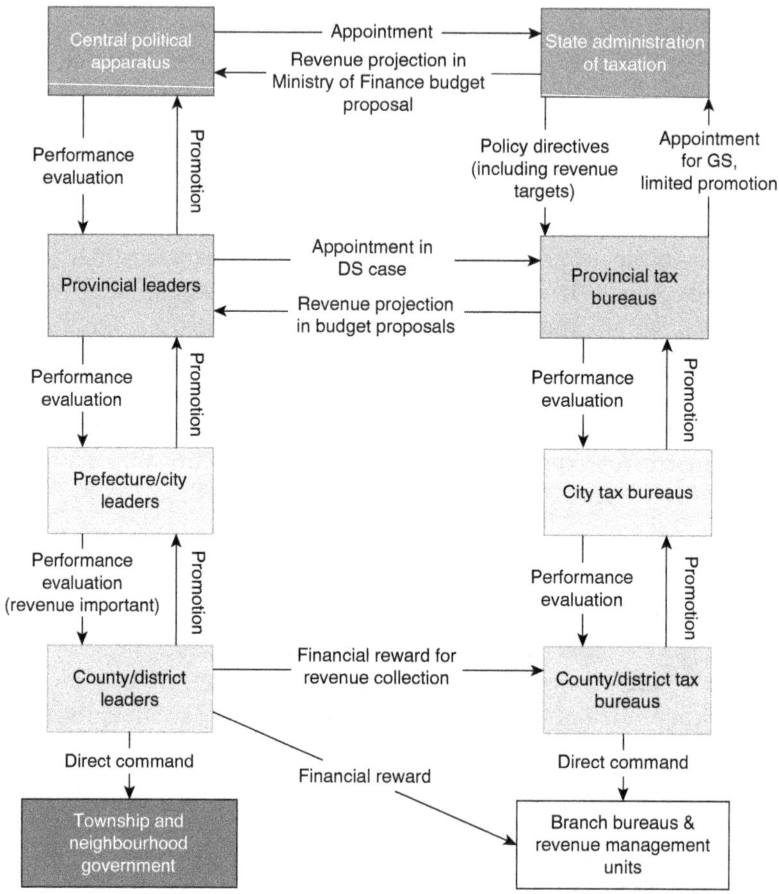

Figure 5.1 The transmission of incentives for meeting revenue targets

should be tax exempt) to remit tax to the government (*kongzhuan xushou*), and "buying" tax revenue from businesses outside one's jurisdiction by issuing tax payment certificates at a heavy discount.[34] The idea common to all such techniques is to secretly and illegitimately channel local government funds from other accounts into the tax revenue account. As recently as 2015, the SAT urged local tax agencies to monitor "abnormal tax payment" by taxpayers, and to decline accepting funds when the payment is not

[34] The last practice was reported to be so popular in the 1990s and early 2000s that it became an unspoken collective understanding among county-level officials across the country. The mechanics of such illicit activities are laid out in a book-length journalistic investigation (Tian and Zhao 2008).

genuinely due.[35] In cases where local governments improperly intervene in tax collection, the SAT suggested that tax agencies should "work on communicating and explaining [proper policies], in order to gain understanding and support" from local political leaders. In the meantime, they should "report such problems to superior tax agencies."

The need for fabricating revenue for local political leaders generally arises because revenue targets are set too high in their performance evaluations. Although this tends to happen more often in poor counties where the tax bases are perennially inadequate, it is also not uncommon even in more prosperous regions.[36] Interestingly, from the local governments' perspective, the main drawback with adulterations of revenue is that the practice is unsustainable: revenue targets are generally set by reference to revenue receipts in prior years (usually adjusted by a projected increase), thus meeting an unrealistic target through fabrication in one year generally results in the need to continue such fabrication in the next year.[37] Remarkably, the incentive to fabricate revenue is often taken as a given, problematic not so much in itself as because of its consequences. Thus, some cities in China implement performance contracts with lower-level governments to guarantee the quality of revenue,[38] while others give out rewards to government units for meeting standards in the quality of revenue.[39]

The fabrication of revenue also appears to be more prevalent for nontax revenue: making up revenue by moving government funds from one account to another is easier without having to go through tax agencies as gatekeepers. Thus, when local governments themselves express the resolve to improve the quality of revenue, they generally

35 SAT, "Notice regarding Further Normalizing Order in Tax Collection and Improving the Quality of Tax Revenue" (*Shuizonghan* [2015] 79, February 5, 2015).

36 See, for example, Guangzhou People's Government, Forwarded Notice from the Provincial Government Regarding Further Strengthening the Collection of Non-Tax Revenue and Improving the Quality of Non-Tax Revenue (*Huifu* [2006] 28, July 27, 2006).

37 This problem is explicitly discussed in Maoming City (Guangdong Province) People's Government Office, "Opinions regarding Improving the Quality of the City's Fiscal Revenue' (*Maofuban* [2010] 48, October 12, 2010).

38 See, for example, Pingxiang City (Jiangxi Province) People's Government, "Notice regarding Strictly Following the Law in Taxation and Improving the Quality of Local Tax Revenue" (*Fupingzi* [2005] 15, May 16, 2005).

39 Jiangxi Provincial Department of Finance, "Notice regarding Implementing Rewards and Subsidies for Maintaining the Quality of Fiscal Revenue in Counties, Cities and Districts" (*Caiyu* [2013] 54, September 9, 2013).

emphasize increasing the share of tax revenue in total revenue.[40] Assuming that the incentives to fabricate revenue remain the same, however, this merely increases the pressure to guard the "quality" of tax revenue.

The logic of Figure 5.1 also implies that in incentivizing frontline tax collectors, higher-level tax agencies and the lowest tiers of governments need to coordinate. Rather precise evidence for this can be found in Jiangsu's tax administration reform, which I discussed in Chapter 4. The ambitious reorganizations of tax administration carried out in Jiangsu between 2012 and 2015 involved separating taxpayer service from other revenue management functions, reducing contact with taxpayers, and formalizing audit functions. The provincial reformers foresaw the risk that this would disrupt the normal channels of communication between the lowest tiers of governments and revenue management units. Such channels of communication were previously quite direct. As captured in the illustration of the traditional paradigm of atomistic coercion in Figure 3.1, local politicians directly monitor revenue targets through communication with the grassroots revenue management units in tax agencies (and perhaps promptly make up for shortfalls with fabricated revenue). After the reform, how to keep such communication open was left unresolved (see Figure 4.1).

The solution that Jiangsu's tax agency leaders proposed was to organize new channels of communication. Heads of county- or district -level tax bureaus would reach out to political leaders in township (rural) or neighborhood (urban) governments, whereas heads of city-level tax bureaus would communicate with political leaders in county (rural) or district (urban) governments. Through such new communication channels, the tax bureaus could push through agency reorganization without undermining local politicians' revenue expectations. What is exquisitely informative is the matching of hierarchies. County and district bureau chiefs supervise the lowest revenue management units, and such latter units normally respond to the lowest-ranked politicians, below the county level. City bureaus supervise the next-lowest revenue management units usually at the county level, which respond to the next-lowest-ranked politicians also at the county level. This makes it explicit that

[40] Heze City (Shandong Province) People's Government, "Notice regarding Improving the Quality of Fiscal Revenue and Preventing Fake Fiscal Revenue" (*Hezhengzi* [2009] 20, April 14, 2009).

revenue managers at the bottom tier of the tax bureaucracy respond to two sets of government actors: tax agency superiors and bottom-tier actors in the political branch of the state.

The Political Determinants of Tax Administration

While replacing the direct links between local politicians and revenue management units with new channels of communication, Jiangsu's reformers still acknowledged the status quo: the most powerful incentives for realizing revenue targets are found at the bottom layer of the state. There is one precondition for this grassroots incentive scheme to work: the frontline tax collectors who are financially rewarded for meeting revenue targets must be able to deliver the goods. What makes it possible for them to locate "good-quality" tax revenue on demand? What is the enforcement capacity that generates results in this core aspect of the state's tax effort?

The answer, I believe, lies in the mode of enforcement that Chapter 3 described as atomistic coercion. In traditional-style revenue management, revenue managers have extensive contact with, and have relatively close observations of, taxpayers. Moreover, revenue managers enjoy a tremendous amount of discretion, in two senses. First, they can vary the weights given to different administrative tasks and enforcement tools: for the taxpayers assigned to them, they handle a large range of tasks ranging from registration, monitoring return filing and payment, and collections, to taxpayer services. They thus enjoy freedom to choose the most effective means for extracting revenue: for example, not imposing penalties may be more effective than doing so. Second, they exercise discretion on how much taxpayers pay, in the sense that tax payments are not exclusively or even primarily tied to taxpayers' truthful reporting on tax returns. Instead, revenue managers can communicate expectations for payment based on general observations of taxpayers, while neglecting the accuracy of particular tax return entries. By tolerating both literal and substantive noncompliance on a routine basis, revenue managers thus always reserve the capacity to extract additional revenue. Indeed, this capacity seems to be proven by the popular practice of mandatory taxpayer self-inspections (discussed in Chapter 2), and by the success of self-audits in Jiangsu's formalized audit system (analyzed in Chapter 4).

One should not overstate the capacity of close observations of taxpayers and tolerance for routine noncompliance to generate a "strategic reserve" of revenue. There are certainly many cases in which revenue targets are set too far above the local tax base for discretionary extraction to make up the difference. Otherwise, we would not see so many instances of local governments fabricating revenue. Even within tax administration, higher-level agency leaders regularly denounce (though they rarely truly discipline) the over-collection of tax revenue through techniques such as requiring taxpayers to pre-pay tax that is not due until later periods. These "illegal" techniques would not be necessary if current year tax liabilities are sufficiently elastic to revenue managers' discretion. However, atomistic coercion may generate just enough such elasticity for financial incentives offered by the lowest-ranked politicians to be worthwhile.

Indeed, a cynical perspective would be that the lowest ranks of the Chinese tax bureaucracy have strong incentives to preserve the discretion inherent in atomistic coercion. Such discretion allows tax collectors not only to extract bribes from taxpayers but also to extract surplus from local political leaders.[41] This would help explain why in places like Jiangsu, many revenue managers and low-level bureau leaders strongly resisted reform that emphasized centralized information and formalized audits. In Jiangsu, the quintessential debate between proponents and opponents of the tax administration reform was the appropriate personnel allocations between "basic management" and "intermediate risk response." Reform proponents claimed that while "intermediate risk response" was necessary to modernize Chinese tax administration, "basic management" tasks such as annual manual verifications of taxpayer accounts imposed unnecessary burdens on the tax agency workforce. Reform opponents argued that, to the contrary, "basic management" was essential to securing revenue targets. This latter argument of reform opponents is hard to counter, for two reasons. First, it comes from the employees who actually collect the revenue. Second, under the regime of atomistic coercion, the higher-ups are uninformed as to what it takes to secure revenue targets from one period to the next. How bargains are struck with taxpayers is a black box; one can only incentivize the negotiators.

The discretion inherent in atomistic coercion helps us to grasp the rich meaning of the phrase "organizing revenue," widely used by Chinese tax administrators to describe their mission. When I first encountered this phrase, I was struck by its connotation that tax is not simply remitted by

[41] Higher-level tax bureaucrats may be seen as complicit in such latter extortion.

taxpayers – nor is it even just collected by tax administrators. It is instead "organized": the state's intake of revenue is both proactive and deliberate. But there is another subtlety in the term. "Organizing revenue" was used historically by China's government to refer to any way in which the socialist state generated revenue in its operations. Production in state-owned enterprises, the collection of user fees by government offices (e.g. notaries and business registration), and prices charged by government-owned nonbusiness units (e.g. research labs) were all regarded as ways to "organize revenue." Consequently, tax bureaus were not the only or, prior to the late 1980s, even the main government agencies engaged in organizing revenue. The phrase emphasizes the perspective of the state's budget, and elevates the budgetary goals of the state above the means by which they are achieved.

It is possible that, in the 1980s, when Chinese tax agencies were young and just beginning to assume a greater role, "organizing revenue" was a way to emphasize their own importance to other agencies: it was a kind of grandiose talk, using big words to glorify the mundane task of tax collection. Interestingly, as China's tax system grew and the centrality of taxation became indisputable, "organizing revenue" has remained an appealing slogan. This may be because it is particularly appropriate for mobilizing civil servants at the lowest bureaucratic ranks: it extols their role in the state by invoking the paramount political objective of raising revenue. Ironically, it is also a fitting signal for the political importance of their task, given the material rewards political actors are willing to give for it.

Revenue managers, of course, pursue more than just the revenue objective (associated with a pompous slogan and hidden material rewards). Instead, within tax agencies, they are subject to their own performance metrics – similar to the SAT's 1999 quality of tax administration index discussed in the first section of this chapter, but much more extensive and detailed today. In Chapter 3 (Table 3.1), we saw that Chinese taxpayers display extraordinarily high levels of tax registration, timely return filing, and timely payment; I could have provided statistics on many other outcomes, such as delinquency management, prompt taxpayer service, and surveys of taxpayer satisfaction, on which Chinese tax agencies appear to excel. All these are outcomes that revenue management units are evaluated on. Constant efforts are needed to keep them at their high levels year after year. Like the provincial and city evaluation schemes discussed earlier, metrics tailored for revenue management units are used to monitor achievements among the lowest work units (e.g. branch bureaus), although the rewards for high achievement are scant.[42]

While the revenue objective may seem natural from the government's perspective, the rationality of setting high targets for these other administrative outcomes may seem less apparent. We saw in Chapter 3 that a high level of taxpayer registration in China is also associated with a high level of zero-reporting. If a substantial proportion of taxpayers fail to provide a single item of financial information on their tax returns, it is also not surprising that their contributions to revenue often prove negligible. Why did the Chinese government decide to expend resources to bring so many small firms into the tax net? Why register so many firms when most of their transactions remain informal? These questions were raised at the end of Chapters 3 and 4. One answer can now be considered that synthesizes several findings from this and earlier chapters.

Recall from Chapter 1 that the nationwide tax administration reform launched in 1997 already met with sharp internal criticism in the early 2000s, before it was abandoned in the mid-2000s. The criticism accused the design of the 1997 reform as over-relying on taxpayer self-compliance, and as leading to "the neglect of management and the weakening of accountability." The concern about the "weakening of accountability" may be understood in terms of a particular human resource problem in the late 1990s. On the one hand, administration reform centralized many tax collection tasks, especially payments and the filing of tax returns. Therefore, the number of outpost offices was reduced, and grassroots staff became concentrated in branch bureaus. On the other hand, overall government personnel reform led to cuts in the personnel size of provincial bureaus (and some city bureaus); it was becoming clear that the tax administration workforce, already getting older (especially in the GS system), would forever be kept at below-county ranks. While the type of door-to-door tax collection of the 1980s was certainly a thing of the past, the future of the tax administration workforce, especially in light of further introductions of information technology, was uncertain.

[42] When divisions within a low-level bureau – for example, a county bureau or a city-level bureau with no subordinate bureaus – are evaluated, different metrics are applied to different divisions depending on the functions they perform. Consequently, it is harder to rank units on the basis of the same metrics – to compare revenue management units, for example, with an IT/data division or the bureau's general office. Revenue managers sometimes complain that they are disadvantaged in any ranking, because their tasks are more complex and challenging.

The logic of the critics of the 1997 tax administration reform was that the more tax administrators "manage" taxpayers, the more tax administrators would also become "accountable." That is, by expanding the range of tax administrators' *ex ante* interventions in tax compliance, there would also be a wider range of measurable outcomes to evaluate individual and collective performance with. Such evaluations would give personnel management a semblance of objectivity and meritocracy, and support instruments of discipline. They would also stake out norms and expectations – all businesses should be registered, all taxpayer accounts should be annually verified, all tax returns should be timely filed, and so forth – that sustain a sense of mission, and therefore morale, among the rank and file.

One can see how this solution to the personnel problem might have led to the literally impossible job description for the revenue manager reviewed at the beginning of Chapter 3. The impossibility of carrying out all of the listed tasks of a revenue manager implies substantial discretion in their execution. The fact that some of the outcomes are measurable (and routinely measured) also provides a solution to the multitasking problem: revenue managers can simply aim to do well on the measured outcomes while neglecting others. But the real "advantage" of the revenue management system is that the vast discretion enjoyed by revenue managers renders tax revenue elastic to tax efforts. This elasticity is highly valued by local politicians chasing revenue targets, which stabilizes an arrangement that, from many other perspectives, may seem irrational.

Obviously, in this explanation, two institutions are completely exogenous to the design of tax policy. The first is a political hierarchy in which the lowest-level politicians are most motivated to meet revenue targets – such targets are not just budgetary abstractions but actually affect career outcomes. The other is a bureaucratic hierarchy where most employees, by historical accident, are situated at grassroots units. The design of revenue management serves the political needs of the former institution and the management needs of the latter. Even if the revenue management system subverts the logic of self-assessment inherent in the modern taxes China transplanted in the 1990s, it can survive and even thrive, generating a compliance landscape the extraordinary features of which have only been surveyed in part in the chapters so far.

6

Policy Making without Information

Despite the enormity and vital world importance of the Chinese economy, the study of Chinese tax policy is still in its infancy.[1] This chapter advances a perspective on the subject that aims to shed light on its theoretical complexity. I start with an idea familiar to scholars in tax and development, namely that tax administration capacity is a critical determinant of tax policy choices. On the surface, China's tax structure bears much resemblance to those found in other low- or middle-income countries. This makes it tempting to explain Chinese tax policy in terms of certain structural features of the Chinese economy that, in other countries, have also led to widespread noncompliance, narrow tax bases, and high tax rates. This amounts to what the political economists Tim Besley and Torsten Persson call the "standard economic view" of fiscal capacity.[2]

However, a critical takeaway from this book's previous chapters is that tax capacity is determined not by economic structure alone, but is highly dependent on other political institutions and historical factors. For instance, the fact that China rapidly built up a tax apparatus to collect revenue from state-owned enterprises in the 1980s, before abandoning its planned economy and adopting a modern tax system (Chapter 1), is

[1] There are many possible explanations. To begin, tax policy is technical: features that specialists see as fundamental in tax systems can easily elude the attention or memory of non-specialists because of their opaque logic and interactions. Further, economists studying Chinese tax policy must navigate through conflicting scholarly and policy discourses. Among empirically oriented scholars, many feel compelled to demonstrate general relevance or "external validity" for their findings and therefore deemphasize what may be perceived as unique to the Chinese context. Meanwhile, as illustrated by narratives in this chapter and the next, the logic of policy discourses inside China can be highly unusual by international standards. Another potentially critical fact is that, although tax policy making can be extremely political, there is a shortage of widely accepted theories of the politics of taxation regarding either democracies or authoritarian regimes. As Western social scientific interest in China has historically focused on the political, interest in Chinese taxation is predictably subdued when there are no obvious takeaways regarding tax policy's implications for Chinese politics.

[2] See Besley and Persson 2013. I discuss their view at length in Chapter 8.

already striking. It suggests that the tasks of managing and motivating an army of grassroots tax collectors in low-ranked offices have unique historical roots. These tasks must also be coordinated within an evolving personnel system sustaining China's Party state (Chapter 5). The government's decisions first to adopt a set of modern taxes but, subsequently, to systematically abandon the approach of taxpayer self-assessment commonly associated with such taxes (Chapter 1), are both unusual and unexpected. These and other facts presented earlier support the theory that political institutions also determine fiscal capacity.[3]

This chapter explores a particular extension of this last view: not only might politically determined tax administrative capacity influence economic outcomes, it could also shape the policymaking process – the politics of tax policy – itself. That is, the relation between tax administration and tax policy is highly endogenous: policy decisions directly affect the structure of tax administration, which in turn determine how policy decisions are made.[4] Specifically, I explain how politically determined tax administration shapes the state's capacity to gather information, which in turn becomes an important factor for both specific tax policy decisions and overall policy stability. Limits on the state's ability to gather information both constrain policy and are the products of policy: they are *endogenous information bottlenecks.*

I first illustrate this idea through two taxes that tend to be the most important and most politically salient in developed economies – the personal income tax (PIT) and mandatory employment-based social insurance (SI) – but which have remained insecure in China even after decades of development. I then turn to the seemingly less political sphere of business taxation that the Chinese government has most extensively relied on. I argue that the structures of relentless delegation and governance through atomistic coercion discussed in the preceding chapters – all of which have political origins – generate subtle yet pervasive information constraints. These constraints imply that policy makers rarely apply efficiency considerations even in the context of business taxation. The resulting policy instability gives fodder to further politics.

[3] A tax administration approach that secures high firm formality even while tolerating high transactional informality (Chapter 3) is also not readily anticipated in the tax and development literature.

[4] This can be viewed as a variant of what Besley and Persson call the "extended approach" to analyzing political institutions' relation to tax systems, which they allude to but do not elaborate (Besley and Persson 2013, 55–56).

Dismantling the Personal Income Tax

The PIT plays a minor role in China's tax system: its revenue pales not only against revenues from taxes on goods and services and the corporate income tax (CIT), but even in comparison with SI contributions – which can be seen as simply another set of taxes on wage income (Figure 6.1). By contrast, among OECD countries, the PIT generated 23.5 percent of tax revenue in 2016 on average.[5] Yet, at the same time, the PIT plays an outsized role in the imagination of China's affluent urban class: the rich in China talk about the PIT as though they live in a country where the PIT matters. Unfortunately, these two facts are not unrelated: the opposition to the PIT by China's rich has been breathtakingly successful in undermining the tax during the past decade.

The PIT is typically a minor source of government revenue in developing countries.[6] There are two standard explanations for this. First, since its initial adoption in industrialized countries in the early twentieth century, the PIT has tended to generate most of its revenue from the taxation of wages, that is, from employers' withholding of the tax from

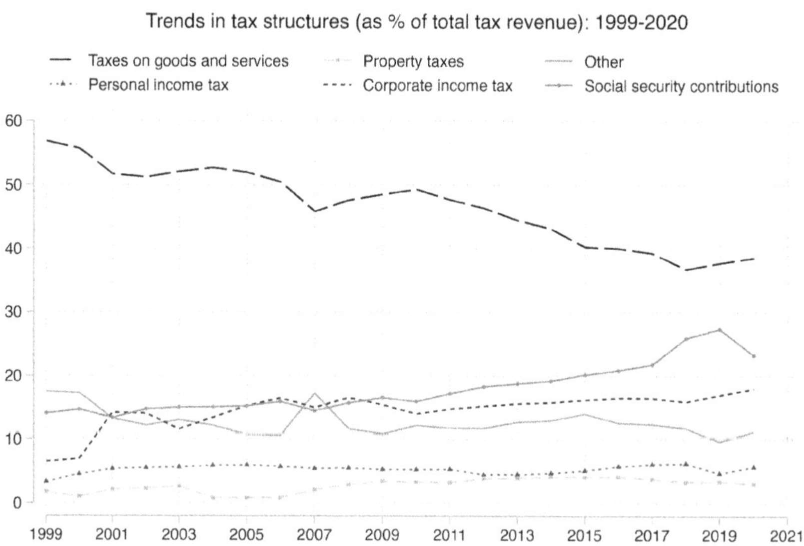

Figure 6.1 The changing composition of tax revenue in China, 1999–2020

[5] In countries like the United States and Canada, this portion can reach above 40 percent. See OECD 2020 for a recent overview of the evolution of tax structures in OECD countries.

[6] See Bird and Zolt 2005.

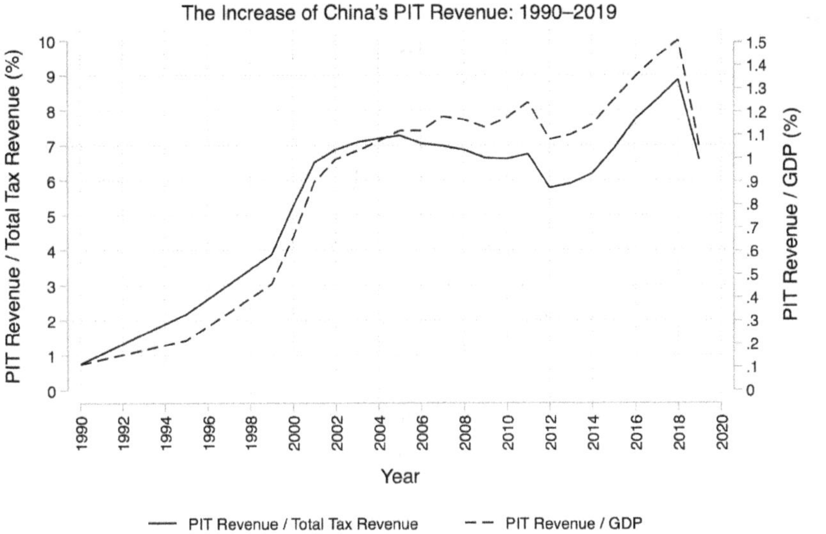

Figure 6.2 Trend in PIT revenue relative to total tax revenue and GDP

paychecks written to employees. In many developing countries, the formal employment sector is small, and therefore the wages of formally employed workers yield a relatively small tax base. Moreover, perhaps because of their lack of capacity in making social transfers to the poor, poorer countries tend to set their PIT exemptions high relative to the income distribution so that a greater portion of the population is exempt from the PIT.[7] Second, notwithstanding the possibility of a "flat tax," it is often believed that the PIT must possess certain features – for example, progressive tax rates, certain types of deductions, and so forth – that make the tax administratively complex.[8] Thus, low administrative capacities in developing countries further handicap revenue-raising through the PIT.

These standard explanations, however, are largely irrelevant for developments in China's PIT in the past twenty-five years. As Figure 6.2 illustrates, China's PIT revenue rapidly rose between 1994 and 2005 as percentages of total tax revenue, from 2 percent to over 7 percent. In a study completed in 2006, Thomas Piketty and Nancy Qian predicted that the PIT would become a "mass tax" in China, which would have major implications for the evolution of the country's

[7] As countries get richer, the proportion of the population exempt from the PIT also tends to decrease. See Jensen 2019.

[8] See the United States Treasury 2003; Keen, Kim, and Varsano 2006.

income inequality.[9] Yet this prediction turned out to be wrong: China's PIT languished after 2006, at around 6 percent of total tax revenue and 1 percent of GDP. The trend since 2006 clearly bears no relationship to the rising income of the Chinese people or the maturity of Chinese tax administration. Instead, China's PIT began to follow a trajectory that Piketty and Qian had found for the PIT in India: it seems doomed to remain an "elite tax."

Tax lawyers and accountants can attest to the fact that at least before 2018, the Chinese PIT was not unduly complex. While wage and business incomes are taxed at progressive rates, capital income is taxed at lower flat rates, implementing the type of "dual income tax" standardly recommended by international organizations.[10] Even for business and self-employment income, simplified rules are extensively adopted.[11] The administrability of the tax is further strengthened by extensive reliance on third-party withholding rather than individual self-declarations.[12] Certain aspects of tax enforcement have also steadily improved in recent years. For example, a 20 percent PIT on capital gains realized by owners of private companies on the sale of their company shares represents a rapidly increasing source of PIT revenue due to better monitoring of such transactions.

The primary factor that explains the stagnant revenue contribution of the Chinese PIT since 2006 is the changing amount of monthly wage income that is exempt from the tax.[13] In taxing wage income, the Chinese PIT imposes a progressive rate structure on monthly wage income above an exemption threshold. Between 1994 and 2006, this threshold was set at CNY 800. As urban wage income grew, more and more employees began to be subject to PIT withholding. Even so, the average PIT rate on wage income faced by urban households only increased from 1.1 percent to 3.1 percent from 1997 to 2005.[14] In comparison, the general VAT rate was 17 percent throughout this period and most consumer services were subject to Business Tax at 5 percent. Taxes on consumer expenditures thus bore much, much more heavily on the purchasing power of Chinese taxpayers than the PIT.

Nonetheless, the NPC raised the PIT exemption threshold for wages to CNY 1,600 in 2006, and just one year later, to CNY 2,000. The result was

[9] Piketty and Qian 2009.

[10] See Cui 2006; Bird and Zolt 2011.

[11] Cui 2007b.

[12] Cui 2007a.

[13] The State Council also eliminated the PIT on bank deposit interest in 2008, which in 2007 had contributed 16 percent of total PIT revenue.

[14] Ma, Xu, and Li 2015 at 494 (Table 2).

that the lowest six deciles of wage earners in urban China paid nearly no PIT in 2008.[15] Notably, because the urban population was only 45 percent of China's total population in 2007 but by far the richer, urban households already represented the richer half of Chinese people. Any further increase of the monthly exemption threshold would only benefit the richest 18 percent of Chinese individuals.

But that was exactly what the government chose to do. In 2011, Premier Wen Jiabao requested the NPC to raise the monthly exemption amount to CNY 3,500: within just five years, the exemption level increased by 337 percent. The Ministry of Finance estimated at the time that this reduced the number of PIT taxpayers from 28 percent of urban wage earners to 12 percent.[16] Moreover, the 2011 PIT change broadened rate brackets, such that even in 2013, less than 3 percent of urban wage earners faced marginal tax rates higher than 20 percent, and a vanishing portion faced marginal rates higher than 25 percent.

The 2011 legislative change to the PIT was devastating to PIT administration in China. Many cities lost almost all of their PIT revenue from wages. One city where I recently conducted research ranked in the top third decile of Chinese cities in per capita GDP terms in 2017 (its GDP per capita level was 117 percent of China's national average). In that year, 86.1 percent out of all returns filed by wage withholding agents (i.e. employers) reported zero PIT remittable. In terms of individual wage earners reported on these withholding returns, only 36.4 percent had a positive PIT liability. This was after urban average wages increased 80 percent from 2011 to 2017! Because the PIT generates so little revenue, most local tax agencies cannot afford to invest in auditing individual taxpayers and compiling databases about them. Therefore, even the government itself has little information about individuals' income.

[15] Cui 2008. Zhan, Li, and Xu 2019 showed that in 2007, the median individual wage income in an urban household lay below the CNY 19,200 amount that corresponded to the CNY 1,600 monthly exemption applicable that year. Xu, Ma, and Li 2013 calculate that in 2008, the lowest six deciles of urban earners of income contributed 5.4 percent of total PIT revenue – as compared with 4.4 percent in 1997 and 11.5 percent in 2005. Their calculation includes PIT revenue on all sources of income (e.g. sole proprietor business income, interests, etc.) and not just wages, and suggests that all of the PIT revenue gains from increasing urban wages before 2008 were wiped out by the lifting of the exemption threshold that year to CNY 2,000.

[16] Research carried out by independent scholars using the urban household survey confirmed that even in 2013, the median wage income was clearly below CNY 42,000 – the annual amount exempted under the 2011 PIT change. Zhan, Li, and Xu 2019.

In 2018, the Chinese government took this information-destroying tax policy further, and raised the monthly exemption again to CNY 5,000, corresponding to an annual amount of CNY 60,000. Only two provincial jurisdictions, Beijing and Shanghai, had average individual income above that level in that year. The 2018 PIT legislation also moved further up the rate brackets, so that one needed to earn CNY 204,000 a year (USD 32,380) to face even a 20 percent marginal tax rate. Moreover, on top of the generous exemptions and wide rate brackets, the 2018 PIT legislation introduced "additional special deductions" for high-income households, such as the mortgage interest expense and children's education deductions. This means that rich Chinese families can send children to study abroad and claim a PIT deduction for a portion of the expense. Researchers have calculated that these special deductions may further remove 5 percent of the urban wage-earning population from the PIT tax base.[17]

In summary, since 2008, China has steadily cut the PIT for the highest 10 percent or 5 percent of wage earners in the country. Contrary to observations from cross-country studies and studies of countries with long histories of PIT, China's exemption from the PIT moved *up* – as opposed to down – the income distribution as China got richer in the past two decades. This has led to a dramatic reduction in the redistributive effect of the Chinese PIT.[18]

The government's repeated undercutting of the PIT since 2006 went against the preferences of bureaucrats in the Ministry of Finance and the State Administration of Taxation. *How* the rich in China have been so successful in persuading the decision-makers in China's State Council to enact the tax cuts is a puzzle.[19] One might speculate that two factors are likely relevant. First, the regions that benefit most from the tax cuts are the rich cities hosting the highest wage earners – Shenzhen, Shanghai, Beijing, and so forth. These cities have engaged in tax competition for many years

[17] Id.

[18] That effect was already very small to begin with. By one calculation (Zhan, Li, and Xu 2019), the Chinese PIT had the most redistributive impact in its history in 2018, prior to the PIT change that year: the PIT reduced the income Gini coefficient in China by about 1.9 percent. This is far smaller compared to advanced economies: Canada's PIT, for example, reduces the Gini coefficient by about 4 percent. However, had the Chinese PIT been left intact, an increasing portion of the high urban wage earners would have become subject to the PIT, which would have increased the amount of redistribution in the entire population. The 2018 (and earlier) tax cuts trounced this expectation. Zhan, Li, and Xu 2019 project that the 2018 legislation sets back the PIT enough that its redistributive effect will not recover to 2017 levels even by 2025.

[19] Most scholars of public finance in China either offered faint praise for the tax cuts or remained silent, perhaps to avoid public derision for asserting that the PIT should remain higher.

by handing (borderline illegal) PIT tax breaks to bankers and entrepreneurs.[20] They have also continuously sponsored a media misinformation campaign claiming that the low PIT rates in Hong Kong and Singapore are the international norm, and that China needs to cut its top marginal tax rates to be "internationally competitive." One might thus conjecture that the State Council has been particularly influenced by these regions in making tax policy. Second, the Chinese government has tolerated public attacks on the PIT, as though complaints about taxation represent one subject where public dissent is permitted. The PIT thus appears to be a preferred way for China's political leadership to cut deals with the country's economic elite.

Whatever one thinks of these speculations, one consequence seems clear: the Chinese PIT has been, and may remain for the foreseeable future, an invisible subject for both academic and policy purposes. By wiping out tax agencies' incentives to invest in collecting information about individual income, China's PIT policy has made it easy for media catering to the urban affluent to obfuscate basic facts about the distribution of income in China, such as who is rich enough to be subject to tax. A priori, one might think that income inequality in China is just as important a topic as income inequality in the United States, yet the subject has become impossible to study using the prevalent tax-returns-based methodologies deployed in the United States and other Western countries. Researchers studying income inequality in China thus can only rely on infrequent, government-organized household surveys.[21] The dismantling of the PIT deprived researchers of critical tools for studying the tax – and, perhaps simultaneously, helped to conceal this very act of dismantling.

Whither Social Insurance?

Figure 6.1 shows that employer and individual SI contributions have rapidly gained prominence in China's tax structure since the mid-2000s.

[20] Cui 2011b.

[21] Piketty, Yang, and Zucman 2019 use national and provincial reports (during 2006–2015) of the total number of individuals required to file annual PIT returns (i.e. those with annual income greater than CNY 120,000, see Cui 2007a) in analyzing recent income inequality in China. This very limited tax data already allows the authors to conclude that urban household surveys underestimate top income. But even the information reported on the annual PIT returns is likely to be highly inaccurate, as there is little auditing of such returns in light of the limited contribution of PIT to total revenue. In the middle-income city I described a few paragraphs back, annual return filers declared PIT liabilities that represented only 1.13 percent of the city's total PIT revenue in 2017.

They are now the second largest source of government revenue after taxes on goods and services, ahead of even the CIT. SI contributions also represent almost six times the amount of China's PIT revenue.[22] But like the PIT, China's SI regime remains unpredictable in its development, and the government's capacity in sustaining it is frequently questioned. The reasons for such unpredictability and challenge again have more to do with politics than economics.

A few policy details must be set out before I explain the politics of SI. The two largest components of SI in terms of taxpayer contributions are urban employment-based pension insurance and health insurance.[23] These are followed by the smaller unemployment and workplace injury insurance schemes.[24] From its inception, redistribution was a central purpose of Chinese pension and health insurance. In the mid- to late-1990s, as China transitioned from a planned economy to a market economy, many workers at state-owned enterprises were laid off and faced grim prospects in the private sector. Establishing a publicly-sponsored pension and health insurance system was thus critical for the welfare (even livelihood) of this vast population. In response, China adopted a "pay-as-you-go" system in which younger generations of workers would help meet the retirement needs of workers who had earned low wages in the planned economy but who must now live the rest of their lives in a market economy.[25] This redistributive design dominated two other conventional purposes of SI: the need to implement compulsory saving for the nation – private saving rates in China have remained relatively high – and health risk pooling.[26]

This initial redistributive design substantially explains the high tax rates and narrow tax base initially chosen for China's SI regime. SI funding

22 This tax revenue composition is observed not only at the aggregate level but also at the firm level: as documented using firm-level data in Chen et al. 2020a (for the period 2007–2011) and Cui, Hicks and Norton 2020b (for 2016), SI contributions represent the second largest category of remittance that businesses make to the government, after the VAT and other taxes on goods and services.

23 See Fang and Feng 2018. In recent years, China has also dramatically expanded both urban, residence-based (i.e. non-employment-based) pension and health SI, as well as rural pension and health SI. See Feng et al. 2018; Feng and Zhao 2019; Huang and Zhang 2021. However, government subsidies dominate individual contributions in these new insurance schemes, in contrast to the pay-as-you-go structure of urban employment-based SI.

24 Qian 2014. Unemployment and workplace injury insurance are entirely employment-based. A fifth employment-based scheme, maternity/reproductive insurance, has been gradually folded into the health insurance scheme.

25 Feng and Zhao 2019 cite World Bank 1994 as laying out the set of policy recommendations that China incorporated in its initial SI design.

26 Song et al. 2015; Feng and Zhao 2019.

would mainly come from employer contributions. As recently as 2016, the central government set the employer contribution rate for pension SI at 20 percent of wages, and for health SI at 8 percent. All employer contributions would go to the locally pooled SI fund instead of being credited to individual employee's accounts. Only employees' contributions – at 8 percent for pension and 2 percent for health SI – are recorded in individual accounts. In the aggregate, a tax of 38 percent was imposed on a worker's wage by these two types of SI alone. Unemployment and injury insurance increased the tax rate further, and some local jurisdictions, especially in the first decade of SI operations (i.e. the 2000s), adopted even higher rates. In 2009, the American business magazine *Forbes* infamously ranked China No. 2 on its global Tax Misery Index, purely as a result of adding the nominal aggregate SI contribution rates temporarily adopted in Shanghai (>60 percent) to the top rates of other taxes in China – which all stood around or below the OECD average.

The rich expat readers of *Forbes* in China actually had little to fear from China's SI regime. China's central government capped the SI tax base at three times the region-specific average wage income of urban workers: wages above that amount bear no SI contribution liabilities (for either employer or employee). It is instead low-wage earners that faced extraordinarily high effective tax rates: the government also put a floor on contributions, so that the taxable wage of an employee registered for SI is deemed to be no less than 60 percent of the region-specific average wage. For small businesses that pay low wages, the floor in contributions means that the effective tax rate on wages paid to participating employees could exceed 100 percent.[27] The SI rate structure is thus highly regressive, and would, if complied with, impose extraordinary costs on small businesses and their employees.

While these and other inefficient choices in China's SI policy leave much room for improvement, they are also not uncommon among countries that have young SI systems.[28] As younger generations of workers enter the SI system, the average participant's time for accumulating contributions in the system would lengthen, and their capacity for private savings would also increase, relative to earlier generations. It should thus become gradually feasible to cut SI contribution rates, reduce benefit payouts, extend retirement ages, and rationalize participation requirements.[29] Indeed, it is

27 Cui, Hicks, and Norton 2020b.
28 Bird and Smart 2012; International Social Security Association 2017.
29 Fang and Feng 2018.

reasonable to expect China to move away from the pay-as-you-go funding structure for SI, as the central planning era recedes into the past.

But an important set of *political* choices renders these policy improvements harder to achieve. These are the central government's decisions to dictate a nationwide set of SI policies, and to adopt the ultimate policy goal of establishing a national SI system – even though subnational governments have been left to fund and operate SI systems indefinitely. As of 2019, only one province (Shaanxi) claimed to have a provincial pension SI system. Pension SI is organized at the prefectural (city) or lower, county level in most of the country, and health insurance budgetary units are even more decentralized. Consequently, commentators generally describe SI in China as "fragmented."[30]

But in using that term, one might already be implicitly accepting an unfounded premise: namely, that there *should* be national SI in China. In reality, decentralized insurance systems can work quite well. In countries like Canada, so-called "nationalized," "single-payer" health insurance schemes are operated substantially by provinces or similar subnational units. In pension systems that rely on individual accounts (e.g. privatized pensions), whether the public component of the system is run by a national, provincial, or other government unit makes even less difference. Experiences in other countries also demonstrate that decentralized SI can be compatible with labor mobility and the portability of insurance benefits; a unified SI regime is not a prerequisite for a national labor market.

The most compelling reasons for China to set SI policy again relate to redistribution. The decision to move toward a market economy, for instance, was clearly a national one, and the corresponding need to compensate older workers arguably required national action. Similarly, reducing regional disparities may be regarded as nationally desirable. Still, redistribution does not require setting the same terms of insurance across the country, nor pooling the resources for redistribution within a single employment-based system. Indeed, China's own experience amply illustrates the latter point: it has been able to introduce rural and urban non-employment-based SI mainly through fiscal subsidies funded by general tax revenue, without taking the position that these SI schemes must ultimately be merged with urban employment-based insurance.[31]

In short, there is no fundamental policy reason why China must adopt national pooling in its pension or health insurance schemes. Indeed, even

[30] Id; Li et al. 2021.

[31] See literature cited in note 2, supra.

for a social planner who possesses perfect information and is unencumbered by fiscal politics, designing such schemes can be challenging. For example, there will inevitably be regional differences in preferences: citizens in richer cities may desire higher retirement or health benefits and are willing to pay for them; they would naturally hesitate to subsidize the payment of similar benefits to citizens in poorer regions, especially if the latter may value them less (e.g. because of lower costs of living). In light of these difficulties, it is unsurprising that the Chinese central government has never been able to table any concrete plans for a national SI system.

Such considerations, however, are rarely mentioned in Chinese policy and academic discussions. Instead, the government and scholars *insist* on the ultimate goal of national pooling. It is as though maintaining central government control over SI has become an end in itself. This suggests that one should think of the goal of central government control as a *political* objective.

Yet this political position immediately and perversely leads to the following provincial response: few provinces would invest in setting up their own (fiscally sustainable) SI programs, since such programs can at any moment be disrupted by a national scheme. In particular, the richer provinces in China would have the lowest incentives in establishing provincial pooling: any surplus in a provincial system would very likely be skimmed away by the central government. Therefore, one can trace the persistent "fragmentation" of the SI system in China to provincial abdications from investing in such systems. This abdication in turn can be traced to the political objective of retaining central government authority, the economic rationales of which have not been articulated.[32]

This combination of an inadequately justified goal of central control and provincial abdication goes a long way toward explaining the instability of SI in China – and the apparent puzzle of weak state capacity when it comes to collecting SI contributions. It is widely agreed that there are major gaps in participation in China's nominally compulsory employment-based SI schemes. Official statistics suggest that participants (workers) as a percentage of total urban employees was only 68.7 percent in 2017 (though this was already an increase from 45.1 percent in 2000).[33] A government think tank estimates that in 2015, 70 percent of all firms that participated in

[32] In fact, the national government's insistence on dictating SI policy gives an excuse to provincial governments for disengagement.

[33] Fang and Feng 2018.

SI under-contributed relative to statutory requirements.[34] In one province my coauthors and I have studied using administrative data, as many as 54 percent of active firms in 2016 did not participate in SI at all.[35]

It is tempting to attribute these large compliance gaps to the exorbitant nominal SI tax rates.[36] However, scholars have also remarked that non-enforcement may be just as important a factor in China's SI compliance outcomes. Numerous explanations have been offered for such nonenforcement. One is that local officials – who may control the intensity of enforcement – are likely to limit enforcement, as this mitigates the adverse effect of SI collection on business formation and growth.[37] Another is that Chinese provinces may designate either tax agencies or local SI administrations to collect SI contributions, and that the latter may be less capable of enforcement.[38] Yet these explanations appear, even on their face, partial. For example, *all* taxes may have potentially adverse effects on business formation and growth; why are local government agencies particularly lax in enforcing SI? In fact, given that China's SI regimes are decentralized, local agencies should be *more* zealous in enforcement, since they are collecting revenue that benefit local SI budgets, whereas the revenue from many other taxes are shared with higher levels of government.[39]

As to whether collection by tax agencies would improve SI compliance, the empirical evidence is mixed.[40] There is also one important institutional fact to consider: tax agencies merely *collect* – and do not actively assess – the SI liabilities already determined for firms by local SI administrations.[41] Therefore, even if tax bureaus have greater experience with enforcement

34 Feng and Zhao 2019. See also Tang and Feng 2019 for additional citations. Li et al. 2021 report a median effective contribution rate of only 0.9 percent in the sample for firms they study.

35 Cui, Hicks, and Norton 2020b. In our sample, while non-participation is especially high among small firms – only 22 percent of the smallest decile of firms make any SI contributions – only 78 percent of even the top decile of firms contribute.

36 Feng 2013 suggests that for firms already participating in SI, lower tax rates may lead to incrementally greater compliance in terms of reducing under-contributions.

37 Li et al. 2021; Qian and Wen 2020. This is tantamount to a political explanation of the non-deployment of existing state capacity.

38 Tang and Feng 2019.

39 Scholars have otherwise been willing to adopt the conjecture that local tax enforcement is very sensitive to the local share of tax revenue. See, for example, Cai, Chen, and Wang 2018. This logic should extend to the collection of SI contributions.

40 Tang and Feng 2019 suggest that provinces that switched to SI collection by tax agencies witnessed greater participation by new firms, but already-participating firms did not demonstrate improved compliance through higher levels of contribution (i.e. lower under-contribution).

41 Feng and Zhao 2019.

against delinquent taxpayers and greater capacity for monitoring other aspects in the financial operations of firms, they would not be able to collect more SI than local SI administrations require firms to pay.[42]

I believe an alternative explanation of lax SI enforcement lies in the following fact. Local government agencies – whether SI administrations or tax bureaus – are enforcing a nationally imposed set of requirements, but the enforcement outcomes only matter to the budgetary health of each member of a very decentralized set of SI regimes. To use a concept from previous chapters, Chinese tax agencies do not face top-down revenue targets in SI collection: such targets are determined locally. The discrepancy between legally required and actual participation, therefore, may issue directly from the gap between central government policies and local fiscal realities. Enforcement efforts may depend on local fiscal preferences, instead of national requirements or enforcement capacity – such local preferences could reflect both the solvency of the local SI regime and the transfers that local governments can expect to negotiate from higher levels of government.[43]

Currently, these competing explanations of SI compliance patterns are all difficult to verify: China's SI system is notorious for its lack of transparency. In fact, the lack of transparency, not weak enforcement, is likely the key vulnerability of the system. When provinces report their SI budgets to the national government, they are merely aggregating budget reports generated by cities, which in turn may be aggregating budgetary reports from counties and other lower units. The more layers there are in this aggregation process, the more information is lost regarding the types of populations that are contributing or receiving benefits, the amounts of these benefits, the sources and nature of government subsidies being implemented, and the investment or other uses of any accumulated surplus. This lack of information radically undermines the central government's ability for policy planning, but – here is the irony – it may be in part the very goal of central control that is destroying information.

The combination of central control and lack of information has destabilizing consequences.[44] In 2020, in response to the COVID-19 pandemic,

[42] Cui, Hicks, and Norton 2020b observe high levels of non-participation even in a province that switched to SI collection by tax agencies many years ago.

[43] For example, richer regions may under-enforce SI not only because it may be good for businesses, but because local surpluses resulting from greater enforcements may prove disadvantageous in future bargaining.

[44] Only since 2016 has the central government started to recognize that SI contributions represent a major burden on small businesses and urged local governments to cut

the central government required all provinces to suspend, for eleven months of the year, employer contributions to pension, unemployment, and work injury SI for all but the largest 1 percent of for-profit businesses. This represented by far the largest component of the Chinese government's policy interventions in the COVID-induced economic crisis. While this clearly benefitted China's small businesses, it further weakened local SI units around the country. The power of the central government to disrupt the operation of SI regimes with a stroke of the pen – much as it has done with the PIT – is abundantly clear. However, the goals that guide the central government's monopolized exercise of authority are not.

Endogenous Information Bottlenecks

The PIT and SI examples demonstrate that economic factors in themselves – including even the limitations on enforcement capacity implied by economic factors – are insufficient in explaining features of China's tax system. It is politics that shapes state fiscal capacity, and it is politics that determines what type of information is available to political actors.

Political economists have studied a variety of ways in which politics can shape information acquisition. Consider a well-known paradigm,[45] where a principal charges agents to gather information for making decisions. When information gathering takes effort, agents may refrain from undertaking such efforts if they fear that, once armed with the information, the principal will take actions against the agents' preferences. One can easily imagine such behavior on the part of rich provinces in China: information about their SI surpluses, for example, could facilitate appropriation – if the (perceived) central government's objective is interprovincial redistribution, then the rich provinces should minimize information gathering efforts. But insofar as the central government's preferences are unclear, even less wealthy provinces may refrain from undertaking costly information acquisition.

But there are more complex ways in which decision-making processes and governance techniques determine the information available in such processes and governance. In Chapter 3, I argued that the atomistic aspect of the revenue management system – the primacy of the assigned revenue manager in determining a Chinese taxpayer's compliance – implies that

contribution rates. However, it has undertaken very limited steps to enhance intergovernmental transfers to mitigate the fiscal distress experience by some local SI regimes.

45 Aghion and Tirole 1997.

much taxpayer information lays dormant in the government's databases. Because the use of such information by anyone other than the assigned revenue manager is infrequent, local tax offices find it irrational to invest in making such information accessible. Consequently, individual revenue managers' close monitoring of taxpayers does not translate into systematic information that the government can use. What is more, the revenue management system's penchant for *ex ante* interventions also reduces taxpayers' accountability for providing accurate information. As a result, taxpayer information can be significantly degraded, even in county or city tax bureaus that have relatively well-maintained IT systems.

Now, because information is generated – and most frequently used – at the grassroots level, China's provincial tax bureaus have both less control over the quality of taxpayer information and fewer uses for it. In fact, until the past decade, many provinces simply did not have province-wide taxpayer databases. Since the SAT can obtain taxpayer information only from provincial bureaus, there is also, to this day, no nationwide taxpayer database. This fact is highlighted by the existence of the National Taxpayer Survey (*quanguo shuishou diaocha*, NTS), a source of data that economists inside and outside of China have recently used to produce empirical studies on Chinese taxation.[46] The NTS produces taxpayer datasets that the SAT shares only with a small number of researchers. It is assembled literally through annual surveys: each of hundreds of thousands of taxpayers surveyed across the country is asked to complete a form with over 600 entries.[47] Most of the survey entries correspond to items on a taxpayer's income and other tax returns as well as financial statements (i.e. balance sheets, income statements, and cash flow statements). Still, subnational bureaus continue to organize these surveys, instead of simply pulling most of the needed information from existing tax returns. This is why NTS datasets are taxpayer samples biased toward large taxpayers, who are more likely to have the capacity to complete the extraordinarily lengthy form.[48] They also cover only businesses and not individuals. While a wonderful resource for the few researchers who can use it, it is striking that it is through this national survey, not actual tax returns, that the SAT currently has access to the most detailed taxpayer-level information. By contrast, even in many poorer

[46] See, for example, Chen et al. 2018, 2019, and 2020; Liu and Mao 2019; Fan and Liu 2020.

[47] See www.stats.gov.cn/tjfw/bmdcxmsp/bmzd/201901/t20190121_1645931.html for an official description of the survey. For instructions on completing the survey, see www.zhckw.com/show-108-7971-1.html.

[48] Taxpayer information in the NTSD is also not audited – no rational tax administration would audit surveys – but this itself does not detract from the value of the survey.

developing countries, tax administrators have boasted of comprehensive national taxpayer databases.[49]

To be fair, the lack of a national taxpayer database does not by itself necessarily handicap policy making. In reality, even the NTS data is little used by the SAT. This is because for most types of tax policy analyses and revenue projections, governments all around the world do not rely on granular, taxpayer-level data. Instead, aggregate statistics about different taxpayer populations are often sufficient.[50] Traditionally, the main use of tax return data was thought to be the analysis of taxpayer compliance. Even then, how much of the government's ability to detect noncompliance depends on systematic data, as opposed to the individual experience and skills of auditors, is unclear.[51] In this sense, accurate taxpayer data can be seen as simply a by-product of the compliance process; it is not indispensable to policy making or to the goal of securing compliance.

Nonetheless, the absence of national or often even provincial taxpayer databases in China shows that obstacles to information gathering are often not technological, but institutional. In Chinese business taxation, they are the direct byproduct of the fiscal state's structure, in which the task of tax collection is relentlessly pushed down to the bottom rank. The erosion of norms of truth reporting, and the lack of incentives to maintain the information system, are further byproducts of the system of atomistic coercion. This system has the consent of the highest-level policy makers, likely because it is one through which they can try to maximize their command and the obedience of subordinates. No lower-tier bureaucrat is *hiding* taxpayer information – instead, information is simply foregone, given the incentives imposed on grassroots tax administrators and the strategies they choose in response.

Chinese tax administrators complain more often about other forms of information failure. For one, the use of revenue targets essentially accepts – and perpetuates – a state of incomplete information on the

49 Recent studies based on taxpayer databases in Africa include, for example, Mascagni et al. 2020 (Rwanda), Lediga, Riedel, and Strohmaier 2020 (South Africa), Santoro and Mdluli 2019 (Eswatini), and Alumnia et al. 2020 (Uganda). Of course, many of these countries are more like provinces or even cities in China in terms of the size of their taxpayer populations.

50 Statisticians at the SAT routinely request summary statistics from provincial tax bureaus about taxpayer characteristics.

51 In China, the analysis of taxpayer compliance has largely been the provenance of provincial or city-level tax bureaus. And as we saw in Chapter 4, although the use of tax-return-based risk identification is increasing in some provinces of China, the government has used many other means for ensuring basic compliance.

part of policy makers. Actual tax revenue reflects both taxpayer business conditions and tax administrator efforts, whereas revenue targets mainly aim to incentivize tax collection efforts. By being forever willing to manipulate this lever – any diminution of the tax base needs to be made up by collection effort – the SAT and senior leaders in the state's political branch essentially accept a perpetual state of ignorance about the actual tax base. There is thus an obvious sense in which the higher-ups are complicit in the fabrication of information.

China's policy makers' lack of information also hurts ordinary bureaucratic operations in many other ways. When I described the use of comprehensive evaluations of city tax bureaus and individual employees in Chapter 5, I omitted relating the complaints that lower-level employees make about the impracticality, inappropriateness, and alienating effect of many evaluation metrics. Nor did I dwell on complaints that tax inspectors and revenue managers have about the uselessness of the "taxpayer risk indicators" they receive.[52] Although it is difficult to pinpoint the causal impact of information failures on policy making systematically, case studies can illuminate this impact. Some such case studies, relating to some of China's smaller taxes, include Christian Göbel's superb account of the abolition of the agriculture tax[53] and my own earlier research on the vehicle and vessels tax.[54] In the next section, I highlight how information failures may explain crucial missteps in policy design in the largest source of tax revenue in China: the VAT.

Muddling Up the Largest Source of Revenue

In November 2008, in response to the Global Financial Crisis, China's State Council delivered a major tax cut through a reform of the country's VAT.

[52] Those I interviewed told me that it was futile to tell their superiors that the latter's metrics were wrong, as one was more likely to be rewarded by going out of the way to demonstrate that the superiors were right.

[53] Göbel 2010. In Göbel's narrative, the central government systematically vetoed local governments' proposals to reform the agricultural tax in the mid-1990s, while giving the subject low policy priority. When the central government took up the cause of reforming the agricultural tax in the late 1990s, it dictated national policies before adequate fact-finding. The course of reform abruptly changed after the central government – Premier Zhu Rongji in particular – came to recognize its mistakes.

[54] Cui and Wang 2015 offer evidence of tax mimicking in provincial decisions to set rates for the vehicle and vessels tax, which can be explained by provinces' lack of information and incentives in designing a tax that made no impact on provincial budgets.

The change was technically narrow and can be explained in simple terms. Under a normal VAT regime (as adopted in many developed economies), a business (X) selling goods or services to another business (Y) is required to charge and collect VAT on such sales. But when Y later makes its own sales and charges VAT to its customers, it can reduce its VAT remittance to the government by the amount that it previously paid on purchases from X and other suppliers. This way, VAT charged on business-to-business (B2B) transactions serves simply as a way of withholding, in advance, the VAT that would eventually be charged when the production chain ends – when sales are made to final consumers.[55] But before the 2008 reform, the Chinese VAT denied most VAT taxpayers the ability to reduce VAT remittance by previously-collected VAT on equipment purchases. This meant that equipment purchases generally bore a hefty 17 percent tax cost.[56] The November 2008 policy removed this large, unusual tax and allowed taxpayers to claim input credit.

Economists have recently demonstrated that the 2008 policy change was highly successful. As equipment purchases became 17 percent cheaper, equipment manufacturers ramped up their production and invested in better technology to meet increased demand. Other businesses either increased their investments in equipment or applied the freed-up cash flow from previously planned investments to productive use.[57] Small, privately owned, and cash-constrained firms responded especially well to the policy change. The reform even increased competition in some affected industries.[58] While novel in their empirical rigor and precision, these recent findings are generally consistent with conventional economic theories. An important question, however, is to what extent the likelihood of these outcomes mattered to the government's decision-making in adopting the policy.

55 The VAT is thus equivalent to a retail sales tax but is administered differently. For the basic logic and mechanics of the VAT (also known as the Goods and Services Tax), see Chapters 2–3 of Schenk, Thuronyi, and Cui 2015.

56 By taxing B2B transactions so heavily, the Chinese VAT was a "value added tax" only in name. The Chinese VAT has substantially deviated from international norms throughout its history – see chapter 14 of Schenk, Thuronyi, and Cui 2015.

57 Chen et al. 2019; Liu and Mao 2019.

58 China's November 2008 tax cut package – of which the VAT reform was the most important part – amounted to CNY 500 billion of foregone revenue. While this was only one eighth of the size of the famous four-trillion-yuan stimulus spending package that the Chinese government also announced at the time, both the short-term and long-term impacts of that latter giant spending spree are much more controversial – see Bai et al. 2016.

The answer is ambiguous. Just a few months before the announcement of the 2008 VAT change (and before the US subprime mortgage crisis began to generate global impact), China's policy experts debated about this reform in entirely different terms.[59] Reform proponents pointed to the stunning tax revenue growth in China – the growth rates in 2007 and the first half of 2008 were close to 34 percent – to argue that the government could finally afford any revenue shortfall that might come as a cost of rationalizing the VAT. In their view – correct as far as it goes – the VAT was never intended to tax business purchases. The denial of input VAT credits for investments in equipment had been adopted only out of earlier political expediencies that were no longer relevant. Opponents argued, however, that tax revenue was growing fast partly because the Chinese economy was becoming frothy, and the 17 percent tax on equipment purchases could help dampen pockets of investment frenzy. More generally, should China really worry about seemingly distortionary taxes when the economy appeared to be doing well? Reform advocates seemed simply to promote a doctrine without much evidence on their side. Although tax specialists fussed about the deadweight losses generated by taxation – especially high taxes on narrow tax bases – those concerns occupied few others in China.[60]

In fact, the State Council had already implemented the 2008 VAT policy on an "experimental" basis in select regions several years prior.[61] But the government specifically chose economically troubled regions as experimental pilots, betraying a presumption that the removal of the 17 percent tax would stimulate investment. It is not clear that the government thought it necessary to test this assumption (nor were the experiment pilots best designed for conducting such tests). At the same time, nothing in the regional experiments was designed to address the macroeconomic issues that seemed to really sway decision-makers. From all appearances, these "experiments" themselves appeared to be further products of political expediency – that is, to provide a tax preference to aid regional economic development – rather than genuine attempts at fiscal reform.

In any case, the muddle of this earlier policy debate allowed China to respond to the Global Financial Crisis with a type of fiscal stimulus not

[59] For a summary of this debate, see Cui 2012b.

[60] It is not implausible to think that tax-induced inefficiencies could be of lesser significance in a country undergoing major structural transformations. In addition, conflicting evidence regarding the micro and macroeconomic consequences of investment incentives also features in other countries. See Hines and Park 2019 for a discussion of the American case.

[61] Zhang, Chen, and He 2018.

available anywhere else.[62] What one *can* say, with greater hindsight, is that the 2008 policy change failed to teach the right lessons to China's political leaders for the next round of VAT reform.

The biggest distortion in China's VAT system in 2008 was not the unusual tax on equipment purchases, but the overall narrow base of the VAT: it applied only to the manufacturing and sales of goods, but completely left out service sectors, including large industries such as construction, real estate, financial services, education, and health care. Businesses in all of these sectors paid a turnover tax called Business Tax (*yingyeshui* or BT), under which all taxes on all input purchases, whether they were for equipment, inventory, or services, were final and non-creditable. Their sales to other businesses also bore a tax cost that was not allowed to reduce the buyer's taxes on subsequent sales. The BT ensured that there was a tax cost paid at every chain of production. As a consequence, BT taxpayers – and their suppliers and customers – were strongly motivated to arrange production and sales to reduce such costs. Such actions distorted business decisions.[63] But it was only after the Global Financial Crisis that policy makers in China finally began to consider replacing the BT with the VAT.[64]

If the 2008 VAT change taught policy makers anything, it should have been that making the tax on B2B transactions creditable under the VAT would remove the tax burden on such transactions. While the government would lose revenue in the short term, taxpayers would be allowed to make undistorted business decisions and likely become more productive. In evaluating whether these tax reductions and efficiency gains justified the comprehensive replacement of turnover taxes with the VAT, policy makers might normally have considered three major issues: first, whether any lost tax revenue should be made up through revenue increases elsewhere, such as tax rate increases; second, the potential impact of the first decision on general prices in the economy; and third, what impact such reform would have on national and subnational government finances.[65]

When China embarked on its reform to replace the BT with the VAT in 2012, however, it not only appeared to have no plan to answer any of

[62] If China had had a more typical tax structure, the VAT reform option would not have been available. Conversely, Cui 2012b shows that because of the idiosyncrasies of China's tax structure in 2008, some of the policy measures commonly deployed in other countries also could not be used.

[63] In these respects, the BT exemplifies the type of turnover taxes that the VAT was initially invented to replace.

[64] Cui 2009.

[65] James 2007; Bird and Smart 2009.

these questions, but also seemed to completely ignore the lessons that might have been learned from the 2008 reform.

In the series of policies implemented during 2012–2016, the State Council first chose – seemingly in customary fashion – a "regional experiment" approach. Initially only in Shanghai, BT taxpayers in several service sectors that mainly provided B2B services started paying the VAT. The trouble was that this regional experimental pilot was clearly going to reveal nothing about the economy-wide policy questions mentioned earlier. How much China as a whole would need to adjust tax rates to compensate for revenue loss through the reform could not be answered by an experiment in Shanghai alone, both because of Shanghai's atypical economy and the fact that the budgetary impact of the reform could show up elsewhere (e.g. input tax credits claimed in other provinces). Similarly, any price effects of the reform also would not be observable in Shanghai, given the integration of domestic markets. Finally, Shanghai generally operated with a fiscal surplus and transferred tax revenue to the central government. Its fiscal preparedness for VAT reform thus revealed little about the preparedness of other jurisdictions.

Choosing Shanghai to start the reform had one predictable consequence: it made Shanghai businesses more competitive service providers than businesses elsewhere in China, since the VAT charged on their sales was creditable by buyers, whereas the previous BT was not. Shanghai's unilateral reform seemed to put other provinces at a large economic disadvantage. This incentivized other provinces to join the reform "experiment." Barely a few months after Shanghai's reform pilot began in January 2012, the State Council announced that eight other provinces would also launch "reform pilots" in 2012. By August 2013, the regional pilot phase of the VAT reform ended and sectoral-specific reform expanded to the entire country.[66] Although the regional experiment approach may have made it easier to achieve national consensus that *some* form of VAT reform would be carried out, it is all but certain that, from the perspective of gathering information for designing policy, the approach was fruitless.

Yet this aspect of China's reform to replace the BT was arguably harmless in the long run, compared to a more basic, yet egregiously misguided, goal Premier Li Keqiang set for the reform. Soon after the Shanghai reform pilot's commencement, the State Council began to take the view that the reform's success depended on whether firms in the pilot industries would be remitting less tax under the VAT than they did under

[66] Cui 2014.

the BT. This was motivated by a conception that VAT remittances to the government represented "tax burdens" on businesses, which went completely against the traditional conception of the VAT (as a tax on final consumption). It also disregarded both the rationale and lessons of the earlier 2008 reform: converting a turnover tax to a VAT can itself both cut taxes and generate efficiency gains, making it unnecessary for any particular business to demonstrate reduced remittance.[67]

Once this objective was set, the State Council required pilot jurisdictions to ensure its achievement, and even to prepare to provide subsidies to pilot sector firms if their tax remittances increased.[68] Notably, taxpayer data about tax remittances were unavailable from most of the pilot jurisdictions. Local tax agencies and finance departments handed out surveys to businesses about the impact of the reform. Many businesses, seeing the opportunity to bargain for subsidies, claimed that they were hurt by the reform, even while the government reported substantial foregone revenue (and actual lower revenue growth).

Just a year into the reform, the idea that replacing the BT with the VAT would generate efficiency gains was all but sidelined. The State Council instead instructed the Ministry of Finance to design policies for the subsequent phases of the reform according to the objective of reduced tax remittance, measured at the level of individual firms. This led to a set of VAT rules that are highly unconventional by international standards, the economic impact of which has also turned out to be particularly difficult to analyze.[69] Moreover, to comply with the State Council's policy objective, the Ministry of Finance decided to grant widespread exemptions from the VAT. In recent years, only 20 percent of businesses supposedly subject to the VAT pay it in a regular fashion – charging VAT on sales and claiming input tax credit for purchases – while the remaining businesses are either exempt or pay a low-rate turnover tax instead.

By the time the BT was nominally folded into the VAT in 2016, China had developed one of the most idiosyncratic VAT systems in the world, combining unusual rules from two different eras: the pre-2012 period in

[67] For example, equipment manufacturers after the 2008 reform – and service providers in the reform replacing the BT with the VAT – could be remitting more tax because of increased sales, but such increased VAT remittance would largely be claimed as input credits by their customers.

[68] Cui 2014.

[69] Most notably, China's VAT rates differ even for B2B transactions, whereas in other countries, VAT rates vary only for consumer goods and services. See Shen and Krever 2017.

which the VAT had a narrow base and therefore could not realize its efficiency properties,[70] and the post-2012 period in which reductions in firm-level tax remittance, rather than efficiency gains, drove policy design. Chinese tax professionals joke that instead of a reform that replaced the BT with the VAT, the BT succeeded to replace the VAT. This is all the more remarkable because China had introduced the VAT – considered to be one of the simplest modern taxes adopted by most countries in the world – ahead of nations like Singapore and Canada, and therefore has had a long time to learn about the functioning of the tax.

This outcome is difficult to reconcile with any notion that the central government's policy making is driven by policy expertise, or that it is able to assemble policy-relevant information. It is, instead, more consistent with the view that China's tax collection apparatus generates revenue at the expense of gathering information. A vast army of atomistic tax collectors can be relied on to diligently monitor taxpayers, but smart policies that rely on systematic information are beyond reach.

This assessment has fundamental implications for the development of Chinese tax policy in the coming decade. The government has come to view cutting taxes as one of the most important ways to help the country meet its ample economic challenges. It now faces the awkward task of incentivizing a tax bureaucracy that is trained to meet revenue targets to deliver tax preference instead. But more critically, it lacks the means of delivering tax cuts in smart ways and where it matters. Because fiscal politics had kept the PIT and SI regimes in states of under-development, cutting taxes through the VAT and CIT represents the main policy option. As the distortionary features of the Chinese VAT lead to persistent pressures of rate reduction, the CIT could be expected to sustain an increasing share of total revenue. This places China in an opposite policy trajectory from most developed economies, where the CIT is increasingly regarded as distortionary in a globalized world, while the VAT, an efficient tax on consumption, is viewed as enjoying room for growth. How China will navigate its unique trajectory against the background of accumulating information deficits is an open question with serious consequences.

[70] Cui and Wu 2012.

7

The Rhetoric of Law

Understanding the roles that law plays in taxation is essential both for analyzing Chinese fiscal politics and, arguably, for grasping the more general relationship between law and taxation in the development of state capacity. But scholars pursuing such understanding face an enormous obstacle: familiar discourses about law can be highly manipulable; the political functions of rhetoric about law make such rhetoric an especially unreliable guide to reality. Both in China and elsewhere, law is often discussed in connection with certain institutions of public decision-making. For example, in the sphere of taxation, the rule of law is often associated with exercises of parliamentary authority. The legitimacy of taxation is often assumed to be based on legislation – the *Magna Carta* being a symbol that resonates worldwide. Likewise, when economists attach significance to law, they tend to invoke the role of courts, which, like parliaments, can exercise constraints on the executive. But as this chapter shows, it is possible for a state to make significant investments in parliamentary and judicial institutions – and to sustain a discourse about the power of these institutions – without them actually exercising meaningful authority. The result is a striking juxtaposition: the legal system matters very little to the lives of ordinary people but matters greatly in political discourse.

Indeed, for anyone who studies official documents, directives, and speeches in China to understand policy priorities, skipping discussions of law would require passing over some of the most prominent, persistent, and lengthy parts of official discourse. Consequently, discounting official emphasis on law can lead to the neglect of essential politics. But taking such emphasis at face value can create a severely distorted view of everyday governance.

This chapter lays out a path through this conceptual quandary. A basic proposition I begin with is that every legal system needs to have certain basic *rules of recognition*: commonly known criteria for determining which rules that the public is expected to follow are *legal* rules, the compliance or noncompliance with which has *legal* consequences.

I demonstrate that such a set of rules of recognition exists in China and is consistently acknowledged by government officials themselves, notwithstanding the fact that common folk and scholars alike often fail to comprehend them. Given the existence of this set of rules, it follows that the Chinese government holds both legal and nonlegal instruments for adopting and implementing policy – much like governments elsewhere. What is notable about China is that politicians and bureaucrats show a remarkable lack of interest in the use of legal instruments. This is likely because top-town bureaucratic command often appears to serve as an adequate substitute, but whatever the explanation, a critical observation is that the disuse of legal instruments cannot be easily corrected by legislatures and courts. As a consequence, even though China's legislative bodies and courts are not allocated fewer resources for their activities than one could generally expect, their roles are sharply curtailed simply by political leaders' disuse of law.

Instead, legal institutions tend to be invoked in China for specific political purposes. For example, in recent years, a claim widely embraced by Chinese scholars and the media, namely that the NPC must endorse any tax policy for it to be lawful – the doctrine that taxation must be provided by legislation (*shuishou fading*) – has been opportunistically used for the anti-tax agenda of the country's rich. A more basic example of the selective appeal to legal institutions is the successful conflation of the authority of law with the central government's monopoly on policy making. The assertion of central political authority both gives life to the rhetoric of law in China and renders it deeply incoherent.

The Rules of Recognition

On January 26, 2011, Premier Li Keqiang convened an executive meeting of China's State Council that adopted broad policy measures for controlling rapidly rising housing prices in China, including significant measures under existing turnover taxes that applied to real estate transfers. The next day, after the State Council General Office released the meeting's official summary, Chinese media began to report on what appeared *not* to have happened. It had been rumored for a year that two provincial-level cities, Shanghai and Chongqing, sought central government authorization for experimenting with some new form of property tax on personal residences.[1] The introduction of a new property tax had been

1 Deng and Zhao 2011.

widely debated, but no mention of it was made in the official, published record of the January 26 cabinet meeting. Since no State Council authorization was given, journalists inferred that the idea had been punted on.

Yet in the evening of January 27, a young broadcaster on China Central Television's main news channel (CCTV-13) looked into the camera and declared: "According to our own information, the recently-held State Council Executive Meeting agreed that some cities may carry out pilot reforms to levy a property tax on individually owned residences; the specific measures are to be adopted by the People's Governments of the pilot provinces, autonomous regions, or municipalities directly under the Central Government according to their circumstances." An hour later, reports came from Chongqing that Mayor Huang Qifan held a press conference to publicly announce Chongqing's version of the new property tax, which was to begin collection the next day. Without even a news conference, Shanghai also began to collect its own property tax the next day. The announcement and the collection of the taxes were thus separated by a mere four hours.

In the early hours of January 28, the report of a "press conference" with the MOF, the SAT, and the Ministry of Construction appeared on another official website, People's Daily. It was not clear whether a meeting with the press was actually held, nor whether the questions that ministries offered written answers to actually came from reporters. The press release also provided few policy details, and seemed intended to address one specific question: "What is the legal basis of the pilot programs?" This question had been prominently raised by opponents of new property taxes in the preceding weeks.[2] The answer given by China's central ministries was identical to the one-liner read on television a few hours earlier.

The prominent news magazine *Caixin* offered this commentary about the sequence of events:

> Obviously, on the pilot reform of the real property tax, the Central Government has deliberately kept itself behind the scene. The posture of the Central Government is to "devolve" power to local governments and have the latter make "voluntary" decisions about whether or not to perform the pilot reform. The pilot programs are to be designed by local governments, and even the announcement of the launching of the reform pilots was to be done by the latter. The underlying message of the Central Government was: "You bear the responsibility: if trouble arises, you hold the bag."[3]

[2] Ye 2011; Zhai 2011.

[3] Wang 2011a.

In other words, to those who closely observed these developments in January 2011, what happened was not very subtle. Not only did the central government decline to coordinate local experiments of a new property tax, it even refrained from giving public authorization for them – claims of such authorization were backed only by hearsay, and not by documented evidence. This raises the questions: Were the new property taxes in Shanghai and Chongqing legally imposed?[4] Did their legality depend on the central government's authorization? And if central government authorization was required for legality, how did the obvious infirmity in the actual authorization affect the two cities' abilities to collect the new taxes?

To answer these questions, it is useful to recognize that, from a legal point of view, the Chongqing City Government and the Shanghai City Government actually took different approaches to announcing their new taxes. The Chongqing government issued a formal "local government regulation" (*difang zhengfu guizhang*) that was dated January 27, 2011 and came into force the next day.[5] The formal nature of Chongqing's rules is immediately discernible. First, they were issued pursuant to a decree (*ling*) of the Chongqing City Government, which (as was required for such decrees) bore the signature of the mayor (Huang Qifan in 2011) and was numbered along with other formal decrees of the city government. Second, the decree addressed the public instead of government departments. Third, because it was a formal legal instrument, the decree's subsequent change had to go through formal legal procedures. When Chongqing decided to expand the scope of the tax a few years later,[6] it adopted a formal amendment of the 2011 decree in January 2017 through a decree signed by a new mayor.[7]

[4] Caixin Magazine reached the clear conclusion that they were not: see Wang 2011b. Fourteen Chinese legal scholars also submitted a petition to the NPC to review the legality of the new property taxes. See Xiong et al. 2011. However, the topic essentially disappeared from Chinese media, initially because of censorship and subsequently because of lack of interest.

[5] Chongqing Municipal People's Government Decree No. 247, *Interim Measures for the Pilot Reform of Levying Property Tax on Some Individual Residential Properties and the Detailed Rules for the Implementation of the Administration of Individual Residential Property Tax Collection in Chongqing Municipality* (January 27, 2011, effective January 28, 2011).

[6] Individuals who did not work or reside in Chongqing had been subject to the city's property tax only on their second housing purchase under the 2011 decree. The 2017 amendment expanded the tax to these individuals' first purchase of a Chongqing residence.

[7] Chongqing Municipal People's Government Decree No. 311, January 13, 2017.

By contrast, Shanghai's new property tax rules were announced through a "notice" from the City Government, addressed only to that government's internal actors.[8] Instead of the public, the notice was directed to the chief executive offices of district and county governments in Shanghai, as well as the city's various government agencies. The notice did not contain the name of the mayor or any other individual official. Moreover, while Shanghai's rules were given the title of "interim measures" just like Chongqing's rules – though neither set of measures limited the duration of their respective property tax's imposition – the duration of the validity of Shanghai's rules was apparently not regarded as certain. Shanghai has issued internal government notices confirming the continued application of the 2011 notice no fewer than five times (roughly at two-year intervals) since January 2011.[9]

Chongqing's and Shanghai's property tax rules exemplify two basic types of Chinese government policy announcements, governed by two markedly different regimes. Formal government regulations of the kind adopted by Chongqing are part of a formal legal regime, which is guided by procedures and norms set out in the country's highest laws and the Constitution. Specifically, the State Council's Rules on Procedures for the Adoption of Regulations govern all formal regulations promulgated by executive branch entities in China, from national ministries to People's Governments in provinces and cities.[10] The State Council's Rules are in turn based on the Law on Legislation (*lifafa*), a quasi-constitutional statute first enacted in 2000. Within this regime, formal regulations can be amended or annulled only by equivalent or higher legal instruments, which is why the continued application of Chongqing's property tax regulation required no ongoing affirmation. Further, changes to general procedures and norms for the adoption of formal regulations affect all specific instances of such regulation. For example, beginning in 2018, the adoption of most formal regulations requires a minimum thirty-day period for giving notice to and soliciting comments from the public. Chongqing imposed the property tax in 2011 and expanded it in 2017

[8] Shanghai Municipal People's Government, *Notice on Issuing the Interim Measures of Shanghai Municipality for Levying Property Tax on Some Individual Residential Properties on a Pilot Basis* (*Hufufa* [2011] 3, January 27, 2011).

[9] These internal notices were issued in December 2012 (*Hufufa* [2012] 105), December 2014 (*Hufufa* [2014] 78), January 2017 (*Hufufa* [2017] 1), November 2018 (*Hufugui* [2018] 23), and December 2020 (*Hufugui* [2020] 33).

[10] State Council Decree No. 322, November 16, 2001 (originally effective January 1, 2002, amended on December 22, 2017 by State Council Decree No. 695 and effective as amended on May 1, 2018).

without going through such notice and comment, but if and when further changes are made to the Chongqing regulation in the future, such notice and comment would be required.

Shanghai's property tax rules, by contrast, are an archetypical instance of government policy announcements commonly referred to as "normative documents" (*guifanxing wenjian*) or "red letterhead documents" (*hongtou wenjian*) in China. Such documents come from government sources, but there are no general rules (let alone publicly known ones) about how and when they are deployed. They often serve purposes other than announcing rules to be followed by the public, including purposes so limited to government internal affairs that they are not publicly available at all.[11] Moreover, there are almost no procedural constraints on their issuance: there is no general rule, for example, requiring deliberation among the leaders of the issuing body, nor rules on authorization. The personal anonymity of such documents – in contrast to the need of formal regulations to have identified, authoritative signatories – reflects such lack of procedural conditions. Their informality and their frequent use for purely internal organizational purposes are two sides of the same coin.

The distinction between formal regulations and informal policy announcements has been easily detectable and uniformly followed in the practices of Chinese government agencies since 2000, as observed through government publications, websites, and so forth. Although the City Government of Chongqing issues plenty of informal policy announcements, it chose a more elevated, formal legal instrument to promulgate the 2011 property tax rules. Conversely, while the City Government of Shanghai adopts a significant number of formal regulations, it seemed to find it unnecessary or inappropriate to impose its 2011 property tax rules in this fashion. Regardless of such choices, the existence and legal meaning of this distinction are black and white.

The consistency with which government entities across China follow this distinction is not accidental: it is a *legal* distinction that reflects a necessity, inherent in all legal systems, to have a set of rules of recognition for identifying valid legal rules. The idea of rules of recognition is intuitive. People living in modern societies follow many rules – for example, the rules in their workplaces, in the social organizations to

[11] For instance, while Shanghai Government Notice No. 3 in 2011 announced the property tax rules, Notice No. 7 named a new chief of the city government's news office, Notice No. 42 announced an award of lifetime achievement to the basketball player Yao Ming, and Notice No. 4 is nowhere to be found.

which they belong, and in various social, ethnic, and religious communities. But only some of these rules are *legal* rules, and any legal system must be able to distinguish legal rules from nonlegal ones. Consequently, legal systems typically contain a classification scheme that identifies certain rules as having the force of law. Such a scheme would also generally set out how valid changes to legal rules may be made, and how conflicts among seemingly conflicting rules are resolved.

In China, this classification scheme is generally thought to be set out in the Law on Legislation, which specifies what rules adopted by government entities have the force of law, the hierarchy of superior and subordinate legal norms, and how conflicting rules of the same hierarchical rank are reconciled. A direct implication of this scheme of legal norms is that red letterhead documents – informal policy announcements from government agencies like the one used by Shanghai to announce its property tax reform – are not rules with the effect of law.[12] This implication, importantly, is recognized not only by government bureaucrats responsible for implementing legal procedures, but also, as I will discuss later, by the Chinese judiciary.

Ordinary people often fail to grasp the distinction between formal regulations and informal policy announcements: indeed, I have encountered many *scholars* of Chinese law whose grasp of the distinction is tenuous. This does not undermine the validity or even importance of the distinction: it is sufficient that the distinction is observed by those who are responsible for sustaining China's legal system.[13] In fact, the distinction is legally significant even if it seems to matter little in real world practice. Did the implementation of property tax in 2011 proceed differently in Chongqing than in Shanghai, because only the former chose to enact a formal regulation for the new tax?[14] The answer, as far as I know, is "No," notwithstanding initial protests by legal scholars. If a taxpayer in Shanghai challenged the city's property tax rules in a court, the judge

[12] See Cui 2011; Cui, Cheng and Wiesner 2019.

[13] The legal philosopher who invented the concept of rules of recognition, H. L. A. Hart, famously argued that rules of recognition only need to be grasped by the "officials" of a legal system. Ordinary people need not know these "secondary" rules – rules about the validity of rules – and only need to know the "primary rules" regarding appropriate conduct. At the same time, Hart thought that for there to be a legal system, the officials of the system must be *committed* to the rules of recognition: in Hart's own terminology, they must follow the rules not because of coercion by others, but because they are intrinsically motivated to do so. See Hart 1961; Shapiro 2013.

[14] Bai, Li, and Ouyang 2014 provide a study of the two cities' property taxes on housing prices.

would have needed to ask whether the effort at tax collection had any legal basis. But no such legal challenge seems to have been mounted. The taxpayers and tax administrators in Shanghai proceeded as though the property tax rules were legally binding, even though they were not. This kind of behavior – governments promulgating legally nonbinding rules with private citizens following the rules because they are "practically" binding – is common in advanced legal systems as well. Legal scholars hold different views about how problematic it is for governments to use legally nonbinding rules extensively.[15] But such disagreements do not create any doubt that, for there to be a legal system at all, there must be a distinction between rules with and without legal effect.

What is perhaps notably different about Chinese governance from governance in most countries with developed legal systems is how little government agencies rely on legal instruments. To the question, "Was the property tax legally imposed in Shanghai in 2011?", the proper answer is that the Shanghai government did not even *try* to do this; it introduced the tax by a casual administrative fiat. In doing so, however, the Shanghai government acted no differently from other Chinese government entities – including most central government ministries and the State Council itself. In fact, the vast majority of tax policies announced by the MOF and SAT are promulgated not through formal regulations, but through informal policy documents.[16] The VAT reforms discussed in Chapter 6, for instance – whether it was the 2009 tax change that converted China's VAT from a "production type" to a "consumption tax", or the wholesale replacement of the Business Tax by the VAT between 2012 and 2016 – were all pursued without any change to legislations and formal regulations.[17] Such skirting of the law exists even in areas where the government officially avows the doctrine that taxation must be based on parliamentary legislation, as I will detail subsequently.

That the Chinese government announces tax policies (as well as policies in many other areas) overwhelmingly in ways that are not recognized by China's legal system as binding is simply a statement of fact. I will soon demonstrate that this has radical consequences: it largely

[15] For a long-standing controversy about this phenomenon in the United States, see Anthony 1992; Parrillo 2019.

[16] Cui 2011.

[17] Nor are the MOF and SAT alone in such nonchalance about legal form. See Cui 2019 for a survey of the use of formal regulations versus informal policy directives among China's national ministries.

undermines the relevance of legislatures and courts. But another feature of the rules of recognition in the Chinese legal system needs to be noted first. Ironically, whether the property tax was legally imposed in 2011 is a question that can be more meaningfully asked in Chongqing, where the city government did choose to deploy a formal legal instrument.[18] While as a provincial-level city (a "municipality directly under the Central Government"), the Chongqing government had the power to make law generally,[19] a further question is whether it possessed the power to introduce new tax rules.

This question may seem odd. Property taxes are levied by local governments around the world; the idea that a major Chinese city may not have the power to legislate its own property tax could be a surprise. But, as we will discuss subsequently, China's central government does reserve the power to legislate on tax matters to itself, and has written this reservation into the Law on Legislation. Therefore, the possibility for subnational governments to introduce new taxes hinges on some form of delegation from the central government. Without the ability to trace a tax rule to central authorization, no such rule can be recognized as legally valid.

The parameters of such permissible delegation of taxing power are a topic of some interest to Chinese legal scholars. But one need not learn such legal niceties to recognize that for the property tax "pilot reforms" in 2011, the delegation was botched in a spectacular way. All that Chongqing and Shanghai were able to obtain from the State Council, it seems, was some private instruction to CCTV and some central ministries to tell the public that delegation was given. Whatever legally permissible or valid delegation is, *this* cannot be it: the end result is little different from the two cities (and other observers) merely *claiming* delegation. Therefore, even in Chongqing's case, one cannot say that the property tax was introduced legally. Indeed, Shanghai's choice of informality seems savvy in light of the failure of formal delegation from the central government, as it calls less attention to the latter.

To reiterate, neither the failure of formal delegation nor the lack of legal effect of the chosen policy instrument has impeded tax collection in

[18] The Chongqing government also invested more into providing public guidance for the implementation of its property tax than Shanghai. The Interim Measures in Chongqing contained more detailed provisions than the Shanghai Interim Measures, and were more than twice as long.

[19] Before 2015, most prefecture-level cities in China lacked any lawmaking power – a striking oddity of the Chinese legal system. See Cui and Wan 2019a.

Chongqing and Shanghai during the past decade. The property tax in the two cities has received acquiescence from all parties, including the State Council and the central ministries. The significance of law can be found only in the political spectacle in January 2011, when it first appeared that legality required central government authorization. No one could have anticipated that the State Council would grant authorization by the most conspicuously nonlegal means, with this choice conveying a critical political message.

Parliament

The distinction between formal regulations and informal policy announcements issued by the Chinese executive branch is concededly subtle, even apart from the fact that its existence is specialized knowledge. Under the Law on Legislation and subsidiary State Council rules, for an executive branch entity to adopt a formal regulation, only certain procedural formalities need to be followed. Aside from the promulgation formalities mentioned earlier, the main additional procedural requirements are for leaders of the executive branch body issuing the regulation (such as the People's Government of a province or city) to meet and deliberate before adopting a regulation, and since 2017, for there to be a period of public notice and comment.[20] To non-lawyers, this may seem trivial and not something that would change the substance of the rules adopted.[21]

For this and other reasons, some readers may balk at the proposition that a relatively unknown classification system, deeming some official documents as having legal effect and others as having none, is what defines law: is law not associated with more prominent and well-established institutions, such as parliaments and courts? Instead of examining whether the executive branch uses formal regulations or

[20] For the key features of formal regulations under the Law on Legislation, see Cui 2011. Another relevant legal detail is that the consistency of formal regulations with higher legal instruments can be challenged in certain institutionalized ways before they are enforced: the validity of formal regulations depends on such consistency (though pre-enforcement challenges to the validity of regulations are rare in China). Informal policy documents, if they are inconsistent with formal legal rules, can be rejected in implementation as having no basis in law. But since they do not purport to be legally valid in the first place, the legal system cares less about their inconsistency with valid legal rules, and provides no channel for pre-enforcement review. I return to this issue in the discussion of judicial review later.

[21] The general rate of public participation during notice and comment periods in formal regulation making in China is very low.

informal policy directives to implement policy, it seems more relevant to ask what legislatures do in the sphere of taxation.

But from both a political and, surprisingly, a legal perspective, parliamentary legislation in China can also be viewed as a matter of formality. Politically, it is generally recognized (even within China) that China's parliamentary bodies, from the NPC to provincial, city, and county People's Congresses, are not constituted through competitive elections. Delegates are carefully vetted – when not directly chosen – by the CCP's organizational apparatus, and display little political diversity.[22] Moreover, as delegates congregate only once a year, most parliamentary legislations are left to "standing committees" of People's Congresses, which comprise government officials whose resumes look little different from other senior government bureaucrats.[23] Finally, the key decision-making bodies in each congressional entity – the "presidium" of the full congress and the chairpersons' meeting of the standing committee – closely follow the directions of the CCP leaders within each congress. The entire mission of these congressional CCP leaders, in turn, is to implement the directives of CCP leaders in the region (and in the case of the NPC, of the CCP's central leadership). Although it is certainly the CCP's intention to use parliaments to legitimize its rule, the Party also makes no secret of the fact that it is in charge of the nation's parliaments.

This familiar narrative about the political characteristics of Chinese parliamentary bodies has one critical legal implication. Since the same political party controls both the parliamentary and executive branches, policy making mainly originates in the executive branch – as does legislation. In this respect, China's NPC and subnational legislatures resemble legislatures in many parliamentary democracies governed by strong majority parties: the executive branch proposes legislation to parliaments, and for the most part, the latter enact legislation as proposed.[24] This type of parliamentary "rubber-stamping" behavior can be perfectly compatible with authentic democratic politics: it simply reflects the fact that elections and the need to form political coalitions are the main democratic constraints on what policies are enacted. But once elections and coalition formation are done, it is not unusual for parliaments to cease to be a significant locus of politics. Parliamentary

[22] Potter 2003; Manion 2015.
[23] Dowdle 1997.
[24] Moe and Caldwell 1994; Huber and Shipan 2002; Jensen and McGrath 2011.

members of the majority party should have little interest in challenging their own party leaders in the process of legislative enactment.[25]

In other words, when Chinese congressional bodies routinely enact legislation proposed by executive branch entities, their operations are not necessarily being subverted by the CCP's authoritarian overreach. Chinese parliaments simply do not have an "independent" will from the executive branch, any more than majority-party-controlled legislatures in genuine democracies have independent wills from the executive branch headed by majority party leaders.[26]

It follows that legislation is simply another way for Chinese political leaders in the national and subnational governments to promulgate policy, as an alternative to the adoption of formal regulations and the issuance of informal policy directives. Although parliamentary legislation possesses much more formality, and correspondingly holds higher ranks in the hierarchy of legal norms, the same political actors are behind all three types of policy announcements. While it is good to query how such actors make these choices, the question of why politicians choose legislation is not fundamentally different from the question of why they choose formal regulation over informal policy directives. One should not fall for the illusion that completely different actors and interests are necessarily involved in legislation than in executive-branch rulemaking.[27]

It is from this perspective that one can begin to appreciate how remarkable and strange it is that the Chinese government has elevated the symbolism of legislation in the realm of taxation. In 2015, the NPC amended the Law on Legislation. One widely lauded achievement of the amendment was the codification of the purported principle that taxation must have legislative basis: "the establishment of any category of tax, determination of tax rates, tax administration and other basic taxation rules" must be governed by national, parliamentary statutes.[28] By a popular narrative, the enshrinement of the principle in a foundational statute would protect Chinese taxpayers from the whims of bureaucrats who were otherwise unrestrained in raising taxes. "Taxation according to

[25] See Docherty 1997 and Docherty 2005 for accounts of the limited nature of parliamentary activities during periods of strong majority rule in Canada.

[26] This reasoning contradicts the presumption of some political scientists that the absence of genuine politics in parliamentary legislative activity has to be explained by authoritarianism. See Williamson and Magaloni 2020.

[27] Cui 2019 and Cui and Wan 2019b discuss when Chinese executive branch leaders may pursue legislation.

[28] Article 8(6) of the Law on Legislation, as amended by Presidential Decree No. 30 (March 15, 2015).

legislation" seemed to have become that rare doctrine embraced by both the CCP and China's economic elite.

But if law is invoked only against proposals to raise taxes, law may be dispensable if the government wants to *cut* taxes. This appears to be the true logic of "taxation according to legislation" in China. Because the Chinese government has been keen to cut taxes in the past ten years, the idea of "taxation according to legislation" has been much easier to find in Chinese media commentaries than in the law itself.

A most jarring example comes from the 2018 amendment of the Personal Income Tax Law (PITL). As discussed in Chapter 6, that amendment substantially shrank China's PIT tax base and reduced tax rates. It also restructured the PIT, most significantly by introducing an astounding array of personal deductions – for children's education and continuing education expenses, major medical expenses, home mortgage interest and rental expenses, and expenses for elderly dependents – almost unparalleled in PIT systems elsewhere. The amended PITL only stated that such deductions would be available, and delegated the specification of their "scope, standard, and gradual introduction" to the State Council. While such delegation might seem to immediately conflict with the norm of promulgating tax rules by legislation, the Law on Legislation permits delegation of parliamentary lawmaking powers when certain conditions are satisfied.[29] Specifically, the statute prohibits the State Council from re-delegating NPC-delegated authority to others, and requires the State Council to exercise any delegated legislative authority through the promulgation of administrative statutes (*xingzheng fagui*) – a form of secondary legislation specifically defined under the Law on Legislation.[30]

After the PITL amendment in August 2018, the MOF and SAT drafted rules on special personal deductions and circulated them for public comment in October 2018. But since the State Council was, in theory, not permitted to further delegate lawmaking power regarding taxation to others (including ministries), its own action was required. On December 13, 2018, the State Council issued a "notice" – an informal policy document not recognized as having the effect of law by the Law on Legislation – to announce the finalized personal deduction rules.[31] This

[29] Articles 9–13 of the Law on Legislation, as amended.

[30] Moreover, delegation of NPC lawmaking powers must be limited in duration.

[31] State Council, Notice Regarding the Issuance of Interim Measures for Special Additional Deductions under the Person Income Tax (*Guofa* [2018] 41, December 13, 2018). The informality and internal bureaucratic character of a State Council notice (*guofa*) is recognizable by some familiar features: it bears no individual signature, is addressed to

was clearly a deliberate choice: just five days later, Premier Li Keqiang signed an amendment of a previous administrative statute, the Implementation Measures for the PITL, which did have the effect of law.[32] The line between formality and informality is clear. The personal deduction measures simply appeared, for whatever reason, not to deserve the imprimatur of the Premier or elevation to formal deliberation.[33]

This unabashed breach of the Law on Legislation, after the pomp and circumstance that hailed the codification of "taxation according to legislation," suggests that legislation – in the very basic sense of giving policies legally valid form – and not taxation, is the *real* matter of whim for the Chinese government. For the State Council, proposing legislation that substantially delegates authority back to itself, adopting an administrative statute independently of the NPC, or issuing an informal directive, are almost perfectly substitutable options for adopting tax policy.

I want to offer one more extended example to illustrate the sham of the "taxation according to legislation" doctrine, both because of the example's intense irony and because it happens to be one of the most important pieces of tax policy China adopted in recent years. In January 2019, the State Council announced a panoply of "inclusive" tax cuts intended to apply to over 95 percent of all Chinese businesses. The appeal to "inclusivity" (*puhuixing*) is uncommon in tax policy anywhere and marked a new phase in the development of Chinese public finance under President Xi Jinping. One measure adopted was a CIT rate reduction that would be made available for three years.[34] Prior to 2019, Chinese firms with fewer than eighty employees and RMB ten million of assets effectively enjoyed a 10 percent rate on their taxable income, if such income, as normally computed, was less than RMB one million. The nominal tax rate applicable to such firms was 20 percent, but qualified

government entities only, and is very often not publicly available (at least 10 percent of the State Council notices in 2018 cannot be accessed). For example, it was through a State Council notice that the 1997 tax administration reform discussed in Chapter 1 was launched – that State Council directive contained no component that addressed the public.

32 State Council, The Amended Implementation Measures for the Personal Income Tax (State Council Decree No. 707, December 18, 2018).

33 According to a report by the Finance Minister Liu Kun to the NPC Standing Committee on December 24, 2018, the special deduction rules "received the approval" of both the State Council and the Central Committee of the CCP. Such vague phrasing, however, usually implies some informal approval, and the absence of formal deliberation by the approving bodies.

34 MOF and SAT, Notice Regarding Inclusive Tax Reduction and Exemptions for Small and Micro-Enterprises (*Caishui* [2019] 13, January 17, 2019).

firms only needed to include half of their income as normally computed. The 2019 "inclusive tax cut" extended this preferential rule to all firms that had less than 300 employees, RMB fifty million in assets, and RMB three million in taxable income. Moreover, firms earning less than RMB one million of taxable income a year only had to include a quarter of their income when computing tax liability, and therefore could effectively enjoy a 5 percent tax rate.

The MOF and SAT called firms entitled to such generously preferential treatment "small and micro-profit enterprises" (*xiaoxing wenli qiye*). Some might be struck that a firm with up to 300 employees can still be regarded as "small", or that firms with three million yuan of profit as "micro-profit." But the central ministries' use of the term is also odd in a *legal* sense: the same words were a defined term in China's Enterprise Income Tax Law (EITL), the basic statute governing the CIT since 2008. Yet the MOF and SAT were using the term in their informal policy announcements as though the statutory term did not exist.

The statute (EITL Article 28) provides that a "small and micro-profit enterprise" (SMPE) is entitled to a reduced 20 percent rate as opposed to the regular CIT rate of 25 percent. To specify the scope of the preferential rate's application, the 2008 Enterprise Income Tax Law Implementation Regulations (EITLIR, Article 92) defined SMPEs in terms of certain employee, asset, and profit thresholds. The EITLIR is a State Council administrative statute; hence the SMPE concept has a specific definition under a formal legislative instrument. Before 2017, the MOF and SAT appeared to take the view that any CIT policy adopted must at least nominally be consistent with the EITL and EITLIR. This was not least because the EITL, enacted in 2008, was one of only two substantive tax statutes China had before 2011, and, by being an exception, represented the idea of "taxation according to legislation." This was why the 10 percent effective CIT rate was initially introduced in 2009 (for firms earning less than 30,000 yuan in annual profit) through the device of half income inclusion: there was no 10 percent statutory tax rate, after all.

In a series of subsequent tax cuts, the government continued to lower the rate for SMPEs through the legal device of half-income inclusion between 2010 and 2016. By 2016, all businesses describable as SMPEs under the EITL's definition became entitled to include only half of their taxable income in computing tax liability. Effectively, at that point, no Chinese firm was paying the 20 percent tax rate. But the government could still describe the 10 percent tax rate as a policy applied to statutorily defined SMPEs.

In 2017, however, the State Council wanted to extend the 10 percent tax rate to more firms. It apparently had no appetite for doing so through amending legislation or even its own administrative statute. Instead, the MOF and SAT announced, in an informal policy circular, that "SMPEs" with annual income up to 500,000 yuan could claim a 20 percent tax rate and half income inclusion.[35] This seemed sloppy, to put it mildly, since by statutory definition (per EITLIR Article 92), a firm with more than 300,000 yuan of annual income could not be an SMPE. Consequently, the SAT, in providing further guidance under this new policy, stated that "SMPE" meant *either* firms defined under Article 92 of the EITLIR or the 2017 informal circular.[36]

As though emboldened by the fact that no one in China seemed to take notice of this legal inconsistency, the MOF and SAT, acting at the direction of the State Council, increased the "SMPE" income threshold to one million yuan in July 2018.[37] And in January 2019, the State Council lifted both the employee and asset thresholds for applying the low business tax rates. This meant that the SMPE term became completely unanchored from its definition in the EITLIR, carrying both a statutory and an extra-statutory meaning (with the latter defining policy after 2017).

Do the State Council, MOF, and SAT have authority to bypass the EITL and EITLIR in this way? Lawyers point to two provisions of the EITL as relevant. EITL Article 35 states that "the specific measures for the preferential tax treatments as mentioned in this Law shall be formulated by the State Council." Article 36 further provides that, "where the national economic and social development so requires, or the business operations of enterprises have been seriously affected by emergencies and other factors, the State Council may formulate special preferential policies concerning the enterprise income tax and submit them to the Standing Committee of the National People's Congress for

35 MOF and SAT, Notice Regarding Expanding the Scope of Income Tax Preferences for Small and Micro-Profit Enterprises (*Caishui* [2017] 43, June 6, 2017).

36 SAT Bulletin [2017] 23, Bulletin Regarding Administrative Issues in the Implementation of Expanding the Scope of Income Tax Preferences for SMPEs (June 7, 2017). One charitable reading of this sloppy drafting is that in 2017, only the taxable income threshold increased, while the employee and asset thresholds remained the same as before. A firm earning half a million of annual income could thus still be recognized as an SMPE by virtue of meeting the other EITLIR requirements. The break from the EITL was thus not total.

37 MOF and SAT, Notice Regarding Inclusive Tax Reduction and Exemptions for Small and Micro-Enterprises (*Caishui* [2019] 13, January 17, 2019).

archival purposes." In respect of a wide range of issues, the State Council and its agents have acted as though these provisions allow them to interpret or change CIT law as much as they please. The evolution of the SMPE concept since 2017 implies that Article 36 may even be taken as authorization to the executive branch to rewrite the EIT law altogether, using the very same terms as the original statute.

Political scientists debate about whether legislatures in authoritarian regimes are merely ceremonial,[38] but tend to look only to parliamentary voting and other legislative procedures in isolation to assess such claims. Unfortunately, a "rubber-stamping" parliament does not have to be ceremonial, and often one needs to investigate what statutes actually say – and the surrounding actions taken by the executive branch – to assess the significance of legislation. In pursuing the shortest route to implementing tax policies, the CCP has left no doubt that legislation is often merely symbolic.

It is vital to interrogate the meaning of such symbolism. But before doing so, we need to consider the other seemingly essential legal institution: courts.

Courts

The Chinese government's general disuse of formal legal instruments for promulgating and implementing policies has a profound implication for the country's courts. China's judicial system is of the civil law, as opposed to common law, variety.[39] This means, among other things, that it is by and large not the role of Chinese judges to create generally applicable legal norms when they render decisions on individual disputes: they are only to *apply* the law to particular cases and not *make* law that is to be complied with by parties other than the litigants.[40] As a result, civil law judicial decisions do not have precedential value, in contrast to common law decisions. Additionally, civil law judges generally cannot invalidate formal legal instruments. In adjudicating each case, they can reject purported legal rules that conflict with legal rules and principles of superior status, but they cannot preempt legal rules from being enforced

[38] Gandhi, Noble, and Svolik 2020.

[39] See, for example, Chow 2015. See Damaska 1991 for a classic account of the organizational differences between common law and civil law judiciaries.

[40] The most important exception to this statement is the Chinese Supreme People's Court's (SPC) ability to issue general interpretations of statutes that are binding on the country's judiciary.

outside of adjudication. An even more fundamental consequence of this inability to make law is that when government policies are barely embedded in legal rules in the first place, there will be little to no law for judges to apply. The power of the judiciary is thus automatically diminished. This describes the situation of Chinese judges in matters of taxation, as well as other regulatory areas where government use of formal legal instruments is perfunctory.[41]

The obvious fact that judges must apply the law underscores the indispensability of classification schemes that distinguish between rules with and without legal effect. Although the distinction between formal regulations and informal policy documents may be unfamiliar to some readers, the distinction is critical for Chinese judges: judges need to know what law they must apply, and not everything the government announces is law.[42] But this legal necessity also generates the following predicament for judges: when very little of what the government announces is law, there is also little basis for determining whether government actions are in accordance with law or not. Since most Chinese tax policy is announced through the MOF's or SAT's informal policy directives, how should Chinese judges approach such directives when adjudicating disputes between taxpayers and tax administrators?

If an informal policy directive is offered as the legal basis of government action in such a dispute, the judge may examine whether the nonbinding directive is consistent with existing law.[43] There are certainly instances where the MOF's or SAT's policy announcements are in breach of statutory and other explicitly legal rules, but such instances are rare overall. Consider the State Council's informal rules for special PIT deductions (for education, elderly dependents, etc.) announced in December 2018. The only relevant provision in the PITL is a delegation of lawmaking power regarding these deductions to the State Council. The entire substantive regime for such deductions is thus based on the State Council's notice (and subsequent informal announcements by the MOF

41 Such other regulatory areas include food and drug safety, education, and so forth. See Cui and Wan 2019b. The indirect disabling of judicial institutions through the shortage of legislation and formal regulations is thus a general – and also generally under-studied – phenomenon in Chinese governance.

42 The hierarchy of legal norms set out in the Law on Legislation is thus well mirrored in various statutes and judicial interpretations governing adjudication, including especially the Administrative Litigation Law. See Cui, Cheng, and Wiesner 2019.

43 Indeed, after an amendment of the Administrative Litigation Law in 2015, a judge is required to do so if the taxpayer plaintiff requests the court to review the legality of the informal policy document. Id.

and SAT).[44] Consequently, there is no substantive formal law for judges to follow. The same is true for the extra-statutorily prescribed CIT preference for SMPEs, all of the VAT reform rules that applied to Business Tax taxpayers during the 2012–2016 reform, and so on. Even if one dismissed these as extreme examples (which would be brave, given that they represent some of the most important tax policies China adopted in recent years), it is still the case that China's tax statutes and formal regulations generally provide little substantive detail, and the question of whether a tax is correctly assessed is most frequently resolvable only by reference to informal policy documents.[45]

There is another possible approach to the judicial review of informal policy announcements: a judge may give effect to them only when he or she deems them to be reasonable and appropriate. That is, since informal agency guidance is not legally binding, Chinese judges may decline to apply it even if it is not in violation of any law, simply on the ground that it is unreasonable.[46] But to ask them to exercise such discretion against government agencies would be to ask more of them than even common law judges accustomed to making law: faced with the complex multitude of policies in the modern state, most judges would choose deference to the executive branch when there is no clear violation of law.

The radical limitation of the civil law judge's powers in this context has been little recognized by commentators on the Chinese judiciary. Chinese courts have long been the most prominent topic for those interested in promoting the rule of law in China: the conventional wisdom is that a key to the advance of law is to give courts enough resources so that they can act independently from the government and the CCP. The irony, however, is that by various objective measures, China's political leaders grant courts rather extensive resources. For

44 Because the State Council's announcement is informal, neither the MOF nor the SAT can make formal regulations regarding the same subject matter: such regulations would neither have a basis in the PITL (which delegated lawmaking authority only to the State Council) nor claim a basis in an informal State Council notice.

45 Cui 2011, 2017b.

46 This was especially the case before 2018, when the SPC issued new guidance on the application of the Administrative Litigation Law as amended in 2015. The latter amendment gave plaintiffs the right to request courts to review the legality of informal agency guidance. While legal scholars and commentators in China claimed that this change enhanced the right of private citizens, an unintended consequence was that judges were soon required to give force to any informal agency guidance that is not in violation of law – they can no longer reject guidance that is not illegal but unreasonable. See Cui, Cheng, and Wiesner 2019 for discussion.

instance, the total number of judges in China stands at close to 200,000, which implies a significantly higher number of judges per capita than even the United States and France, and almost ten times the ratio in India.[47] Even more relevantly, each of China's general courts – there are over 3,500 of them at the county, prefecture, and provincial levels – has an administrative law tribunal dedicated to adjudicating disputes between government agencies and private citizens. This means that in 2017, the average annual caseload for each administrative law tribunal in the country was less than 100 (the total number of first-instance and appeals cases that year was 338,531): this is especially light given that Chinese judges only apply the law to resolve disputes and need not write lengthy opinions that might have precedential value.[48]

These final statistics point to yet another distinct, but equally profound, reason why Chinese courts hold little relevance in the field of taxation. For judges (even of the common law variety) to exercise influence and constrain government action, private citizens need to bring lawsuits in the first place. In Chinese taxation, this rarely happens. The highest number of lawsuits brought against Chinese tax agencies in a year was 2,069 (in 1998),[49] and that number has remained under 1,000 since 2004 (reaching a low of 293 cases in 2008). Therefore, the vast majority of Chinese courts have no opportunity to adjudicate tax disputes, let alone to "hold the government accountable" in tax collection. The low volume of tax litigation is unlikely to be explained by the lack of formal law that taxpayers can appeal to: in addition to the substantive provisions in various parts of tax law, there are plenty of procedural issues that could generate disputes and that Chinese judges could opine on.[50] Instead, Chinese taxpayers' lack of interest in litigation is likely to have much more to do with Chinese tax administration's approach of atomistic coercion. As analyzed in Chapter 3, this approach encourages quasi-compliance among a wide swath of the taxpayer population: businesses only need to heed the commands of grassroots tax administrators rather than the letters of the law to be deemed compliant. The physical

[47] Ng and He 2017.

[48] Cui, Cheng, and Wiesner 2019. See Cui and Wang 2017 for statistics on the long-term evolution of patterns of litigation against government agencies in China.

[49] As discussed in Chapter 1, this was during the transient period after the launching of the 1997 tax administration reform; the emphasis on taxpayer self-assessment was abandoned in the early 2000s.

[50] Cui 2017a discusses various proposed explanations of the low level of tax litigation in China.

accessibility of decentralized tax agencies and the resulting opportunity for personal familiarity with tax collectors further diminish the probability of litigation. Thus, even if the courts are well resourced – and even if Chinese citizens hold courts in relatively high esteem – they could hardly make law more relevant.

Central Political Authority

This chapter's arguments so far suggest that although the Chinese government has undermined the rule of law in taxation, it has done so not through manipulation or subversion of parliaments or courts, but through two other extraordinary practices. First, much ordinary governance is conducted outside the realm of legal norms and institutions altogether. Second, while marginalizing law in this way, political actors also invoke law selectively: law becomes pertinent when new taxes are introduced or tax rates increased, but not when taxes are cut; law is germane when the central government desires to withhold approval in respect of subnational policies, but not when it grants approval.

Political invocations of the idea of "taxation according to law" (*yifa zhishui*) in fact go back at least four decades: by the early 1980s, it had already become a prominent slogan in tax policy debates within the Chinese government. It bears stressing how remarkable this little-known fact is: it means that Chinese political leaders and top bureaucrats argued about "taxation according to law" well before they came to know about the VAT and other modern taxes introduced during and after the 1994 tax reform, well before most of the NPC's activities in the tax area, and well before Chinese courts gained systematic authority to adjudicate disputes between the government and taxpayers.[51] Why did law seem important for taxation so early on, when the country's legal and tax systems were barely starting to develop?[52]

An important part of the explanation is that certain essential features of law render it uniquely suitable for modern governmental functions. For example, when China's central government introduced new tax rules in the early 1980s (applicable mostly to state and collectively owned enterprises), the planned economy was still in full swing; firms in different industries had their own supervising ministries setting production

[51] The Administrative Litigation Law was enacted in 1989.

[52] The next few paragraphs summarize the findings in Cui 2013. I refer readers to that earlier work for extensive historical references documenting the various uses of the concept of law in Chinese taxation before 1994 (or see Cui 2012a for references in Chinese).

plans. The Ministry of Finance encountered difficulty getting firms to follow the tax rules it announced, because other ministries also wanted to make decisions about taxes. The MOF thus found it useful to stress that there was something called taxation according to *law*: not just anyone could announce law; only the agency authorized by the State Council to make tax rules (i.e. the MOF) was the source of tax law. Because the concept of law intrinsically conveys the ideas of an identifiable authority and of a consistent set of rules, it was the right concept for asserting the MOF's authority.

Moreover, the MOF emphasized the procedural aspects of law's adoption. It acknowledged that other government agencies and subnational governments may disagree with the rules it promulgated, but argued that such disagreement should be elevated to the State Council for resolution. Before those who held different opinions could sway the "lawmakers," the law that had already been adopted must be obeyed. The possibility of making changes to rules, combined with the obligatory nature of rules before they are changed, is another quintessential feature of legal systems.

Another intrinsic feature of law that appealed to China's tax policy makers in the early 1980s is its public-facing nature: law needs to be publicly known, and there is a public expectation for law to be followed. This was likely why Article 56 of China's 1982 Constitution, the only constitutional provision addressing the subject of taxation, states that citizens have the obligation to pay tax according to the law. The aim of this provision was neither to enable nor to limit the government's taxing power within a constitutional framework, but simply to announce that by having basis in law, the government's exercise of taxing power expects compliance. And more generally, invocations of law in tax matters were often made in the 1980s in connection with the publicity of law: tax administrators were eager to support legal education (*pufa*) campaigns, and referred to Chinese citizens' lack of awareness of the obligatory nature of tax rules as a major obstacle to tax collection.

It is not coincidental that, during the 1980s, China's tax administration workforce was just beginning to build up (see Figure 1.1). As I argued in Chapters 3 and 4, once the revenue management regime and its approach of atomistic coercion became entrenched in the early 2000s, taxpayers' lack of awareness of the content of law became more acceptable to tax agencies. And as mentioned earlier in this chapter, the MOF and SAT have also largely lost interest in announcing tax policy through formal legal instruments and giving publicity to new policies through the levers of law. But in the 1980s, China's army of grassroots tax collectors was not yet a very effective substitute for legal mechanisms. This is reflected in another reason why the government often appealed to law in taxation: strong taxpayer resistance to tax collection emerged in the late 1980s among both private firms and state-owned enterprises. In 1989, the Supreme People's Court reported that there had been 8,017 incidents of violent attacks on tax administrators since 1986, with "11 individuals killed, 26 individuals physically disabled, and 713 individuals severely injured." The Commissioners of the SAT reported in 1992 that incidents of "mob siege, abuse, humiliation and injuring of tax administrators and threats, retaliation, and persecutions against tax administrators and their family members" exceeded 3,000 a year. In this context, tax agencies' appeals to "law" allowed courts and especially the police to be mobilized against tax protestors. In 1989, the SPC even issued a directive explicitly calling on China's courts to *favor* tax agencies in adjudicating disputes with taxpayers – so beleaguered were tax administrators when carrying out their missions.[53]

These reasons for making appeals to law – ensuring the consistency and publicity of rules, and commanding compliance with the coercive powers of the state – may not be obvious at first, but they are directly based on the fundamental nature of law. Yet their significance in Chinese tax administration has receded; they are no longer the main reasons why official documents endlessly exhort taxation according to law. Instead, in the 1980s, there was *another* reason why China's central government promoted this concept – one that was more prominent and more controversial, and that had little to do with the intrinsic nature of law. But it is the position that survived and holds sway in Chinese political discourse today: only the central government, not subnational governments, can dictate tax policy. Lawmaking power in matters of taxation must be reserved to the national government.

Current Chinese political discourse so thoroughly conflates law with central government authority that it can be difficult for those immersed in it to distinguish between two claims: (1) that law must be sponsored by a public authority and (2) that law must be sponsored by a national authority. This latter claim is hard to justify, and is refuted by the fact that even under China's own Constitution, subnational People's Congresses (and the governments they form) are sui generis sources of state power and of law (even if the national government claims supreme power).[54] China's central

[53] Cui 2012a.

[54] Articles 2, 96, and 105 of the Constitution of the People's Republic of China. From an international perspective, subnational governments also almost uniformly possess some inherent lawmaking power, whether in federalist or unitary countries.

government has downplayed this fact, partly by exploiting the ambiguity in the Chinese word *guojia* – which at once connotes the idea of state or public authority and the idea of a nation. Yet in the sphere of tax policy in the 1980s, the idea that only the central government could make law struck many as nearly absurd, not because of its logical fallacy, but because it flew in the face of political reality.

The most direct reason for this was that China had emerged from the Cultural Revolution in a state of deep decentralization. Before 1976, the central government had been largely paralyzed by the political turmoil Mao Zedong created; provincial governments determined their own budgets and adopted their own tax policies. And as Deng Xiaoping launched a new era of economic reform, the country went through a long period – from 1977 all the way to 1993 – of "fiscal contracting" between provinces and the central government: provinces claimed a large degree of fiscal autonomy and were only responsible to remit fixed amounts of tax revenue to the central government.[55] When provinces bargained with the State Council and MOF only about the amounts of fiscal transfers to the central government each year, why should the central government care about *how* each province collected taxes, and *what* the rules by which taxes were raised were? The claim that a nationally uniform set of tax rules needed to be followed seemed completely unmoored to fiscal practice.

Moreover, most of the tax rules that the MOF adopted throughout the 1980s did not work. Subnational governments championed economic reform and opening to foreign investments during this period, and the national government relied on and encouraged their experimentations. Economic policy was thus very decentralized. The MOF's tax rules, however, failed to keep pace with and often conflicted with local economic policies (e.g. by requiring firms to pay much more taxes to subnational governments than subnational policy makers desired). It was thus unsurprising that most of these national tax rules were quickly abandoned, sometimes even before implementation. With such poor credentials, the State Council's and MOF's attempt to monopolize tax policy making seemed poorly conceived.

Yet if China's central government was not particularly good in the 1980s at devising tax policy for the country, it was better than subnational governments at invoking the idea of law. It certainly had an advantage in doing so, being the most prominent public authority in the country. But

[55] Oksenberg and Tong 1991; Wong 1991; Jin, Qian and Weingast 2005.

it is also true that no subnational government in China invoked the concept of law in the 1980s as often as the central government did. Although they contested the center's attempt to monopolize tax policy making, they did not pursue their own legislations. Consequently, when the central government ultimately succeeded in consolidating China's public finance by securing provincial agreements to the 1994 tax reform, it encapsulated this victory in the language of law. The State Council's *Decision to Implement the Revenue Sharing System of Public Finance Management* proclaimed: "The power to legislate with respect to central government taxes, shared taxes, and local taxes shall all be held exclusively by the central government, so as to guarantee the uniform implementation of central government policies and command, and to protect a single national market and allow enterprises to compete fairly."[56]

Once the name of law is adapted to embody and legitimize the central government's claim of monopoly on tax policy making, invocations of law become inescapable in official documents. Indeed, all of the important policy directives I have cited in this book regarding tax administration,[57] as well as countless other internal documents originating from the MOF, SAT, and provincial tax bureaus, began with exhortations about taxation according to law. Critically, the vast majority of these directives are aimed at civil servants and not the public. "Taxation according to law" thus has nothing to do with parliamentary or judicial constraints on the executive, or with citizens' obligations to comply; it has all to do with obedience, on the part not of citizens but of political actors within the state, to the central government's political authority. The radical subversion of law comprises first in the building of a vast state machinery that substitutes for legal mechanisms in tax collection, and second in the wholesale adaptation of the language of law for maintaining political control within that machinery.

[56] *Guofa* [1993] 85, December 15, 1993. This doctrine initially appeared in Article 3 of the Law on the Administration of Tax Collection (Presidential Decree No. 60, September 4, 1992), and was subsequently codified in Article 8 of the Law on Legislation (Presidential Decree No. 31, March 15, 2000).

[57] These include those that launched the 1997 tax administration reform (Chapter 1), established the performance evaluations in the organization of revenue (Chapter 5), entrenched the revenue management system (Chapter 3), and promoted specialization within revenue management in more recent years (Chapter 4).

8

Varieties of State Capacity

One single fact crucially distinguishes China's tax system, as it has evolved since the 1980s, from tax systems in other countries: China has collected standard modern taxes – income taxes, VAT, broad-based excise taxes, and so forth – that are designed to be administered through self-assessment, while *minimizing* reliance on self-assessment. This is a radical and unique experiment. The Chinese case allows us to study what follows from decoupling the taxes familiar to modern economies from a collection method that many have assumed to be immutable.

This basic modification of the modern taxation paradigm has extraordinary implications. It reveals something that has been little recognized by previous scholarship: how extensively our conventional depictions of tax administration and compliance rest on the practice of self-assessment, and how substantially altered such depictions must be when self-assessment is not present. In this chapter, I first argue that this calls for significant revisions to economic theories of tax administration and compliance. Because self-assessment is quintessentially about complying with legal norms, modern taxation is deeply intertwined with legal systems, and the Chinese case demonstrates how a tax system becomes profoundly different when severed from a legal system's support. Significantly, although there are long-standing controversies about the explanatory power of economic theories of tax compliance, few have recognized that these theories' shortcomings might originate from their neglect of the central role of law.

A second aim of this chapter is to draw out the implications of this book's study for the theory of tax and development. By the account given in previous chapters, China's revenue management system has complex political origins, and derives its resilience and vitality from the political ecosystem of the contemporary Chinese state. Stated abstractly, this book's narrative suggests that (1) politics is a key determinant of both tax policy and the structure of tax administration and (2) the structure of tax administration is a key determinant of both the design and outcomes of tax policy. These claims are consistent with an ambitious theory advanced by the political economists Tim Besley and Torsten Persson, which hypothesizes that to properly study tax and development, one must not only consider state capacity in tax collection, but also view such state capacity as endogenous with politics.[1] This book provides a rare, detailed case for examining Besley and Persson's hypothesis. In particular, Besley and Persson posit that investments in legal systems and taxation – which they regard as the two forms of state capacity that represent the twin "pillars of prosperity" in modern economies – are complementary. My account partially affirms, but also enriches, that hypothesis in two ways. First, China's case demonstrates that state-sponsored social ordering without law can also complement tax capacity. Second, I suggest that law's complementarity to taxation should be understood not in terms of the benefits of contractual enforcement and property rights protection, but in terms of the public knowledge and voluntary compliance afforded by a legal system.

Because the Chinese experiment with modern taxation is fairly recent, one may query whether its distinctive features will erode in the future – whether it will evolve to converge with more familiar paradigms of modern taxation. I believe that, instead, technological developments could strengthen China's policy preference for its current tax system. Will we, then, see other countries converge toward China's model? This question is important both theoretically and from a policy perspective. A third task of this chapter is to revisit the claim that there are fundamentally different types of state capacity in taxation, and to consider the policy implications of these choices.

Law, Social Norms, and Economic Theories of Tax Compliance

Self-assessment is one of the most fundamental – yet rarely recognized – ideas of modern taxation. The concept is simple: taxpayers and other private parties (such as agents responsible for withholding) acquaint themselves with the rules that determine their liabilities and obligations under tax law; they then apply the rules to themselves and make declarations and payments to the government. Self-assessment is the primary method by which most modern taxes – the VAT, sales taxes, income taxes, and payroll taxes – are collected. However, it is generally mentioned only in practical discussions of tax administration, and even there, its seeming simplicity prevents it from receiving further elaboration.

[1] Besley and Persson 2013.

It helps to be more precise about self-assessment's meaning. Compare it with a more commonly used term, "voluntary compliance." Two differences should be noted. First, self-assessment is a *legal* obligation: it is both enforceable and enforced by government and private parties. "Voluntary" compliance, by contrast, can be a confusing term. To many, it suggests that private parties behave in accordance with legal requirements without regard to whether the requirements are enforced (through surveillance, punishment, etc.); it thus seems an oxymoron to speak of *enforcing* voluntary compliance, when parties supposedly act purely out of pro-social motives. Second, self-assessment implies that the applicable rules by which self-assessments are made are knowable in advance. In contrast, some may not associate "voluntary compliance" with rules: one can comply with the calls of some leader or authority, doing "whatever one is asked to do," without obligations spelled out in advance.

This conceptual reflection highlights something critical: following publicly announced rules of law is the essence of self-assessment. Any discussion of tax administration that assumes the practice of self-assessment thereby assumes the existence of a background legal system. This includes the foundational economic model of tax evasion advanced by Michael Allingham and Agnar Sandmo, which studies an individual's "tax declaration decision."[2] In this classic setting, the taxpayer chooses whether to fully declare his or her actual income, facing uncertainty that any underreporting may be detected under audit. The taxpayer knows what income is required by law for disclosure; the tax authority assumes that the taxpayer knows such requirements; and sanctions are threatened on the basis of such common knowledge. This means that the problem of income tax evasion, as economists have come to conceptualize it, would not even make sense to anyone unacquainted with legal systems. Moreover, since the concept of audits assumes self-assessment, it also assumes that a background legal system exists.

Unable versus Unwilling to Cheat

To probe the logic of self-assessment further, note that the government interventions that enforce it are necessarily *ex post*: taxpayers declare tax liabilities on tax returns first, followed by audits (and punishment in the

[2] Allingham and Sandmo 1972. A casual scan of the vast literature that followed will confirm the universal acceptance of the implicit setting – that tax evasion is conceived of as misreporting within a paradigm of self-assessment. See, for example, Andreoni, Erard, and Feinstein 1998; Slemrod and Yitzhaki 2002; Slemrod 2019.

case of violations) from tax administrators. A common notion that captures this idea is that audits generate deterrence: taxpayers decide what to do, in light of what might happen *after*. A lesser known, but rather illuminating, take on the *ex post* nature of audits is that the sanctions threatened by audits are intended to make taxpayers *unwilling* to cheat, instead of making them completely *unable* to do so.

The dichotomy between being unwilling versus unable to cheat on taxes has been recently invoked in a widely cited study by Hendrik Kleven and several other economists.[3] Like economists before them, the study's authors noted that the level of tax compliance in advanced economies is generally very high – enough to allow some governments to collect more than 40 percent of GDP as tax revenue. But neither the probabilities of audits nor the magnitudes of penalties in these countries seem high enough to deter rational individuals who are bent on maximizing their own incomes from underreporting their taxable earnings. There is a large gap between the actual observed levels of compliance, and the deterrence powers that can be plausibly attributed to actual audit and penalty practices. To bridge this gap, many claim that most taxpayers feel a sense of obligation to pay their taxes, and do not engage in calculations about the personal costs and benefits of tax evasion. But Kleven and his coauthors argued that economic and noneconomic motives that make people unwilling to cheat are not the only mechanisms in play.

Very often, they argue, the government can observe how much income taxpayers have earned through reports submitted by third parties. For sources of income subject to third-party information reporting (TPIR), taxpayers may not really have a choice – the probability of detection and penalty could be close to 100 percent. In these cases, taxpayers are essentially disabled from cheating. Kleven et al.'s study shows that even in Denmark – a country known for its high taxes and law-abiding citizens – the rate of accurate income reporting is much higher for types of income subject to TPIR than those that are not. Therefore, the ability of governments to intervene in advance and *disable* noncompliance may be just as (or more) important than the threats of audits and other, noneconomic factors.

Although the Danish study emphasizes information reporting's effect on compliance – a subject to which I will return – a broader lesson one can draw is that the availability of *ex ante* interventions in tax compliance could render *ex post* interventions superfluous. Consider, for instance,

[3] Kleven et al. 2011.

property tax assessments based on the market value of real properties. Suppose that the government's ability to determine a property's market value is no worse (or even better) than that of the property owner. In this case, there would be no need to ask the taxpayer to assess his or her own tax liability and conduct audits to verify whether there is underreporting: the government can make the assessment directly. Similarly, suppose some income from financial transactions (e.g. dividend or capital gain) is taxed at a flat rate without regard to personal circumstances. Suppose further that it is just as easy for the government to observe the tax base as it is for taxpayers (e.g. financial institutions need to produce the relevant information either way, whether to the government or to individuals). Again, the government can dispense with self-assessments and audits, and directly engage in assessment and collection.

A substantial range of tax administration tools can be seen in this light. As further examples, tax authorities can automatically register businesses for tax purposes, based on registration with other government authorities, without waiting for the businesses to do so;[4] the government can also "pre-populate" individual tax returns with information obtained from third parties and leave taxpayers only a chance to identify inaccuracies; the government can even require taxpayers to deposit funds into bank accounts from which the government automatically deduct amounts, which would substantially secure timely tax payments periodically.

In what circumstances might a government be limited to *ex post* interventions? Economists studying tax administration have rarely considered this question, but there is a relevant – though not completely satisfactory – answer from another area of scholarship, namely law and economics.[5] In the terms used in this latter literature, audits enforce a kind of "liability rule" – tax evasion is not prohibited, taxpayers simply have to bear the consequences of tax evasion. *Ex ante* interventions, by contrast, can be analogized to "property rules," which categorically prohibit regulated subjects from certain activities. Property rules are often enforced with very high penalties or direct coercion (e.g. injunctions, imprisonment). Choosing liability rules over property rules in controlling harmful activities is typically justified by law and economic scholars on two grounds. First, private parties may possess better information about the social benefits of the activities being regulated: liability rules allow the benefits of such activities to be weighed against their

4 Lediga, Riedel, and Strohmaier 2020 study such practices in South Africa.

5 Kaplow and Shavell 1996; Shavell 2004.

harm.[6] Second, property rules are sometimes unenforceable because the government lacks the power of observation to make *ex ante* interventions. In such cases, liability rules play an important role, either by leveraging private parties' power of observation (e.g. allowing victims to sue for damages), or by making the regulated subject responsible for all consequences of its actions, without the need to observe the precise nature of the actions.[7]

It is generally assumed that, when taxes are properly designed, only private benefits, but no social benefit, accrue to tax evasion. Therefore, the first standard justification for liability regimes would not explain the adoption of self-assessment and audits. This leaves the second justification: it must be that the government is often not able to intervene *ex ante*, either for the lack of the power of observation or the power to intervene in a cost-effective way, or both. If, say, one becomes convinced on reflection that the government's power of *ex ante* interventions in taxation is *inherently* limited, then one would have an explanation of why *ex ante* interventions cannot completely substitute for self-assessment and audits.

However, the extent to which *ex ante* interventions can substitute for *ex post* ones to secure tax compliance clearly depends on tax design and available technologies. If taxing real property generated sufficient revenue for a government, for example, it would have no need for self-assessment regimes. So one might well resist the idea that limitations on the government's power of observation and intervention are immutable. Kleven et al.'s hypothesis, that much of the tax compliance observed in advanced economies may be due to *ex ante* interventions that "disable" tax cheating, can be (and has been) taken to suggest that the more governments extend their power for *ex ante* interventions, the greater their taxing power becomes. In fact, one can read much of the recent economic literature on tax administration (inspired by the Danish study) as following this suggestion.[8] The striking intuition is that what holds the greatest promise for tax compliance is finding substitutes for self-assessment and audits, that is, administrative tools that would make self-assessment and audits irrelevant.

6 For instance, the social benefits of a polluter's production may be greater than the social harms generated by his or her pollution. When the government only observes pollution's harms but not production's benefits, it may be socially optimal not to prohibit pollution, but only to hold polluters liable for harm.

7 For example, negligence rules require judges to determine whether a defendant exercised the proper level of care, whereas strict liability rules are less demanding on the judge's ability to make sure determinations.

8 See Pomeranz 2015; Brockmeyer et al. 2019; Naritomi 2019.

This is exactly the approach that Chinese tax administration has taken. In Chapter 3, we saw that the (reported) timely filing and timely payment rates of Chinese taxpayers had reached above 90 percent even in the early 2000s. This could only be explained by the fact that tax agencies largely disabled taxpayers from filing returns and paying taxes late: if necessary, revenue managers would file the returns and arrange the payments for taxpayers. The notion that the government should intervene as early as possible to prevent noncompliance, instead of waiting to detect and punish wrongdoers, is precisely what animated the revenue management system (Chapters 3–4) and fueled the critique of the 1997 tax administration reform (Chapter 1). We have also seen that, at least in the past, Chinese practice has also revealed certain limits of the *ex ante* approach. High compliance can be secured where observation and intervention are feasible. Yet when this becomes the only reason why taxpayers comply, compliance on other margins – such as providing accurate information on tax returns – can fall significantly. Limits on the government's power of observation or intervention translates immediately into dismal compliance.

The critical question for economic theories of tax compliance is not whether the Chinese approach – and the strategy of maximizing the power of government observation and intervention to improve tax compliance – is doomed to failure. Instead, it is whether this is the *only* strategy available – or whether the high compliance levels we currently observe in advanced economies can be explained by something else. If the account of Chinese tax administration offered in this book sounds unfamiliar – even alien – then there must be something suspect about explaining tax compliance in rich countries like Denmark by the government's ability to disable tax cheats.

Tax Morale versus Legal Norms

Traditional economic theories of tax compliance portray government sanctions as the only source of "economic" or pecuniary incentives against tax evasion. Many economists concede that nonpecuniary motives may also drive citizens to comply with tax law (e.g. "moral sentiments, guilt, reciprocity, and social norms") and label them as the "intrinsic" motivations for tax compliance.[9] However, economists also hesitate, for good reason, to embrace the idea that "intrinsic" motivations

[9] Dwenger et al. 2016. See also Luttmer and Singhal 2014; Alm 2019; Besley, Jensen and Persson 2019; Besley 2020.

offer the primary explanation for the generally high levels of tax compliance in advanced economies. In studies that precisely measure compliance based solely on intrinsic motivations, the compliance level observed tends to be quite low.[10] And when multiple motivations are in play, the prevalence and strengths of purported "intrinsic" motivations are difficult to confirm empirically. Most importantly, even in high-compliance countries, it is well known that taxes that are poorly enforced – whether these are employment taxes that ought to be remitted when hiring childcare providers at home ("the nanny tax"), sales or use taxes that consumers are theoretically required to remit on purchases from foreign vendors, or income taxes that ought to be collected on individuals' barter transactions – are rarely complied with. Nonetheless, there continues to be substantial social scientific and policy interest in the phenomenon of "tax morale," which is defined as "the intrinsic willingness to pay tax."[11]

Yet this familiar dichotomy between the extrinsic and intrinsic motivations behind tax compliance ignores something quite fundamental. As I argued earlier, self-assessment is distinct from voluntary compliance. While the latter is largely synonymous with positive tax morale, the former is not. This is because self-assessment is in the first place a legal (not moral or cultural) obligation. Acts of self-assessment display adherence to a very specific type of norm – that is, rules spelled out in the law about what information or remittance needs to be sent to the government – rather than general moral principles or social mores. As a result, taxpayers with very different moral or political orientations can adhere to the same self-assessment requirements: they can, for example, engage in proper self-assessment even without feeling a "warm glow" from knowing that taxpayer dollars are contributing to worthy public goods, or thinking that one is fulfilling one's part of some social contract, and so forth.

The specificity of the norms that inform self-assessment is neatly captured by a recent study of German church tax compliance by Nadja Dwenger et al.[12] The study finds that among the minority of German

[10] For instance, Dwenger et al. 2016 found that when the German church tax was not actively enforced, only 20 percent of individuals liable for the tax were fully compliant, and most individuals were fully noncompliant. This is especially remarkable because church tax liability is calculated based on income as reported on personal income tax returns, suggesting that most individuals fully evade the church tax even as they comply with the PIT.

[11] OECD 2019. See also Luttmer and Singhal 2014 for an earlier review of the academic literature on tax morale.

[12] Dwenger et al. 2016.

taxpayers who voluntarily paid the church tax when there was no enforcement, more than half paid exactly the amount that the law required them to pay – no more and no less. Since, in the absence of enforcement, there was no "extrinsic" motivation for taxpayers to focus on this amount, the authors label the "intrinsic" motivation displayed the "duty-to-comply preference." They show that this preference did not vary according to the quality of services offered by the parish or other features of the taxpayer's local community – features that could lead to variations in local tax morale – but seemed instead to be trained on a *specific* object: the amount of tax that the law said was due. There is no reason why these specific dollar amounts (which were a function of individual income) would feature in taxpayers' psychology other than that they were dictated by specific legal rules.

Specificity is a distinct feature of legal norms: to find out what the law requires, one does not need to observe what other people do, engage in moral reasoning, or reflect on one's past experiences of guilt or shame; one only needs to consult the law.[13] Notably, public enforcement of the law through audits and penalties tracks such specificity of law. It is thus striking that when scholars consider "intrinsic" (as opposed to "extrinsic") motivations for compliance, they neglect this specificity and fall back on broader social norms and moral sentiments: indeed, it is assumed that all types of normative considerations may contribute to or detract from tax morale.

I believe this is partly because saying that tax compliance relies on intrinsic motivations to comply with *the requirement of law* sounds no more, and perhaps even less, enlightening than appealing to intrinsic motivations to adhere to other social norms. Scholars who have tried to analyze individuals' motivations to adhere to legal norms have focused on mechanisms such as the influence of personal reputation (e.g. "it is honorable to pay your taxes").[14] This attention to individuals acting in private capacities, however, not only seems arbitrary on reflection, but may also render the appeal to legal norms implausible. In many advanced economies, very few people other than tax administrators know how a particular individual completes their personal tax returns. People who cheat on their taxes are rarely publicly shamed. Thus, even if reputational concerns could motivate individuals to adhere to certain social norms, they do not seem particularly relevant in the field of individual tax

[13] Shavell 2004, Chapter 26.
[14] Besley, Jensen, and Persson 2019; Posner 2000.

compliance. I suspect this is why, to explain tax compliance in terms of intrinsic motivations, it has seemed necessary to invoke stronger sentiments, such as the drive to follow moral principles or attitudes about the government.

However, the significance of legal norms becomes unmistakable when one considers their complementarity with *business firms*. The reputational concerns associated with whether individuals adhere to the law or not are likely much stronger when strangers come together to work together in an organization, especially in business firms. This is because, outside of criminal gangs, people come together in a business to pursue lawful gains and divide up the gains in an orderly manner. Such collective efforts become much simpler when the participants in the firm can mutually expect adherence to the law. And the larger the firm (and the more complex its internal coordination), the more likely it is that compliance with legal norms matters. A regularity that economists have observed is that larger business firms are more likely to be tax compliant, and countries with a greater share of large firms in their economies tend to raise taxes more easily.[15] But it is likely that this merely reflects a more fundamental regularity, namely that large business firms are more compliant with a wide range of legal rules (i.e. not just tax rules): they rely on the legal system more, and therefore display greater tendencies for intra-firm enforcement of legal norms.[16]

There are important reasons to believe that the tendencies of business firms – and not of individuals in their personal capacities – to comply with legal norms are critical to modern tax administration. Earlier, I referred to the conjecture that TPIR preempts much of tax noncompliance by providing the government with the required information. Such information reporting (and, equally importantly, the withholding of taxes) is overwhelmingly carried out by business firms: for instance, employers and financial institutions report on wage and financial income paid to employees and investors, businesses withhold the VAT on other businesses, and so forth. But TPIR is hardly an explanation of

[15] See Kleven, Kreiner, and Saez 2016.

[16] Kleven, Kreiner, and Saez 2016 interpret the size gradient of compliance in terms of the greater risk of whistleblowing by insiders to a firm when firm size increases. The appeal to whistleblowing can be analogized to arguments made by law and economics scholars regarding how liability rules strengthen the enforcement of law by allowing private litigants to bring infringers to court. See Shavell 2004, Chapter 25. However, whistleblowing has played a negligible role in the history of modern taxation. It is more likely that private social sanctions, without the involvement of public authorities, are sufficient to enforce most legal norms in business firms.

compliance, since the acts of the "third parties" filing information returns and remitting withheld taxes are *acts of self-assessment in themselves.* Unless business firms are somehow preempted from noncompliance, their performance of self-assessment obligations equally represent instances of unwillingness to cheat. And if such compliance happens at levels above what can be predicted from government deterrence alone, some other explanation must be offered of why businesses do not cheat as much as they could. In other words, a critical error committed by economists advocating the benefits of TPIR is that they have conflated institutions of self-assessment with institutions of *ex ante* government interventions.

Noting the complementarity between legal norms and the institutional setting of business firms is vitally important, because it breaks down the dichotomy between extrinsic and intrinsic motivations of compliance. That dichotomy characterizes individuals only in their private capacity (i.e. as citizens and individual taxpayers). But because the administration of modern taxes relies extensively on business firms, modern tax compliance may have primarily *institutional* foundations: individuals may be substantially more motivated to comply with the law in organizational rather than private (or non-organizational and cultural) settings. Since individuals often enter business ventures (or the workplace) with pecuniary motivations, it is not fully accurate to say that they act mainly on nonpecuniary motives in complying with the law in their business or employment. Yet at the same time, it is also true that individuals pursuing business or employment in firms do not comply with the law only when there is a specific individual pecuniary benefit for the act of compliance: instead, complying with the law may be a general condition for entering into or staying at a business venture for pecuniary gain.[17]

My purpose here is not to conclusively establish the primacy of one general explanation of tax compliance (e.g. the greater likelihood of adherence to legal norms in the context of business firms) over others. Instead, my suggestion is that the idea that tax compliance in advanced economies is essentially based on adherence to legal norms is much more plausible than considerations of individual tax compliance have revealed, because compliance with the law often has an institutional, rather than individual, basis. Further, the centrality of legal norms is what makes self-assessment and audits such fundamental institutions of modern taxation. Prior economic theories of tax compliance thus commit at least three

[17] I develop this view in Cui 2018.

errors in their analyses: (1) failing to recognize the centrality of legal norms to self-assessment and audits; (2) failing to recognize the complementarity between business firms and legal norms; and (3) mistaking self-assessment performed by business firms for *ex ante* interventions by the government against noncompliance.

One payoff of recognizing the centrality of legal norms in modern tax administration is that it allows us to identify what is truly radical about China's approach to collecting modern taxes. As I showed in Chapters 2 and 3, Chinese tax collection substantially puts the norm of truthful reporting out of play: taxpayers are generally not held accountable for their declarations required by law. Even when tax collection depends on private information held by taxpayers (and not just on the government's own ability to observe the tax base), tax administrators rely on informal bargaining, and not legally prescribed sanctions. Further, tax administrators are willing *not* to rely on large organizations' capacity to achieve full compliance, and instead tolerate a substantial degree of "quasi-compliance." At the same time, strenuous efforts are made to expand the government's range of observation and capacity for *ex ante* interventions. The substitution of such intervention for self-assessment and legal norms is genuinely put into practice, as opposed to being merely a scholarly misinterpretation of the facts.

If one asks, "How high is tax morale in China?", the answer, I believe, is indeterminate. "Voluntary compliance" seems low, as the government's prodding and handholding are extensive, and the norm of truthful reporting is widely disregarded. But it is unclear that Chinese taxpayers' noncompliance with self-assessment obligations is any greater than taxpayer noncompliance in rich countries with unenforced legal norms (such as the previously described "nanny tax"). In the meantime, taxpayer satisfaction in China may be high, as a result of easily accessible taxpayer services. What is unambiguously true, however, is the decisive disregard for legal norms.

Optimal Tax Administration

In the preceding discussion (and in Chapters 2–4) I proposed to classify administrative tools for securing compliance into (1) *ex ante* interventions, based on the government's power of observation and (2) *ex post* interventions, in response to taxpayers' prior compliance decisions. Among the latter, I further distinguish between interventions (such as audits) that enforce legal norms like truthful reporting, and other interventions (such as mandatory taxpayer self-inspections) that aim at raising revenue but disregard legal norms. While these are simple categories, they already stand in contrast with the way economists and other scholars ordinarily depict tax administration tools – basically, as an unstructured array. In the traditional economic literature on tax enforcement, audits are simply assumed to be the primary manner in which tax administrators exercise coercive power. While some economists have recently shown interest in studying a broader range of tax administration tasks – for example, taxpayer registration,[18] efforts to increase the rate of return filing and the timely payment of taxes,[19] and enforcement against delinquent taxpayers[20] – few have tried to articulate the relationship of these tasks to audits, or an overall framework by which the relative importance of these tasks can be evaluated.[21]

Yet in designing tax administration, questions about the relations among administrative tools are inevitable. For instance, researchers have recently confirmed that increasing taxpayer registration may have the consequence of lowering the rate of tax return filing, or decreasing the frequency of truthful reporting.[22] Does this require us to reevaluate the benefits of taxpayer registration? Similarly, recent research examining taxpayer services – sending out letter, email, or text reminders about filing tax returns or paying overdue taxes – recognizes that while enhanced services may improve some compliance outcomes, more coercive tactics may be required to raise revenue in environments characterized by high noncompliance.[23] Given limited government budgets, should resources be invested in more coercive tactics instead of taxpayer services – and are audits the only such coercive tactics?

In trying to answer these questions, it is tempting to take revenue collection as the ultimate yardstick of success. According to an important

[18] Bruhn and McKenzie 2014; De Giorgi, Ploenzke, and Rahman 2018; Floridi, Demena, and Wagner 2019.

[19] Brockmeyer et al. 2019, Gillitzer and Sinning 2020.

[20] Ortega and Scartascini 2020.

[21] In some sense, improving government performance in all these tasks strengthens state capacity in taxation. The International Monetary Fund (IMF) developed the Tax Administration Diagnostic Assessment Tool (TADAT) that encompasses these and many other tax administration outcomes. The OECD's Tax Administration Comparative Information Series likewise compiles extensive information comparing outcomes in different stages of tax administration.

[22] Lediga, Riedel, and Strohmaier 2020; Mascagni et al. 2020.

[23] Carrillo, Pomeranz, and Singhal 2017.

theory about tax administration,[24] the best approach is, essentially, to choose the administrative tool that yields the greatest "bang for the buck." More specifically, the theory of optimal tax administration contemplates that for each administrative tool, one can define (and potentially measure) its "enforcement elasticity" – the marginal revenue yield from the more intensive use of that tool. The more this marginal revenue yield exceeds the marginal cost of using the tool, the more desirable is its use.

Implementing this abstract theoretical conception faces substantial technical challenges. There are few estimates of the "enforcement elasticities" of tax enforcement techniques. Estimates of such elasticities relative to other tax administration techniques within the same context seem virtually impossible to find. And it is not meaningful to transpose enforcement elasticities across contexts – given that the theory of optimal tax administration explicitly recognizes that the enforcement elasticity of one administrative technique may be endogenous with tax policies and other administrative techniques.[25] Yet some economists seem to believe that more empirical research will advance what one might call the technological frontier envisioned by optimal tax administration theory.

However, there may be a more fundamental conceptual problem with choosing administrative tools based on their (net) revenue yields. This problem arises when the impact of government interventions on compliance is fundamentally mediated by social norms. For example, if audits fail to make the social and legal norm of truthful reporting prevalent, the direct revenue gain from audits may be quite high, because taxpayers are very non-compliant: Chapter 4 showed 95 percent of taxpayers in a Chinese province faced positive adjustments when subject to "intermediate risk response" (a type of audit). But as the Chinese case illustrates, the gain from informal negotiations with taxpayers may be even higher. After all, the chief reason why Chinese tax administrators choose self-inspections, self-audits, or other forms of bargaining for tax payments is that they yield higher revenue at lower cost.

On the other hand, if audits succeed in sustaining a norm of truthful reporting, the direct revenue gain from audits may be low compared to

[24] See Keen and Slemrod 2017. Keen and Slemrod's apparatus is attractive due to both its theoretical rigor and its off-the-shelf nature. Basri et al. 2020 and Brockmeyer et al. 2020 have already applied it to developing country contexts, although both studies examine the choice between varying tax administration efforts and changing statutory tax rates, and not between tax administration techniques.

[25] Basri et al. 2020 acknowledges this point in applying Keen and Slemrod 2017.

audits in a noncompliant environment, because taxpayers are already compliant. But such gain may still be higher than the gain from informal bargaining, if such bargaining is unacceptable to taxpayers adhering to legal norms. In other words, both the absolute and relative magnitudes of "enforcement elasticities" of government interventions may critically depend on the presence or absence of social norms.

A point commonly acknowledged is that one should not assess audits only by the adjustments made to audited taxpayers and the tax collected directly and immediately from them; one must also consider an audit's indirect deterrence effects. That is not my point here. Instead, my argument is that the indirect deterrence effects may be essentially mediated by the social norm of truthful reporting that audits aim to support. Whether such norms are sufficiently prevalent do not depend on audits alone. That is why, without considering the strength of the social norms sustained, the enforcement elasticity of revenue with respect to audits (even if indirect effects could be measured) may not be well defined. Moreover, the presence of social norms of tax compliance should not be taken as a given, the way individuals' "intrinsic motivations" are taken as a given in standard theories of compliance. Instead, because the social norms of tax compliance are intrinsically legal norms, public and private enforcement are mutually dependent.

Accounting for the deep connections between modern taxation and legal systems requires major revisions to traditional theories of tax compliance: this critical proposition can be further evaluated in connection with a new theory of tax and development.

Theories of Tax and Development

The theory of optimal tax administration derives its impetus from the theory of optimal taxation, which is a body of modern economic theory that analyzes the consequences of tax policies on economic efficiency, the distribution of income, and social welfare. Many logically possible tax policies are not realistically implementable. Even those tax instruments studied in economic theory that are familiar-sounding are only idealizations of real-world taxes, which may misrepresent the latter when abstracting from tax administration. In response, some economists have aimed to make optimal tax theory more relevant to policy making by incorporating administrative considerations: the theory of optimal tax administration is the result. Importantly, both standard optimal tax theory and its variant incorporating tax administration share two significant features. First, both are technocratic exercises, depicting how a benign social planner would design policies (and organize tax collection) to maximize social welfare. Second, economists tend to postulate that economic factors ultimately determine feasible administrative instruments. For example, an economy characterized by a greater presence of large firms and greater use of financial intermediation provides better support for certain tax collection technologies (e.g. TPIR and withholding). Tax administration is, in the end, apolitical.

Tim Besley and Torsten Persson have recently argued for going beyond this "standard economic view" in the study of taxation and development.[26] Advances in broader social scientific research, they suggest, show that major modern economic institutions are dependent on *political institutions*. A nation's capacity to collect tax – its "fiscal capacity" – may also be fundamentally dependent on the incentives of *political* actors. Therefore, changes in economic structures alone cannot determine a country's approach to tax administration; neither economic development nor the development of tax systems should be taken as exogenous to politics.

Besley and Persson's theory provides two highly relevant observations for interpreting the Chinese experience. First, they explicitly propose that a government's investments in building and supporting a legal system and in fiscal capacity are complementary.[27] This hypothesis emanates from a cluster of intuitions: legal institutions are critical to economic development; legal institutions depend on political actors' willingness to maintain such institutions; political actors are more willing to invest in legal institutions if they can extract economic surplus from the fruit of such institutions (including through taxation); and legal institutions lower the cost of investments in fiscal capacity.[28] If the complementarity between legal systems and modern taxation is strong, then the idea that political institutions determine fiscal capacity becomes much more plausible (and intriguing). After all, many view political institutions as critical determinants of legal systems; if legal systems are in turn robustly complementary with modern taxation, then it would be surprising if investment in fiscal capacity were insensitive to the nature of political institutions.

[26] Besley and Persson 2013 at 52–54.

[27] Id, at 78. As evidence for this conceptual hypothesis, they show that measures of fiscal capacity (e.g. share of total tax collected through the income tax) and measures of legal capacity (the International Country Risk Guide's index of property rights protection) are strongly positively correlated in cross-country data.

[28] Id, at 76–79.

Besley and Persson's claim regarding the complementarity between law and modern taxation clearly has a similar ring to my earlier claim this chapter: legal systems form the essential background of modern taxation through the institution of self-assessment. It is thus useful to consider how their claims differ from mine. For Besley and Persson, the significance of legal systems for economic development lies in contract enforcement and property rights protection, illustrated by the courts' adjudication of contractual disputes and public land registries delineating property rights. Suppose we accept these familiar examples – taken from mainstream institutional economics – about how law facilitates economic development.[29] Still, how do such institutions increase the cost of evading income taxation – the main way in which Besley and Persson imagine legal systems to lower the cost (or increase the return) of investment in fiscal capacity? Here, they draw on another popular metaphor in institutional economics: to access the legal mechanisms of contract enforcement and property rights protection (including accessing credit markets), firms need to enter the *formal sector*. In the formal sector, "transactions and employment relations are recorded," making it "very hard for an individual to simultaneously be largely invisible to the tax system and take full advantage of the formal legal system."[30] The legal system increases the return of being in the formal sector, and therefore makes firms more willing to be subject to forms of taxation feasible only for this sector.

I believe there are two general ways in which this narrative can be improved. The first is that it is best not to conflate being in the formal sector with behavior adhering to legal norms. As discussed in Chapter 3, formality is a multifaceted concept: "firm formality" can coexist with labor or transactional informality. Insofar as formality is thought of as simply being on the government's radar, whether particular economic activities are "formal" will vary with the extent and nature of government interventions.[31] Such variations, however, do not generally track the actual reach of legal systems, since legal norms can also be privately enforced.[32] Conversely, government monitoring can also lead one away

[29] A more general view is that law facilitates complex coordination, and the causal channels go beyond particular types of law (e.g. contract and property) and particular legal institutions (e.g. courts). See Hadfield 2016.

[30] Besley and Persson 2013 at 78–79.

[31] Even within economic scholarship, there has been increasing recognition of the different margins of formality and the different types of corresponding government interventions. See Ulyssea 2018.

[32] It is not clear whether our concept of the formal sector requires us to say, for example, that when the *lex mercatoria* allowed medieval trade to flourish in Europe (Greif 2006), or

from law-abiding behavior: for example, being the target of government negotiations for tax payments and other purported regulation may require taking actions at odds with the law.[33]

Second, what Besley and Persson describe as behaviors in the formal sector (e.g. recording transactions and employment relations) are in themselves actions guided by legal norms. The point of recording transactions and employment relationships is for individuals to confirm that their legally protected expectations are fulfilled. Taking such actions may also be beneficial for economic pursuits, by allowing individuals to enter complex transactions both across and within firms. It is unnecessary to assume that the benefits of a legal system accrue only when justiciable disputes arise, or when some specific type of property rights (e.g. those that can go into a public registry) are at issue. If being "formal" simply means ordering one's economic affairs according to legal norms, then it makes no sense to speak of *first* entering the formal sector and *then* being allowed to access the benefits of law.

In other words, Besley and Persson seem to postulate that enabling government monitoring of economic agents in some basic way (i.e. bringing firms into the "formal sector"), using legal institutions as the "hook," facilitates other forms of government monitoring (e.g. reducing tax evasion). What I argue instead is that the key connection between legal norms and modern taxation is that the former makes self-assessment possible. When economic agents spontaneously order their affairs around legal norms – whether or not we describe this as a matter of entry into the formal sector – the institutional foundations of self-assessment are already established. With this foundation, the government's role in taxation becomes one of initiating occasional *ex post* interventions. The complementarity between law and modern taxation thus runs much deeper than is depicted by Besley and Persson – and without an intermediate and arbitrary concept of formality.

The refinement I propose to Besley and Persson's arguments critically bears on a second major aspect of the theory. If political institutions determine investment in fiscal capacity, how might different political institutions lead to different outcomes? For Besley and Persson, investment in fiscal capacity can vary only in two ways: a government may choose to invest in the income tax (and its associated administrative

when property rights regimes emerged on the Labrador Peninsula (Demsetz 1967), the formal sector expanded in these parts of the world.

33 Indeed, the Chinese case shows that the interaction between the government and regulated subjects can systematically deviate from legal norms.

infrastructure) or simply relying on trade taxes (e.g. tariffs); and once the income tax is chosen, a government can vary the intensity of its fiscal capacity investment. Within this narrow set of choices, Besley and Persson make various predictions: for instance, a government experiencing greater political turnover will invest less in fiscal capacity, whereas a government characterized by cohesiveness and inclusivity – or common interest – will invest more in fiscal capacity.[34]

This book has highlighted the Chinese government's apparently unwavering resolve to invest in some forms of fiscal capacity since the 1980s. Even when the country operated mainly under the 1980s planned economy, a large army of tax collectors was already hired to administer taxes for state-owned enterprises. Further, substantial investments in taxpayer services were made starting in the late 1990s, and in information technology since the 2000s. Although the personal income tax languished for seemingly political reasons (see Chapter 6), revenues from the corporate income tax and social insurance contributions have been robust. Such patterns of investment seem to indicate a collective political horizon that is relatively long, or "low turnover" in Besley and Persson's terms. By their theory, these patterns may even be taken to reflect sufficiently *cohesive* institutions, insofar as vital public goods are produced (e.g. juggernaut physical infrastructures and several waves of social insurance regimes that facilitated the country's vast economic transformation). It is unlikely that Besley and Persson's classification of cohesive and inclusive political regimes was intended to encompass China's political institutions. The predictions of the theory, therefore, seem ambiguous.

The imprint of political institutions on China's contemporary fiscal capacity is, however, unmistakable. It seems almost unimaginable, in a democratic polity, to systematically offer yearly incentives to subnational politicians to meet revenue targets. It seems even more unimaginable to charge civil servants with impossible portfolios of tasks (Chapter 3) – and to selectively implement those tasks according to the ever-changing wishes of bureaucratic superiors (Chapter 5) – without an ideological and political iron grip in the state apparatus. However, it is probably also unsurprising that tax farming – the granting of substantial pecuniary rewards to frontline tax collectors based on the amount of tax collected – thrives in China but not in modern democracies. Every

34 Less cohesive institutions use tax revenue to redistribute resources from one group to another instead of securing public goods, and the corresponding incentives to invest in state capacity depend on expectations about political turnover (in contrast to the incentives in cohesive institutions).

element of the system of atomistic coercion seems to bear the mark of authoritarianism.

To acknowledge the political imprint on state capacity requires recognition of a greater variety of fiscal capacities. The Chinese approach shows that social institutions coordinated through law are not the only possible complements to investments in fiscal capacity. Building a bureaucratic apparatus that is sufficiently decentralized, but still extensively disciplined and incentivized, may be a way to support enough *ex ante* government interventions to substitute for law-abiding behavior among private parties. In taxation, when *ex ante* government interventions replace self-assessment, law is rendered largely irrelevant. State capacity based chiefly on *ex ante* interventions thus centers on what the state can do by itself. In contrast, state fiscal capacity built upon legal norms – through the combination of self-assessment and *ex post* interventions – is only partly about state power. The critical role played by private individuals' willingness to adhere to legal norms, especially in the context of business firms and other large private organizations, implies that the government actually possesses limited oversight on such matters.[35]

I have endeavored to show how China's approach to tax administration is substantially explained by the country's political institutions. For one, a decentralized tax administration reflects a generally decentralized bureaucratic structure; it also complements a political promotion structure (in place since the 1980s) in which revenue targets are used to evaluate the performance of politicians at the lowest levels. Similarly, the reliance on *ex ante* interventions is not just a response to taxpayer noncompliance – it is applied even to large or state-owned institutions that are unquestionably in the formal sector – but also a means of facilitating the evaluation and incentivization of civil servants. Such a fine calibration of tax administration techniques to politics affirms Besley and Persson's general theory of tax and development. It also implies that the type of state capacity exemplified by the Chinese model deserves an important place in this theory's ongoing elaboration.

State, Statistics, and Fundamental Choices

At the end of Chapter 1, I briefly described China's investment in the Golden Tax Project. This involved the wide adoption of a VAT anti-fraud

[35] This is why Besley and Persson's claim about the complementarity between the state's investment in law and in fiscal capacity is so perceptive and intriguing.

technology that, though obscure, brilliantly illustrates the anti-thesis of self-assessment. Registered VAT taxpayers (i.e. those who could claim VAT input credits) were required to obtain special software from tax bureaus as well as accessory hardware (in particular, an integrated circuit [IC] card). To issue VAT invoices to other taxpayers, they had to enter transactional information in government software, which encrypted the information to preclude tampering while producing encrypted codes on VAT invoices. Each month, taxpayers had to go to local tax offices to upload encrypted information from these IC cards to the government's IT system. While taxpayers also filed regular VAT returns – like VAT returns in most countries, these contained only aggregate monthly information – tax bureaus generally had no use for them: they only cared about the IC cards when it came to determining the value of taxpayer sales. Similarly, to claim input VAT credits, buyers were required to bring the encrypted invoices to local tax bureaus for verification. Only the validation of an invoice through de-encryption – and no other evidence of the purchase, including contracts, evidence of payments, and the physical goods purchased – was sufficient to permit the input credit claim. Once information about a transaction was reported from the seller and buyer sides through this specialized invoice system, the government would then match invoices to detect any VAT fraud. The *truthfulness* of tax returns had no import. Only the government's eye, in the form of the IC cards and the special invoices it generated, was relevant to compliance.[36]

Instead of this VAT practice, I have focused on the revenue management system as the most important example of the dis/replacement of self-assessment in China. This is not only because revenue management has been adopted for the administration of *all* Chinese taxes, but also because an assessment of the merits of VAT invoice cross-matching is complicated by certain technical issues.[37] Yet, at least internationally,

36 This system is detailed in chapter 14 of Schenk, Thuronyi, and Cui 2015. While in recent years China has substantially moved to e-invoicing and encryption technology that is consistent with online information submission and invoice verification, the basic idea of automatic invoice cross-matching remains the same.

37 The issues can be roughly summarized as follows. The invoice-credit VAT is designed as a system where businesses withhold tax that would be applied to downstream transactions and ultimately, to sales to final consumers (Ebrill et al. 2001; Schenk, Thuronyi, and Cui 2015; Waseem 2020a). In this system, VAT invoices represent a form of financial claims against the government that exist because of previously withheld and remitted taxes. When such claims can be forged at low cost by criminals – that is, when they are presented to the government even when no previous tax was remitted – the government is at risk of

VAT invoice cross-matching is clearly the less obscure phenomenon. It is thus useful to return to the Golden Tax Project as an example of the rejection of self-assessment.[38] The level of VAT fraud in China in the late 1990s was so high that it attracted the death penalty – the ultimate emblem of (attempted) deterrence. The Golden Tax Project may have reduced the level of VAT fraud in the 2000s,[39] enough so that China abolished the death penalty for this offence in 2011. This, in itself, can be viewed as a successful substitution of *ex ante* for *ex post* interventions.

Yet few Chinese tax administrators would claim that China's level of VAT compliance is as high as the levels in advanced economies. Notably, *no* advanced economy – not the European countries that first adopted the VAT, nor the myriad of countries that subsequently adopted and improved the VAT (e.g. the United Kingdom, Canada, Australia, New Zealand, and Singapore) – practices VAT invoice cross-matching. These countries have struggled with VAT fraud in recent decades, but they have been able to implement the VAT on the basis of self-assessment. This stark reality has been ignored in recent economic scholarship suggesting that invoice cross-checking is the essence of the VAT: it is now extremely popular among economists to claim that the VAT's credit invoice system creates a paper trail that allows governments to monitor market transactions against noncompliance, and that stronger state capacity consists of the greater frequency and effectiveness with which governments carry out VAT invoice cross-matching. Yet the reality is that the world's rich countries have *never* invested in such state capacity.

Notwithstanding this inconvenient fact, claims that governments can improve their state capacity by acquiring more information strike many as self-evident.[40] When technology lowers the cost of state monitoring and permits governments to assemble seemingly infinite amounts of

losing huge amounts of money. While criminal VAT frauds in advanced economies are associated with particular types of cross-border transactions (Keen and Smith 2006), in developing countries they are rampant even in purely domestic settings (Waseem 2020b). To collect the VAT, therefore, governments in developing countries especially feel the pressure to invest in anti-fraud techniques. VAT invoice cross-matching may thus seem necessary, even though in the VAT's original design – in which businesses were merely supposed to withhold taxes to be collected from consumers (and were thus indifferent to the VAT on B2B transactions) – VAT cross-matching would be completely pointless.

[38] The IMF explicitly identifies China's Golden Tax Project as abandoning self-assessment for the VAT. See Harrison and Krelove 2005, at 27.

[39] Fan et al. 2018.

[40] See the opposing views in Pomeranz 2015 and Cui 2018.

data, what is the downside of monitoring everything? In fact, this idea has recently gained traction in China, as the SAT has attempted to justify new investments in the Golden Tax Project: through VAT invoices, the government can monitor the entire economy at the transactional level[41] – and as a subtext, the SAT would become a valued source of economic data independent from the other arms of the state's statistical apparatus. Companies selling IT equipment and services to governments around the world also peddle this type of reasoning.

The gamble that technology will replace self-assessment has recently received endorsement from China's top leadership. In March 2021, the CCP and the State Council announced a new plan for tax administration "reform" – which, however, reads more like an ambitious vision to rely on technological upgrades to entrench the current system.[42] The government now touts the goal of "intelligent taxation" (*zhihui shuiwu*), in the sense of applying large-scale data processing, artificial intelligence (AI), and automation in tax administration. A central theme is to use "big data" and newly available computing power to perpetuate the current tax system while addressing its shortcomings. For example, the atomistic approach to tax administration has led to difficulties (discussed in Chapter 3) in keeping a single taxpayer file even at grassroots bureaus, let alone across jurisdictions. The 2021 tax administration "reform" plan contemplates that AI will permit unified taxpayers files to be created by 2022. Further, each tax bureau and even each tax administrator's actions will be sorted by AI into single files by 2023. The type of risk analysis that Mr. Chen Jianpu experimented with in Huai'an and Jiangsu Province before 2016 will supposedly become possible (and even automated) because of "big data." As e-invoices reduce the cost of verifying and matching VAT invoices, a universal e-invoice system is regarded as the "breakthrough" in this comprehensive technological upgrade.

Interestingly, performance evaluations of individual tax collectors will also be automated. At the same time, the tax administration "reform" announced in 2021 gives significant emphasis to the *reduced* use of penalties against breaches of law. A general principle of "no penalty for the first offence" is to be extended to a range of previously penalizable

[41] Chen et al. 2020b. However, criminals in China continue to find new ways to score gains against the government's anti-fraud system, while the Golden Tax Project continues to enrich many companies selling equipment and IT services to tax bureaus.

[42] General Office of the Chinese Communist Party Central Committee and the General Office of the State Council, *Opinions Regarding Further Deepening Tax Administration Reform*, March 24, 2021.

violations. Further, taxpayer services will be enhanced: individuals are supposed to be able to manage all compliance tasks "in their palms" (i.e. through smart phone apps) in the near future, online services are supposed to be available 24/7, and in-person services are supposed to be tailored to individual taxpayers. Nanny-style tax administration, in other words, will experience a second revival after its first renewal in the revenue management system – now through AI-driven customization.

One take on this vision of "intelligent taxation" – one that I am certainly inclined to offer – is that it consists of much wishful thinking, and simply adds to the many examples offered in Chapter 6 of how out of touch the Chinese central government is from grassroots reality. The vision, for example, ignores the poor quality of tax return data and the incompleteness of VAT transaction-level data. However, it cannot be denied that some elements of extensive data sharing and AI may strengthen Chinese tax authorities' surveillance power. Such power, when combined with other techniques of surveillance and social control (such as the Social Credit system that already preclude tax delinquents from purchasing plane or train tickets or from leaving the country), may well discourage some tax cheats and cajole other taxpayers into quasi-compliance. The more important point, though, is that the arrival of AI has emboldened the Chinese government to treat the revenue management system as a permanent, rather than transient, institution. Contrary to Mr. Chen Jianpu's theory, nanny-style tax administration is not the past, but the future.

The complementarity – real or perceived – between technology and *ex ante* government observation and intervention is of first-order importance for thinking about the future of tax administration, both in China and elsewhere. This is why it is critical to point out how modern tax administration in advanced economies has operated *without* the government access to information now envisioned by proselytizers of information reporting – there is a risk for scholars studying state capacity to forget this fact. Such forgetfulness has already befallen the Chinese experience. China's 1997 tax administration reform brought about substantial investment in state capacity – especially in taxpayer services – but it was soon forgotten that the aim of such services and investments was to *enable* taxpayer self-assessment. Instead, a substitute for self-assessment, in the form of 600,000 tax collectors stationed at post office-like proximity to taxpayers, was both readily available and in fact politically expedient to deploy. A mongrel language was quickly normalized to describe tax administration: tax administrators needed to "manage" taxpayers, taxpayers should be allowed to "self-inspect" and "self-audit," "taxpayer evaluations" and "risk management" could be put in place without the imposition of penalties, revenue needed to be "organized," and so on. Willy-nilly, self-assessment receded from the scene. As a legal scholar who has studied the VAT, I regard claims that the VAT may be "self-enforcing," creates "paper trails," and solves the problem of "no taxation without information" as similarly obscuring the VAT's original nature as founded upon self-assessment.[43]

The forces pushing for the expansion of governments' powers of observation and capacity for *ex ante* interventions go beyond commercial interests on the part of the IT industries and partial conceptions of state capacity. Scholarly biases have also contributed to the view that the government is empowered by information. As some economists have acknowledged, the term "statistics" has its etymology in the state.[44] In recent economic research, higher standards for empirical rigor have led academics to place greater premium on "big data" that can support sophisticated research design:[45] tax returns and other forms of "administrative data" at the individual or firm levels have become particularly prized. In talking to young economists, I hear expressions such as, "Unfortunately, we don't have transactional-level data" – as though governments' possession of data at the transactional level is natural and desirable. More generally, there is an undertone among empirically oriented scholars that what is good for researchers must also be good for governments (and the only problem is researchers' access to government data).

Yet it is not hard to see how such views are unreflective at best: if one privileges tax return data in the study of state capacity, one is basically predicating such study on the existence of a singular (and not inexpensive) form of state capacity. In fact, scholars' demand for "administrative data" can even be incoherent. As the Golden Tax Project concretely illustrates, the expansion of governments' abilities to make *ex ante* observations (e.g. forcing taxpayers to provide transactional-level data through encryption technology) may render other forms of data (e.g. tax returns) irrelevant, because the self-assessment practices that generate the latter would have been retired. Yet scholars may unwittingly assume that "state capacity" implies having *both* transactional-level data and tax return data.

[43] Ebrill et al. 2001, chapter 13.
[44] Beraja, Yang, and Yuchtman 2020.
[45] Angrist and Pischke 2010.

What lessons does the Chinese experience in tax administration hold for developing countries seeking to build their state capacity? It would be difficult to answer this question without first identifying some of the foregoing intellectual confusion. In summary, I believe the previous chapters suggest a three-part answer to the question.

First, there are fundamentally distinct forms of modern state capacity in tax collection. The most basic distinction is between capacities to carry out *ex post* interventions that support broader social institutions – especially those that encourage individual behavior adhering to legal norms – and capacities to observe private activity and make *ex ante* interventions. This distinction has, unfortunately, been little recognized in mainstream theories of tax compliance, which generally fail to acknowledge the deep connections between legal systems and modern taxation (Besley and Persson's theory being a notable exception). This distinction not only has explanatory power, but also reveals a substantial range of normative choices implicated in the design of tax administration. One obvious type of choice relates to the rule of law. For example, in advanced economies like the United States and Canada, lying on one's personal income tax returns is likely to attract moral disapprobation. In a tax administration approach that values *ex ante* interventions over *ex post* interventions, however, misreporting on one's tax returns may attract as little social or moral sanction as the act of skimming the payment of the "nanny tax," the church tax, or the user tax on out-of-state purchases in advanced economies. Similarly, tolerance for informal bargaining may be much greater in systems that prize *ex ante* interventions. These discomforting reflections show that designing tax administration is far from a predominantly technocratic exercise. But the possibility of irreconcilable normative choices also renders it challenging to sustain discourses about "best practices" in tax administration. Policy advice that urges changes to tax administration on all fronts – to enhance both *ex ante* and *ex post* interventions or to invest in legal institutions (e.g. legislation and formal dispute resolution) and mechanisms that erode legal norms – will likely be ignored.

Second, because of the significant normative choices implicated in tax administration design, it is difficult to say, as a normative matter, whether the Chinese approach is worthy of emulation or is instead utterly dystopian.[46] But what China's (largely inadvertent) experiment has

[46] As I showed in my discussion of Mr. Chen Jianpu's book in Chapter 4, many Chinese tax administrators despise the revenue manager system. But many others – as well as many Chinese taxpayers, especially high-income earners who face little enforcement of the PIT – are fine with it.

shown, as a positive matter, is that it is possible to collect modern taxes without self-assessment. Until recently, this experiment has relied on a historical legacy of grassroots tax offices and tax administrators, and a capacity to incentivize and discipline civil servants that is reminiscent of the revolutionary mobilizations of a Leninist state. However, tax administration that prizes *ex ante* interventions over *ex post* interventions may not need to rely on similar institutions being present in other countries. Instead, technological advances may broadly enhance a government's capacity for observation and intervention. By an accident of its political and bureaucratic apparatuses, China has demonstrated a possibility that is now available for all countries facing the digital revolution. With investments in technology, would investments in self-assessment and audit capacity still be worthwhile? This question again has no ready answer, but it is perhaps one of the most fundamental questions facing tax administrators in developing countries (and perhaps even in developed ones).

Third, if we take seriously Besley and Persson's theory of tax and development – the Chinese case lends ample credence to the theory – choices over tax administration will come to look even less technical. The most fundamental divergences in state capacity are likely to emanate from differences in *political* institutions; even normative preferences about the rule of law may be secondary. But for most people, once where they live is taken as a given, the political systems they live with are substantially beyond their control. They *adapt*, instead of choose. For this reason, the Chinese experience in tax administration does not so much teach a lesson as it holds up a mirror to the system each of us lives in.

9

Pivoting Away from the Rule of Law

A useful analogy can be drawn between China's 1994 tax reform and the country's accession to the World Trade Organization (WTO) in 2001. The tax system established in 1994 allowed China's gross tax ratio to quickly recover after the mid-1990s and, in the ensuing decades, furnished the country's leaders with the means for both substantial social spending and tax cuts – much as joining the WTO set China on a path of accelerated economic growth. Moreover, we now know that China's accession to the WTO fundamentally transformed the global economic order, and brought substantial disruptions to the economic, social, and political lives of citizens in some developed countries.[1] In the meantime, the expectations of the United States and other advanced economies that China would open its markets, liberalize its political regime, and increasingly adhere to the rule of law following the WTO accession have all been sourly disappointed. This book has told a parallel story of unfulfilled expectations, though purely within China's domestic setting. In 1994 – Chinese taxation's "WTO moment" – China's political leaders fully expected that the new tax system would be implemented on the basis of self-assessment and rule of law, following the practice of developed countries. Extensive resources were mobilized during the 1997 tax administration reform precisely for this purpose. But Chinese tax administration moved inexorably in a different direction, dashing the hopes of admirers of the Western taxation paradigm.

But the parallel goes deeper. I believe that the story of Chinese taxation – concededly obscure compared to the story of China's global economic ascendance – may be critical to understanding China's future global role. This is because the economic and ideological contests between China and Western countries will increasingly depend not on who better represents the rule of law, but on who has more inclusive institutions. Should the Chinese government maintain its tax capacity

[1] See, for example, Autor et al. 2016, 2019, and 2020.

and be willing to engage in redistributive social spending on the poor, its domestic legitimacy will strengthen, in comparison to polities that are nominally democratic but cater to only the interests of small groups of elites. If joining the WTO set China on a course of clashes with the West, it is China's tax system, which the 1994 reform launched, that may ultimately determine the outcome of such clashes.

In this chapter, I explain why the analysis of the earlier chapters should point both policy makers and social scientists away from studying the Chinese state's predilections for the rule of law and toward its capacity and willingness for inclusivity and redistribution.

Superstructures without Micro-foundations

In Chapters 7 and 8, I deployed an implicit theory of law in my accounts of law's marginal place in contemporary Chinese taxation and law's centrality in the modern tax paradigm within developed countries. Chapter 7 claimed that every legal system (to be viewed as such) must have a set of *rules of recognition* that determine which set of rules are valid legal rules. I explained that while China's Law on Legislation delineates a set of rules of recognition – indeed, the very operation of Chinese legislatures and courts depends on these rules – governance in areas like tax largely bypasses these rules (and therefore, subverts the legal system through its disuse). Chapter 8 argued that the paradigm of self-assessment in modern taxation depends on the joint enforcement of the norm of truthful reporting (and norms of law following in general) by government and private parties. Because the legal norms associated with self-assessment are enforced by private parties in the context of business firms and other organizations, government enforcement need not bear the entirety – or even most – of the burden in sustaining such norms. What some scholars have erroneously taken to be forms of *ex ante* government intervention (e.g. third-party information reporting) actually reflect the practice of self-assessment and the private enforcement of legal norms.

It is time to make this implicit theory of law explicit. The rules of recognition and the reliance on private enforcement are central to what one might call a minimalist theory of law. Gillian Hadfield and Barry Weingast recently advanced a version of this theory:[2] though it is not widely known, I find it highly illuminating. Hadfield and Weingast begin

[2] See Hadfield and Weingast 2014, 2019; Hadfield 2016.

with a premise widely accepted among legal theorists – namely that legal norms are distinct from many other types of social norms in that they are deliberately adopted and, as a result, can be frequently and purposely modified.[3] This feature of legal norms is explained, according to Hadfield and Weingast, by the existence in every legal system of an authoritative, "centralized classification institution" that pronounces legal norms. Hadfield and Weingast's idea of a classification institution is similar to H. L. A. Hart's "rule of recognition" and other conceptions of legal authority elaborated by legal positivists. Their distinctive insight is that while every legal system requires an authority that *announces* law, it is not necessary for that authority to also *enforce* the law. Instead, the enforcement of rules pronounced by the centralized classification institution can be entirely decentralized and carried out by each member of the "relevant community" intended to be governed by the rules.

Moreover, according to Hadfield and Weingast, it is precisely the reliance on decentralized enforcement that explains why legal systems tend to be characterized by what they call "legal attributes." These are attributes that scholars such as Lon Fuller and John Rawls describe as intrinsically normative aspects of law: law must possess "universality [; ...] publicity; clarity, non-contradiction, and uniqueness; stability; prospectivity and congruence (between classifications as announced and classifications as enforced); generality; impersonal, neutral, and independent reasoning; and openness."[4] It is only by virtue of these attributes, Hadfield and Weingast argue, that a classification institution that does not centralize enforcement can ensure that members of the community are motivated – and know that other members of the community are similarly motivated – to punish those who break the legal norms. A classification institution's possession of these legal attributes can be taken as one definition of the "rule of law." Thus, the rule of law has "micro-foundations" in the decentralized enforcement of centrally announced rules.

One might summarize Hadfield and Weingast's theory as making a two-part claim: (1) the essence of law is public announcement, not public enforcement; and (2) the essence of the rule of law is the robustness of incentives for private enforcement of publicly announced rules. The theory has a corollary. Consider this question: If the centralized

[3] Hadfield and Weingast 2019, at 247. This is related to the specificity of legal norms discussed in Chapter 8.

[4] Id, at 253.

authority is entirely responsible for the enforcement of announced rules, such that the purported legal rules do not need to be enforced by private parties at all, does the announcement of legal rules still need to maintain the (Fullerian) legal attributes Hadfield and Weingast associate with the rule of law? They suggest that the answer is no: the legal attributes would no longer describe a behavioral equilibrium.[5] While private parties would still have incentives to comply with the announced rules (since they will be enforced), the announcers of rules would have incentives to cut corners on these legal attributes when they are not constrained by the need for private enforcement. They can adopt rules that favor some community members at the detriment of others, deviate from transparency, or fail to announce coherent and interpretable rules altogether.

This minimalist theory of law nicely captures the logic of China's approach to tax administration since the early 2000s. We have seen that the revenue management system heavily invests in public enforcement (ranging from taxpayer registration, account verification, and return filing to tax payments). By contrast, truthful reporting and other rules that must rely on private enforcement – as opposed to enforcement through government observation and intervention – are largely neglected. Informal bargaining is used instead to extract more from those suspected of being noncompliant. The substitution of government interventions for self-assessment in turn makes it unnecessary for the government to pronounce tax policy through the formality of lawmaking. Efforts to make tax rules transparent, internally non-self-contradictory, and prospective are minimal.[6] Overall, Hadfield and Weingast's conceptual connection between the legal attributes of classification institutions and private enforcement is distinctly confirmed by the absence of both in China's tax administration.

A question can be raised as to whether a legal system lacking the Fullerian legal attributes – one that relies on centralized announcement and *exclusively* public enforcement – would still count as a legal system. This is, to an extent, merely a semantic question. After all, the legal philosopher John Austin famously claimed that for there to be law, there only needs to exist a sovereign who announces commands and who can secure compliance with those commands through the threat of sanctions.[7]

[5] Id, at 263–267.

[6] Think of Chapter 7's discussion of the conflicting statutory and extra-statutory definitions of "SMPEs," or of the process and format by which property tax rules are adopted in Shanghai.

[7] Austin 1832; Shapiro 2013.

Even though many legal positivists believed Austin to be mistaken in his analysis of the concept of law, he may have at least captured a popular (mis-)conception of law.[8] While philosophers debate about whether such a "statist" conception of law – postulating that the essence of law is a coercive sovereign – does justice to "our" intuitions about law, a more interesting question is whether the minimalist theory of law offers greater explanatory power. Hadfield and Weingast suggest that it does, because the theory helps to explain why so many "rule of law" initiatives have failed in developing countries.[9] Such initiatives focus on establishing what appear to be the right *formal* institutions – legislatures and courts in particular – for the public announcement and enforcement of law. But they fail to recognize that whether the rule of law will take hold depends on whether such institutions provide enough incentives (and mechanisms) for *private* enforcement. Although Hadfield and Weingast propose no account of what the other necessary or sufficient conditions may be for an equilibrium characterized by the rule of law to take hold, recognizing the conceptual gap between such an equilibrium and specific legal institutions is, they suggest, a starting point for exploring an explanation.

I am sympathetic to Hadfield and Weingast's intuition and believe that there are various plausible ways of extending their explanatory project.[10] But for understanding contemporary Chinese governance, it is already helpful to recognize the conceptual gap that Hadfield and Weingast identify. As Chapter 7 showed, China has government authorities announcing and enforcing tax rules on the one hand, and legislatures and courts on the other. The two sets of institutions operate in parallel; neither secures the rule of law in taxation. The former fails to do so because it chooses not to adhere to the legal formalisms that facilitate private enforcement (and often preempts private enforcement). And the latter fails to do so because the micro-foundations of the rule of law are absent. This is the core explanation for the superfluity of ostensible legal institutions in China's giant public finance system.

[8] Even when law and economics scholars speak about the private enforcement of law, they tend to think of private parties enforcing the law at a state-sponsored forum, for example, courts, rather than directly sanctioning one another as in Hadfield and Weingast's conception of private enforcement. See, for example, Shavell 2004, chapter 25.

[9] Hadfield and Weingast 2014.

[10] For example, the presence of large business firms whose continued operation depends on an adherence to legal norms would generate a large array of mechanisms for the private enforcement of such norms.

This problem of the lack of micro-foundations for China's formal legal institutions likely permeates other spheres of Chinese governance. Indeed, scholars of Chinese law have recently adduced much evidence to highlight how even Chinese courts themselves do not apply the law: they implement state directives to preserve social stability or uphold local social orders by reaching for equitable outcomes outside the law.[11] Not surprisingly, scholars have attributed such behavior to Chinese judges' incentive structures within the judicial bureaucracy and the state's political prerogatives – a behavior that is little different from the behavior of Chinese tax administrators depicted in this book. Yet this similarity challenges a general assumption, made by scholars studying China, that one must specifically look at judicial institutions to know the effectiveness of China's legal system. Is it really coherent to imagine a country's judicial institutions as operating within the rule of law while most other government functions do not? On reflection, this assumption seems entirely unwarranted.

Applying the minimalist theory of law to China has two startling implications. First, Hadfield and Weingast concede that "the rule of law" as they define it implies neither democratic governance nor equality of all persons before the law.[12] Instead, their conception of the rule of law emphasizes the capacity of legal ordering to facilitate complex social coordination – its superiority as a form of organizational technology, so to speak. In saying that the rule of law is unable to take hold in many societies, Hadfield and Weingast are arguing that such societies cannot avail themselves of the technology of law.[13] Similarly, when I argue that Chinese tax administrators have little use for the rule of law – much as Chinese judges are reported to often disregard the law – I am not assuming that the law being ignored is just and reasonable, or displays due regard for Chinese citizens' basic moral and political rights. Any critique of what is normatively lacking about Chinese law is irrelevant when legal norms do not guide behavior at all. In other words, the claim made in this book is that in the sphere of Chinese taxation (as in many other spheres of governance), there is no *rule by law*, let alone the *rule of law*.

The "rule by law" versus "rule of law" distinction has been endlessly discussed among scholars of Chinese law in the past three decades both

[11] See, for example, He 2021; Liebman and Stern 2021.

[12] Hadfield and Weingast 2019 at 272 (footnote 25).

[13] Hadfield 2016 mainly argues that, in the context of developed countries, failing to recognize the basic nature of law has resulted in an overreliance on governments to promulgate legal rules, therefore creating an undersupply of such rules.

inside and outside of China.[14] It is often proposed that although the Chinese Communist Party has increasingly embraced "rule by law" in governance, this may not lead to convergence with Western-style governance because the CCP still opposes "thicker" conceptions of the rule of law that imply robust substantive and procedural rights for individuals. It is also claimed that China has developed a form of "authoritarian" legality, perhaps based on its own cultural tradition of legalism and perhaps resembling the governance styles adopted in countries like Singapore. The evidence offered for such claims usually comprises observations about the growing resources and institutional status commanded by Chinese courts, in addition to references to the heavy emphasis on law in the Chinese government's own discourse. However, the types of behaviors I described in Chapter 7 are rarely considered: notably, the central government's strident calls for governance through law, which are merely aimed at securing the obedience of subordinates in the nation's vast bureaucracy, are routinely violated by the central government's own actions; courts, while commanding increasing resources, are given few legal principles to work with and even fewer disputes to hear in many areas of governance; finally, Chinese legislatures serve as ceremonial showpieces and rarely get to decide on what laws to make.

When Western legal scholars postulate the relevance of an ideological debate between authoritarian and more liberal conceptions of legality in China, I believe they have already accepted a central component of the Chinese government's propaganda, namely that law is a main instrument by which the Chinese state governs. Such a declaration is inconsistent with careful analyses of the Chinese state's actual operations and the application of basic notions of what law comprises. It also goes against much of the lived experiences of Chinese citizens, who, in taxation and many other areas, usually have no difficulty in recognizing that they do not live under the "governance of rules," but under the governance of particular authorities. In depicting China as choosing a thin conception of law, legal scholars err precisely in their judgment about this basic fact.

The second startling implication of the conclusion that the rule of law, in a minimalist sense, is lacking in Chinese governance is the following: scholars like Hadfield and Weingast see the rule of law as a fundamental approach to social organization and essential for modern nations' prosperity. Securing social order through law is a practice with a longer history than the modern nation-state, let alone large-scale democracies.

[14] For representative examples, see Peerenboom 2009 and Chen 2019.

If one claims that China has not adopted the rule of law in some robust, "thick" notion of the term, then one is usually expressing a normative judgement – that China has not embraced some of the most cherished values in Western democracies that are widely believed to be universal human values. But if one claims that China does not have the rule of law in the minimalist sense, this identifies China's difference in terms of not just important normative dimensions, but a fundamental, positive dimension. How can China organize economic and social activities at such vast scales without what we believe to be a fundamental technology of modernity? How is basic social order achieved? After all, the value of the rule of law would not seem to have any grip in a society that does not even need rule by law. If the principles and practices of social organization may diverge in this elemental fashion, what hope do powerful countries adopting different principles and practices have for engaging in normative dialogues?

The State as a Substitute for Law

The one-party state is not China's invention. The Nationalist Party (*kuomintang*), which first embarked on building such a state in China in the early twentieth century, as well as the CCP that toppled and succeeded it, were organized like revolutionary parties in many other countries. One-party states around the world have long since challenged democratic norms and human rights and rejected many values that citizens in liberal democracies associate with the idea of the rule of law. My account of Chinese taxation documents a much lesser-known fact about the one-party state, namely that it can generate a relatively robust substitute for law even in areas of governance where law may have seemed critical. This finding is important because if law is indispensable to modern taxation or to other areas of modern governance – for example, regulation of the environment, labor, services, consumer protection, finance and trade, and so forth – then authoritarian rulers may either need to embrace law at least partially or reject law at a substantial cost. But if substitutes for law are widely feasible, then the cost of rejecting the rule of law can turn out to be much lower.

The idea of political institutions substituting for legal ordering echoes an earlier literature on "market-preserving federalism."[15] That literature began with a notion popular in institutional economics, namely that

[15] See Montinola et al. 1995; Weingast 1995; Jin, Qian, and Weingast 2005.

formal legal institutions – courts that enforced contracts, land registries that publicly delineated property rights, and so forth – are critical to modern economic development. How, in light of this notion, did China manage to achieve a high rate of economic growth until the mid-1990s without any of these formal institutions in place? The theorists of market-preserving federalism argued that this was a puzzle, and that it was solved by recognizing that political decentralization in China reduced the risks of government expropriations. The central government lacked the power, and the subnational government lacked the incentives in the face of inter-jurisdictional competition, to prey on private economic actors. Thus, if the main role of legal institutions is to mitigate the risk of government expropriation, then political institutions that also mitigate such risk can be viewed as a substitute for law.

It is possible to disagree with the premises of the theory of "market-preserving federalism" while being sympathetic to the main question it raises.[16] Most importantly, it is highly unlikely that the main relevance of law to economic development is its impact on the likelihood of government expropriation. Instead, law facilitates large-scale social coordination among private parties, and state rulers often can gain much more from sponsoring legal systems in their territories than from victimizing their subjects. Protection against government expropriation is only one of many – and likely not the defining – facet of the rule of law. Moreover, the significance of law for economic development goes far beyond contract enforcement and property rights protection. Taxation and effective regulation are equally important for economic prosperity; they require complex social coordination, and have rested, in Western countries, on the rule of law. The failure of the rule of law can thus have systematically adverse consequences even in the absence of a predatory state. The question remains, though, whether state institutions can substitute for the rule of law in its more fundamental roles.

The case study of Chinese taxation suggests that the answer, surprisingly, may be affirmative. Insofar as this finding can be generalized to other areas of Chinese governance, it constitutes, I believe, a genuinely new insight into the Chinese state. In the past two decades, social scientists have made substantial progress investigating the inner workings of the CCP, especially by studying promotional tournaments and forms of

[16] The theory of market-preserving federalism has been disputed by other scholars, especially on the claim that decentralization was sufficient to reduce the risk of government expropriations. See Rodden and Ackerman 1997.

factionalism within the Party.[17] Many of these studies have identified relations between such political arrangements and particular economic outcomes, ranging from GDP growth and infrastructure spending to famine, mine safety regulation, environmental protection, and tax collection.[18] Incentives within the CCP political apparatus thus clearly have an impact – of both the positive and negative kinds. A crucial question, however, is whether this political system can have a more systemic effect beyond particular policy areas. One such effect would be the replacement of law as a basic principle or means of social organization. By looking at the organization of grassroots tax administration – which fits into and supports the same political system that other scholars have studied the higher echelons of – I believe that one can plausibly claim that such an effect exists.

A state's ability to create substitutes for law, of course, depends on the internal cohesion of the state apparatus. The CCP has over ninety-one million members. If most members can be expected to adhere to the Party's internal commands, then the CCP's capacity as an organization to secure social order among 1.4 billion Chinese people may not be so mysterious. How internal cohesion is sustained within the CCP, therefore, is an important subject for investigation.[19] Similarly, while the administrative arm of the Chinese state is far smaller than CCP membership – 7.19 million in 2016[20] – it is important to understand what ensures cohesion and effective command within this organization as well. One observation relevant to answering this question is that the Chinese bureaucracy may be relatively meritocratic and grants sufficient

[17] For recent studies that review prior findings, see Landry, Lü, and Duan 2018 (for promotional tournaments), Francois, Trebbi, and Xiao 2016 and Fisman et al. 2020 (for factions), and Jiang 2018 (on the interaction between promotional tournaments and patronage networks).

[18] See Kung and Chen 2011; Lü and Landry 2014; Fisman and Wang 2015; Yu et al. 2016; Jia and Nie 2017; Chen et al. 2018a.

[19] Do legal norms within the CCP's organization contribute to its cohesion? The minimalist conception of law discussed earlier in this chapter is especially apposite for studying this question, since there are no obvious counterparts to legislatures and courts within the CCP. I believe law-like norms play no significant role within the CCP. Indoctrination, political loyalty, and strong incentive regimes involving rewards and punishment are much more fundamental, and the CCP displays little of the internal publicity and transparency that is needed for any legal norm to operate.

[20] MOHRSS 2016. Ang 2016 includes public employees (including state-funded institutions such as universities and hospitals) in describing the size of China's "bureaucracy" (over fifty million so measured). I believe this is at odds with standard definitions of the scope of government bureaucracies, but public employment, including among individuals who are not CCP members, is certainly another instrument for social ordering in China.

autonomy to civil servants – and is *perceived* to do so by its members.[21] The study of Chinese tax administration strongly supports this observation. As we saw in Chapter 5, performance evaluation is widely adopted, and the combination of collective and individual evaluations injects strong meritocratic components into leaders' and managers' careers. Autonomy, on the other hand, is inherent in many of the results-oriented arrangements and persistent, even relentless, decentralization.

The presence of meritocracy and autonomy, however, does not mean that China's state apparatus is "Weberian."[22] As this book has documented, at least two features of what Weber deemed essential to modern democracies are lacking in China's tax bureaucracy. First, decision-making is not rule based; performance metrics and official discretion replace rules. Second, at least among the vast portion of the bureaucracy at the lowest ranks, there is little specialization. Revenue managers and tax inspectors bear greater resemblance to soldiers in China's revolutionary army in earlier times – working tirelessly to implement the ever-changing commands of superiors – than to government bureaucrats in nineteenth-century Germany or most developed countries today. This is not a mere quibble about when to invoke the name of the great German sociologist: what is of interest is that meritocracy and autonomy may be sufficient to generate a sense of cohesion and even legitimacy within a bureaucracy, even if Weber thought that legal-rational authority is what imparts modern bureaucracies with legitimacy.

The idea of substitutes for law in social organization is, in some ways, thoroughly familiar to both legal scholars and social scientists. Within small-scale communities characterized by stable membership, familial/tribal/clan norms, local customs, and religious and cultural beliefs can also displace the need for law. But law has been thought to be less replaceable for very large-scale social cooperation.[23] Contemporary governance in China suggests that this may not be the case. This presents an enormous normative challenge: when legal norms are unnecessary for social cooperation, social values expressed *only* in legal terms lose their traction.

21 Boittin, Distelhorst, and Fukuyama 2016.

22 Boittin, Distelhorst, and Fukuyama 2016 use meritocracy and autonomy as measures of the Weberian quality of Chinese governance, following Evans and Rauch 1999. Evans and Rauch 1999 explicitly recognize that their "Weberian" metric (pertaining specifically to meritocracy) does not consider other Weberian features such as rule-based governance and specialization.

23 Shapiro 2013; Hadfield 2016.

Paths to Legitimacy

In 2020, with minimal legislative or judicial involvement, China mobilized its vast urban network of grassroots, publicly funded "neighborhood offices" and "resident committees," as well as the giant membership of the CCP, to curb the domestic spread of COVID-19.[24] Along with the use of new surveillance technology,[25] this crusade seems to have saved the country, for the time being, from the devastations of a pandemic that had its start in the calamitous outbreak in Wuhan – even though China's medical technologies for COVID vaccination and treatment still lag significantly behind countries like the United States, United Kingdom, and Germany. China's economy grew at 2.3 percent in 2020, in contrast to the severe setbacks in the world's other major economies. Even more remarkably from the public finance and political perspectives, the Chinese government pressed ahead with a poverty eradication campaign in 2020 despite enacting substantial tax cuts at the same time and expectations of plummeting tax revenue. In late 2020, the CCP announced that extreme poverty had been eradicated from rural China.[26]

The form of state capacity underlying Chinese taxation analyzed in this book bears strong resemblances to, and likely shares the same institutional sources, as these other recent demonstrations of state capacity. They are all likely to provoke two natural reactions. The first is simple disbelief. Do we really know that COVID cases were brought under control to the extent indicated by official statistics, or that the level of extreme poverty declined substantially because of the CCP campaign? Such skepticism is applicable to all spheres of Chinese governance, and is fueled by not just the lack of transparency, but also the peculiarity of the mechanisms that supposedly secured the purported outcomes. In the case of taxation, even after reading this book, some readers may still wonder: can a large country really successfully raise revenue without relying on self-assessment, audits, penalties, and compliance with published rules, but through negotiations with and coercion of individual taxpayers instead? One aim of this book has been to show that the effectiveness of such seemingly alien mechanisms may be less implausible than it first appears. Either in-person authority or impersonal technology may intervene in private activities with sufficient force to create social order, and thereby mitigate the need for rule-based behavior and robust

[24] Hessler 2020.
[25] Xiao 2020.
[26] The Economist 2021.

legal norms.[27] In disease control and targeted social assistance, the effectiveness of a state's in-person or technological interventions may in fact be even more plausible.

The second reaction is judgment and reproach. The Chinese approach to tax administration, for example, may seem terribly inefficient.[28] What is the sense in devoting so much administrative resource to micro-taxpayers that generate little revenue? Why is the target for timely return-filing set so high when the returns are unreliable and infrequently examined? Why inflict the Golden Tax Project on taxpayers when the technology was never good enough for real-time invoice cross-matching and thus left large berth for maneuver to criminals? Isn't a tax system very ineffective when taxpayers either evade so much tax already or know so little about tax law that they do not respond to tax incentives?[29] The list of such questions goes on, and a similarly long list of criticisms can be made regarding China's tax policies. It is easy to imagine similar findings emerging from analyses of China's policies in other areas, including pandemic control and poverty eradication. In many ways, approaches based on the rule of law seem vastly more efficient. With self-assessment in place, taxpayers can learn about the law through market-based professional services, and the law can be fashioned in many ways to achieve policy objectives in ever-changing circumstances. Indeed, the fact that legal systems have widely spread across the world in the past millennia seems to provide overwhelming evidence of its virtues as an efficient form of social organization. Foregoing the efficiencies of law, just like foregoing the efficiencies of markets, seems gravely misguided.

Such criticisms of or misgivings about Chinese governance because of its inefficiencies may be entirely valid, but they only go so far, when considered in light of China's remarkable success in engineering sustained economic growth. The human and environmental costs of economic development can be very high in all places, and there at least is no consensus yet that such costs generated by China's current political institutions are far greater in proportion to their benefits than in other

[27] Lest it is thought that a culture of obedience to authority is sufficient to have kept Chinese citizens in line with COVID safety protocols, it should be remembered that such culture never succeeded to ensure that Chinese taxpayers accurately report on their tax returns or generally display tax compliance on their own, nor that urban residents obey traffic rules without extensive surveillance.

[28] As we saw in Chapters 3 and 4, this was the view taken by many Chinese tax administrators themselves.

[29] Fan and Liu 2020; Cui et al. 2020a.

countries. In many instances, apparently inefficient arrangements may potentially be rationalized because of some existing distortions. We simply do not have enough information to conclusively make appraisals about the impact on social welfare of various Chinese policies.

In summary, a distrust of the Chinese state on account of its eschewal of legal norms – whether the distrust rests on abstract efficiency considerations or moral commitments to the rule of law – may be amply justified, but it must also be placed in its proper place. The Chinese government has raised substantial revenue consistently since the 1990s, and spent at least a portion of this revenue to improve the welfare of a broad population through the provision of public goods and services and through cash and in-kind transfers to the needy. Any normative assessment of this performance depends critically on what one takes the counterfactuals to be. On the one hand, a government that is bent on promoting economic growth and distributing the benefits of such growth broadly across the population may have accomplished even more by making more extensive use of legal norms. On the other hand, a government that serves the interests only of the political and economic elite could have taxed and redistributed far less, and thereby dramatically limited the beneficiaries of economic growth (even more so than has been the case in China), or failed to provide enough public goods to stimulate economic development.[30] In fact, such latter government could even have relied on law as a governing instrument more, but used such instrument to carry out the same or even greater amount of political repression than the CCP has done.[31]

This book has not tried to assess the impact of China's tax and transfer system on the country's income or wealth inequality, or the inclusiveness of its tax policies. Instead, I have focused on the difference between China's approach to revenue extraction and those familiar in developed countries – and on the *affinities* of China's approach with popular depictions (especially by economists) of what modern tax capacity consists in. A basic point of this exercise is to motivate a fundamental distinction in the typology of modern tax capacity – between capacity based mainly on the rule of law and capacity based mainly on state power. But a further point is to clear the ground for further studies of the politics of taxation in China. The interests of China's economic elite are already

[30] See Albertus and Menaldo 2018.

[31] One only needs to consider China's adoption in 2020 of the National Security Law and its immediate use to crack down on dissent in Hong Kong to be reminded of the potential of law as an instrument for repression.

being advanced in the name of law: like economic elites elsewhere in the world, the affluent in China has equated taxation with the taking of private property. In the balance between the Chinese state's coercive substitutes for law, on the one hand, and the cockeyed appeal to law on the part of the economic elite, on the other, lies the Chinese polity's legitimacy and inclusivity. Just as the complementarity between law and modern taxation in Western democracies requires much better theorizing than we possess today,[32] grasping the possible connections between authoritarianism and redistributive policies is critical for understanding democracies' powerful rivals.[33]

[32] See Besley and Persson 2013.
[33] See Albertus, Fenner, and Slater 2018; Jia, Roland, and Xie 2021.

REFERENCES

Acemoglu, D., S. Johnson, and J. Robinson. 2005. "Institutions as the Fundamental Cause of Long-Run Growth." in *Handbook of Economic Growth*, edited by P. Aghion and S. Durlauf, 385–472, Oxford: North Holland.

Aghion, P. and J. Tirole, 1997. "Formal and Real Authority in Organizations." *Journal of Political Economy*, 105(1): 1–29.

Albertus, M., S. Fenner, and D. Slater. 2018. *Coercive Distribution*. New York: Cambridge University Press.

Albertus, M. and V. Menaldo. 2018. *Authoritarianism and the Elite Origins of Democracy*. Cambridge: Cambridge University Press.

Allingham, M. G. and A. Sandmo. 1972. "Income Tax Evasion: A Theoretical Analysis." *Journal of Public Economics*, 1: 323–338.

Alm, J. 2019. "What Motivates Tax Compliance?" *Journal of Economic Surveys*, 33 (2): 353–388.

Alm, J. and Y. Liu. 2013. "Did China's Tax-for-Fee Reform Improve Farmers' Welfare in Rural Areas?" *Journal of Development Studies*, 49: 516–532.

Alumnia, M., J. Hjort, J. Knebelmann, and L. Tian. 2020. "Strategic or Confused Firms? Evidence from 'Missing' Transactions in Uganda." NBER Working Paper No. 29059.

Andreoni, J. 1991. "The Desirability of a Permanent Tax Amnesty." *Journal of Public Economics*, 45(2): 143–159.

1992. "IRS as Loan Shark Tax Compliance with Borrowing Constraints." *Journal of Public Economics*, 49: 35–46.

Andreoni, J., B. Erard, and J. Feinstein. 1998. "Tax Compliance." *Journal of Economic Literature*, 36(2): 818–860.

Ang, Y. Y. 2016. *How China Escaped the Poverty Trap*. Ithaca: Cornell University Press.

Angrist, J. and J. Pischke. 2010. "The Credibility Revolution in Empirical Economics: How Better Research Design Is Taking the Con out of Econometrics." *Journal of Economic Perspectives*, 24(2): 3–30.

Anthony, R. A. 1992. "Interpretive Rules, Policy Statements, Guidances, Manuals, and the Like—Should Federal Agencies Use Them to Bind the Public?" *Duke Law Journal*, 41: 1311–1384.

Austin, J. 1832. *The Province of Jurisprudence Determined.* London: John Murray.

Autor, D., D. Dorn, and G. Hanson. 2016. "The China Shock: Learning from Labor-Market Adjustment to Large Changes in Trade." *Annual Review of Economics*, 8: 205–240.

2019. "When Work Disappears: Manufacturing Decline and the Falling Marriage Market Value of Young Men." *American Economic Review: Insights*, 1(2): 161–178.

Autor, D., D. Dorn, G. Hanson, and K. Majlesi. 2020. "Importing Political Polarization? The Electoral Consequences of Rising Trade Exposure." *American Economic Review*, 110(10): 3139–3183.

Baer, K. E. and E. Le Borgne. 2008. *Tax Amnesties. Theory, Trends, and Some Alternatives.* Washington, DC: International Monetary Fund.

Bai, C.-E., C.-T. Hsieh, and Z. Song. 2016. "The Long Shadow of China's Fiscal Expansion." *Brookings Papers on Economic Activity*, 47(2): 129–181.

Bai, C.-E., Q. Li, and M. Ouyang. 2014. "Property Taxes and Home Prices: A Tale of Two Cities." *Journal of Econometrics*, 180(1): 1–15.

Bardhan, P. 2016. "State and Development: The Need for a Reappraisal of the Current Literature." *Journal of Economic Literature*, 54(3): 862–892.

Basri, M., M. Felix, R. Hanna, and B. Olken. 2020. "Tax Administration vs. Tax Rates: Evidence from Corporate Taxation in Indonesia." NBER Working Paper No. 26150.

Bayer, R.-C., H. Oberhofer, and H. Winner. 2015. "The Occurrence of Tax Amnesties: Theory and Evidence." *Journal of Public Economics*, 125: 70–82.

Beraja, M., D. Y. Yang, and N. Yuchtman. 2020. "Data-intensive Innovation and the State: Evidence from AI Firms in China." NBER Working Paper No. 27723.

Bernstein T. P. and X. Lü. 2003. *Taxation without Representation: Peasants, the Central and the Local States in Reform China.* Cambridge: Cambridge University Press.

Besley, Timothy. 2020. "State Capacity, Reciprocity, and the Social Contract." *Econometrica*, 88(4): 1307–1335.

Besley, T. and T. Persson. 2013. "Taxation and Development." in *Handbook of Public Economics Vol 5*, edited by A. Auerbach, R. Chetty, M. Feldstein, and E. Saez, 51–110, Amsterdam: North Holland.

2014. "Why Do Developing Countries Tax So Little?" *Journal of Economic Perspectives*, 28(4): 99–120.

Besley, T., A. Jensen and T. Persson. 2019. "Norms, Enforcement, and Tax Evasion." NBER Working Paper No. 25575.

Bird, R. M. 2004. "Administrative Dimensions of Tax Reform." *Asia-Pacific Tax Bulletin*, 10(3): 134–150.

Bird, R. M. and M. Smart. 2009. "The Economic Incidence of Replacing a Retail Sales Tax by a Value-Added Tax: Evidence from Canadian Experience." *Canadian Public Policy*, 35(1): 85–97.

2012. "Financing Social Expenditures in Developing Countries: Payroll or Value Added Taxes?" ICEPP Working Papers No. 58.

Bird, R. M. and J. Martinez-Vazquez, eds. 2014. *Taxation and Development: The Weakest Link?* Cheltenham, UK: Edward Elgar.

Bird, R. M. and E. Zolt. 2005. "The Limited Role of the Personal Income Tax in Developing Countries." *Journal of Asian Economics*, 16(6): 928–946.

2011. "Dual Income Taxation: A Promising Path to Tax Reform for Developing Countries." *World Development*, 39(10): 1691–1703.

Boittin, M, G. Distelhorst, and F. Fukuyama. 2016. "Reassessing the Quality of Government in China," Osgoode Legal Studies Research Paper Series 197.

Brockmeyer, A., A. Estefan, K. Ramirez, and J. C. Suárez Serrato. 2020. "Taxing Property in Developing Countries: Theory and Evidence from Mexico." NBER Working Paper No. 28637.

Brockmeyer, A., S. Smith, M. Hernandez, and S. Kettle. 2019. "Casting a Wider Tax Net: Experimental Evidence from Costa Rica." *American Economic Journal: Economic Policy*, 11(3): 55–87.

Brondolo, J. and Z. Zhang. 2016. "Tax Administration Reform in China: Achievements, Challenges, and Reform Priorities." IMF Working Paper No. WP/16/68.

Bruhn, M. and D. J. McKenzie. 2014. "Entry Regulation and Formalization of Microenterprises in Developing Countries." *World Bank Research Observer*, 29: 186–201.

Brys, B., S. Matthews, R. Herd and X. Wang. 2013. "Tax Policy and Tax Reform in the People's Republic of China." OECD Taxation Working Paper No. 18.

Burgess, R. and N. Stern. 1993. "Taxation and Development." *Journal of Economic Literature*, 31(2): 762–830.

Cai, J., Y. Chen, and X. Wang. 2018. "The Impact of Corporate Taxes on Firm Innovation: Evidence from the Corporate Tax Collection Reform in China." NBER Working Paper No. 25146.

Carrillo, P., D. Pomeranz, and M. Singhal. 2017. "Dodging the Taxman: Firm Misreporting and Limits to Tax Enforcement." *American Economic Journal: Applied Economics*, 9(2): 144–164.

Chen, A. 2019. *An Introduction to the Chinese Legal System* (5th ed.). Hong Kong: LexisNexis.

Chen, J. 2011. *On the Road: Innovative Exploration and Thinking of Tax Management.* 陈建浦,《在路上——税务管理创新探索与思考》, 江苏: 江苏人民出版社, 2011。

Chen, S. X. 2017. "The Effect of a Fiscal Squeeze on Tax Enforcement: Evidence from a Natural Experiment in China." *Journal of Public Economics*, 147: 62–76.

Chen, Y., P. Li, and Y. Lu. 2018a. "Career Concerns and Multitasking Local Bureaucrats: Evidence of a Target-Based Performance Evaluation System in China." *Journal of Development Economics*, 133: 84–101.

Chen. Z., Z. Liu, J. C. S. Serrato, and D. Y. Xu. 2018b. "Notching R&D Investment with Corporate Income Tax Cuts in China." NBER Working Paper No. 24749.

Chen, Z., X. Jiang, Z. Liu, J. C. S. Serrato, and D. Y. Xu. 2019. "Tax Policy and Lumpy Investment Behavior: Evidence from China's VAT Reform." NBER Working Paper No. 26336.

Chen, Z., Y. He, X. Jiang, Z. Liu, J. C. S. Serrato, and D. Y. Xu. 2020a. "The Structure of Business Taxation in China." in *Tax Policy and the Economy*, Vol. 35, edited by R. A. Moffitt. Chicago: University of Chicago Press.

Chen, Z., P. Li, L. Liao, and Z. Wang 2020b. "Assessing and Addressing the Coronavirus-Induced Economic Crisis: Evidence From 1.5 Billion Sales Invoices," PBCSF-NIFR Research Paper.

Chow, D. C. K. 2015. *The Legal System of the People's Republic of China in a Nutshell*. 3rd ed., St. Paul, MN: West Academic.

Cui, W. 2006. "Should China's Personal Income Tax Aim to Measure Precisely the Ability to Pay?" 《准确衡量支付能力应该是个税改革的目标吗?》 《月旦财经法杂志》2006年12月第7期.

2007a. "China's New Personal Income Tax Return-Filing Regime." *Tax Notes International*, 45: 977–985 (March 12, 2007).

2007b. "The Prospect of New Partnership Taxation in China." *Tax Notes International*, 46: 625–634 (May 7, 2007).

2008. "Raising the Income Tax Threshold Has Limited Effect in Boosting Domestic Demand." 崔威,《提高个税起征点拉动内需作用有限》,《第一财经日报》/2008 年12 月4 日第 A07 版。

2009. "Business Tax: China's Quasi-VAT." *International VAT Monitor*, 20(4): 291–295.

2011a. "What Is the 'Law' in Chinese Tax Administration?" *Asia Pacific Law Review*, 19(1): 75–94.

2011b. "Fiscal Federalism in Chinese Taxation," *World Tax Journal*, 2011(3): 455–80.

2012a. "The Historical Origin of Tax Legislative Centralization." [Journal Article]. 崔威,《税收立法高度集权模式的起源》,《中外法学》, 第24期。

2012b. "China's Tax Policy Response to the Global Financial Crisis." in *China and the Global Economic Crisis: A Comparison with Europe*, edited by J.-P. Cabestan et al., 84–98, London: Routledge.

2013. "The Origin of the High Centralization of Tax Legislative Power." *Peking University Law Journal*, 1(1): 105–131 (English translation of Cui 2012a).

2014. "China's Business-Tax-to-VAT Reform: An Interim Assessment." *British Tax Review*, 2014(5): 617–641.
2015. "Administrative Decentralization and Tax Compliance: A Transactional Cost Perspective." *University of Toronto Law Journal*, 65(3): 186–238.
2017a. "Does Judicial Independence Matter? A Study of the Determinants of Litigation Patterns in an Authoritarian Regime." *University of Pennsylvania Journal of International Law*, 38(3): 941–998.
2017b. "The Legal Maladies of 'Federalism, Chinese-Style'." in *The Beijing Consensus? How China Has Changed the Western Ideas of Law and Economic Development and Global Legal Practices*, edited by W. Chen, 97–118, Cambridge: Cambridge University Press.
2018. "Taxation without Information: The Institutional Foundations of Modern Tax Collection." *University of Pennsylvania Journal of Business Law* 20(1): 93–146.
2019. "When Do Chinese National Ministries Make Law?" Working Paper, available at https://commons.allard.ubc.ca/fac_pubs/512/.
Cui, W., J. Cheng, and D. Wiesner. 2019. "Judicial Review of Government Actions." *China Perspectives*, 2019(1): 29–38.
Cui, W. and J. Hicks. 2021. "The Extent and Determinants of Zero-Reporting: Evidence from China." Working Paper, available at https://papers.ssrn.com/sol3/papers.cfm?abstract_id=3914479.
Cui, W., J. Hicks, and J. Xing. 2020a. "Cash on the Table? Imperfect Take-up of Tax Incentives and Firm Investment Behavior." CESifo Working Paper No. 9413.
Cui, W., J. Hicks, and M. Norton. 2020b. "How Well-Targeted Are Payroll Tax Cuts as a Response to COVID-19? Evidence from China." Working Paper, available at https://papers.ssrn.com/sol3/papers.cfm?abstract_id=3686345.
Cui, W. and J. Wan. 2019a. "Decentralizing Legislation in China's Law on Legislation Amendment." *Hong Kong Law Journal*, 49(2): 665–696.
2019b. "When Do Chinese Subnational Governments Make Law?" Working Paper, available at https://papers.ssrn.com/sol3/papers.cfm?abstract_id=3467703.
Cui, W. and R. Wang. 2019. "Tax Whistleblowing in China," Presentation at the 4th International Conference on Taxpayer Rights, University of Minnesota School of Law.
Cui, W. and Z. Wang. 2015. "The Inefficiencies of Legislative Centralization: Evidence from Provincial Rate-Setting." *China: An International Journal*, 13(3): 49–67.
2017. "The Selection of Litigation against Government Agencies: Evidence from China." *Review of Law and Economics*, 13(3): 1–41.
Cui, W. and M. Wei. 2021. "Registered Capital and Firm Entry." Working Paper, available at https://papers.ssrn.com/sol3/papers.cfm?abstract_id=3914483.

Cui, W., M. Wei, W. Xie, and J. Xing. 2021. "Corporate Tax Cuts for Small Firms: What Do Firms Do?" Oxford University Centre for Business Taxation Working Paper 21/16.

Cui, W. and A. Wu. 2012. "The Chinese VAT." in *The Future of Indirect Taxation: Recent Trends in VAT and GST Systems around the World*, edited by T. Ecker et al., 159–189, Amsterdam: Kluwer Law International.

Damaska, M. R. 1991. *The Faces of Justice and State Authority: A Comparative Approach to the Legal Process*. New Haven, CT: Yale University Press.

De Giorgi, G., M. Ploenzke, and A. Rahman. 2018. "Small Firms' Formalisation: The Stick Treatment." *The Journal of Development Studies*, 54(6): 983–1001.

De Simone, L., R. Sansing, and J. Seidman. 2013. "When are Enhanced Relationship Tax Compliance Programs Mutually Beneficial?" *The Accounting Review*, 88(6): 1971–1991.

Demsetz, H. 1967. "Toward a Theory of Property Rights." *The American Economic Review Papers and Proceedings*, 57(2): 347–359.

Deng, L. and F. Zhao. 2011. "Shanghai's Property Tax: Exemptions under Discussion with the Ministry of Finance." [news article] 邓丽、赵飞飞, 《上海房产税: 起征点正与财政部沟通》, 《21世纪经济报道》 2011年01月11日。

Di Porto, E. N. P., N. Persico, and N. Sahuguet. 2013. "Decentralized Deterrence, with an Application to Labor Tax Auditing." *American Economic Journal: Microeconomics*, 5(1): 35–62.

Docherty, D. C. 1997. *Mr. Smith Goes to Ottawa: Life in the House of Commons*. Vancouver, BC: UBC Press.

2005. *Legislatures*. Vancouver, BC: UBC Press.

Dowdle, M. W. 1997. "The Constitutional Development and Operations of the National People's Congress." *Columbia Journal of Asian Law*, 11(1): 1–125.

Dwenger, N., H. Kleven, I. Rasul, and J. Rincke. 2016. "Extrinsic and Intrinsic Motivations for Tax Compliance: Evidence from a Field Experiment in Germany." *American Economic Journal: Economic Policy*, 8(3): 203–232.

Ebrill, L., M. Keen, J.-P. Bodin, and V. Summers. 2001. *The Modern VAT*. Washington: International Monetary Fund.

The Economist. 2021. "Extreme Poverty is History in China, Officials Say." January 2, 2021.

Evans, Peter B. and James E. Rauch. 1999. "Bureaucracy and Growth: A Cross-National Analysis of The Effects of 'Weberian' State Structures on Economic Growth." *American Sociological Review*, 64(5): 748–765.

Fan, Z. and Y. Liu. 2020. "Tax Compliance and Investment Incentives: Firm Responses to Accelerated Depreciation." *Journal of Economic Behavior and Organization*, 176(C): 1–17.

Fan, H., Y. Liu, N. Qian, and J. Wen. 2018. "The Dynamic Effects of Computerized VAT Invoices on Chinese Manufacturing Firms." NBER Working Paper No. 24414.

Fang, H. and J. Feng. 2018. "The Chinese Pension System." NBER Working Paper No. 25088.

Fang, H. and J. Zhang. 2013. "The snatching hand, the helping hand, and the GDP-surpassing growth of China's taxation revenue." [Journal Article] 方红生、张军,《攫取之手、援助之手与中国税收超GDP 增长》,《经济研究》, 2013年第3期。

Feng, J. 2013. "The Incentive of Participation in Urban Social Insurance System in China: A Study Based on Manufacturing Firms." [Journal Article] 封进,《中国城镇职工社会保险制度的参与激励》,《经济研究》, 2013年第7期, 104–117。

Feng, J., Z. Wang, and H. Song. 2018. "Self-choice and Medical Expenses in China's Medical Insurance System——A Research Based on the Insured Behavior of Flexible Employment." [Journal Article] 封进, 王贞, 宋弘:《中国医疗保险体系中的自选择与医疗费用——基于灵活就业人员参保行为的研究》,《金融研究》, 2018年第8期。

Feng, J. and F. Zhao. 2019. "70 Years of New China Pension Insurance: Experience, Problems and Prospects." [Journal Article] 封进、赵发强,《新中国养老保险70 年: 经验、问题与展望》,《社会保障研究》2019 年第6 期。

Finan, F., B. A. Olken, and R. Pande. 2017. "The Personnel Economics of the Developing State." *Handbook of Economic Field Experiments*, 2: 467–514.

Fisman, R., J. Shi, Y. Wang, and W. Wu. 2020. "Social Ties and the Selection of China's Political Elite." *American Economic Review*, 110(6): 1752–1781.

Fisman, R. and Y. Wang. 2015. "The Mortality Cost of Political Connections." *The Review of Economic Studies*, 82(4): 1346–1382.

Floridi, A., B. A. Demena, and N. Wagner. 2019. "Shedding Light on the Shadows of Informality: A Meta-Analysis of Formalization Interventions Targeted at Informal Firms." ISS Working Papers – General Series 642.

Francois, P., F. Trebbi, and K. Xiao. 2016. "Factions in Nondemocracies: Theory and Evidence from the Chinese Communist Party." NBER Working Paper No. 22775.

Gandhi, J., B. Noble, and M. Svolik. 2020. "Legislatures and Legislative Politics Without Democracy." *Comparative Political Studies*, 53(9): 1359–1379.

Gillitzer, C. and M. Sinning. 2020. "Nudging Businesses to Pay their Taxes: Does Timing Matter?" *Journal of Economic Behavior & Organization*, 169: 284–300.

Göbel, C. 2010. *The Politics of Rural Reform in China: State Policy and Village Predicament in the Early 2000s*. Abingdon/New York: Routledge.

Gordon, R. 2010. *Taxation in Developing Countries.* New York: Columbia University Press.

Gordon, R. H. and W. Li. 2009. "Tax Structures in Developing Countries: Many Puzzles and a Possible Explanation." *Journal of Public Economics*, 93(7): 855–866.

Greif, A. 2006. *Institutions and the Path to the Modern Economy: Lessons from Medieval Trade.* New York: Cambridge University Press.

Hadfield, G. 2016. *Rules for a Flat World: Why Humans Invented Law and How to Reinvent It for a Complex Global Economy.* New York: Oxford University Press.

Hadfield, G. and B. R. Weingast. 2014. "Microfoundations of the Rules of Law." *Annual Review of Political Science*, 17: 21–42.

2019. "Is Rule of Law an Equilibrium without (Some) Private Enforcement?" *NOMOS: American Society for Political and Legal Philosophy*, 60: 246–275.

Harrison, G. and R. Krelove. 2005. "VAT Refunds: A Review of Country Experience." IMF Working Paper No. WP/05/218.

Hart, H. L. A. 1961. *The Concept of Law.* Oxford: Oxford University Press.

He, X. 2021. *Divorce in China: Institutional Constraints and Gendered Outcomes.* New York: New York University Press.

Hessler, P. 2020. "How China Controlled the Coronavirus: Teaching and Learning in Sichuan during the Pandemic." *The New Yorker*, August 10, 2020.

Hickman, K. E. and G. Kerska. 2017. "Restoring the Lost Anti-Injunction Act." *Virginia Law Review*, 103: 1683–1767.

Hines, J. R. and J. Park. 2019. "Investment Ramifications of Distortionary Tax Subsidies." *Journal of Public Economics*, 172: 36–51.

Huang, W. and C. Zhang. (2021). "The Power of Social Pensions: Evidence from China's New Rural Pension Scheme." *American Economic Journal: Applied Economics* 13 (2): 179–205.

Huber, John D. and Charles R. Shipan. 2002. *Deliberate Discretion? The Institutional Foundations of Bureaucratic Autonomy.* Cambridge: Cambridge University Press.

International Monetary Fund. 2011. *Revenue Mobilization in Developing Countries.* Washington: International Monetary Fund.

2015a. *Current Challenges in Revenue Mobilization: Improving Tax Compliance.* Washington: International Monetary Fund.

2018. *People's Republic of China: Tax Policy and Employment Creation.* Country Report No. 18/92.

International Social Security Association. 2017. *Social Security Programs Throughout the World: Asia and the Pacific, 2016.* Washington: SSA Publication No. 13–11802.

James, K. A. 2007. "We of the Never Ever: The History of the Introduction of a Goods and Services Tax in Australia." *British Tax Review*, 2007(3): 320–348.

Jensen, A. 2019. "Employment Structure and the Rise of the Modern Tax System." NBER Working Paper No. 25502.

Jensen, C. B. and R. J. McGrath. 2011. "Making Rules about Rulemaking: A Comparison of Presidential and Parliamentary Systems." *Political Research Quarterly*, 64(3): 656–667.

Jia, R., M. Kudamatsu, and D. Seim. 2015. "Political Selection in China: The Complementary Roles of Connections and Performance." *Journal of the European Economic Association*, 13(4): 631–668.

Jia, R. and Nie H. 2017. "Decentralization, Collusion and Coalmine Deaths." *Review of Economics and Statistics*, 99(1): 105–118.

Jia, R., G. Roland, and Y. Xie. 2021. "A Theory of Power Structure and Institutional Compatibility: China vs. Europe Revisited." NBER Working Paper No. 28403.

Jiang, J. 2018. "Making Bureaucracy Work: Patronage Networks, Performance Incentives, and Economic Development in China." *American Journal of Political Science*, 62(4): 982–999.

Jin, H, Y. Qian and B. Weingast. 2005. "Regional Decentralization and Fiscal Incentives: Federalism, Chinese Style." *Journal of Public Economics*, 89(9–10): 1719–1742.

Kaplow, L. and S. Shavell. 1994. "Optimal Law Enforcement with Self-Reporting of Behavior." *Journal of Political Economy*, 102: 601–03.

1996. "Property Rules versus Liability Rules: An Economic Analysis." *Harvard Law Review*, 109(4): 713–790.

Keen, M. 2013. "Taxation and Development—Again." in *Studies of Critical Issues in Taxation and Development*, edited by C. Fuest and G. Zodrow, 13–41, Cambridge: MIT Press.

Keen, M., Y. Kim, and R. Varsano. 2006. "The 'Flat Tax(es)': Principles and Evidence." IMF Working Paper WP/06/218.

Keen, M. and J. Slemrod. 2017. "Optimal Tax Administration." *Journal of Public Economics*, 152: 133–142.

Keen, M. and S. Smith. 2006. "VAT Fraud and Evasion: What Do We Know, and What Can Be Done?" *National Tax Journal*, 59: 861–887.

Khan, A. Q., A. Khwaja, and B. Olken. 2016. "Tax Farming Redux: Experimental Evidence on Performance Pay for Tax Collectors." *Quarterly Journal of Economics*, 231(1): 219–271.

2019. "Making Moves Matter: Experimental Evidence on Incentivizing Bureaucrats through Performance-Based Postings." *American Economic Review*, 109(1): 237–70.

Kleven, H. J. 2014. "How Can Scandinavians Tax So Much?" *Journal of Economic Perspectives*, 28(4): 77–98.

Kleven, H. J., M. B. Knudsen, C. T. Kreiner, S. Pedersen, and E. Saez. 2011. "Unwilling or Unable to Cheat? Evidence from a Tax Audit Experiment in Denmark." *Econometrica*, 79(3): 651–692.

Kleven, H. J., C. Kreiner, and E. Saez. 2016. "Why Can Modern Governments Tax So Much? An Agency Model of Firms as Fiscal Intermediaries." *Economica*, 83: 219–246.

Kung, J. and S. Chen. 2011. "The Tragedy of the Nomenclature: Career Incentives and Political Radicalism during China's Great Leap Famine." *American Political Science Review*, 105(1): 27–45.

Landry, P., X. Lü, and H. Duan. 2018. "Does Performance Matter? Evaluating the Institution of Political Selection along the Chinese Administrative Ladder." *Comparative Political Studies*, 51(8): 1074–1105.

Langenmayr, D. 2017. "Voluntary Disclosure of Evaded Taxes—Increasing Revenue, or Increasing Incentives to Evade?" *Journal of Public Economics*, 151: 110–125.

Lediga, C., N. Riedel, and K. Strohmaier. 2020. "What You Do (and What You Don't) Get When Expanding the Net – Evidence from Forced Taxpayer Registrations in South Africa." Working Paper available at: https://papers.ssrn.com/sol3/papers.cfm?abstract_id=3616808.

Li, J. 2013. "Is the Administration of Tax Collection the Reason for the Rapid Growth of Tax Revenue?" [Journal Article] 李建军,《税收征管是税收收入高速增长的原因吗？》,《税务与经济》, 2013年第2期。

Li, H. and L. Zhou. 2005. "Political Turnover and Economic Performance: The Incentive Role of Personnel Control in China." *Journal of Public Economics*, 89(9–10): 1743–1762.

Li, L., K. Z. Liu, Z. Nie, and T. Xia. 2021. "Evading by Any Means? VAT Enforcement and Payroll Tax Evasion in China." *Journal of Economic Behavior & Organization*, 185, 770-784.

Li, R. and G. Ma. 2017. "Personal-Income-Tax Reforms and Effective-Tax Functions in China." *FinanzAchiv: Public Finance Analysis*, 73(3): 317–340.

Liebman B. and R. Stern. 2021. "Fairness Beyond Law: How Contemporary Chinese Courts Smooth Financial Loss and Repair Emotional Rupture." Working Paper.

Liu, K. and K. Jia, eds. 2009. *Thirty Years of Chinese Fiscal and Tax Reform: Personal Accounts and Retrospections*. [Book] 刘克崮、贾康编,《中国财税改革三十年亲历与回顾》, 经济科学出版社。

Liu, Y. and J. Mao. 2019. "How Do Tax Incentives Affect Investment and Productivity? Firm-Level Evidence from China." *American Economic Journal: Economic Policy*, 11(3): 261–91.

Lockwood, B. and F. Porcelli. 2013. "Incentive Schemes for Local Government: Theory and Evidence from Comprehensive Performance Assessment in England." *American Economic Journal: Economic Policy*, 5(3): 254–286.

Lou, J. and S. Wang. 2008. *Public Finance in China*. Washington, DC: World Bank.

Lü, B. and Q. Guo. 2012. "Why China's Tax Revenue Is Likely to Maintain Its Rapid Growth: An Explanation within the Framework of Tax Capacity and Tax Effort." *Social Sciences in China*, 33(1): 108–126.

Lü, X. and P. F. Landry. 2014. "Show Me the Money: Interjurisdiction Political Competition and Fiscal Extraction in China." *American Political Science Review*, 108(3): 706–722.

Luttmer, E. F. P. and M. Singhal. 2014. "Tax Morale." *Journal of Economic Perspectives*, 28(4): 149–168.

Ma, G., J. Xu, and S. Li. 2015. "The Income Distribution Effect of China's Personal Income Tax: What the Micro-data Say." *Contemporary Economic Policy*, 33 (3): 488–498.

Malik, A. S. and R. M. Schwab. 1991. "The Economics of Tax Amnesties." *Journal of Public Economics*, 46(1): 29–49.

Manion, Melanie. 2015. *Information for Autocrats: Representation in Chinese Local Congresses*. Cambridge: Cambridge University Press.

Ministry of Human Resource and Social Security (MOHRSS). 2016. Statistical Bulletin on the Development Human Resources and Social Security. 《2016年度人力资源和社会保障事业发展统计公报》.

Montinola, G., Qian, Y., and Weingast, B. 1995. "Federalism, Chinese Style: The Political Basis for Economic Success in China." *World Politics*, 48: 50–81.

Mascagni, G., F. Santoro, D. Mukama, J. Karangwa, and N. Hakizimana. 2020. "Active Ghosts: Nil-filing in Rwanda." ICTD Working Paper No. 106.

Moe, T. M. and M. Caldwell. 1994. "The Institutional Foundations of Democratic Government: A Comparison of Presidential and Parliamentary Systems." *Journal of Institutional and Theoretical Economics* 150(1): 171–195.

Naritomi, J. 2019. "Consumers as Tax Auditors." *American Economic Review*, 109 (9): 3031–3072.

Ng, K. H. and X. He. 2017. *Embedded Courts: Judicial Decision-Making in China*. New York: Cambridge University Press.

Oksenberg, M. and J. Tong. 1991. "The Evolution of Central-Provincial Fiscal Relations in China, 1971-1984: the Formal System." *The China Quarterly*, 125: 1–35.

Organization for Economic Co-operation and Development. 2013. *Co-operative Compliance: A Framework from Enhanced Relationship to Co-operative Compliance*. www.oecd.org/tax/administration/co-operative-compliance.htm.

2015. *Tax Administration 2015: Comparative Information on OECD and Other Advanced and Emerging Economies*. Paris: OECD.

2019. *Tax Morale: What Drives People and Businesses to Pay Tax?* Paris: OECD.

2020. *Revenue Statistics 2020*. www.oecd.org/ctp/revenue-statistics-2522770x.htm#:~:text=Tax%20to%20GDP%20ratio%3A%20New,of%20GDP%20relative%20to%202018.

Ortega D. and C. Scartascini. 2020. "Don't Blame the Messenger. The Delivery Method of a Message Matters." *Journal of Economic Behavior & Organization*, 170: 286–300.

Parrillo, N. 2019. "Federal Agency Guidance and the Power to Bind: An Empirical Study of Agencies and Industries." *Yale Journal on Regulation*, 36: 165–271.

Peerenboom, R. 2009. *China's Long March toward Rule of Law*. Cambridge: Cambridge University Press.

Peng, X., Y. Liu, and H. Lin. 2015. "Does Collection Agency Change Influence the Effectiveness of Social Security Contributions Enforcement? Evidence from Enforcement Agency Change from Social Security Office to Local Taxation Administration in China." [Journal Article] 彭雪梅、刘阳、林辉,《征收机构是否会影响社会保险费的征收效果》,《管理世界》, 2015年第6期, 63–71.

Piketty, T. and N. Qian. 2009. "Income Inequality and Progressive Income Taxation in China and India, 1986-2015." *American Economic Journal: Applied Economics*, 1(2): 53–63.

Piketty, T., L. Yang, and G. Zucman. 2019. "Capital Accumulation, Private Property, and Rising Inequality in China, 1978–2015." *American Economic Review*, 109(7): 2469–2496.

Pomeranz, D. 2015. "No Taxation without Information: Deterrence and Self-Enforcement in the Value Added Tax." *American Economic Review*, 105(8): 2539–2569.

Posner, Eric. 2000. "Law and Social Norms: The Case of Tax Compliance." *Virginia Law Review*, 86: 1781–1819.

Potter, P. 2003. *From Leninist Discipline to Socialist Legalism: Peng Zhen on Law and Political Authority in the PRC*. Stanford: Stanford University Press.

Qian, J. 2014. "Unemployment Insurance in China." EAI Background Brief No. 903.

Qian, J. and Z. Wen. 2020. "Institutional Constraints for the Extension of Social Insurance Coverage to Informal Economy Workers in China." ILO Brief. www.ilo.org/wcmsp5/groups/public/–asia/–ro-bangkok/–ilo-beijing/documents/briefingnote/wcms_761658.pdf.

Robinson, L. and J. Slemrod. 2012. "Understanding Multidimensional Tax Systems." *International Tax and Public Finance*, 19(2): 237–267.

Rodden, J. and S. Rose-Ackerman. 1997. "Does Federalism Preserve Markets?" *Virginia Law Review*, 83(7): 1521–1572.

Rose-Ackerman, S. 1999. *Corruption and Government: Causes, Consequences, and Reform*. Cambridge: Cambridge University Press.

Santoro, F. and W. Mdluli. 2019. "Nil-Filing in Eswatini: Should the Revenue Administration Be Concerned?" ICTD African Tax Administration Paper 6, Brighton: Institute of Development Studies.

Schenk, A., V. Thuronyi, and W. Cui. 2015. *Value Added Tax: A Comparative Perspective*, 2nd ed. New York: Cambridge University Press.

Shapiro, S. 2013. *Legality*. Cambridge, MA: Harvard University Press.

Shavell, S. 2004. *Foundations of Economic Analysis of Law*. Cambridge, MA: Harvard University Press.

Shen, S. Y. and R. Krever. 2017. China's VAT Reform: Experiences and Lessons Learned. *International VAT Monitor*, 28(2): 147–153.

Slemrod, J. (1990). "Optimal taxation and optimal tax systems." *Journal of Economic Perspectives*, 4(1): 157–178.

2019. "Tax Compliance and Enforcement." *Journal of Economic Literature*, 57 (4): 904–954.

Slemrod, J. and S. Yitzhaki. 2002. "Tax Avoidance, Evasion and Administration." in *Handbook of Public Economics Vol 2*, edited by A. Auerbach and M. Feldstein, 1423–1470, North Holland: Amsterdam.

Song, Z., K. Storesletten, Y. Wang, and F. Zilibotti. 2015. "Sharing High Growth across Generations: Pensions and Demographic Transition in China." *American Economic Journal: Macroeconomics*, 7(2): 1–39.

Tang, J. and J. Feng. 2019. "Collecting System of Social Insurance and Contribution Compliance–Evidence from Chinese Firm-Level Data." [Journal Article] 唐珏、封进,《社会保险征收体制改革与社会保险基金收入———基于企业缴费行为的研究》,《经济学(季刊)》, 2019年第3期, 833–854。

Tian, S and Z. Fan. 2016. "Tax Sharing, Tax Effort and Corporate Tax Evasion–Evidences from the Income Tax Reform." [Journal Article] 田彬彬、范子英,《税收分成、税收努力与企业逃税—来自所得税分享改革的证据》,《管理世界》, 2016年第12期。

Tian, X. and X. Zhao. 2008. *Tax in the Country Village*. 田毅、赵旭,《他乡之税》, 北京:中信出版社, 2008。

Ulyssea, G. 2018. "Firms, Informality, and Development: Theory and Evidence from Brazil." *American Economic Review*, 108(8): 2015–2047.

U.S. Department of the Treasury. 2003. "Return-Free Tax Systems: Tax Simplification Is a Prerequisite." https://home.treasury.gov/system/files/131/Report-Return-Free-2003.pdf.

Wang C. 2011a. "Property Tax: The Government's Challenge Truly Begins." [News report] 王长勇,《房产税: 政府的挑战真正开始》, 财新网, 2011年1月28日.

2011b. "Property Tax Pilots Dodge Legal Requirements." [News report] 王长勇,《房产税试点游走于法律边缘》, 财新网, 2011年1月31日.

Waseem, M. 2020a. "The Role of Withholding in the Self-Enforcement of a Value-Added Tax: Evidence from Pakistan." Forthcoming in *Review of Economics and Statistics*.

Waseem, M. 2020b. "Overclaimed Refunds, Undeclared Sales, and Invoice Mills: Nature and Extent of Noncompliance in a Value-Added Tax." CESifo Working Paper No. 8231.

Weigel, J. 2020. "The Participation Dividend of Taxation: How Citizens in Congo Engage More with the State when It Tries to Tax Them." *Quarterly Journal of Economics*, 135(4): 1849–1903.

Weingast, B. 1995. "The Economic Role of Political Institutions: Market-Preserving Federalism and Economic Development." *Journal of Law, Economics, & Organization*, 20(1): 1–31.

Williamson, S. and B. Magaloni. 2020. "Legislatures and Policy Making in Authoritarian Regimes." *Comparative Political Studies*, 53(9): 1525–1543.

Winn, J. and A. Zhang. 2013. "China's Golden Tax Project: A Technological Strategy for Reducing VAT Fraud." *Peking University Journal of Legal Studies*, 4: 1–33.

World Bank, 1990. China: Revenue Mobilization and Tax Policy Issues and Options. Washington, DC: World Bank.

1994. *Averting the Old Age Crisis: Policies to Protect the Old and Promote Growth*. New York: Oxford University Press.

Wong, C. P. W. 1991. "Central-Local Relations in an Era of Fiscal Decline: The Paradox of Fiscal Decentralization in Post-Mao China." *The China Quarterly*, 128: 691–715.

Xiao, K. 2020. "The Value of Big Data in a Pandemic." Working Paper, available at http://dx.doi.org/10.2139/ssrn.3583919.

Xie, Z and Z. Fan. 2015. "Chinese Tax Sharing System, Centralized Central Tax Collection and Taxation Competition." [Journal Article] 谢贞发、范子英: 《中国式分税制、中央税收征管权集中与税收竞争》,《经济研究》, 2015年第4期。

Xiong, W. et al. 2011. "Recommendations to Propose a Review of the Legality of the Property Tax Pilots." [book chapter] 熊伟、翟继光、杨小强: 《关于提请对房产税改革试点进行合法性审查的建议》， 载熊伟主编:《税法解释与判例评注》（第2卷）, 法律出版社2011年版.

Xu, J., G. Ma, and S. Li. 2013. "Has Personal Income Tax Improved China's Income Distribution?: A Dynamic Evaluation Based on Microdata from 1997 to 2011." [Journal Article] 徐建炜、马光荣、李实:《个人所得税改善中国收入分配了吗——基于对1997—2011年微观数据的动态评估》,《中国社会科学》, 2013年第6期。

Yao, Y., and M. Zhang. 2015. "Subnational Leaders and Economic Growth: Evidence from Chinese Cities." *Journal of Economic Growth* 20: 405–436.

Ye, S. 2011. "Member of Political Consultative Conference Strongly Opposes Property Tax, Asks for Respect for the Constitution." [News article] 叶石界, 《政协委员强烈反对征房产税 请给宪法留面子》,《21世纪经济报道》2011年1月27日.

Yu, J., L. Zhou, and G. Zhu. 2016. "Strategic Interaction in Political Competition: Evidence from Spatial Effects across Chinese Cities." *Regional Science and Urban Economics*, 57: 23–37.

Zhai, J. 2011. "Shanghai and Chongqing Launch Property Taxes: The Government Directly Faces Huge Challenges from Taxpayers." [News commentary] 翟继光,《上海重庆开征房产税: 政府直面纳税人挑战很大》, 《中国青年报》, 2011年2月13日。

Zhan, P., S. Li, and X. Xu. 2019. "Personal Income Tax Reform in China in 2018 and Its Impact on Income Distribution." *China & World Economy*, 27(3): 25–48.

Zhang, L., Y. Chen, and Z. He. 2018. "The Effect of Investment Tax Incentives: Evidence from China's Value-Added Tax Reform." *International Tax and Public Finance*, 25: 913–945.

Zhou L. 2008. *Local Government in Transition: Incentive and Management of Officials*. [Book] 周黎安《转型中的地方政府：官员激励与治理》, 格致出版社。

Zhou L., C. Liu, and X. Li. 2011. "The Mystery of Tax Effort, Taxation Bureaus and Tax Growth." [Journal article] 周黎安, 刘冲, 厉行, 《税收努力, 征税机构与税收增长之谜》, 《经济学 （季刊）》第11卷第1期。

INDEX

www.ingramcontent.com/pod-product-compliance
Lightning Source LLC
LaVergne TN
LVHW011808200926
848484LV00005B/1110
9781108491426